Get Updates and More on Nolo.com

Go to this book's companion page at:

www.nolo.com/back-of-book/RUNS.html

When there's an important change to the law affecting this book, we'll post updates. You'll also find articles and other related materials.

More Resources from Nolo.com

Legal Forms, Books, & Software

Hundreds of do-it-yourself products—all written in plain English, approved, and updated by our in-house legal editors.

Legal Articles

Get informed with thousands of free articles on everyday legal topics. Our articles are accurate, up to date, and reader friendly.

Find a Lawyer

Want to talk to a lawyer? Use Nolo to find a lawyer who can help you with your case.

NOLO
LAW for ALL

NOLO The Trusted Name

(but don't take our word for it)

"*In Nolo you can trust.*"
THE NEW YORK TIMES

"*Nolo is always there in a jam as the nation's premier publisher of do-it-yourself legal books.*"
NEWSWEEK

"*Nolo publications…guide people simply through the how, when, where and why of the law.*"
THE WASHINGTON POST

"*[Nolo's]…material is developed by experienced attorneys who have a knack for making complicated material accessible.*"
LIBRARY JOURNAL

"*When it comes to self-help legal stuff, nobody does a better job than Nolo…*"
USA TODAY

"*The most prominent U.S. publisher of self-help legal aids.*"
TIME MAGAZINE

"*Nolo is a pioneer in both consumer and business self-help books and software.*"
LOS ANGELES TIMES

17th Edition

Legal Guide for Starting & Running a Small Business

Attorneys Fred S. Steingold and David M. Steingold

SEVENTEENTH EDITION	APRIL 2021
Editor	AMY LOFTSGORDON
Cover Design	SUSAN PUTNEY
Book Design	SUSAN PUTNEY
Proofreader	LINDA FOUST
Index	RICHARD GENOVA
Printing	BANG PRINTING

ISSN: 2163-0321 (print)

ISSN: 2325-3975 (online)

ISBN: 978-1-4133-2860-8 (pbk)

ISBN: 978-1-4133-2861-5 (ebook)

This book covers only United States law, unless it specifically states otherwise.

Please note

We know that accurate, plain-English legal information can help you solve many of your own legal problems. But this text is not a substitute for personalized advice from a knowledgeable lawyer. If you want the help of a trained professional —and we'll always point out situations in which we think that's a good idea— consult an attorney licensed to practice in your state.

Acknowledgments

Special thanks to Nolo publisher Jake Warner—the cheerful perfectionist whose ideas infuse every page of this book—and to Nolo editor Mary Randolph, who deftly whipped the early manuscripts into final shape.

Thanks, too, to the rest of the remarkable Nolo family for their invaluable contributions—especially Steve Elias, Robin Leonard, Barbara Hodovan, Jackie Mancuso, Tony Mancuso, Barbara Kate Repa, Beth Laurence, Ilona Bray, Catherine Caputo, Betsy Simmons, JinAh Lee, and Marcia Stewart.

I am indebted to Attorney David Steingold for bringing the subsequent editions up to date.

In addition to the folks at Nolo, these other professionals generously shared their expertise to make this book possible:

- Attorneys Charles Borgsdorf, Douglas Ellmann, Larry Ferguson, Sandra Hazlett, Peter Long, Michael Malley, Robert Stevenson, Nancy Welber, and Warren Widmayer

- Certified public accountants Mark Hartley and Lonnie Loy, and

- Insurance specialists James Libs, Mike Mansel, and Dave Tiedgen.

Finally, thanks to my small business clients, who are a constant source of knowledge and inspiration.

—Fred S. Steingold

About the Authors

Fred S. Steingold, the original author of this book, practiced law in Ann Arbor, Michigan, for more than 50 years. His main practice areas were business law, estate planning law, and real estate law. Fred also authored many other Nolo books, including *Legal Forms for Starting & Running a Small Business*, *The Employer's Legal Handbook*, *Negotiate the Best Lease for Your Business*, *The Complete Guide to Buying a Business*, and *The Complete Guide to Selling a Business*. His death in 2017 was a great loss to Nolo.

David M. Steingold practices law in Ann Arbor, Michigan. His main practice areas are business law, real estate law, and estate planning and probate law. He has updated the most recent editions of this book. He also is the author of Nolo's *Guide to Single-Member LLCs*.

Table of Contents

Appendix

Index

Your Legal Companion for Starting and Running a Small Business

Starting and running a small business can be both profitable and emotionally satisfying. Being an entrepreneur offers rewards of many sorts: the opportunity to spread your wings and use your natural talents, the freedom of being your own boss, the possibility of huge financial success, and more. And in an era when job security can seem like a relic of a bygone era, owning a business means you will never be fired or outsourced at someone else's whim.

At the time of writing, millions of people had lost their jobs due to the coronavirus (COVID-19) crisis. If you've suddenly found yourself unemployed and are thinking about—or are in the planning stages of—starting your own business out of necessity, you've come to the right place.

Every businessperson runs into legal questions. Maybe you're just looking to start (or buy) a small retail, service, or manufacturing business, alone or with others, online or off, and are wondering how to structure your ownership. Maybe you're considering setting up a corporation or LLC if doing so would be legally advantageous. You might have questions about taxes or employees.

In plain English, this book covers all those issues and lots of others—all the major legal issues that a small business is likely to face, in fact. You'll learn about preliminary issues such as raising money, forming the business, and choosing and protecting a business name. There's also lots of good information about how to get the business up and running, including hiring employees, getting permits and insurance, and negotiating a lease. The book also covers the maintenance of your business—paying taxes, dealing with customers and problem employees, and resolving legal disputes.

Other Useful Nolo Books, Forms, and Resources for Small Businesses

Throughout this book, we recommend other Nolo books (all available as hard copy and e-book) to help you handle a specific business issue or task, from forming an LLC to hiring employees. One especially useful title is *Legal Forms for Starting & Running a Small Business*, also by Fred S. Steingold. The *Legal Forms* book includes over 60 of the most important forms you'll need to run your small business—from borrowing money to writing contracts of various sorts to preparing corporate bylaws.

For more information and lots of free articles on business issues, see Nolo's Small Business section at www.nolo.com/legal-encyclopedia/small-business. Also, be sure to check out the Business Formation: LLCs & Corporations section at www.nolo.com/legal-encyclopedia/llc-corporations-partnerships; here you'll find many articles of interest to small business owners, including state requirements for forming an LLC or establishing a sole proprietorship, and links to the best state and federal resources for small businesses.

Finally, if you're looking for a lawyer, asking for a referral to an attorney from someone you trust can be a good way to find legal help. Also, two sites that are part of the Nolo family, Lawyers.com and Avvo.com, provide excellent and free lawyer directories. These directories allow you to search by location and area of law, and list detailed information about and reviews of lawyers. Whether you're just starting your lawyer search or researching particular attorneys, visit www.lawyers.com/find-a-lawyer and www.avvo.com/find-a-lawyer.

Adjusting Your Business Practices During the COVID-19 Emergency

Following the coronavirus outbreak in early 2020, many companies and aspiring entrepreneurs have had to rethink their usual in-person business methods. Throughout this book, we discuss various tactics and strategies that might involve dealing with customers and other individuals in person. While the pandemic continues, use appropriate precautions when in these situations, like wearing a mask and practicing social distancing. You might also consider whether you can accomplish your goal using an alternate communication method, like phone, email, text, or videoconferencing.

Legal Guide for Starting & Running a Small Business will help you take key preventive measures that will dramatically cut the number of expensive visits you'd otherwise make to a lawyer's office. You'll know exactly where you might be vulnerable to lawsuits so you can wisely take steps to reduce the risks. And you'll know when it makes sense to call in a lawyer or a tax pro for special assistance before small problems turn into big ones. You'll be able to spend your time on what really counts: running a sound and successful business.

Of course, starting a business involves some risk. Demographic changes, pandemics, recessions, changing tastes and styles, new technologies—any of these or a hundred other factors can challenge even the most astute and experienced businessperson. That's why it's so important to increase your chances of success not only by working hard and planning

carefully but also by knowing how the law affects your business. It can help you avoid many costly risks.

Congratulations on taking the first steps toward owning and running your own enterprise. You have a lot of hard work ahead of you, and Nolo is here to help you along the way. So roll up your sleeves and dig in.

Get Updates and More at This Book's Companion Page on Nolo.com

When important changes to the information in this book happen, we'll post updates online, on a page dedicated to this book (what we call the book's companion page):

www.nolo.com/back-of-book/RUNS.html

In early 2019, the most sweeping changes to federal tax laws in roughly 30 years were just beginning to take effect.

Some of the key changes effective for the 2018 tax year were:

- lower federal income tax rates and the elimination of brackets for corporations
- adjustments in tax deductions for businesses and individuals, including a significant new deduction for most owners of pass-through businesses such as limited liability companies (LLCs)
- elimination of the alternative minimum tax (AMT) for corporations, and
- a cap on write-offs for business losses on individual returns.

We'll keep you up to date on these and other changes on the update page for this book at www.nolo.com/ back-of-book/RUNS.html.

Which Legal Form Is Best for Your Business?

When you start a business, you must decide on a legal structure for it. Usually, you'll choose either a sole proprietorship, a partnership, a limited liability company (LLC), or a corporation. There's no right or wrong choice that fits everyone. Your job is to understand how each legal structure works and then pick the one that best meets your needs.

The best choice isn't always obvious. After reading this chapter, you might decide to seek some guidance from a lawyer or an accountant.

For many small businesses, the best initial choice is either a sole proprietorship or—if more than one owner is involved—a partnership. Either of these structures makes especially good sense in a business where personal liability isn't a big worry—for example, a small service business in which you are unlikely to be sued and for which you won't be borrowing much money. Sole proprietorships and partnerships are relatively simple and inexpensive to establish and maintain.

Forming an LLC or a corporation is more complicated and costly, but it's worth it for some small businesses. The main feature of LLCs and corporations that is attractive to small businesses is the limit they provide on their owners' personal liability for business debts and court judgments against a business. Another factor might be income taxes: You can set up an LLC or a corporation in a way that lets you enjoy more favorable tax rates. In certain circumstances, your business might be able to stash away earnings at a relatively low tax rate. In addition, an LLC or a corporation might be able to provide a range of fringe benefits to employees (including the owners) and deduct the cost as a business expense.

Given the choice between creating an LLC or a corporation, many small business owners will be better off going the LLC route. For one thing, if your business will have several owners, the LLC can be more flexible than a corporation in the way you can parcel out profits and management duties. Also, setting up and maintaining an LLC can be a bit less complicated and expensive than a corporation. But sometimes a corporation will be more beneficial. For example, because a corporation—unlike other types of business entities—issues stock certificates to its owners, a corporation can be an ideal vehicle if you want to bring in outside investors or reward loyal employees with stock options.

Keep in mind that your initial choice of a business form doesn't have to be permanent. You can start out as sole proprietorship or partnership and, later, if your business grows or the risks of personal liability increase, you can convert your business to an LLC or a corporation.

RELATED TOPIC

For some small business owners, a less common type of business structure might be appropriate. While most small businesses will find at least one good choice among the four basic business formats described above, a handful will have special situations in which a different format is required or at least desirable. For example, a pair of dentists looking to limit their personal liability might need to set up a professional corporation or a professional limited liability company. A group of real estate investors could find that a limited partnership is the best vehicle for them. These and other special types of business organizations, including benefit corporations, are summarized at the end of this chapter.

SEE AN EXPERT

You might need professional advice in choosing the best entity for your business. This chapter gives you a great deal of information to assist you in deciding how to best organize your business. Obviously, however, it's impossible to cover every relevant nuance of tax and business law—especially if your business has several owners with different and complex tax situations. And for businesses owned by several people who have different personal tax situations, sorting out the effects of "pass-through" taxation (where partners and most LLC members are taxed on their personal tax returns for their share of business profits and losses) is no picnic, even for seasoned tax pros. The bottom line is that unless your business will start small and have a very simple ownership structure, before you make your final decision on a business entity, check with a tax adviser after learning about the basic attributes of each type of business structure (from this chapter and Chapters 2, 3, and 4).

Ways to Organize Your Business		
Type of Entity	**Main Advantages**	**Main Drawbacks**
Sole Proprietor	Simple and inexpensive to create and operate Owner reports profit or loss on personal tax return	Owner personally liable for business debts
General Partnership	Simple and inexpensive to create and operate Owners (partners) report their share of profit or loss on their personal tax returns	Owners (partners) personally liable for business debts
Limited Partnership	Limited partners have limited personal liability for business debts as long as they don't participate in management General partners can raise cash without involving outside investors in management of business	General partners personally liable for business debts More expensive to create than general partnership Suitable mainly for companies that invest in real estate
C Corporation	Owners have limited personal liability for business debts Fringe benefits can be deducted as business expense Corporate profit can be split among owners and corporation, resulting in lower overall tax rate	More expensive to create than partnership or sole proprietorship Paperwork can seem burdensome to some owners Separate taxable entity
S Corporation	Owners have limited personal liability for business debts Owners report their share of corporate profit or loss on their personal tax returns Owners can use corporate loss to offset income from other sources	More expensive to create than partnership or sole proprietorship More paperwork than for a limited liability company, which offers similar advantages Income must be allocated to owners according to their ownership interests Fringe benefits limited for owners who own more than 2% of shares
Professional Corporation	Owners have no personal liability for malpractice of other owners	More expensive to create than partnership or sole proprietorship Paperwork can seem burdensome to some owners All owners must belong to the same profession
Nonprofit Corporation	Corporation might not have to pay income taxes Contributions to certain charitable corporations are tax deductible Fringe benefits can be deducted as business expense	Full tax advantages available only to groups organized for the following purposes: charitable, scientific, educational, literary, religious, testing for public safety, fostering national or international sports competition, and preventing cruelty to children or animals Property transferred to corporation stays there; if corporation ends, property must go to another nonprofit

	Ways to Organize Your Business (continued)	
Type of Entity	**Main Advantages**	**Main Drawbacks**
Limited Liability Company	Owners have limited personal liability for business debts even if they participate in management Profit and loss can be allocated differently than ownership interests IRS rules allow LLCs to choose between being taxed as partnership or corporation	More expensive to create than partnership or sole proprietorship A member's entire share of LLC profits might be subject to self-employment tax
Professional Limited Liability Company	Same advantages as a regular limited liability company Owners have no personal liability for malpractice of other owners Gives state-licensed professionals a way to enjoy those advantages	Same as for a regular limited liability company Members generally must all belong to the same profession or related professions.
Limited Liability Partnership	Mostly of interest to partners in old-line professions, such as law, medicine, and accounting Owners (partners) aren't personally liable for the malpractice of other partners Owners report their share of profit or loss on their personal tax returns	Unlike a limited liability company or a professional limited liability company, owners (partners) remain personally liable for many types of obligations owed to business creditors, lenders, and landlords Not available in all states Often limited to a short list of professions

RESOURCE

Need help choosing the legal structure for your business? Take Nolo's quiz at www.nolo.com/business-formation-quiz to find out what the best form of business ownership is for you.

Sole Proprietorships

The simplest form of business entity is the "sole proprietorship." If you choose this legal structure, then legally speaking, you and the business are the same. You can continue operating as a sole proprietor as long as you're the only owner of the business.

Establishing a sole proprietorship is cheap and relatively uncomplicated. While you do not have to file articles of incorporation or organization (as you would with a corporation or an LLC), you might have to obtain a business license to do business under state laws or local ordinances. States differ on the amount of licensing required. In California, for example, almost all businesses need a business license, which is available to anyone for a small fee. In other states, business licenses are the exception rather than the rule. But most states do require a sales tax license or permit for all retail businesses. Dealing with these routine licensing requirements generally involves little time or expense. However, many specialized businesses—such as an asbestos removal service or a restaurant that serves liquor—require additional licenses, which might be harder to qualify for. (See Chapter 7 for more on this subject.)

In addition, if you're going to conduct your business under a trade name such as Smith Furniture Store rather than John Smith, you'll have to file an assumed name or fictitious name certificate at a local or state public office. This is so people who deal with your business will know who the real owner is. (See Chapter 6 for more on business names.)

From an income tax standpoint, a sole proprietorship and its owner are treated as a single entity. Business income and business losses are reported on your own federal tax return (Form 1040, Schedule C). If you have a business loss, you might be able to use it to offset income that you receive from other sources. (For more tax basics, see Chapter 8.)

Personal Liability

A potential disadvantage of doing business as a sole proprietor is that you have unlimited personal liability on all business debts and court judgments related to your business.

EXAMPLE 1: Liam is the sole proprietor of a small manufacturing business. Believing that his business's prospects look good, he orders $50,000 worth of supplies and uses them up. Unfortunately, there's a sudden drop in demand for his products, and Liam can't sell the items he's produced. When the company that sold Liam the supplies demands payment, he can't pay the bill.

As sole proprietor, Liam is personally liable for this business obligation. So the creditor can sue him and go after not only Liam's business assets, but his other property as well. This can include his house, his car, and his personal bank account.

EXAMPLE 2: Sara is the sole proprietor of a flower shop. One day Rex, one of Sara's employees, is delivering flowers using a truck owned by the business. Rex strikes and seriously injures a pedestrian. The injured pedestrian sues Rex, claiming that he drove carelessly and caused the accident. The lawsuit names Sara as a codefendant. After a trial, the jury returns a large verdict against Rex—and Sara as the owner of the business. Sara is personally liable to the injured pedestrian, which means the pedestrian can go after all of Sara's assets, business and personal.

One of the major reasons to form a corporation or an LLC is that, in theory at least, you'll avoid most personal liability. (But see Chapter 12 for a discussion of how a good liability insurance policy could be enough to protect a sole proprietor from personal liability if someone is accidentally injured.)

Income Taxes

As a sole proprietor, you and your business are one entity for income tax purposes. The profits of your business are taxed to you in the year that the business makes them, whether or not you remove the money from the business. This is called "flow-through" taxation, because the profits "flow through" to the owner. You report business profits on Schedule C of Form 1040.

If you form an LLC or a corporation, you have a choice of two different types of tax treatment:

- **Flow-Through Taxation.** One choice is to have the IRS tax your LLC or corporation like a sole proprietorship or partnership. The owners report their share of LLC or corporate profits on their own tax returns, whether or not the money has been distributed to them.
- **Entity Taxation.** The other choice is to make the business a separate entity for income tax purposes. If you form an LLC and make that choice, the LLC will pay its own taxes on the profits of the LLC. And as a member of the LLC, you won't pay tax on the money earned by the LLC until you receive payments as compensation for services or as dividends. Similarly, if you form a corporation and choose this option, you as a shareholder won't pay tax on the money earned by the corporation until you receive payments as compensation for services or as dividends. The corporation will pay its own taxes on the corporate profits.

Later in this chapter, I'll explain the mechanics of choosing between these two methods. For now, just be aware that this tax flexibility of LLCs and corporations offers some tax advantages over a sole proprietorship if you're able to leave some income in the business as "retained earnings." For example, suppose you want to build up a reserve to buy new equipment, or your small label-manufacturing company accumulates valuable inventory as it expands. In either case, you might want to leave $50,000 of profits or assets in the business at the end of the year. If you operated as a sole proprietor, those "retained" profits would be taxed on your personal income tax return at your marginal tax rate. But with an LLC or corporation that's taxed as a separate entity, the tax rate will almost certainly be lower.

Fringe Benefits

If you operate your business as a sole proprietorship, tax-sheltered retirement programs are available. A Keogh plan, for example, allows a sole proprietor to salt away a substantial amount of income free of current taxes. So does a one-person 401(k). You can't really do any better by setting up an LLC or a corporation.

When it comes to medical expenses for you and your family, however, there can be a tax advantage to setting up a corporation or an LLC. As a sole proprietor, you can take a tax deduction for the entire amount of your health insurance premiums, but you can deduct only part of your medical expenses not covered by insurance. The situation is different if you form a corporation or an LLC and choose to have the corporation or LLC taxed as a separate entity. Your corporation or LLC could hire you as an employee and—if you're the only employee—the business could set up a medical reimbursement plan that pays for your health insurance premiums and 100% of other health costs incurred by you, your spouse, and your dependents. However, if you prefer to be a sole proprietor and you're married, you can reach a similar result by hiring your spouse as an employee. See "Hiring Your Spouse Can Have Tax Benefits," below, for details.

Hiring Your Spouse Can Have Tax Benefits

If you choose to do business as a sole proprietor, there's a way you can deduct more of your family's medical expenses. First, hire your spouse at a reasonable wage. Then, set up a written health benefit plan covering your employees and their families. Your business can then deduct 100% of the medical expenses it pays for you, your spouse, and your dependents. (**Caution:** Don't do this if you plan to hire additional employees. It only works if your spouse is your sole employee.)

But balance whether such a plan can save you enough money to justify the effort. There may be some expense for setting up the plan and handling the associated paperwork. And remember that your business will be obligated for payroll taxes on your spouse's earnings. (See Chapter 8 for information on payroll taxes.) But this isn't all bad, because your spouse will become eligible for Social Security benefits, which can be of some value—especially if your spouse hasn't already worked long enough to qualify.

If you're audited, the IRS will look closely to make sure your spouse is really an employee and performing needed services for the business.

 **RESOURCE**

To learn about how a person qualifies for Social Security benefits, see *Social Security, Medicare & Government Pensions*, by Joseph Matthews (Nolo).

Also, check out Nolo's Social Security Center at www.nolo.com/legal-encyclopedia/social-security for useful articles on the subject.

Routine Business Expenses

As a sole proprietor, you can deduct day-to-day business expenses the same way an LLC, corporation, or partnership can. Whether it's car expenses, meals, or travel, the same rules apply to all of these types of business entities.

You'll need to keep accurate books for your business that are clearly separate from your records of personal expenditures. The IRS has strict rules for tax-deductible business expenses (covered in Chapter 8), and you need to be able to document those expenses if challenged. One good approach is to keep separate checkbooks for your business and personal expenses—and pay for all of your business expenses out of the business or a separate credit card you use only for business expenses and pay for from a business checking account.

It's simple to keep track of business income and expenses if you keep them separate from the start—and challenging if you don't.

Partnerships

If two or more people are going to own and operate your business, you must choose between establishing a partnership, a corporation, or an LLC. This section looks at the "general partnership," which is the type of partnership that most small businesses will be considering. The limited partnership is described toward the end of this chapter.

The best way to form a partnership is to draw up and sign a partnership agreement (discussed fully in Chapter 2). Legally, you can have a partnership without a written agreement, in which case you'd be governed entirely by either the Uniform Partnership Act or the Revised Uniform Partnership Act (explained in Chapter 2).

Beyond a written agreement, the paperwork for setting up a partnership is minimal—about on a par with a sole proprietorship. You might have to file a partnership certificate with a public office to register your partnership name and you might have to obtain a business license or two. The income tax paperwork for a partnership is marginally more complex than that for a sole proprietorship.

Personal Liability

As a partner in a general partnership, you face personal liability similar to that of the owner of a sole proprietorship. Your personal assets are at risk, in addition to all assets of the partnership. In other words, you have unlimited personal liability on all business debts and court judgments related to your business.

Law From the Real World

First Things First

Ellen, Molly, and Brianna—all superb cooks—planned to open a catering business. They would hold on to their day jobs until they could determine whether the new business could support all three of them.

At a planning meeting to discuss the equipment they would need for a commercial kitchen, Ellen said she wanted the business to be run as professionally as possible. To her, that meant promptly incorporating or forming an LLC. The discussion about equipment was put off while the three women tried to decide how to organize the legal structure of their business. After several frustrating hours, they agreed to continue the discussion later and to do some research about the organizational options in the meantime.

Before the next meeting, Ellen conferred with a small business adviser, who suggested that the women refocus their energy on the kitchen equipment they needed and getting their business operating, keeping its legal structure as simple as possible. One good way to do this, she suggested, was to form a partnership, using a written partnership agreement. Each partner would contribute $10,000 to buy equipment and contribute roughly equal amounts of labor. Profits would be divided equally.

Later, if the business succeeded and grew, it might make sense to incorporate or form an LLC and consider other issues, like a health plan, retirement plan, and other benefits. But for now, real professionalism meant getting on with the job—not consuming time and dollars forming an unneeded corporate or LLC entity.

In a partnership, any partner can take actions that legally bind the partnership entity. That means, for example, that if one partner signs a contract on behalf of the partnership, it will be fully enforceable against the partnership and each individual partner, even if the other partners weren't consulted in advance and didn't approve the contract. Also, the partnership is liable, as is each individual partner, for injuries caused by any partner while on partnership business.

EXAMPLE 1: Ted, a partner in Argon Associates, signs a contract on behalf of the partnership that obligates the partnership to pay $50,000 for certain goods and services. Esther and Helen, the other partners, think Ted made a terrible deal. Nevertheless, Argon Associates is bound by Ted's contract even though Esther and Helen didn't sign it.

EXAMPLE 2: Juan is a partner in Universal Contractors. Elroy, one of his partners, causes an accident while using a partnership vehicle. Juan and all the other partners will be financially liable to people injured in the accident if the car isn't covered by adequate insurance. The same would be true if Elroy used his own car while on partnership business.

In both of these situations, the personal assets (home, car, and bank accounts) of each partner will be at stake, in addition to partnership assets. But remember that a partnership can protect against many risks by carrying adequate liability insurance.

Partners' Rights and Responsibilities

Each partner is entitled to full information—financial and otherwise—about the affairs of the partnership. Also, the partners have a "fiduciary" relationship to one another. This means that each partner owes the others the highest legal duty of good faith, loyalty, and fairness in everything having to do with the partnership.

EXAMPLE: Wheels & Deals, a partnership, is in the business of selling used cars. No partner is free to open a competing used-car business without the consent of the other partners. This would be an obvious conflict of interest and, as such, would violate the fiduciary duty the partners legally owe to one another.

Unless agreed otherwise, a person can't become a new partner without the consent of all the other partners. However, in larger partnerships, it's common for partners to provide in the partnership agreement that new partners can be admitted with the consent of a certain percentage of the existing partners—75%, for example.

State laws regulating partnerships dictate what occurs if one partner leaves your partnership and you don't have a partnership agreement that provides for what happens. In about half the states, the partnership is automatically dissolved when a partner withdraws or dies; the business is then liquidated. In such a state, it's an excellent idea to put a provision in your partnership agreement that allows the business to continue without interruption, despite the technical dissolution of the partnership. A partnership agreement, for instance, may contain a provision that calls for a buyout if one of the partners dies or wants to leave the partnership, avoiding a forced liquidation of the business. (Traditionally, these have been known as "buy-sell" agreements, but now we generally refer to them as "buyout agreements.")

EXAMPLE: Tom, Dylan, and Maya are equal partners. They agree in writing that if one of them dies, the other two will buy the deceased partner's interest in the partnership for $50,000 so that the business will continue. (Be aware that often a partnership agreement doesn't fix a precise amount as the buyout price but uses a more complicated formula based on such data as yearly sales, profits, or book value.) To fund this arrangement, the partnership buys life insurance covering each partner in an amount large enough to cover the buyout. If Tom dies first, under the terms of the agreement, his wife and children will receive $50,000 from the partnership to compensate them for the value of Tom's ownership interest in the business. Technically, the remaining partners would operate as a new partnership, but the important point is that the business would keep functioning.

Other states—generally those that have adopted the revised version of the Uniform Partnership Act—follow a slightly different rule. In those states, if your partnership was created to last for a fixed length of time or was created for a specific project, and a partner leaves before the fixed time expires or the project is done, the partnership isn't automatically dissolved. Instead, the remaining partners have the opportunity to continue the existing partnership rather than having to form a new one. But even if your state follows this more flexible approach, you'll still want to use buyout provisions to specify how the departing partner—or the family of a partner who's died—gets compensated for that person's partnership interest.

 RELATED TOPIC

More on buyouts. Chapter 5 discusses buyout provisions in greater detail.

Income Taxes

In terms of income and losses, the tax picture for a partnership is basically the same as that of a sole proprietorship. A partnership doesn't pay income taxes. It must, however, file an informational return that tells the government how much money the partnership earned or lost during the tax year and how much profit (or loss) belongs to each partner. Each partner uses Schedule E of Form 1040 to report the business profits (or losses) allocated to each and then pays income tax on this share,

whether or not this income was actually distributed during the tax year. If the partnership loses money, each partner can deduct the proportional share of losses for that year from income earned from other sources (subject to some fairly complicated tax basis rules—see "Investment Partnerships," below).

Special Tax Status Available for a Husband-and-Wife Business

Ordinarily, if you and your spouse jointly own an unincorporated business, your business is classified as a partnership for federal tax purposes. This means you need to file an annual partnership tax return—IRS Form 1065—as well as IRS Form 1040. But a better option may be available. You may elect to be classified as a "qualified joint venture"—and avoid having to file an additional tax return—if you meet all of the following requirements:

- You and your spouse co-own the business.
- You and your spouse are the only owners of the business, and you file a joint tax return.
- You both materially participate in running the business—joint ownership of business property isn't enough.
- You both elect for your business not to be treated as a partnership.
- Your business isn't held in the name of a partnership or an LLC.

Being classified as a qualified joint venture also helps ensure that each of you gets proper Social Security credit.

To get these benefits, you and your spouse should each file a Schedule C with your joint Form 1040. In your separate Schedule C forms, you'll list your respective shares of profit or loss based on your ownership interests in the business. Most husband-and-wife businesses are owned 50-50.

You'll find more information on qualified joint ventures at the IRS website at www.irs.gov. Look for the pages titled *Husband and Wife Business* and *Election for Husband and Wife Unincorporated Businesses.*

Investment Partnerships

A partner's share of the partnership's losses from income earned through other sources can be deducted only if that partner actively participates in the business of the partnership. If, instead, a partner is a passive investor (as is often the case in partnerships designed to invest in real estate) or receives income from passive sources (such as royalties, rents, or dividends), any loss from the partnership business is treated as a passive loss for that partner. That means that for federal income tax purposes the loss can be deducted only from other passive income—not from ordinary income.

Fringe Benefits and Business Expenses

When it comes to fringe benefits (such as retirement plans and medical coverage) and business expenses, the IRS treats partnerships like sole proprietorships. The discussion about "Fringe Benefits" and "Routine Business Expenses" for sole proprietorships, above, applies to partnerships as well.

CAUTION

Put it in writing. If you go the partnership route, I strongly recommend that the partners sign a written partnership agreement, even though an oral partnership agreement is legal. The human memory is far too fallible to rely on for the details of important business decisions. Chapter 2 contains basic information on how to write a partnership agreement.

Corporations

If you're concerned about limiting your personal liability for business debts, you'll want to consider organizing your business as either an LLC or a corporation. (Of course, you might have other reasons in addition to limited liability for considering these two business structures.) Because the corporation has a longer legal history, I'll deal with it first, but the LLC—covered next—might well be preferable for your particular business, despite its relative newness.

This book deals primarily with the small, privately owned corporation. I'll assume that all of the corporate stock is owned by one person or a few people and that all shareholders are actively involved in the management of the business—with the possible exception of friends and relatives who have provided seed money in exchange for stock. Because there are many complexities involved in selling stock to the public, I don't discuss public corporations.

The most important feature of a corporation is that, legally, it's a separate entity from the individuals who own or operate it. You may own all the stock of your corporation and be its only employee but—if you follow sensible organizational and operating procedures—you and your corporation are separate legal entities.

All states have adopted legislation that permits a corporation to be formed by a single incorporator. All states permit a corporate board that has a single director, although the ability to set up a one-person board may depend on the number of shareholders. (See Chapter 3 for more details.) In addition, many states have streamlined the procedures for operating a small corporation to permit decisions to be made quickly and without needless formalities. For example, in most states, shareholders and directors can take action by unanimous written consent rather than by holding formal meetings, and directors' meetings can be held by telephone.

Limited Personal Liability

One of the main advantages of incorporating is that, in most circumstances, it limits your personal liability. If a court judgment is entered against the corporation, you stand to lose only the money that you've invested. Generally, as long as you've acted in your corporate capacity (as an employee, officer, or director) and without the intent to defraud creditors, your home, personal bank accounts, and other valuable property can't be touched by a creditor who has won a lawsuit against the corporation.

EXAMPLE: Andrea is the sole shareholder, director, and officer of Market Basket Corporation, which runs a food store. Ronald, a Market Basket employee, drops a case of canned food on a customer's foot. The customer sues and wins a judgment against the business. Only corporate assets are available to pay the damages. Andrea is not personally liable.

CAUTION

Liability for your own acts. If Andrea herself had dropped the case of cans, the fact that she is a shareholder, officer, and director of the corporation wouldn't protect her from personal liability. She would still be personally liable for the wrongs (called torts, in legal lingo) that she commits.

So much for theory. In practice, incorporating might not actually give you broad legal protection. In the real world, banks and some major corporate creditors often require the personal guarantee of individuals within the corporation. So the limited liability gained from incorporating isn't always as valuable a legal shield as it first seems.

EXAMPLE: Market Basket Corporation borrows $75,000 from a bank. Andrea signs the promissory note as president of the corporation, but the bank also requires her to guarantee the note personally. The corporation runs into financial difficulties and can't repay the debt. The bank sues and wins a judgment against the business for the unpaid principal plus interest. In collecting on the judgment, the bank can go after Andrea's assets as well as the corporation's property. Incorporation offers no advantage over a sole proprietorship when an owner personally guarantees a loan.

As mentioned above, liability insurance can protect against many of the risks of doing business. Because of this, many businesses can structure themselves as sole proprietorships or partnerships without worrying about unlimited personal liability. But if you operate a high-risk business—childcare center, chemical supply house, asbestos removal service, or college town bar—and you can't get (or can't afford) liability insurance for some risks that you're concerned about, incorporation might be the wisest choice.

EXAMPLE: Loren is afraid that a clerk at his After Hours beverage store might inadvertently sell liquor to an underaged customer or one who has had too much to drink. If that customer got drunk and hurt someone in a car accident, there might be a lawsuit against the business.

Loren contacts his insurance agent to arrange for coverage but learns that his liquor store can afford only $50,000 worth of liability insurance. Loren buys the $50,000 worth of insurance but also forms a corporation—After Hours, Inc.— to run the business. Now if an injured person wins a large verdict, at least Loren won't be personally liable for the portion not covered by his insurance.

The lesson of these examples is clear: Before you decide to incorporate your business primarily to limit your personal liability, analyze what your exposure will be if you simply do business as a sole proprietor (or a partner in a partnership).

The limited liability feature of corporations can be valuable, protecting you from personal liability for:

- debts that you haven't personally guaranteed, including most routine bills for supplies and small items of equipment, and
- injuries suffered by people who are injured by business activities not covered adequately by insurance.

Also, for a business with more than one owner, incorporating can offer a great deal of protection from the misdeeds or bad judgment of your co-owners. In contrast, in a partnership, as noted above, each partner is personally liable for the business-related activities of the other partners.

EXAMPLE: Ted, Mona, and Maureen are partners in Mercury Enterprises. Mona writes a nasty letter about Harold, a former employee, which causes Harold to lose the chance of a good new job. Harold sues for defamation and wins a $60,000 judgment against the partnership. Ted and Maureen are each personally liable to pay the judgment even though Mona wrote the letter.

If Mercury Enterprises had been a corporation, Mona and the corporation would have been liable for the judgment, but Ted and Maureen would not. Ted and Maureen would lose money if the assets of the corporation were seized to pay the judgment, but their own personal assets would be safe.

CAUTION

Payroll taxes. Limited liability doesn't protect you if you fail to deposit taxes withheld from employees' wages—especially if you have anything to do with making decisions about what bills the corporation pays first. Also, because unpaid withheld taxes aren't dischargeable in bankruptcy, you want to pay these before you pay other debts (most of which can be wiped out in bankruptcy) in case your business goes downhill.

Income Taxes

Federal taxation of corporations is a very complicated topic. Here I deal only with basic concepts.

The federal tax laws distinguish between two types of corporations. A "C corporation" is treated as a tax-paying entity separate from its investors and it must pay corporate federal income tax. By contrast, a corporation that chooses "S corporation" status doesn't pay federal income tax; instead, income taxes are paid by the corporation's owners.

 Law From the Real World

Going With Your Gut

Several years ago, John took over his dad's rug cleaning business as a sole proprietor. He didn't expect the business to ever grow beyond its status as a small local facility with six employees and $400,000 in annual sales. But grow it did—first to ten, then to 25 employees, operating in four suburban cities and taking in $3.5 million a year.

About this time, John and his wife bought a nice house, put a few dollars in the bank, and finished paying off the promissory note to his dad for the purchase of the business. Things were going so well that John began to worry about what would happen to his personal assets if the business were sued for big bucks. He reviewed his insurance coverage and sensibly increased some of it. He reviewed his operations and improved several systems, including the one for storing, handling, and disposing of toxic materials. Still, he felt vaguely disquieted.

Finally, even though he couldn't identify any other risks likely to result in a successful lawsuit against his company, John decided to incorporate, to limit his personal liability for the business's debts. He tried to explain his gut feelings of worry to his father but felt he wasn't quite making sense. The older man interrupted and said, "I think you're trying to say that things have been going so well lately that something is bound to mess up soon. And if they do, you want as much of a legal shield between your personal assets and those of the business as possible."

"Precisely," John said. "But I've already protected myself against all obvious risks, so I can't logically justify a decision to incorporate."

His father replied, "John, business decisions are like any other—if your gut tells you to be a little extra careful, go with it. Running a small business means being ready to trust your own intuition."

S Corporations

Electing to do business as an "S corporation" lets you have the limited liability of a corporate shareholder but pay income taxes on the same basis as a sole proprietor or a partner. Among other things, this means that as long as you actively participate in the business of the S corporation, business losses can be used as an offset against your other income—reducing, maybe even eliminating, your tax burden. But be aware that under a federal tax law that took effect as of 2018, there is a cap on the amount of business losses you can claim. The corporation itself doesn't pay taxes, but files an informational tax return telling what each shareholder's portion of the corporate income is.

EXAMPLE: Paul decides to start an environmental cleanup business. Because insurance isn't available to cover all of the risks of this business, he forms a corporation called Ecology Action, Inc. This limits Paul's personal liability if there's a lawsuit against the corporation for an act not covered by insurance.

Paul is also concerned about taxes. He expects his company to lose money during its first few years; he'd like to claim those losses on his personal tax return to offset income he'll be receiving from consulting and teaching work. He registers with the IRS as an S corporation. Unless he changes that tax status later, his corporation won't pay any federal income tax. Paul will report the corporation's income loss on his own Form 1040 and will be able to use it as an offset against income from other sources.

For many years, if you wanted to limit the personal liability of all owners of your business and have the income and losses reported only on the owners' income tax returns, you would have no choice but to create an S corporation. Today, you can accomplish the same goal by creating an LLC. Because an LLC offers its owners the significant advantage of greater flexibility in allocating profits and losses, it's generally better to structure your business as an LLC than

as an S corporation. (But see "Choosing Between a Corporation and an LLC," below, for a discussion of when it might be better to create an S corporation.)

SEE AN EXPERT

Limits on deductions. You can deduct S corporation losses on your personal return only to the extent of the money you put into the corporation (to buy stock) and any money you personally loaned to the corporation. Also, if you don't work actively in the S corporation, there are potential problems with claiming losses, because they might be considered losses from passive activities. For the most part, you can use losses from passive activities only to offset income from passive activities. See your tax adviser for technical details.

Shareholders pay income tax on their share of the corporation's profits regardless of whether they actually receive the money or not. If the corporation suffers a loss, shareholders can claim their share of that loss.

EXAMPLE: Assume the same facts as in the previous example, except that there are two other shareholders in Ecology Action, Inc. Paul owns 50% of the stock, and Ellen and Ted each own 25%. Paul would report 50% of the corporation's profit or loss on his personal tax return, and Ellen and Ted would each report 25% on theirs.

Most states follow the federal pattern in taxing S corporations: They don't impose a corporate tax, choosing instead to tax the shareholders for corporate profits. About half a dozen states, however, do tax an S corporation the same as a C corporation. The tax division of your state treasury department can tell you how S corporations are taxed in your state.

RELATED TOPIC

To be treated as an S corporation, all shareholders must sign and file IRS Form 2553, *Election by a Small Business Corporation.* For more information on this and other requirements for electing S corporation status, see Chapter 8.

C Corporations

Under federal income tax laws, a "C corporation" is a separate entity from its shareholders. This means that the corporation pays taxes on any income that's left after business expenses have been paid.

As you saw earlier in this chapter, a sole proprietorship doesn't pay federal income tax as a separate entity; the owner simply reports the business's income or loss on Schedule C of Form 1040 and adds it to (or, in the case of a loss, subtracts it from) the owner's other income. Similarly, a partnership doesn't pay federal income tax; rather, the partnership annually files a form with the IRS to report each partner's share of yearly profit or loss from the partnership business. Each partner then adds his or her share of partnership income to other income reported on his or her personal tax return (the familiar Form 1040) or deducts his or her share of loss. And an S corporation is treated as a sole proprietorship or partnership for federal income tax purposes, depending on the number of owners.

A C corporation is different. It reports its profits on Form 1120 and pays corporate tax on that income. In addition, if the profits are distributed to shareholders in the form of dividends, the shareholders pay tax on the dividends they receive (creating the much-feared "double-taxation" scenario).

In practice, however, a C corporation might not have to pay any corporate income tax even though it is a separate taxable entity. Here's how: In most incorporated small businesses, the owners are also employees. They receive salaries and bonuses as compensation for the services they perform for the corporation. The corporation then deducts this "reasonable" compensation as a business expense. In many small corporations, compensation to owner-employees eats up all the potential corporate profits, so there's no taxable income left for the corporation to pay taxes on.

Should Your Corporation Elect S Corporation Status?

For federal tax purposes, it's often best for a start-up company to elect to be an S corporation rather than a C corporation. To make sure an S corporation is best for you, speak to a knowledgeable accountant or other tax adviser. Also keep in mind that an LLC might be an even better choice than either type of corporation.

Starting as an S corporation rather than a C corporation could be wise for several reasons:

- Because income from an S corporation is taxed at only one level rather than two, your total tax bill will likely be less. (But be aware that the two-tier tax structure for C corporations can sometimes be an advantage. See the discussion below on how a C corporation can achieve tax savings through income splitting.)
- Your business might have an operating loss the first year. With an S corporation, you generally can pass that loss on to your personal income tax return, using it to offset income that you (and your spouse, if you're married) might have from other sources. Of course, if you're expecting a profit rather than a loss—because, for example, you're converting a profitable sole proprietorship or partnership to a corporation—this pass-through for losses won't be an advantage to you.
- Interest you incur to buy S corporation stock is potentially deductible as an investment interest expense.
- When you sell the assets of your S corporation, you might be taxed less on your gain than if you operated the business as a C corporation (because of the dual taxation structure of corporations).

Your decision to elect to be an S corporation isn't permanent. If you later find there are tax advantages to being a C corporation, you can easily drop your S corporation status, but timing is important.

EXAMPLE: Zoey forms a one-person catering corporation, Zoey Enterprises Ltd. She owns all the stock and is the main person running the business. The corporation hires her as an employee with the title of president. The corporation pays her a salary plus bonuses that consume all of the corporation's profits. Zoey's salary and bonuses are tax deductible to the corporation as a corporate business expense. There are no corporate profits to tax. Zoey simply pays tax on the income that she receives from the corporation, the same as any other corporate employee.

The End of Tax Savings Through Income Splitting?

Prior to 2018, you might have wanted to consider leaving some corporate income in the corporation to finance the growth of your business rather than paying out all the corporate profits in the form of salaries and bonuses. Doing so could often save tax dollars because, under the longstanding system of corporate tax brackets, for the first $50,000 of taxable corporate income, the tax rate and actual taxes paid would generally be lower than what you'd pay as an individual.

You can see how the federal government taxed corporate income prior to 2018 in the chart below. Note that the corporate tax rate reached a high of 39% for taxable income between $100,000 and $335,000, and then dropped down once taxable income exceeded $335,000.

Pre-2018 Corporate Tax Rates

Taxable income over	Not over	Tax rate
$0	$50,000	15%
$50,000	$75,000	25%
$75,000	$100,000	34%
$100,000	$335,000	39%
$335,000	$10,000,000	34%
$10,000,000	$15,000,000	35%
$15,000,000	$18,333,333	38%
$18,333,333		35%

Corporate Taxation Now: A Flat Rate and No Brackets

As of 2018, all profits for traditional (C-type) corporations are taxed at a flat rate of 21%. After roughly 80 years of at least some bracketing of corporate tax rates, now there are no tax brackets for corporation profits.

Here's an example of how, prior to 2018, a small incorporated business could split income between the corporation and its owners, retaining money in the corporation for expenses and lowering the corporation's tax liability to an amount that's actually less than what would have to be paid by the principals of the same business if it were not incorporated.

EXAMPLE 1: Sally and Randy run their own incorporated lumber supply company, S & R Wood, Inc. In 2016, their sales increased to $1.2 million. After the close of the third quarter, Sally and Randy learned that S & R Wood was likely to make $110,000 net profit (net taxable corporate income) for the year. They decided to reward themselves and other key employees with moderate raises in pay, give a small yearend bonus to other workers, and buy some needed equipment.

This reduced the company's net taxable income to $40,000—an amount that Sally and Randy felt was prudent to retain in the corporation for expansion or in case next year's operations were less profitable. Taxes on these retained earnings were paid at the lowest corporate rate, 15%. If Sally and Randy had wanted to take home more money instead of leaving it in the business, they could have increased their salaries and paid individual income taxes at a rate of at least 10% but more probably 25% or 28% or higher, depending on their tax brackets.

CAUTION

Watch out for a double-tax trap.
C corporation shareholders (like Sally and Randy) can also consider taking some income in the form of dividends rather than salary. Doing so, however, will often increase the tax burden because both the corporation and the shareholder will have to pay income tax on the distributed funds. Still, in some situations, taking some dividends in place of salary might make sense—for example, if in 2018 or later, the corporation pays the flat 21% tax and the shareholder is in the 28% (or higher) bracket. In that case, the money saved on income and Social Security taxes will more than offset the fact that the corporation can't deduct the dividend payment for tax purposes. But this gets complicated. Let a tax pro help you figure it out.

EXAMPLE 2: Now assume S & R Wood is not incorporated but instead is operated as a partnership. Now the entire net profits of the business ($110,000 minus the bonuses to workers and deductible expenditures for equipment) are taxed to Sally and Randy. The result is that the $40,000 (which was retained by the corporation in the above example) is taxed at their individual rate of 25%, 28%, or higher rather than the flat 21% corporate rate (effective as of 2018).

For a more detailed explanation of how income-splitting can be an advantage to owners of small corporations, see *How to Form Your Own California Corporation* or *Incorporate Your Business: A Step-by-Step Guide to Forming a Corporation in Any State*, both by Anthony Mancuso (Nolo).

The main point to remember is that once your business becomes profitable, doing business as a C corporation allows a degree of flexibility in planning and controlling your federal income taxes that is unavailable to partnerships and sole proprietorships. To determine whether or not favorable corporate tax rates are a compelling reason

for your business to incorporate, you'll need to study IRS regulations or go through an analysis with your accountant or other tax adviser.

Tax savings might be a largely theoretical advantage for the person just starting out. If your business is like many start-ups, your main concern will be generating enough income from the business to pay yourself a reasonable wage. Retaining profits in the business will come later. In this situation, the tax advantages of incorporating are illusory.

EXAMPLE: In its first year of operation, Maria's store, The Bookworm, has a profit of $25,000. As the sole proprietor, Maria withdraws the entire $25,000 as her personal salary, which for 2018 means part of her income is taxed at 10% and part at 12% after she subtracts her deductions and personal exemption. It doesn't make sense for Maria to incorporate to take advantage of income-splitting techniques—even if she could get by on say, $20,000 a year, if she left the remaining $5,000 in the corporation, it would be taxed at the flat 21% corporate tax rate, so her total tax bill would be higher.

21% Flat Rate Doesn't Apply to S Corporations

The 21% flat rate for retained earnings doesn't apply to S corporations because, as discussed above, an S corporation does not pay taxes on earnings. Individual shareholders in an S corporation pay taxes on their portion of corporate earnings at their personal income tax rates (as if they were partners in a partnership). This is true whether or not those earnings are distributed to them, meaning that even if the shareholders do leave some earnings in the corporation, the shareholders will be taxed on those earnings at their regular tax rates.

However, because an S corporation is a pass-through entity, in most cases, shareholders will be entitled to deduct 20% of their S corporation income as of 2018.

Fringe Benefits

The tax rules governing fringe benefits are complicated. Generally, however, if your business will be offering fringe benefits to its employees, you can enjoy a tax advantage if you organize as a C corporation. The business can pay for employee benefits and then take these amounts as business expense deductions. You and the other shareholders who work as employees of your corporation can have the corporation pay for employee benefits such as:

- deferred compensation plans
- group term life insurance
- reimbursement of employee medical expenses that are not covered by insurance, and
- health and disability insurance.

But the real advantage is how these fringe benefits are treated on your personal tax return. As a shareholder, you won't be personally taxed for the value of these employment benefits. That's because employees of a C corporation—even if they're owners—do not have to pay income tax on the value of the fringe benefits they receive. So, for example, your corporation may decide to provide medical insurance for employees and to reimburse employees for uninsured medical payments. The corporation can deduct these payments as a business expense—including the portion paid for the corporation's owner-employees—and you and the other owner-employees are not taxed on these benefits.

Other types of business entities can also deduct the cost of many fringe benefits as business expenses, but owners who receive these benefits will ordinarily be taxed on their value. That's because the tax laws distinguish between an employee and a self-employed person. The tax laws say that you're a self-employed person—and therefore are taxed on your fringe benefits—if you're a sole proprietor, a partner in a partnership, a member of an LLC that's taxed as a partnership, or an owner of more than 2% of the shares of an S corporation. An owner-employee of a C corporation, however, isn't classified as a self-employed person. So when it comes to the taxation of fringe benefits, owner-employees of a corporation enjoy a unique advantage.

This favorable tax treatment might seem like a powerful reason to organize your business as a C corporation. Not so fast. Obviously, there's no advantage unless your business provides these benefits to employees in the first place. And that might be too expensive for some new businesses—especially because many types of employee benefits must be provided on a nondiscriminatory basis to a wide range of employees or to none, and must not be designed to primarily aid the business owner. If you put together a fringe benefit package that favors you and the other owner-employees, the IRS will require you and the other owners to pay taxes on the value of the benefits received. Few new businesses can afford to carry expensive benefit programs—a cost that typically more than offsets any tax advantage to the owners of a C corporation.

Here are some of the IRS ground rules for fringe benefit plans:

- **Medical Reimbursement Plans.** Your business can set up a plan that will reimburse your employees for certain ancillary health benefits that are not covered by health insurance—for example, dental and vision coverage, long-term care, and disability coverage. Your plan can also include reimbursement of such expenses incurred by the spouse and dependents of each employee. Many technical rules apply to medical reimbursement plans, so you'll certainly want to consult with an experienced CPA or a benefits lawyer before creating such a plan. But here's some good news: If you're the only employee of your corporation, you're not limited to reimbursing for ancillary benefits. You can reimburse all health expenses not covered by health insurance for yourself, your spouse, and your dependents.

- **Group Life Insurance.** Your business can provide up to $50,000 of group term life insurance tax free to employees (including yourself) if you meet certain conditions. Generally, for life insurance to qualify as a group plan, you must provide it to at least ten full-time employees during the year. As an owner-employee of a small corporation, you'll probably be a "key employee" under the tax laws. A key employee is an officer who is paid more than $185,000 a year (this figure is revised periodically), an owner of at least 5% of the company, or an owner of at least 1% of the company who is paid more than $150,000 a year. If you are a key employee and want to deduct the cost of the insurance from your gross income, you must demonstrate that your plan doesn't favor key employees. You can show, for example, that your plan benefits at least 70% of your employees, or that at least 85% of the participating employees are not key employees. For more details, consult IRS Publication 15-B, *Employer's Tax Guide to Fringe Benefits* (available at www.irs.gov).

Retirement Plans

It used to be that by incorporating, you could set up a better tax-sheltered retirement plan than you could get as a sole proprietor, a partner, or a shareholder-employee of an S corporation. There are no longer any significant differences. See the discussion of "Fringe Benefits" for sole proprietorships, above, for more information.

Attracting Investors

To start and successfully run a small business, you might need more money than you can muster from your own savings or the cash generated by the enterprise. As explained in greater depth in Chapter 9, you have two basic options in raising money from outside sources: borrowing it or getting it from investors. If you expect to seek money from investors—even if they're family members, friends, or business associates—there's a substantial advantage in forming a corporation.

Unlike a lender who, in return for providing money, receives a promise that you'll repay it with interest, an investor becomes a part-owner of the business. Although it's possible to form a partnership and make an investor a partner or to form an LLC and make an investor a member, it's often more practical to form a corporation and make the investor a shareholder. That little piece of paper that the corporation issues—the "stock certificate"—is tangible proof of the shareholder's ownership interest in the business and it's something that most investors have come to expect. Put another way, if you offer an investor a partnership interest or an LLC interest, you're more likely to run into resistance than if you offer stock in a corporation.

Keep in mind that shareholders don't necessarily have to have equal rights to elect the board of directors or to receive dividends. To distinguish between various types of shareholders, you can issue different classes of stock with different rights, for example:

- common, voting shares to the initial owners who will be working in the business
- nonvoting shares for key employees to keep them loyal to the business, or
- nonvoting preferred shares to outside investors, giving them a preference if the corporation declares dividends or is sold.

To repeat this key point, the fact that the corporate structure makes it relatively easy to distinguish between different investors by issuing different classes of stock is a real advantage.

 TIP

Stock options can motivate employees. Issuing stock options to employees at a favorable price can be a great way to motivate them, especially for a business that sells stock to the public or plans to do so. That's because employees who hold options know that if the business is profitable and its stock price goes up, they'll be able to cash in their options at a substantial profit. This can motivate them to help make the business successful. Also, employees who get stock options are often willing to work for a slightly lower salary, making investment capital go farther in the early days of business life.

Illusory Incorporation Advantages

What, in addition to limited liability and some marginal tax advantages, can you gain by incorporating? In drumming up enthusiasm for incorporating, lawyers and accountants often point to additional supposed benefits—but these advantages are rarely all they're cracked up to be.

Illusory Benefit: Easy Transfer of Corporate Stock If You Sell the Business. The sales pitch is that if you want to sell your interest in the corporation (which may be as much as 100% if you own all of the stock), you simply endorse your stock certificate on the back and turn over the certificate to the new owner. The corporation then issues a new stock certificate in the new owner's name to replace the one that you endorsed.

Reality: There's not much of a market for a small company's stock. And most small business owners go to great lengths to restrict the transferability of their stock. Moreover, in many sales of a corporate business, the corporate assets are transferred rather than the stock. (See Chapter 10.)

Illusory Benefit: Continuity of Business. A corporation continues even if an owner dies or withdraws. Plus, there may be a buyout agreement— perhaps funded by insurance—in which the corporation's co-owners have the right to buy out your inheritors. Either way, the corporation stays alive, in contrast to sole proprietorships or partnerships, which are automatically dissolved when the owner or a partner dies.

Reality: The death of a principal is traumatic whether you're a sole proprietorship, a partnership, or a corporation. Usually the factors that allow a business to survive are personal and have nothing to do with its formal legal structure. You don't need to incorporate to ensure that your business will continue after your death. A sole proprietor can use a living trust or will to transfer the business to his or her heirs, and partners frequently have insurance-funded buyout agreements that allow the remaining partners to continue the business. (See Chapter 5.)

Illusory Benefit: Centralized Management. In corporations with a number of shareholders, management is typically centralized under a board of directors. With a partnership consisting of many partners, management can become fragmented.

Reality: If you are a partner in a partnership, it doesn't take a board of directors to centralize the management; chances are that you and the other owners will make all decisions over a cup of coffee.

Conclusion: In weighing the pros and cons of incorporation, concentrate on whether you believe you have a real need to limit your personal liability and also on whether you can get substantial tax benefits by retaining some earnings in the corporation and setting up fringe benefit plans. If you conclude that it would be beneficial to form a business entity that offers limited liability, the LLC is often your best choice. And for many new businesses—especially those that won't run up significant debt or expose their owners to the threat of lawsuits—a sole proprietorship or partnership might be a perfectly adequate way to go, keeping in mind that you can always incorporate the business or form an LLC later.

Structuring your business as a corporation is not only advantageous but actually essential if—like many small business owners—you dream of someday attracting investors through a public offering. And, fortunately, it's become far easier than it used to be for a small business to do just that without turning to a conventional stock underwriting company. Congress and state legislatures have rules—often called "private offering exemptions"—that allow a small corporation to raise from $1 million to $5 million annually without having to meet the usual IPO requirements.

RELATED TOPIC

Forming and running a corporation is discussed in more detail in Chapter 3.

Limited Liability Companies

The LLC is the newest form of business entity. It has enjoyed a meteoric rise in popularity among both entrepreneurs and lawyers—and for good reason. It's often a very attractive alternative to the traditional ways of doing business, which are described above.

Once you've decided that your business should be organized as an entity that limits your personal liability for business debts, you'll have to weigh the pros and cons of forming an LLC against the pros and cons of forming a corporation. Sometimes one or the other will clearly emerge as the better choice. Other times the differences are more subtle—which often means that either will suit your needs equally well. After you've absorbed the information on both legal formats, see "Choosing Between a Corporation and an LLC," below, for help in choosing between the two.

RESOURCE

For an in-depth discussion of LLCs and step-by-step guidance on creating one, see *Form Your Own Limited Liability Company,* by Anthony Mancuso (Nolo).

Limited Personal Liability

As with a corporation, all owners of an LLC enjoy limited personal liability. This means that being a member of an LLC doesn't normally expose you personally to legal liability for business debts and court judgments against the business. Generally, if you become an LLC member, you risk only your share of capital paid into the business. You will, however, be responsible for any business debts that you personally guarantee (of course, you can reduce your risk to zero by not doing this) and for any wrongs (torts) that you personally commit (a good insurance policy should help here—see Chapter 12).

By contrast, as discussed above, owners of a sole proprietorship or general partnership have unlimited liability for business debts, as do the general partners in a limited partnership (and limited partners who take part in managing the business—discussed below).

Number of Owners

Every state allows an LLC to be formed by just one person. This means that if you plan to be the sole owner of a business and you wish to limit your personal liability, you have a choice of forming a corporation or an LLC.

RESOURCE

For an in-depth discussion of single-member LLCs and step-by-step guidance on creating one, see *Nolo's Guide to Single-Member LLCs: How to Form & Run Your Single-Member Limited Liability Company,* by David M. Steingold **(Nolo).**

Tax Flexibility

If you create a single-member LLC, it will not be taxed as a separate entity, like a C corporation, unless you elect to have it taxed in this manner.

Corporations and LLCs Use Different Language

Although there are many similarities between corporations and LLCs, there are many differences as well—especially when it comes to terminology, as shown in the following chart:

Concept	Corporation Word	LLC Word
What an owner is called	Shareholder	Member
What an owner owns	Shares of stock	Membership interest
What document creates the entity	Articles of Incorporation (or, in some states, Certificate of Incorporation or Charter)	Articles of Organization
What document spells out internal operating procedures	Bylaws	Operating Agreement

Normally, you won't choose corporate-style taxation, preferring to have your single-member LLC report its profits (or losses) on Schedule C of your personal return, just as a sole proprietorship would. Technically, the IRS refers to this kind of single-member LLC as a disregarded entity.

Similarly, if you have an LLC with two or more members, it will be treated as a partnership for tax purposes, with each partner reporting and paying income tax on his or her share of LLC profits unless you elect to have the LLC taxed as a corporation. Again, you normally won't elect to do this, preferring to have your multimember LLC follow the partnership tax route. This means that the LLC will report its income (or loss) on Form 1065, an informational return that notifies the IRS of how much each member earned (or lost). Each member will then report his or her share of profits or losses on that member's personal Form 1040.

Occasionally, the members of an LLC will conclude that there's an advantage to being taxed like a C corporation, with two levels of tax—one at the business entity level (for company profits) and another at the owners' personal income tax level (for salaries and dividends). LLCs that are taxed like C corporations are able to split monies between business owners and the business itself, which might result in a significant overall tax saving. (See "Tax Savings Through Income Splitting," above, for a discussion of income splitting in the corporate context.)

If, after reviewing all the financial implications—and after perhaps seeking the advice of a tax pro—you elect to have your LLC treated as a C corporation, you'll do this by filing IRS Form 8832, *Entity Classification Election*. Where the LLC has two or more members, those members can all sign the form or authorize one member or manager to sign.

The IRS also allows an LLC to elect to be taxed as an S corporation, which requires filing IRS Form 2553, *Election by a Small Business Corporation*, instead of Form 8832. This could be a solution to the self-employment tax dilemma discussed below. But by electing S corporation taxation, you'll have to report distributions based on ownership proportions; you'll lose the flexibility in assigning profits and losses that's ordinarily available to an LLC. Don't make this election until you've talked to a CPA or tax lawyer.

For more information on tax elections for an LLC, read IRS Publication 3402, *Taxation of Limited Liability Companies*.

> **TIP**
> **Electing to have your LLC taxed as a C corporation can be advantageous if you want to receive tax-free fringe benefits from the business.** If you follow the usual practice of having pass-through taxation for your LLC—meaning that the business isn't taxed as a separate entity—then as a business owner, you'll be taxed on the value of the fringe benefits you receive from the LLC (unlike other employees). A different rule applies if you elect to have your LLC taxed as a C corporation. In that situation, as long as you meet the IRS guidelines, you can receive fringe benefits as an owner-employee of the LLC and not have to pay tax on the value of those benefits. (For more on the tax treatment of fringe benefits, see the discussion of "Fringe Benefits" for C corporations, above.)

Flexible Management Structure

An LLC member may be an individual or a separate legal entity such as a partnership or corporation that has invested in the LLC. You and the other members jointly run the LLC unless you choose to have it run by a single member, an outside manager, or a management group—which may consist of members, nonmembers, or both. If you decide to form an LLC, I recommend that all the members sign an operating agreement that spells out how the business will be managed. Again, the details of how to do this are covered well in *Form Your Own Limited Liability Company,* by Anthony Mancuso (Nolo).

Flexible Distribution of Profits and Losses

The members of an LLC can divide the LLC's profits and losses any way they want. Although it's common to divide LLC profits and losses according to the percentage of the business's assets contributed by each member, this isn't legally required.

EXAMPLE: Jim, Janna, Jill, and Jerry—certified personal trainers—form 4J Personal Trainers, LLC, to operate a family fitness center. Each contributes $25,000 to the enterprise. Because Jim, who has a strong business background, has put together the LLC, set up a bookkeeping system, arranged for a bank loan to purchase necessary equipment, and negotiated a very favorable lease at a good location, the owners state in their operating agreement that for the first two years, Jim will receive 40% of the LLC's profits and that Janna, Jill, and Jerry will each receive 20%. After that, they'll share profits equally.

By contrast, rules governing corporate profits and losses are considerably more restrictive. A C corporation can't allocate profits and losses to shareholders; instead, shareholders must receive dividends according to the number of shares they own—if they receive dividends at all. (But it is possible, although more cumbersome, to establish two or more classes of stock, each with different dividend rights.) Similarly, in an S corporation, profits and losses are attributed to the shareholders based on their shares: A shareholder who owns 25% of the shares in an S corporation ordinarily must be allocated 25% of profits and losses—no more and no less. Sometimes, however, corporations can get away from this strict formula by adjusting the salaries of shareholders who work in the business.

The easy flexibility allowed to LLCs in distributing profits and losses permits businesses to be creative and even make distributions to members who have contributed no cash.

EXAMPLE: Howard and Saul run a home repair business organized as an LLC. Howard puts up all the money needed to buy a van, tools, and supplies and to pay for advertising brochures and radio commercials. Saul, who has little cash but loads of experience in doing home repairs, will contribute future services to the LLC. Although the owners could agree to split profits and losses equally, they decide that Howard will get 60% for the first three years as a way of paying him back for taking the risk of putting up cash.

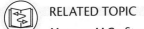
RELATED TOPIC

More on LLCs. Starting and operating an LLC is discussed in more detail in Chapter 4.

Choosing Between a Corporation and an LLC

Let's assume that you've read all the earlier material in this chapter and that you now understand the chief legal, tax, and financial characteristics of the main types of business entities. Let's also assume that you've concluded it would be best to operate your small business through an entity that limits the personal liability of all the owners—even if following this strategy involves a bit more paperwork, complexity, and possible expense.

For the reasons explained earlier in this chapter, you've probably narrowed your choice of entity to either the tried and true corporation or the newer and streamlined LLC. Which is better? There's no answer to this question that applies to every business. Nevertheless, some general principles might be helpful.

For the majority of small businesses, the relative simplicity and flexibility of the LLC makes it the better choice. This is especially true if your business will hold property, such as real estate, that's likely to increase in value. That's because C corporations and their shareholders are subject to a double tax (both the corporation and the shareholders are taxed) on the increased value of the property when the property is sold or the corporation is liquidated. By contrast, LLC member-owners avoid this double taxation because the business's tax liabilities are passed through to them; the LLC itself does not pay a tax on its income.

But an LLC isn't always the better choice. Occasionally, other factors might tip the balance toward a corporation. Such factors include the following:

- **You'd like to provide extensive fringe benefits to owner-employees.** Often, when you form a corporation, you expect to be both a shareholder

(owner) and an employee. The corporation can, for example, hire you to serve as its chief executive officer and pay you a tax-deductible salary, which, from a tax standpoint, is far better than paying you dividends, which can't be deducted by the corporation as a business expense and therefore wind up being taxed twice (once at the corporate level and once at the personal level). But corporate employees (including employees of a C corporation who are also owners) don't just receive pay—most also receive fringe benefits. These benefits can include the payment of health insurance premiums and direct reimbursement of medical expenses. The corporation can deduct the cost of these benefits and they are not treated as taxable income to the employees. Having your own corporation pay for these fringe benefits and then deduct the cost as a business expense can be an attractive feature of doing business through a C corporation. These opportunities for you to receive tax-favored fringe benefits are somewhat reduced if you do business as an LLC.

- **You want to entice or keep key employees by offering stock options and stock bonus incentives.** Simply put, LLCs don't have stock; corporations do. While it's possible to reward an employee by offering a membership interest in an LLC, the process is awkward and likely to be less attractive to employees. Therefore, if you plan to offer ownership in your business as an employee incentive, it makes sense to incorporate rather than form an LLC.

- **You plan to sell ownership interests to the public.** The securities industry and securities laws are geared to the selling of corporate shares—not LLC membership interests. So a corporation is the better choice if you'll be going public. If you're not planning to go public immediately but might do so someday, you can start out as an LLC and then convert to a corporation later on.

Choosing Between an LLC and an S Corporation: Self-Employment Taxes Can Tip the Balance

You know that taxes are withheld from employees' paychecks. In 2021, for example, employers must withhold 7.65% of the first $142,800 of an employee's pay for Social Security and Medicare taxes, and 1.45% of earnings above that amount for Medicare taxes. The employer adds an equal amount (to match the employee's share of Social Security and Medicare taxes) and sends these funds to the IRS. The total sent to the IRS is 15.3% on the first $142,800 of wages and 2.9% on earnings above that amount. (See Chapter 8.)

You might not be aware that the IRS collects a similar 15.3% tax on the first $142,800 earned by a self-employed person and a 2.9% tax on earnings above that amount for Medicare alone. For this reason, the Social Security and Medicare tax is often referred to as the "self-employment" tax.

In 2021, there is a Medicare surtax of 0.9% on the wages and self-employment income of high earners. This surtax applies when a single person's earnings exceed $200,000 and when a married couple's earnings exceed $250,000. On earnings above those amounts, the Medicare tax rate becomes 3.8% rather than 2.9%. This surtax does not affect the 1.45% rate paid by an employer.

For an S corporation, the rules on the self-employment tax are well established: As an S corporation shareholder, you pay the self-employment tax on money you receive as compensation for services—but *not* on profits that automatically pass through to you as a shareholder. For example, if your total share of S corporation income is $100,000 in 2021 and you perform services for the corporation reasonably worth $65,000, you would be taxed 15.3% on the $65,000 but not on the remaining $35,000.

If you have a single-member LLC, you'll owe self-employment tax on 100% of your company's profits. The rules for multimember LLCs are more complicated, and, for now, somewhat unsettled. Proposed IRS regulations (which Congress has placed on hold) would impose the self-employment tax on your entire share of LLC profits in any of the following situations:

- You participate in the business for more than 500 hours during the LLC's tax year.
- You work in an LLC that provides professional services in the fields of health, law, engineering, architecture, accounting, actuarial science, or consulting (no matter how many hours you work).
- You're empowered to sign contracts on behalf of your LLC.

Even though these proposed regulations do not have the force of law, the IRS says it won't challenge you if you use them in determining your liability for self-employment tax. This means that if you don't fall into one of the three categories listed above, you can use the same rules that apply to S corporation shareholders. But if you *do* fall into one of the above categories, you should assume that 100% of your income from the business will be subject to self-employment tax (although the amount that's over the current year's Social Security tax cutoff figure—$142,800 in 2021—will be subject only to Medicare tax).

The point is that, in some cases, an S corporation shareholder may pay less self-employment tax than some LLC members with similar income. You'll need to decide whether these potential tax savings are more important than gaining such LLC advantages as flexibility in management structure and in distributing profits and losses.

- **You're concerned about self-employment taxes.** As an S corporation shareholder, you might wind up paying less self-employment tax than you would as an LLC member. This is explained in "Choosing Between an LLC and S Corporation: Self-Employment Taxes Can Tip the Balance," above.

> **RESOURCE**
>
> **More on choosing a business entity.** See *LLC or Corporation? How to Choose the Right Form for Your Business*, by Anthony Mancuso (Nolo).

Special Structures for Special Situations

It's very likely that the best organizational structure for your small business is either a sole proprietorship, partnership, or corporation, or an LLC. There are, however, some situations in which other, less common entities will either offer some tax or other advantage or will be legally required. Your real estate investment group, for example, might find some benefit in creating a limited partnership (described below). Or, you could find that the law in your state requires you to select a less common structure for your business; for example, if you're a doctor or an accountant and you want to limit your personal liability, state law might require you to form a professional corporation, a professional LLC, or a limited liability partnership.

Limited Partnerships

The kind of partnership covered in "Partnerships," above, is a general partnership. It's very different from another form of partnership known as a limited partnership, which, in certain circumstances, can combine the best attributes of a partnership and a corporation.

Most limited partnerships are formed to invest in real estate because of tax advantages for those who are passive investors; the passive investor is often able to personally write off depreciation and other real estate deductions. For the majority of other types of small businesses with more than one owner, chances are that forming either a general partnership, a corporation, or an LLC will be the best way to go.

A limited partnership works like this: There must be one or more "general partners" with the same basic rights and responsibilities as in any general partnership, and one or more "limited partners," who are usually passive investors. The big difference between a general partner and a limited partner is that the general partner is personally liable for the obligations of the partnership and the limited partner is not personally liable for them. The most a limited partner can lose by investing in a limited partnership is the amount that person:

- paid or agreed to pay into the partnership as a capital contribution, or
- received from the partnership after it became insolvent.

To maintain this limited liability, a limited partner may not participate in the management of the business, with very few exceptions. A limited partner who does get actively involved in the management of the business risks losing immunity from personal liability, meaning having the same legal exposure as a general partner.

The advantage of a limited partnership as a business structure is that it provides a way for business owners to raise money from passive investors (the limited partners) without having either to take in new partners who will be active in the business or to engage in the intricacies of creating a corporation and issuing stock.

EXAMPLE: Anthony and Janice's plan is to buy rundown houses, renovate them, and then sell them at a good profit. All they lack is the cash to make the initial purchases. To solve this problem, they first create a partnership consisting of the two of them. Then they establish a limited partnership, with their own partnership as the general partner, and seek others who are willing to invest for a defined interest in the venture. Anthony and Janice figure that they need $100,000 to get started. They sell ten limited partnership interests at $10,000 each. The limited partners are given the right to a percentage of the profits for a specified number of years, but they are not liable for any obligations of the partnership.

A general partnership that's been operating for years can also create a limited partnership to finance expansion.

EXAMPLE: Judith and Aretha have been partners in a small picture frame shop for two years. They want to expand into a bigger store in a much better location, where they can stock a large selection of fine art prints as well as frames. To raise money, they create a limited partnership, offering each investor an 8% interest in the total net profits of the store for the next three years as well as the return of the invested capital at the end of that period in exchange for a $20,000 investment. They sell four limited partnership interests, raising $80,000.

There is a downside to limited partnerships: Doing business as a limited partnership can be at least as costly and complicated as doing business as a corporation. Although limited partnerships don't have to issue stock, state laws typically require that a limited partnership file registration information about the general and limited partners.

CAUTION

Watch out for confusing labels. Despite the similarity in names, there are major differences between a limited partnership (discussed above) and a limited liability partnership (discussed below).

Choices for Professionals

If you are a professional, such as a doctor, a lawyer, or an accountant, your choice of business structure might have to take into account certain additional factors. These include your need to avoid group liability, and state laws or rules of professional ethics governing your choices of business structure.

Professional Corporations

Laws in every state permit certain professionals to form corporations known as "professional corporations" (PCs) or "professional service corporations." In many states, people in certain occupations (for example, doctors, lawyers, or accountants) who want to incorporate their practice can do so only through a professional corporation. In some states, professionals can incorporate as either a professional corporation or a regular corporation; in either event, the shareholders can elect to have the entity receive S corporation status under the federal tax laws.

The list of professionals eligible to incorporate is different in each state. Usually, though, professionals who must create a professional corporation include:

- accountants
- engineers
- health care professionals, such as audiologists, dentists, nurses, opticians, optometrists, pharmacists, physical therapists, physicians, and speech pathologists
- lawyers
- psychologists
- social workers, and
- veterinarians.

Call your state's corporate filing office (usually the secretary of state or corporation commissioner) to see who is covered in your state.

RESOURCE

Find your state secretary of state office. A list is available at the National Association of Secretaries of State website, www.nass.org. Click on "Membership."

Typically, a professional corporation must be organized for the sole purpose of rendering professional services, and all shareholders must be licensed to render that service. For example, in a medical corporation, all of the shareholders must be licensed physicians.

Professional corporations aren't as popular as they used to be. The main reason for professionals to incorporate—favorable corporate taxation rules—has disappeared. Before 1986, professionals who incorporated could shelter more money from taxes than sole proprietors or partners could. This has all changed. Most professional corporations are now classified as "personal service corporations" by the IRS. As of 2018, the corporate income of personal service corporations is taxed at a flat rate of 21%. Tax laws still give favorable treatment to fringe benefits for corporate employees in professional corporations.

The other reason for professionals to consider incorporating is the limitation on personal liability. It's no secret that malpractice verdicts against professionals continue to climb. Although incorporating can't protect a professional against liability for that person's own negligence, it can protect against liability for an associate's negligence.

EXAMPLE 1: Dr. Anton and Dr. Bartolo are surgeons who practice as partners. Dr. Bartolo leaves a medical instrument inside a patient, who bleeds to death. The jury returns a $2 million verdict against Dr. Bartolo and the partnership. There is only $1 million in malpractice insurance to cover the judgment. Dr. Anton (along with Dr. Bartolo) would be personally liable for the $1 million not covered by insurance.

EXAMPLE 2: Drs. Anton and Bartolo create a professional corporation. Dr. Bartolo commits the malpractice described in Example 1. Dr. Anton, a corporate employee, would not be personally liable for the portion of the verdict not covered by insurance. Dr. Bartolo, however, would still be personally responsible for the $1 million excess, because he was the one guilty of malpractice. (In some states, Dr. Anton would be free from personal liability only if the professional corporation carried at least the minimum amount of insurance mandated by state law.)

Insurance is a better alternative for most professionals than is the limited liability offered by incorporation. But with malpractice rates soaring for many professionals, it's often hard to afford all the insurance you could possibly need, so forming a professional corporation can be a useful backup.

As an alternative to incorporating, professionals wishing to limit their personal liability should consider forming a professional limited liability company or limited liability partnership, as described below.

Professional Limited Liability Companies

As explained above, licensed professionals are permitted to incorporate but, in most states, they can do so only by forming a special type of corporation—a professional corporation. Similarly, in many states, licensed professionals who wish to form an LLC are required to use a special type of LLC known as a "professional limited liability company" (PLLC).

Lawyers or doctors in a group practice, for example, may choose to form a PC or PLLC so that each member of the group is legally liable for only that person's own malpractice—not the malpractice of other members of the group, as would be the case in a partnership. Members of a PLLC also won't be personally liable for other business debts, such as obligations owed to business creditors, lenders, and the landlord.

Typically, state laws require that all PLLC members be licensed to practice the same profession—accounting, for example, or engineering.

Especially if the PLLC consists of lawyers, accountants, engineers, doctors, or other health care professionals, state law might require that each member at least carry a specified amount of malpractice insurance or be bonded.

SEE AN EXPERT

Check the law in your state before setting up a PLLC. If you're a professional and considering forming a PLLC, you need to check your state's statute to learn which professionals can and can't form such an entity. There's wide variation from state to state. (For example, in California, many professionals, such as doctors, therapists, engineers, architects, lawyers, and pharmacists, cannot form any type of LLC.) If you're a member of a state professional society, its administrator might know the answer, or you can check the statute online or at a nearby public library. For information on doing legal research, get Nolo's *Legal Research: How to Find & Understand the Law*, by Stephen Elias (Nolo).

Limited Liability Partnerships

In a few states, laws or professional ethics rulings prevent accounting or law firms from doing business as corporations or LLCs. If you're an accountant or lawyer in such a state and would like some limitation on your personal liability for business obligations, look into forming a "limited liability partnership." Unfortunately, the protection it offers is usually less than you'd get by forming a corporation or LLC—but it's better than nothing.

Available in some but not all states, an LLP is simply a general partnership whose partners enjoy some protection from personal liability. LLPs are authorized under state statutes, and there's a bit of variation from state to state.

Typically, partners in an LLP are personally liable only for their own negligence (malpractice) or that of an employee working directly under the partner's supervision; the partner isn't personally liable for the negligence of anyone else in the firm. That's helpful,

but as a partner in an LLP, you're still personally liable for a large variety of partnership debts not involving your own negligent acts—for example, obligations owed to business creditors, lenders, and the landlord—regardless of which partner incurred the obligation for the partnership.

> **EXAMPLE:** Hillary, Edgar, and Paula—all certified public accountants—want to form a new firm, but determine that ethics rules in their state prevent them from forming a professional corporation or PLLC. Instead, they form an LLP. Hillary, during a period of disarray in her personal life, messes up big time on a tax return for a major client, who has to pay huge penalties to the IRS. The client sues for malpractice and is awarded a $25,000 judgment. The LLP and Hillary are liable for paying the judgment. Edgar and Paula are not.
>
> During the same period, Hillary also orders $15,000 worth of fancy office furniture, which the LLP can't afford. All three partners are personally liable for the furniture debt. (By contrast, if local ethics rules had allowed the three accountants to organize their accounting firm as a PC or PLLC and they had done so, none of them would be personally liable for the cost of the furniture unless they personally guaranteed payment.)

CAUTION

Check the law in your state before setting up an LLP. If you're a professional and considering forming an LLP, you need to check your state's statute to learn which professionals can and can't form an LLP, because of the wide variation from state to state. (For example, only architects, accountants, and lawyers can form LLPs in California, where LLPs are referred to as "registered limited liability partnerships," or RLLPs.) If you're a member of a state professional society, its administrator might know the answer, or you can check the statute online or at a nearby public library. For information on doing legal research, get Nolo's *Legal Research: How to Find & Understand the Law*, by Stephen Elias (Nolo).

Limited liability partnerships are entirely different from limited partnerships (discussed above). Here are the differences between these two similar-sounding business entities:

- A limited partnership consists of at least one general partner and one or more limited partners. A general partner in a limited partnership is personally liable for all debts of and judgments against the business—regardless of who incurred the debt or other liability. A limited partner can generally steer clear of personal liability for any debts or judgments by avoiding active participation in the business.

- A limited liability partnership is a special form of general partnership and is usually reserved for professionals such as doctors, lawyers, and accountants. Normally, partners in an LLP aren't personally liable for the negligent acts of other partners, but are liable for their own negligence and for other partnership debts.

The Benefit Corporation

Chances are, your main motivation for starting a business is to make a profit. It's possible, however, that you and the other shareholders will want to achieve other goals as well. In making decisions, you might want to consider the interests of your employees, your community, or the environment. This can be legally chancy in many states—especially if you have outside investors. State laws traditionally have required corporations to make decisions based solely on the financial interests of shareholders.

This means that if the directors use other factors in running the business, investors can sue them, claiming that the directors have violated their duty to maximize profits. Some states do grant directors more latitude in their decision making. In those states—sometimes called "constituency states"—directors can generally consider the impact of their decisions on employees, creditors, suppliers, consumers, and the community at large. They are not required to do so, however.

Most states (see below) have recently passed laws that let you create a "benefit corporation"—one that requires the directors to consider more than the financial interests of the investors. These "B corporations" can be set up to achieve any of several specific goals, for example:

- providing low-income people with beneficial products or services
- preserving the environment
- improving human health, or
- assisting artists and musicians.

If you create a B corporation, you set out your mission in your corporate charter. The directors can carry out the stated mission without being accused of ignoring the financial interests of the shareholders. There can be some additional advantages to setting up a B corporation: some customers might prefer buying goods or services from a business that has a social or environmental mission—and some investors could relish being part of a do-good organization.

The status of a company as a benefit corporation affects only how state law is applied. It has no bearing on the company's federal tax status. For IRS purposes, a B corporation is like any other corporation: it will be taxed as C corporation unless the owners elect passthrough treatment as an S corporation. (How about that for alphabet soup?) As of late 2020, Washington, D.C., and the following states authorize the formation of B corporations: Arizona, Arkansas, California, Colorado, Connecticut, Delaware, Florida, Hawaii, Idaho, Illinois, Indiana, Kansas, Kentucky, Louisiana, Maine, Maryland, Massachusetts, Minnesota, Montana, Nebraska, Nevada, New Hampshire, New Jersey, New Mexico, New York, North Dakota, Oklahoma, Oregon, Pennsylvania, Rhode Island, South Carolina, Texas, Utah, Vermont, Virginia, West Virginia, and Wisconsin. Legislation is pending in Alaska, Georgia, Iowa, and Mississippi.

RESOURCE

More information, including updated legislation on benefit corporations. Check out www.bcorporation.net and www.benefitcorp.net.

Nonprofit Corporations

Each state permits people to form "nonprofit corporations," also known as "not-for-profit corporations." The main reason people form these corporations is to get tax-exempt status under the Internal Revenue Code (Section 501(c)(3)). To get tax-exempt status, the corporation must have been formed for one or more of the following purposes: the pursuit of charitable, religious, educational, scientific, or literary goals; or testing for public safety, fostering national or international amateur sports competition, or preventing cruelty to children or animals.

If a corporation is tax exempt under Section 501(c)(3), not only is it free from paying taxes on its income, but people and organizations who contribute to the nonprofit corporation can take a tax deduction for their contributions. Because many nonprofit organizations rely heavily on grants from public agencies and private foundations to fund their operations, attaining 501(c)(3) status is critical to success.

Tax-exempt status isn't the only benefit available to a nonprofit corporation. The nonprofit label seems to create an altruistic aura around the organization and the people running it. The message is, "We're not in this for the money—we really do love kids (or music or animals)." Also, an organization that plans to do some heavy mailing might be attracted by the cheaper postal rates that qualifying nonprofits are charged.

What kinds of groups should consider becoming nonprofit corporations? Here's a partial list:

- childcare centers
- shelters for the homeless
- community health care clinics
- museums
- hospitals
- churches, synagogues, mosques, and other places of worship
- schools
- performing arts groups, and
- conservation groups.

Most nonprofit corporations are run by a board of directors or trustees who are actively involved in the corporation's work. Officers and employees (some of whom may also serve on the board) usually carry out the corporation's day-to-day business and often receive salaries.

Keep in mind that if you put assets into a nonprofit corporation, you give up any ownership or proprietary interest in those assets. They must be irrevocably dedicated to the specified nonprofit purpose. If you want to get out of the business, you can't sell it and pocket the cash. If the nonprofit corporation does end, any remaining assets must go to another nonprofit.

RESOURCE

Learn more about nonprofits. This book is addressed primarily to people starting and running a business for profit, so you'll find little here on the peculiarities of nonprofit corporations. If you want to learn about such corporations in greater depth, including how to develop a strategic plan and budget and recruit board members, see *Starting & Building a Nonprofit*, by Peri Pakroo (Nolo).

Cooperatives and Cooperative-Type Organizations

Some people dream of forming a business of true equals—an organization owned and controlled democratically by its members.

These grassroots business organizers often refer to their businesses as a group, collective, or co-op—but these are usually informal rather than legal labels. Everyone who starts a business with others needs to select a legal structure. Generally, this means picking one of the traditional formats described in this chapter: a nonprofit corporation, a partnership, a C corporation, or an LLC. However, some states do have specific laws allowing the formation of a "cooperative corporation." For example, in some states, a consumer "co-op" could be created to manufacture and sell arts and crafts.

If a co-op law exists in your state, it can help make the process of democratic ownership go more smoothly. Otherwise, you'll need to make sure your partnership agreement, corporate bylaws, or LLC operating agreement contains the cooperative features that you and the other members feel are appropriate.

RESOURCE

To learn more about cooperative-type organizations and how to start one, visit the website of the National Cooperative Business Association at www. ncba.coop. You can order many helpful publications there.

Structuring a Partnership Agreement

There are two kinds of partnerships: the general partnership and the limited partnership. This chapter discusses forming the more common general partnership. See "Special Structures for Special Situations," in Chapter 1, for basic information about limited partnerships.

Features of the General Partnership

Main advantages. Simple and inexpensive to create and operate. Owners (partners) report their share of profit or loss on their personal tax returns.

Main disadvantage. Owners (partners) are personally liable for business debts.

Why You Need a Written Agreement

When you form a partnership to run a small business, your partners will probably be family members, close friends, or business associates. You might think it's unnecessary to enter into a formal agreement with people you know quite well. Experience proves otherwise. No matter how rosy things are at the beginning, every partnership inevitably faces problems over the years. A well-thought-out written agreement will help you preserve the business, as well as your friendships.

If you don't sign an agreement, you can still have a legally valid partnership. The laws of your state will dictate how that partnership is run. Every state except Louisiana has adopted either the Uniform Partnership Act (UPA) or the Revised Uniform Partnership Act (RUPA). States have sometimes made slight variations in these laws but there is a remarkable amount of consistency from state to state.

These state laws solve many common partnership problems in a sensible way. For example, the UPA says that if you don't have an agreement, each partner shares equally in the profits and has an equal voice in managing the business. In addition, under the UPA, partners are not entitled to receive compensation for services they provide to the partnership.

Although it's possible that your state law provides exactly what you and your partners want, it's usually better to create your own agreement. And you'll probably want to modify at least some of the terms. For example, if one partner contributes more assets than the others, you might want to give that partner a greater share of the profits. Or you might want to allow one or more partners to receive a salary for their services. You might want to include customized provisions on how to value a partner's interest in the business if a partner dies or leaves. In that situation, many partners want to assign some value to the goodwill of the business for tax purposes—something that does not happen automatically under the UPA. With a written partnership agreement, you can tailor your partnership to fit your needs.

There are other benefits to working out the details in a written partnership agreement. It will get you to focus on issues you might not have thought through with your partners—issues that you and your partners might not agree on. For example, what if one partner wants compensation beyond a share of the profits to recognize work performed in the evening or on weekends for the partnership? By getting issues out into the open early, you can nip potential problems in the bud.

Most Partnership Information Is Confidential

The terms of a partnership agreement for a general partnership don't have to be made public. But, in some states, you must file a certificate of partnership, stating the names of the partners, with a county official (such as the county clerk) or state official (such as the secretary of state).

An Overview of Your Partnership Agreement

It's up to you and your partners to create your partnership. A lawyer can help you focus on issues and suggest possible solutions, but you and your partners—not the lawyer—must decide how your partnership will operate.

This section goes through the clauses that are usually included in a partnership agreement for a small business.

Where to Find Help With Partnership Agreements

The Partnerships section in the Business Formation center on www.nolo.com includes detailed advice for each state on how to establish a partnership.

Form a Partnership, by Denis Clifford and Ralph Warner (Nolo), has extensive material on forming, managing, and ending a partnership. The clauses used in this chapter come from that book. Also, *Legal Forms for Starting & Running a Small Business*, by Fred Steingold (Nolo), contains a sample partnership agreement.

Name and Term

Although many partnerships do business using the last names of the partners, it's both legal and common for a partnership to have one name and do business under another name. For example, the partnership of Jones, Gold, and Sanchez could decide to do business as Seafood Express. The name Seafood Express would be an assumed or fictitious name, which you'd have to register with the appropriate state or county office.

RELATED TOPIC

Chapter 6 contains a thorough discussion of business and product names.

Another issue is how long the partnership will last. If you want it to go on indefinitely, include a clause in your partnership agreement such as this:

> The partnership shall last until it is dissolved by all the partners or a partner leaves, for any reason, including death.

On the other hand, if you plan to develop a particular piece of real estate or do some other finite task, you might want a clause with a definite date, such as one of the following:

> The partnership shall commence as of the date of this agreement and shall continue for a period of _____ years, at which time it shall be dissolved and its affairs wound up.

or

> The partnership shall continue until [*specify an event such as "the completion and sale of The Commercial Office Plaza"*], at which time the partnership shall be dissolved and its affairs wound up.

Purpose

The purpose of the partnership should be broadly stated. The advantage of a broad statement of partnership purpose is that you have flexibility if the business evolves. Here are two typical purpose clauses:

> The purpose of the partnership is to operate one or more stores for the sale of CDs, DVDs, or other related merchandise.

or

> The purpose of the partnership is to operate a bookkeeping and tax preparation service for individual clients and small businesses.

On the other hand, if you're sure you're creating your partnership for a short-term, specific purpose, such as presenting one trade show, it would be appropriate to use a more limited purpose clause, such as:

> The purpose of the partnership is to organize and present this year's Builders and Home Improvement Show at the Municipal Convention Center.

Contributions

Your partnership agreement should describe the initial contributions that you and your partners will make. Often, each partner contributes cash only.

The amounts of contributions may be equal, but don't have to be. For example, one partner might contribute $5,000 while another contributes $1,000 and a third contributes a pickup truck. If a partner contributes property, such as a vehicle, tools, a building, a patent, or a copyright, you need to agree on the value of that property. You can also provide that one of the partners will contribute personal services (perhaps painting the business headquarters) in return for a partnership interest. Keep in mind that a partner can sell, lend, lease, or rent property to the partnership too.

Cash Contributions

It's logically neat if each partner contributes an equal amount of cash to a new business. Otherwise, partners who invest more money than the others may feel entitled to a larger voice in making partnership decisions. But in the real world, not all partners are always able to make equal contributions of cash. One way to handle this is to have the partner who contributes more lend the extra amount to the business rather than contribute it outright.

EXAMPLE: Ricardo and Alberta are opening a martial arts training center. Ricardo has just left a job at a corporation and received a handsome severance package. He's willing to put $40,000 into the business. Alberta, on the other hand, is a single mother who wants to start a business precisely because she is short of money. She can raise $10,000. Alberta could contribute $10,000 and Ricardo $40,000, with Ricardo having more say in partnership decisions than Alberta. But an easier and more democratic approach would be for each to contribute $10,000 in cash, with Ricardo lending the partnership the additional $30,000, to be repaid over three years at 10% annual interest.

A basic clause for equal cash contributions reads as follows:

> The initial capital of the partnership shall be a total of $_____ . Each partner shall contribute an equal share amounting to $_____ no later than _____ , 20_____ . Each partner shall own an equal share of the business.

If a partner can't initially contribute the desired amount of cash, another way to handle it is for the business to agree to accept payments over time. Here's a sample clause:

> Arthur Feldman shall be a partner upon making an initial contribution of $1,000 to the capital of the partnership. He will subsequently contribute to the partnership capital, and his capital account shall be credited, in the amount of $100 per month beginning July 1, 20_____ , until he has contributed a total of $5,000 (including the initial $1,000 payment).

Interest on Partnership Investment. Should partners receive interest on their contributions of capital? Generally, no—after all, the money is already at work building a jointly owned business. But whatever you decide, include a specific clause in the partnership agreement that explicitly covers the issue.

Contributions of Services

Sometimes a partner's contribution consists, wholly or in part, of services. For example, if one partner can't contribute as much cash as the others, that partner could agree to work a certain number of hours more than the other partners at a fixed rate (say $30 per hour) until the contributions were equalized. After that, the partners would work an equal amount of hours each week. If a partner is going to contribute services in return for an interest in the business, this should be spelled out in the partnership agreement.

> EXAMPLE: Margaret and Alice form a 50-50 partnership for catering parties. Each will spend equal time on preparing the food and delivering it. Margaret contributes $10,000 to get the business going. Alice agrees to contribute unpaid labor as a bookkeeper and business manager for one year over and above the amount of time she spends on food-related work. Their intention is to equalize the contributions of the partners.

Contributions of Property

Some or all of the partners may contribute property instead of, or in addition to, cash.

_____ shall contribute property valued at $_____ consisting of _____ by _____ , 20____ . [_If the property is difficult to describe, describe it in detail on a separate sheet of paper marked "Exhibit A" and add here, "The property is more particularly described in Exhibit A, attached to this agreement."_]

SEE AN EXPERT

Getting expert help. If you're transferring property to your partnership, you may need the assistance of a tax expert. Such contributions raise questions about what tax basis (value) will be assigned to the property being transferred. The IRS looks at the tax basis in determining how much profit you've gained when the property is later transferred or sold as well as the amount of losses you can claim on your tax return if the business is not profitable. These tax issues are beyond the scope of this book.

Profits, Losses, Draws, and Salaries

You will need to address how the partnership will compensate the partners. The first issue is how you'll divide profits among partners. Then you should decide whether any partners can receive an early "draw" against their share of the profits—that is, be paid a portion of profits sooner than other partners. This might be appropriate if one partner is coming into the partnership with less savings than the others and is counting on partnership income for living expenses.

You'll also need to think about whether any partners will receive a salary for work they do in the business. If equal partners will all work a roughly equal number of hours, there's no need to pay salaries; an equal division of profits should be adequate. But if one partner will work more hours than the others, paying that partner a salary may make sense. Or you could give the harder-working partner a larger share of the profits. If salaries are paid, they're a normal business expense and don't come out of profits.

If profits are shared equally, you could use the following clause:

The partners will share all profits equally, and they will be distributed [_monthly, yearly, etc._]. All losses of the partnership will also be shared equally.

On the other hand, if profits and losses will be shared unequally, here are some sample clauses to consider:

Partnership profits and losses will be shared among the partners as follows:

Name	Percentage
_____	_____
_____	_____
_____	_____

---

or

Partnership profits and losses shall be shared among the partners as follows:

Name	% of Profits	% of Losses
_____	_____	_____
_____	_____	_____
_____	_____	_____

---

or

Partnership profits and losses shall be shared by the partners in the same proportion as their initial contributions of capital bear to each other.

A draw is an advance of anticipated profits paid to a partner or partners. It's easiest if draws are to be made by all partners. But if you want to authorize draws for only certain partners, you could include the following clause:

Partners _____ and _____ are entitled to draws from expected partnership profits. The amount of each draw will be determined by a vote of the partners. The draws shall be paid [_monthly or on any other kind of schedule that you agree to_].

You might also want to provide for the partnership to retain some profits in the business for new equipment, expansion, or employee bonuses.

Here's a sample clause:

In determining the amount of profits available for distribution, allowance will be made for the fact that some money must remain undistributed and available as working capital as determined by [_for example, "all partners" or "a majority of partners"_].

 Law From the Real World

A Profitable Experience

Jan and Mike discussed forming a partnership to open a desktop publishing service aimed at helping small businesses design brochures, flyers, and other promotional material. The idea of sharing the work and profits 50-50 appealed to both of them. There was only one hang-up: The partnership agreement form they looked at provided for profits to be divided at the end of the year. This was okay with Mike, who had received a generous severance package from a former job, but not for Jan, who was trying to put her daughter through college and had no financial cushion.

Recognizing their different circumstances, Jan and Mike agreed that Jan could take a $3,000 monthly draw against her share of anticipated partnership profits. And because they realized a new business needs all the cash it can get its hands on, Mike would wait and take the same total amount at the end of the year. Then Mike and Jan would split any additional profits.

To guard against the possibility that Jan's draw would use up more than half of the profits and shortchange Mike, the partners, after checking the tax consequences with their tax adviser, also agreed that any amount Jan received over her 50% share would be considered a personal loan from the partnership, to be repaid out of her share of future years' profits.

Even though profits are reinvested, you and the other partners are taxed on your share of the profit at your individual rates. (A C corporation may afford tax advantages over a partnership when a business has retained earnings. See "The End of Tax Savings Through Income Splitting?" in Chapter 1 for more information.)

Management Responsibilities

It's wise to address the basic way you'll operate the business. Often, in small business partnerships, all partners are involved in management and supervision:

> All partners shall be actively involved and materially participate in the management and operation of the partnership business.

You can go further if you want every partner to have a veto power:

> All partnership decisions must be made by the unanimous agreement of all partners.

Some small business partnerships distinguish between major and minor decisions, allowing a single partner to make a minor decision but requiring unanimity for major ones. If you decide to go down this road, you have to figure out how to define a major decision. The distinction between major and minor decisions—especially purchases or the undertaking of obligations—is often based on a dollar amount:

> All major decisions of the partnership business must be made by a unanimous decision of all partners. Minor business decisions may be made by an individual partner. Major decisions are defined as all purchases and contracts over $5,000 [*or other definition of major decisions*].

If you want to provide for unequal management powers, here are some clauses to consider:

> Each partner shall participate in the management of the business. In exercising the powers of management, each partner's vote shall be in proportion to that partner's interest in the partnership's capital.

or

> In the management, control, and direction of the business, the partners shall have the following percentages of voting power:
>
> Name _____ Percentage
>
> _____   _____
>
> _____   _____
>
> _____   _____

If the partners are going to contribute different types of skills, you may want to state that in your partnership agreement. And while it may not always make sense to list the hours to be worked, in some situations it may help avoid problems. For that, you could use a clause such as:

> Except for vacations, holidays, and times of illness, each partner will work _____ hours per week on partnership business.

Consider a clause on leaves of absence or sabbaticals. How much time off is allowed? And what happens to a partner's right to receive pay or profits while on leave?

Other financial matters you might want to deal with in the partnership agreement include:

- Can partners borrow money on behalf of the partnership? Is there a dollar limit on how much a partner can borrow on behalf of the partnership without the consent of the other partners?

- Do you want to authorize partner expense accounts for business expenses? If so, is there a limit on the amount that can be spent?
- How many signatures are required on partnership checks and to withdraw money from the partnership bank account?
- How many weeks of paid or unpaid vacation each year are partners entitled to?

The Authority of Partners

Do you want each partner to be able to make decisions that bind the partnership in the normal operation of its business? Or do you want some limitations—for example, that large contracts or purchases must be approved in advance by a majority of the partners? You can address this issue in your partnership agreement. But remember that while a limitation on a partner's authority is binding among the partners themselves, it doesn't necessarily limit liability to outsiders who deal with the partner.

EXAMPLE: Phoebe, Rowan, and Lisa run a bookkeeping and billing service for several doctors, dentists, and clinics. Phoebe, who is a computer whiz, believes that there's no such thing as too much electronic equipment. The partners decide to put a clause in the partnership agreement stating that at least two of the partners must approve any purchase of equipment. Exceeding her authority, Phoebe buys three notebook computers, two laser printers, and other electronic equipment for the partnership. Even though the partners limited liability among themselves, the partnership and each partner are liable for the $12,000 bill. When Phoebe purchased the equipment, the computer store didn't know what was in the partnership agreement—the usual case. And Phoebe appeared to have authority to bind the partnership. The other partners, however, will have a legal claim against Phoebe.

Partners' Outside Business Activities

A key partnership question is whether or not any partner can engage in outside business. In some instances, they must, at least at first, because the partnership business income isn't enough to live on. If a partner can engage in outside business, what types are permitted? You wouldn't want a partner to directly compete with the partnership. That would be a conflict of interest. But how do you define direct competition? If the partners are running a restaurant, can one of the partners own a catering business? Or work in a delicatessen? There are at least four different approaches to this issue. You can:

- Allow partners to engage in one or more other businesses, except for those that directly compete with the partnership business.
- Allow partners to engage in other businesses without any other restrictions.
- List permitted activities.
- Prohibit partners from participating in any other business.

Here's an example of the first approach:

Any partner may engage in one or more other businesses in addition to the business of the partnership, but only to the extent that this activity does not directly and materially interfere with the business of the partnership and does not conflict with the time commitments or other obligations of that partner to the partnership under this agreement. Neither the partnership nor any other partner shall have any right to any income or profit derived by a partner from any outside business activity permitted under this section.

Departure of a Partner—Buyouts

Now we're getting into one of the most essential—and complicated—areas of a partnership agreement: what you'll do if one of the partners voluntarily leaves, becomes disabled, or dies. These things are not easy to think about when you're caught up in the excitement of starting a new business. Still, it's risky to postpone facing them. Sooner or later, the partnership will change, and these issues will come up. A partner might want to leave for any number of reasons—such as to start another business or to move to another part of the country. Or a partner could retire or die. Can the interest of the departing partner be sold? Do the remaining partners or partner have the right to buy it? How is the purchase price determined?

If one partner quits or dies, most partnership agreements very sensibly give any remaining partners the right to buy out the departing partner's share before selling or transferring it to outsiders. Here's a sample "right of first refusal" clause designed to accomplish this:

> If any partner leaves the partnership, for whatever reason, whether by quitting, withdrawing, expulsion, retirement, death, becoming mentally or physically incapacitated or being unable to fully function as a partner, that person or (in the case of a deceased partner) the estate, shall be obligated to sell the interest in the partnership to the remaining partners, who may buy that interest under the terms and conditions set forth in this agreement.

This option protects the remaining partners. But what if the departing partner has found a buyer who is willing to pay a hefty price for that partnership interest? Some partnerships don't compel a departing partner to take a lower price (as predetermined in the partnership agreement) than could be obtained from a bona fide outside buyer; their partnership agreements provide that the existing partners must pay the market price for the departing partner's share. Whatever you decide, be sure to clearly state in your partnership agreement what happens when a partner leaves the partnership.

Law From the Real World

Outside Interests

When Ted M. and Ted Y. formed a partnership and opened a bookstore called Two Teds, they didn't expect to make much money right away. According to their business plan, it would take two to three years for the store to be solidly profitable. In the meantime, both men would have to hold down second jobs. This led to a problem because both men already worked in the book business and they wanted to avoid any conflict of interest between their personal and partnership interests.

Ted Y., a sales rep for a large publisher, explained his store plans to his employer, who agreed to reduce his sales territory and let him work three days per week. He also committed himself to work 30 hours per week at Two Teds. Because selling books to stores and selling them to the public aren't competitive operations, it was easy for the Teds to agree that there was no conflict of interest for Ted Y. to keep his job and also be in the partnership.

Ted M.'s situation was tougher because he was the manager of a secondhand bookstore. No matter how much they thought about it, managing one store while owning part of another in the same city reeked of possible conflicts of interest. To solve this, it was decided that Ted M. would quit his job managing the other store. Initially, at least, he would work 55 hours per week at Two Teds and be paid a reasonable salary for the 25 hours per week he worked more than Ted Y.

Here's a different approach:

> If the remaining partners do not purchase the departing partner's share of the business under the terms provided in this agreement within _____ days after the departing partner leaves, the entire business of the partnership shall be put up for sale and listed with an appropriate sales agent or broker.

Valuing a Partner's Share

One major issue in a buyout clause is how you'll determine the worth of the business and the value of a partner's share. Let's look at some specific valuation methods.

The "asset valuation method" is based on the current net worth of the business (assets minus liabilities). As of the date the departing partner leaves, the net dollar value of all tangible partnership assets is calculated and all outstanding business debts are deducted to determine net worth. Goodwill isn't a tangible asset, so it's not included in this calculation, which means that some established, successful businesses might be undervalued using this method. The departing partner receives an ownership percentage of the net worth, under whatever payout terms are agreed upon.

Under the "book valuation method," you calculate the value of the business based on all partnership assets and liabilities as they're set forth in the partnership accounting books. This basically means that assets are valued at their acquisition cost. Again, book value doesn't include goodwill, so in a successful business, it can have little relation to what the business is really worth. Furthermore, the acquisition cost of property is often not its current worth.

Under the "set-dollar method," the partners agree in advance that if one partner departs from the partnership, the others will buy out that partner's share for a preestablished price. Before adopting this method, be aware that the price selected might be arbitrary. The value of a business can fluctuate dramatically over time, making a predetermined value out of date. You could consider having the partners establish a value in writing for the partnership each year.

A "postdeparture appraisal" means that you agree to have an independent appraiser determine the worth of the partnership when a partner departs. It sounds good in principle, but many small businesses aren't amenable to precise valuation. Even in the hands of an expert appraiser, this method can lead to bitter arguments.

The "capitalization of earnings method" determines what the business is worth based on what it earns. Unless there's an open market to set a price, the best estimate of what a business is worth often depends on its earning capacity. This method works best with a business that's been around for several years. First you need to measure the earnings of the business for a year or more. Then you must agree on a multiplier (often two to five) which, in effect, takes into consideration the fact that a buyer hopes to reap profits in future years. Finally, you multiply the earnings by your multiplier to arrive at a value. But how do you establish the multiplier? Often one is already loosely established in a particular industry. A consultant or trade magazine might tell you that profitable dry cleaning businesses are often sold on the basis of multiplying profits by a certain number. Be aware that this sort of information is at best an estimate, which can change by industry, individual business, and year. If you decide to use this method of valuing your business, you'll need expert advice.

You might want to have a different buyout price depending on when or why a partner departs. For example, a partner who leaves during the initial stages of a business (say, the first one or two years) could be entitled to only the balance in that partner's capital account. After that initial period, the departing partner's interest could be calculated by a method that more accurately reflects the actual operation and success of the business.

You could also have varying formulas depending on why the partner leaves. For example, there could be one formula if the partner becomes disabled, retires over age 65, or dies, and another formula if the partner leaves under other circumstances.

Payments to Departing Partners

Your partnership agreement should provide for a payment schedule if there's a buyout. Otherwise, the departing partner would have the right to collect for the full value of the bought-out interest immediately.

Your decision on payment terms has a close relationship to the method you use for determining the buyout price. If the remaining partners are allowed to pay over a number of years, they're usually willing to pay a higher buyout price than if all the cash is due the day a partner leaves.

One of the best ways to finance the buyout of a partner's interest is through insurance. If a partner dies, the proceeds from the partnership-financed insurance policy are used to pay off his or her share. That way, partnership operating income doesn't have to be used. Many profitable partnerships buy insurance against each partner's serious illness, incapacity, or death. This can be a sensible way of obtaining money to pay off a deceased partner's interest. A term policy, which is relatively cheap, is especially good.

Continuity of the Partnership

If a partnership has more than two members, the remaining partners usually want to continue the business as a partnership when a partner leaves. Here's a clause that you can use to ensure the continuation of a partnership:

> In the case of a partner's death, permanent disability, retirement, voluntary withdrawal, or expulsion from the partnership, the partnership shall not dissolve or terminate, but its business shall continue without interruption and without any break in continuity. On the disability, retirement, withdrawal, expulsion, or death of any partner, the other partners shall not liquidate or wind up the affairs of the partnership, but shall continue to conduct the partnership under the terms of this agreement.

Noncompetition of a Departing Partner

Another issue relating to a partner who leaves the partnership is competition. You might want to prohibit the departing partner from competing against your firm. This could include the protection of your trade secrets and customer lists.

Legally, this is a touchy area. Forbidding a partner from engaging in his or her usual way of earning a living is a drastic act, and courts often refuse to enforce unfairly restrictive terms. To be legal, a "noncompetition agreement" normally must be reasonably limited in both time and geographical area and otherwise must be fair. State laws vary in regard to noncompetition clauses, and it's not always possible to tell whether or not a judge will enforce one. If you're determined to include a noncompetition clause in your agreement, it makes sense to see a lawyer familiar with this area.

This sample clause will give you an idea of how these clauses are often drafted:

> On the voluntary withdrawal, permanent disability, retirement, or expulsion of any partner, that partner shall not carry on a business the same as or similar to the business of the partnership within the [describe area] for a period of [time period you've agreed on].

Control of a Partnership Name

A business name can be valuable. The partnership agreement should spell out what happens to it if a partner leaves. There are a number of ways to handle this, including a clause stating that the partnership continues to own the name, that one partner owns the name, that control of the name will be decided on at a later date, or, finally, that in the event of dissolution, the partnership business name will be owned by a majority of the former partners.

Resolving Partnership Disputes

Suppose there's a serious disagreement between the partners and you can't resolve it by personal discussions and negotiations. You could find yourself in court, which is a costly, time-consuming, and emotionally draining way to deal with a dispute.

Fortunately, there's a way around litigation as a means of resolving disputes. You can provide in your partnership agreement for mediation or arbitration or both. (For information on mediation and arbitration, see Nolo's Mediation, Arbitration & Collaborative Law section at www.nolo.com/legal-encyclopedia/mediation.)

Here's an example of a mediation clause:

Any dispute arising out of this agreement or the partnership business will be resolved by mediation, if possible. The partners pledge to cooperate fully and fairly with the mediator in an attempt to reach a mutually satisfactory compromise to a dispute. The mediator will be _____ . If any partner to a dispute feels it cannot be resolved by the partners themselves, that partner shall so notify the other partners and the mediator in writing. Mediation will commence within _____ days of the Notice of Request for Mediation. The cost of mediation will be shared equally by all partners to the dispute.

RESOURCE

For in-depth guidance on mediation, get Nolo's e-book *Mediate, Don't Litigate: Strategies for Successful Mediation,* by Peter Lovenheim (Nolo) available at www.nolo.com.

To protect yourselves should mediation fail, you can follow up with an arbitration clause that takes over if a dispute can't be mediated to the satisfaction of the parties. The partners are bound by the arbitrator's decision, which can be enforced in court.

If you include both mediation and arbitration clauses in your partnership agreement, you need to decide whether the mediator and arbitrator should be the same person. If you have the same person playing both roles, you don't run the risk of having to present the case twice—first to the mediator and then, if mediation fails, to the arbitrator. On the other hand, the person who has ultimate power to make a decision as an arbitrator might be less effective as a mediator.

Changes in Your Partnership

As your business changes, your partnership agreement will have to change, too. For example, the addition of a new partner requires revision of at least the clauses listing the partners' names and those covering contributions and distribution of profits.

Even if you admit no new partners, the growth of your business might require you to change your agreement. You and your partners may decide to run your expanded business differently than the original business. Or maybe more cash is required, and the partners decide that their contributions should be in proportions different from those originally agreed to.

Any time you make a significant change in the structure or operation of your business, you should change the partnership agreement to reflect it.

The owners of most small partnerships specify that the partnership agreement may be amended only by the written consent of all partners. But you can create any amendment clause you choose. For example, you could specify that the agreement can be amended by vote of 51% of the partners or by 51% of the capital accounts.

At some point, your partnership may decide to add another partner. You might need a new partner's contribution of cash or skills, or you might want to offer a partnership interest to encourage a key employee to stay with the business. Because a partnership technically is dissolved when a new partner joins, it's helpful to include a clause in your partnership agreement such as the following one:

Admission of a new partner shall not cause dissolution of the underlying partnership business, which will be continued by the new partnership entity.

Creating a Corporation

Chapter 1 introduced the basic business entities—the sole proprietorship, the partnership, the limited liability company, and the corporation. This chapter tells you more about setting up a corporation. We'll start with the structure of a corporation, including the roles of the key players: the incorporators, shareholders, directors, officers, and employees. Then we'll look at corporate finance—how you get money into the corporation and how you take it out. Next we'll walk step by step through the procedures for setting up a corporation. Finally, we'll examine some sound corporate business practices.

The material in this chapter applies to most, but not all, new corporations. Generally, this material will apply to you if your proposed corporation fits the following profile:

- A relatively small number of people—about ten or fewer—will own the corporate stock.
- All or most of the owners will participate directly in managing and running the business; investors who don't directly participate will generally be limited to friends or family members.
- All of the owners will live in the state in which you form your corporation and conduct your business.

Lawyers often call a small corporation that fits this profile a "closely held corporation." We'll borrow this term in its most general, nontechnical sense.

Classifying your corporation at the outset is important because if you're a closely held corporation and sell stock to only a few friends or family members, normally you'll be exempt from all but the most routine requirements of federal and state securities laws.

But if you sell stock in your corporation to outside investors—people who won't help run the business or aren't closely tied to people who are—you must comply with those laws. So if you want to sell stock to a wider range of people, especially if any of them live in a different state, you'll need to learn more about the requirements of the securities laws. Many states have generous exemptions that allow sales of stock to as many as 35 investors without complicated paperwork. But because this is such a technical area and laws vary from state to state, you should seek legal advice from a lawyer knowledgeable about securities laws before you offer stock to outsiders.

 Law From the Real World

Keeping a Hand in the Business

Anne opened a small business providing customized bookkeeping software for manicurists. For several years she struggled financially as she tried to convince small nail shops that buying her computerized system would ultimately be far cheaper than keeping records in a shoe box. Finally, when a trade magazine gave her system a rave review, business took off. Suddenly Anne found herself hiring employees, upgrading and customizing her software, and greatly increasing her marketing activities.

Anne soon realized that she couldn't do it all herself. Her key employees were increasingly critical to her success. To help ensure their loyalty and hard work, Anne decided to give them an ownership interest in the business. She accomplished this by forming a closely held corporation, Digital Nail, Inc. Initially Anne owned 100% of the stock, but under the terms of a shareholders' agreement, half a dozen or so key employees receive stock each year.

Although Anne will always remain the majority owner, the longtime employees will gain a significant share of the business over time. If an employee leaves the company, his or her stock must be sold back to Digital Nail at its book (asset) value—considerably less than its market value (assuming the business continued to prosper and was sold or went public). In short, not only does Anne's plan give key employees a stake in the success of the company, it provides a powerful incentive for them to stick with Digital Nail.

RESOURCE

Looking for a lawyer? Asking for a referral to an attorney from someone you trust can be a good way to find legal help. Also, two sites that are part of the Nolo family, Lawyers.com and Avvo.com, provide excellent and free lawyer directories. These directories allow you to search by location and area of law, and list detailed information about and reviews of lawyers.

Whether you're just starting your lawyer search or researching particular attorneys, visit www.lawyers.com/find-a-lawyer and www.avvo.com/find-a-lawyer.

The Structure of a Corporation

Corporations are controlled primarily by state, not federal, law. This means that 50 different sets of rules cover how corporations are created. Terminology differs from state to state. For example, most states use the term "articles of incorporation" to refer to the basic document creating the corporation, but some states (including Connecticut, Delaware, New York, and Oklahoma) use the term "certificate of incorporation." Tennessee calls it a "charter" and Massachusetts uses the term "articles of organization." Fortunately, the similarities in corporate procedure outweigh the differences, so most of what you find in this chapter will apply to your situation. Nevertheless, watch out for the differences.

People involved in a corporation traditionally play different legal roles: incorporator, shareholder, director, officer, or employee. We'll look at those roles here. And, in virtually every state, there's a way that you can set up a corporation in which one or two people play all roles.

RESOURCE

Your state rules on forming a corporation. The Corporations section in the Business Formation center on www.nolo.com includes detailed advice for each state on how to form a corporation.

Incorporators

The "incorporators" (called the "promoters" in some states) do the preparatory work. This might include bringing together the people and the money to create the corporation. It always includes preparing and filing the articles of incorporation—the formal incorporation document that is filed with a state office, such as the secretary of state. Although several people can serve as incorporators and sign the articles of incorporation, only one incorporator is required by law. Once the articles of incorporation are filed, the incorporator's job is nearly done. The only remaining tasks are to select the first board of directors and to adopt the corporate bylaws (although, in some states, bylaws may be adopted by the directors).

Shareholders

The "shareholders" own the stock of the corporation. One person can own 100% of the stock. Among other things, shareholders can:

- elect directors (although the initial board of directors is usually selected by the incorporator or promoter)
- amend bylaws
- approve the sale of all or substantially all of the corporate assets
- approve mergers and reorganizations
- amend the articles of incorporation
- remove directors, and
- dissolve the corporation.

State laws typically require that the shareholders hold an annual meeting. However, in many states, a consent action or consent resolution—a document signed by all of the shareholders—can be used in place of a formal meeting.

For the corporation to elect S corporation status under federal tax laws, all shareholders must sign the election form that's filed with the IRS. (For more on this, see "Eleven Basic Steps to Incorporate," below.)

Directors

The "directors" manage the corporation and make major policy decisions. Directors authorize the issuance of stock, decide on whether to mortgage, sell, or lease real estate, and elect the corporate officers. Directors may hold regular or special meetings (or both). However, in many states, it's simpler and just as effective for the directors to take actions by signing a document called a consent resolution or consent action.

The incorporators or shareholders decide how many directors the corporation will have. The number of directors is usually stated in the articles of incorporation or in the corporate bylaws. Most states specifically permit corporations to have just one director. In the remaining states, the requirement is that there be at least three directors, but there's an exception for corporations with fewer than three shareholders. If there are only two shareholders, the corporation can operate with two directors; if there's only one shareholder, the corporation needs only one director.

> EXAMPLE 1: Anita, Barry, and Clint create a corporation in Michigan. They choose Anita to be the sole director. They can do this because the law in Michigan—as in many other states—permits a corporation to function with a single director regardless of the number of shareholders.

> EXAMPLE 2: Dustin, Erwin, and Faye create a corporation in California. They would like Dustin to be the sole director, but California law requires them to have at least three directors if there are three or more shareholders. Therefore, Dustin, Erwin, and Faye create a three-person board of directors and appoint themselves to those positions.

Officers

The "officers" are normally responsible for the day-to-day operation of the corporation. State laws usually require that the corporation have at least a president, secretary, and treasurer. The "president" is usually the chief operating officer of the corporation. The "secretary" is responsible for the corporate records. The "treasurer," of course, is responsible for the corporate finances, although it's common to hand day-to-day duties to a bookkeeper. The corporation can have other officers—such as a vice president—as well. In most states, one person can hold all of the required offices.

> EXAMPLE: Abdul forms a Texas corporation. He provides for the two corporate offices—president and secretary—that are required by Texas law. He appoints himself to both offices. This is legal in Texas and in most other states.

Employees

Employees work for the corporation in return for compensation. In small corporations, the owners (shareholders) are usually also employees of the corporation.

As a corporate employee, it's through your salary and other compensation that you'll receive most of your financial benefits from the business. Often the person who runs the business day-to-day gets the most compensation. This may or may not be the president.

How It All Fits Together

If you're new to all of this, the numerous components of a corporation might seem unduly complicated for a small business. Fortunately, it all fits together quite smoothly and easily.

> EXAMPLE: Al, Bev, and Carla decide to form a corporation to run a fitness center. Their plan is to invest $10,000 apiece and be equal owners. Because state law requires only one person to sign the papers setting up the corporation, Bev signs the articles of incorporation for ABC Fitness Center, Inc. and sends them to the secretary of state's office along with the filing fee. Bev is the incorporator.

Next, Bev adopts bylaws for the corporation calling for a three-person board of directors. She elects herself, Al, and Carla to serve as the first directors. The three of them then elect Bev to be the president, Al to be the secretary, and Carla to be the treasurer—so the three of them are then the officers of the corporation.

When Al, Bev, and Carla each pay $10,000 into the corporate bank account, they each receive a stock certificate for 10,000 shares of corporate stock; at that moment, they become shareholders.

All three are active in running the business, working 50 hours a week and receiving a salary. Al and Bev, who have experience as personal trainers, take charge of training customers and supervising a small staff of other workers. Carla, who studied business in college, looks after the finances—billing customers, marketing, ordering supplies. In addition to their other roles in the corporation, Al, Bev, and Carla are employees.

Financing Your Corporation

It doesn't take an MBA degree to grasp the fundamentals of corporate finance in the typical small business. Assets come into the corporation in two forms: equity and debt. Let's look at each.

Funding Your Corporation With Equity

Basically, "equity" means shareholders contribute cash, valuable property, or services to the company in exchange for stock in the company. The number of shares issued is somewhat arbitrary, but the customary practice in some places is for new corporations to issue one share for each dollar invested.

The most common way to pay for stock is with cash. For example, you may put $5,000 into the company in return for 5,000 shares of corporate stock. But money isn't the only thing that you can invest in a company in return for stock. You may

also transfer physical assets, such as real estate or equipment, or a copyright, patent, or trademark. Or you may receive stock in return for past services to the corporation.

 CAUTION

Check before you transfer property for stock. Before you transfer property to your corporation in exchange for stock, check with your tax adviser. If you receive stock for property that has increased in value since you bought it, you may owe taxes.

In some states, you can receive stock in return for promising to perform services to the corporation, or in return for a promissory note. In other words, you might receive 5,000 shares of stock in return for your promise to work for the corporation for 200 hours or to pay the corporation $5,000 six months later. Not all states, however, permit stock to be issued based on a promise of future services or money, so check the rules of your state.

Funding Your Corporation With Debt

The other major way to fund a corporation is through debt—that is, by borrowing money. But you should know that if your corporation borrows from a bank or another outside lender, the lender will probably expect you to personally guarantee to repay the debt should the business be unable to.

Leasing Property to the Corporation

Sometimes you'll want to retain ownership of property being used by the corporation. For example, maybe you own a garage or other small building your company will occupy. With real estate, it's usually better, from a tax standpoint, to have your corporation lease the property from you rather than to transfer the property to the corporation.

EXAMPLE: Nino forms New Age Innovators, Inc., to develop some practical new technologies for the plumbing industry. He plans to work out of his garage. He leases the garage to his corporation for $500 a month. On his own personal Form 1040, Nino will report the rent as income and will deduct interest expense (for the mortgage on the building) and depreciation. On its corporate tax return, New Age Innovators, Inc., will deduct its rent payments and operating expenses for the garage.

If you lease property to the corporation, have the directors adopt a board resolution approving a lease. Then have the corporation sign the lease as a tenant, with you, of course, as the landlord. This will be helpful in establishing the existence of a lease if the arrangements are questioned by the IRS.

Compensating Yourself

I've just discussed how you put money into the corporation. Now let's get to the fun part—how you take it out.

Salary and Bonuses

As a corporate employee, you can receive a reasonable salary plus bonuses, which, for tax purposes, are lumped in with salary. (Many corporate owners prefer to pay themselves conservative salaries and then reward themselves with a year-end bonus if it makes sense economically.) Salaries and bonuses are treated as business expenses of the corporation, which means that the corporation owes no tax on what it pays you (apart from withholding employer taxes). You, in turn, report what you receive as income on your personal income tax return just as you would if you worked for any other employer. The IRS has rules on how much salary is appropriate —the primary one is that the salary must be "reasonable." This is a pretty loose standard and, as a practical matter, doesn't affect most small businesspeople, because their businesses can't afford to pay them the sort of stratospheric salaries the IRS might consider unreasonable.

Interest on Loans to the Corporation

If you lend money or property to the corporation in exchange for a promissory note, you'll receive interest on your loans. Hopefully, the corporation will repay you the principal amount of the loans as well. But you'll have to pay tax on only the interest you receive—not on the principal portion.

> **CAUTION**
>
> **Minimum interest.** Any loan between a corporation and an employee or stockholder for more than $10,000 must carry a minimum interest rate. The rate is based on U.S. Treasury Bill rates. The loan type also determines whether other requirements must be met. Check with your tax adviser for details.

Fringe Benefits

Another way to profit from your investment in the corporation is through fringe benefits. For example, your corporation may purchase health insurance for employees and set up a plan under which the corporation reimburses employees for medical expenses not covered by insurance. Health insurance premiums and medical reimbursements paid by the corporation are tax-deductible business expenses for the corporation—and aren't taxable to the employee as personal income. By contrast, if you were to pay for medical expenses with no corporate help, only a limited amount would be tax deductible on your personal income tax return.

S Corporations Note. S corporations are treated differently under the tax laws. Fringe benefits for an owner-employee who owns more than 2% of the stock of an S corporation are not given this favorable tax treatment.

Dividends

You've probably heard about "corporate dividends" paid to shareholders. This is another way that funds can be removed from a corporation for the benefit of its owners. Perhaps surprisingly, it is rarely done in a small corporation. Because the corporation can't deduct dividends as a business expense, dividends add up to double taxation. (This doesn't apply to S corporations; see "Corporations," in Chapter 1.) The corporation is subject to tax on money paid as dividends, and then the shareholder is taxed a second time. To avoid this double taxation, it's much better to take money out of the corporation through the other means previously discussed.

RESOURCE

Incorporate your business online. If you're ready to incorporate, you might be able to do much of the work online—including searching for a company name and filing your articles of incorporation. To get started, go to www.nolo.com/products/business-suite/business-formation.

Do You Need a Lawyer to Incorporate?

It's possible to form your own corporation without professional help. Every day, many entrepreneurs do exactly that by using an incorporation kit. If you're inclined to go this route, check out *How to Form Your Own California Corporation* or *Incorporate Your Business: A Legal Guide to Forming a Corporation in Your State*, both by Anthony Mancuso (Nolo). These books provide information about incorporating, even if you decide not to do it yourself.

The obvious motivating factor for setting up a corporation on your own is to save on legal fees, which can range from $1,000 to $2,000 or more, depending on where you live. But be aware that there's a trade-off: You're subjecting yourself to bureaucratic hassles and, unless you do your homework carefully, possible errors. The paper-filing phase, by itself, isn't all that difficult. But tax and legal liability problems might not be obvious to the do-it-yourselfer. And if you plan to issue stock to other than a few people who will work in the

business or are close friends and relatives, securities laws can be troublesome.

Still, dollars are often precious to people just starting out in business, and you might decide that it's worthwhile to attempt to form your corporation by yourself. If you choose that route, it's a good idea to have a lawyer experienced with small businesses look over the final documents before you file them. You should be able to find a lawyer willing to do this at a fraction of the cost of having the lawyer handle the matter from beginning to end.

RESOURCE

Looking for a lawyer? Asking for a referral to an attorney from someone you trust can be a good way to find legal help. Also, two sites that are part of the Nolo family, Lawyers.com and Avvo.com, provide excellent and free lawyer directories. These directories allow you to search by location and area of law, and list detailed information about and reviews of lawyers.

Whether you're just starting your lawyer search or researching particular attorneys, visit www.lawyers.com/find-a-lawyer and www.avvo.com/find-a-lawyer.

Hiring and Communicating With a Lawyer or Other Professional During the Coronavirus Crisis

At the time of writing, the coronavirus outbreak was accelerating in the United States and throughout the world. Most industries, including the legal profession, were in the process of changing their usual practices of conducting business in response to the virus. Many firms have limited in-person contact with existing and potential clients and found ways to implement sufficient precautions while still providing assistance to those who need it. Many lawyers, accountants, and other professionals offer help while adhering to social distancing and quarantine protocols, like by conducting initial consultations and subsequent communications over the phone, email, text, and videoconferencing.

CAUTION

Beware of securities law. If you'll have a number of shareholders—especially people who won't be working in the business and who are not close relatives living in your state—consult a lawyer to see that you're in compliance with federal and state securities regulations. (See "Overview of Incorporation Procedures," below.) Although most small businesses are considered to be closely held corporations and exempt from these potentially complicated regulations, it's worth spending a few bucks to find out for sure. Anthony Mancuso's how-to-incorporate books, mentioned in "Do You Need a Lawyer to Incorporate?" above, discuss this issue in detail.

Overview of Incorporation Procedures

While there are differences from state to state, the basic procedures that you or your lawyer will follow in creating a corporation are these:

- prepare and file articles of incorporation
- select a board of directors
- adopt bylaws
- elect officers
- issue stock, and
- decide whether or not to elect S corporation tax status.

In a moment, we'll walk through the incorporation process. Before we do, let's look at one additional step to consider before starting to incorporate: a preincorporation agreement. It might be unnecessary if you're planning a one-person corporation or if your corporation consists only of family members. Similarly, a preincorporation agreement is less necessary if you and your associates are incorporating an existing business or if you've done business together before. However, if you're going into business with relative strangers, putting your agreement in written form will help you avoid disputes later or, if an argument does arise, will

provide a basis for resolving it through arbitration or litigation. Your written agreement should include these key points:

- the name of the corporation
- its purpose
- how much stock each person will buy and how each will pay for it
- what loans each person will make to the corporation and the terms of repayment
- what offices (president, vice president, secretary, treasurer) each person will hold
- what compensation each of you will receive
- what expense accounts each of you will have, and
- what fringe benefits will be available.

If the corporation is going to lease real estate or other property from one of the owners, the agreement can also outline the terms of that transaction.

Another major topic to cover in either a preincorporation agreement or a separate buyout agreement is what happens if a shareholder wants to retire from the corporation, gets sick or dies, or just wants to sell his or her stock. Will the corporation or the remaining shareholders be obligated to buy the stock? How will the price be set? Can the stock be sold to outsiders?

These are difficult and important issues—and it's much better to think them through and arrive at a written agreement at the beginning of the corporation's life rather than wait until a crisis arises. If you don't have an agreement in place, you risk the pain of personal and business discord, and possibly even expensive, disruptive litigation.

 RESOURCE

Buyout agreements are discussed in Chapter 5. Also, you can easily put together a solid agreement covering shareholder issues if you consult *Business Buyout Agreements: Plan Now for All Kinds of Business Transitions,* by Bethany K. Laurence and Anthony Mancuso (Nolo).

> ⓘ **CAUTION**
>
> **Where to incorporate—beware the Delaware myth.** Many people are sold on the notion that there's something magical about incorporating in Delaware. The reality is that the best state to incorporate in is the state where your headquarters is located. For the vast majority of small business corporations that means the state where you live. If you incorporate in Delaware, you'll still have to register as an out-of-state corporation to do business in your own state.

Eleven Basic Steps to Incorporate

The following outline will help you understand how to go about forming a corporation for your small business. The procedure for incorporating is similar—but not identical—in every state.

Step 1. Choose a Name

In Chapter 6, you'll find more detail about selecting a business name. But here are a few basics about naming a corporation.

In most states, to alert the public to your corporate status, you must include certain words in your corporate name, such as Incorporated, Corporation, Company, or Limited, or the abbreviations Inc., Corp., Co., or Ltd. And, in some states, there are certain words you can't use in your name, such as National or Federal.

The quickest way to learn what words are required or prohibited in your state is to contact the office where you'll file your articles of incorporation—usually the secretary of state or corporation commissioner's office. You can also check your secretary of state's website (find yours at www.nass.org) or go to a law library and look up the state statute dealing with corporations. The state statutes for all 50 states are also available at Cornell University's Legal Information Institute's website at www.law.cornell.edu/states/listing.

Most states will reject a corporation name that's the same as a name already on file or a name that is confusingly similar to the name of an existing corporation. But even if the secretary of state accepts your corporate name (or tells you it's available in a prefiling name reservation procedure), this doesn't guarantee your right to use it. An unincorporated business might already be using it as its trade name, or a business might be using it as a trademark or service mark to identify products or services. In short, as discussed in Chapter 6, there is a good deal more to do to check out the availability of a particular name.

Before you file your corporate papers, check with your state's corporate filing office. Generally, it can make a preliminary check and tell you if the name is available. If you expect some delay before the papers are actually filed, find out whether your state permits you to reserve a name. Most will reserve a name for you for a month or more.

What happens if you've got your heart set on a name but find that it's too similar to one already in use? One approach is to change it slightly. Most states' name records are computerized, and often a fairly small modification will turn rejection to approval. Or you can ask the owners of the other business to let you use the similar name. Often, you can use such a name if you get the written consent of the corporation that was established earlier.

In many states, a corporation can do business under an "assumed" or "fictitious name." For example, if you incorporate as Miller Manufacturing Company but want to market some of your products under a more specific business name, you can simply file an assumed name certificate for Miller Appliances. Some states require that you file this paper at the same state office where you filed your articles of incorporation (such as the secretary of state's office). In other states, you must file your fictitious or assumed name certificate in the counties where your company is doing business. And some states require that you also publish notice of your assumed or fictitious name in a newspaper.

! CAUTION
Using your corporate name as a trademark.
If you plan to use your corporate name as a trademark or service mark for products or services, you won't want a name that's very similar to someone else's. As explained further in Chapter 6, even if your name was approved by your corporate filing office, it might infringe on another user's trademark or service mark.

Step 2. Prepare and File Articles of Incorporation

In some states, articles of incorporation are called certificates of incorporation, charters, or articles of association. In this discussion, we'll stick with the term articles of incorporation.

In many states, the secretary of state can give you a printed form for the articles of incorporation; all you have to do is fill in some blank spaces. (Find your state office at the National Association of Secretaries of State website, www.nass.org.) In other states, you must prepare the articles of incorporation from scratch.

See "Sample Articles of Incorporation for California," below, for an example of a California corporation's articles of incorporation.

Though details vary from state to state, the typical articles of incorporation include:

- the corporation's name
- its purpose
- the name of the initial agent for service of process (sometimes called a registered agent or resident agent)
- the number of shares authorized, and
- the names and addresses of the incorporators.

The purpose clause might seem confusing—it's as if you're being asked to define what your business will do until the end of time. Fortunately, this isn't necessary, because the statutes in many states allow you to use very general language, such as: "The purposes of this corporation shall be to engage in any lawful act or activity for which corporations may be organized under the business corporation law."

If such a statement is permitted in your state, it's usually best not to be any more specific. This leaves you free to change the nature of your business without amending the articles of incorporation. It also helps you avoid questions of whether you're acting beyond the scope of your stated purpose if you go into a new business.

Most states require you to designate somebody as a "resident agent" or "registered agent" in the articles of incorporation. This is the person who is authorized to receive official notices and lawsuit papers. Normally, you designate the corporate president as this person. If you change the person named or if there's a new address, you need to notify the secretary of state's office by filing a proper form.

It might take a few weeks for your articles of incorporation to be processed by the secretary of state's office. If you need quicker action, check to see if expedited handling is available. In some states, you can file your articles of incorporation in person and have the filing process completed within a day. Sometimes, articles of incorporation sent by UPS, Federal Express, or other overnight means are treated as in-person filings and given expedited treatment. Some states allow you to file your articles of incorporation by fax. Many states also allow you to file online.

If you need to sign contracts, such as a lease, even before the corporation has been formed, it's a good idea to state in the contract that you're acting on behalf of a corporation to be formed and that the contract is subject to ratification by the board of directors of the new corporation. Then, if for some reason the corporation is never formed or if the directors fail to ratify the document, you're free from personal liability. Here is sample language for such a lease.

Landlord acknowledges that Martin Green is signing this lease on behalf of XYZ Corporation (a corporation to be formed) and that this lease is subject to ratification by the corporation's Board of Directors. If the corporation is not formed or if the Board of Directors fails to ratify this lease within 30 days of the present date, this lease will be void. In no event will Martin Green have any personal liability under this lease.

Sample Articles of Incorporation for California

Secretary of State
Articles of Incorporation of a
General Stock Corporation

ARTS-GS

IMPORTANT — <u>Read Instructions</u> before completing this

form. Filing Fee — **$100.00**

Copy Fees – First page $1.00; each attachment page $0.50;
Certification Fee - $5.00

Note: Corporations may have to pay minimum $800 tax to the
California Franchise Tax Board each year. For more information, go to
ftb.ca.gov.

This Space For Office Use Only

1. Corporate Name (Go to www.sos.ca.gov/business/be/name-reservations for general corporate name requirements and restrictions.)

The name of the corporation is _____

_____

2. Business Addresses (Enter the **complete** business addresses.)

a. Initial Street Address of Corporation - **Do not list a P.O. Box**	City (no abbreviations)	State	Zip Code
b. Initial Mailing Address of Corporation, **if different than item 2a**	City (no abbreviations)	State	Zip Code

3. Service of Process (Must provide either Individual **OR** Corporation.)

INDIVIDUAL – Complete Items 3a and 3b only. Must include agent's full name and California street address.

a. California Agent's First Name (if agent is **not** a corporation)	Middle Name	Last Name		Suffix
b. Street Address (if agent is **not** a corporation) - **Do not enter a P.O. Box**	City (no abbreviations)	State **CA**	Zip Code	

CORPORATION – Complete Item 3c. Only include the name of the registered agent Corporation.

c. California Registered Corporate Agent's Name (if agent is a corporation) – Do not complete Item 3a or 3b

4. Shares (Enter the **number of shares** the corporation is authorized to issue. **Do not** leave blank or enter zero (0).)

This corporation is authorized to issue only one class of shares of stock.

The total number of shares which this corporation is authorized to issue is _____ .

5. Purpose Statement (Do not alter the Purpose Statement.)

The purpose of the corporation is to engage in any lawful act or activity for which a corporation may be organized under the General Corporation Law of California other than the banking business, the trust company business or the practice of a profession permitted to be incorporated by the California Corporations Code.

6. Read and Sign Below (This form must be signed by each incorporator. <u>See instructions</u> for signature requirements.)

_____   _____
Signature   Type or Print Name

ARTS-GS (REV12/2020)   2020 California Secretary of State

If this approach is not acceptable to the person with whom you're contracting, another possibility is to sign the contract in your own name—thereby assuming personal liability temporarily—but to specifically reserve the right to assign it to the corporation later, as in the sample that follows:

> Landlord grants to Martin Green the right to assign this lease to XYZ Corporation, a corporation to be formed. Upon Landlord's receipt of written notice that such assignment has been made, Martin Green will automatically be released from any personal liability under this lease.

Incorporation Fees

Each state imposes a fee or a combination of fees for incorporating. Some states also require an initial tax payment. The total amounts vary widely, from $50 to $1,000. To find out your state's fees, check your state's corporate filing office website (usually a branch of the governor's office in your state capital). The official name of the office is typically the Corporations Division of the Secretary (or Department) of State. Find yours at the National Association of Secretaries of State website at www.nass.org. You can also call or email the office with questions.

Step 3. Elect the First Board of Directors

In some states, initial directors are designated in the articles of incorporation. In other states, the incorporator or incorporators appoint the first board of directors. If this is the practice in your state, be sure to document the appointment of the initial directors with a statement or certificate signed by the incorporators. This statement or certificate, which will be inserted into your corporate records book, might look something like the one below.

Step 4. Adopt Bylaws

The "corporate bylaws" contain much more detail than the articles of incorporation. They spell out the rights and powers of the corporation's shareholders, directors, and officers.

Typically, the bylaws state the time and place for the annual meeting of shareholders, how much notice of the meeting must be given, and what constitutes a quorum. There are also provisions for special meetings to consider matters that can't wait for the next annual meeting and a statement about what actions the shareholders can take by written consent without a formal meeting. Bylaws provide how many directors there are, how they're elected, what their powers are, and if and how they're compensated. Titles of the corporate officers (generally, a president, secretary, and treasurer) are listed in the bylaws.

Sample Designation of Directors by Incorporator

Action by Incorporator of XYZ Corporation

The Incorporator of XYZ Corporation, a Pennsylvania corporation, designates the following people to serve as the initial Board of Directors of the Corporation:

    Joyce Barker

    Lloyd Epstein

    Norton Phillips

Dated: _____   _____

                                                   Joyce Barker, Incorporator

Sample Consent Form for Directors

XYZ Corporation Consent of the Board of Directors

The directors of XYZ Corporation consent to the following:

1. Bylaws: The attached bylaws shall be the bylaws of the corporation.

2. Officers: The following people are elected to serve as officers of the corporation for the next year, or until their successors are elected:

   President: _____

   Secretary: _____

   Treasurer: _____

3. Issuance of Stock Certificates: The President and Secretary are authorized and directed to issue stock certificates in the following amounts upon receipt of payment from the designated shareholders:

Name	Number of Shares	Amount to be Paid
1. _____	_____	_____
2. _____	_____	_____
3. _____	_____	_____

4. Lease: The President is authorized and directed to enter into a three-year lease of space in The Village Green on the terms set out in the attached memorandum.

Dated: _____ , 20____   _____
                                      Director #1

Dated: _____ , 20____   _____
                                      Director #2

Dated: _____ , 20____   _____
                                      Director #3

The bylaws may also cover matters such as who is authorized to sign contracts, who has the right to inspect corporate books and records (and under what conditions), the corporation's fiscal year, and how the bylaws can be amended.

In a few states the incorporators must adopt the bylaws; in others, the directors must adopt them. And in still other states, you can choose between the two methods. If the incorporators adopt the bylaws, be sure to document this in a signed statement or certificate. If the directors adopt the bylaws (see "Step 5. Hold a Directors' Meeting," below), reflect this action in the minutes of the first directors' meeting or, if you don't hold a meeting, in a written consent resolution of the directors.

Step 5. Hold a Directors' Meeting

The directors must do a number of things at the beginning to get the corporation on the right track. Corporations usually record these actions in a document called "minutes of the first meeting of the board of directors." These minutes often are written in language reflecting a formal parliamentary procedure that doesn't match the less formal style of most small businesses.

Fortunately, in most states, there's a streamlined method for accomplishing your initial organizational tasks. You or your lawyer can prepare a consent form to be signed by the board of directors such as the one above.

What actions should the board of directors take at its first meeting, either in formal minutes or through a consent resolution? The following are typical:

- adopt bylaws
- designate corporate officers
- approve the form of stock certificate
- adopt the first fiscal year
- authorize issuance of stock
- approve a lease
- approve employment contracts, and
- adopt a shareholders' agreement (also called a buyout agreement—see Chapter 5).

Step 6. Set Up a Corporate Bank Account

Remember, your corporation is a legal entity separate from its shareholders, directors, and officers. For that reason, the corporation needs its own bank account so that its finances can clearly be kept separate.

If you're incorporating an existing business that already has a bank account, it's best to start fresh and set up a new bank account for the corporation. The bank will ask for a corporate board of directors' resolution authorizing the new account and an Employer ID Number (EIN). (EINs are discussed in Chapter 8.)

If you decide to simply continue the old account, do the following:

- Find out the bank's procedures for changing a sole proprietorship or partnership account into a corporate account. Most likely, the bank will want your directors to adopt a specific resolution, using language the bank will supply. The bank will want to see your articles of incorporation and a copy of the banking resolution. You'll also be asked to provide your Employer Identification Number (issued by the IRS). You might not have this immediately,

and the bank will probably let you start using the account for the corporation if you assure them that you've applied for the ID number.

- Keep detailed records showing exactly how much money was in the account when it was changed over to the corporation. Also keep track of any checks that were written by your existing business but haven't cleared yet. These checks should be treated as expenses of the unincorporated business and deducted from the amount considered transferred to the corporation. Preparing and retaining these records will save you headaches a year or two down the road when you try to figure out exactly what was transferred to the corporation.

Step 7. Issue Stock

The corporation should issue a stock certificate to each shareholder. The certificate is evidence of the shareholder's ownership interest in the corporation. Filling out the stock certificate is simple. Your main legal concern is whether you need to do anything to comply with federal or state securities laws.

Federal securities laws are administered by the Securities and Exchange Commission (SEC). In addition, each state has its own law regulating the sale of securities, intended to protect passive investors—people who put money into a corporation but are not active in the day-to-day operations of the business.

The bad news is that both the federal and state requirements are very complicated. The good news is that, as discussed earlier, the typical small corporation—consisting solely of investors who are actively involved in the day-to-day operation of the company, and often their close relatives—is completely exempt from the complicated requirements. Nevertheless, some paperwork might be involved. For example, it's frequently advisable to give a shareholder representation letter to each prospective shareholder, even though it isn't strictly required under the state's securities laws. The letter gives you a way to confirm the purchaser's reasons for believing the transaction is exempt from the state's securities laws.

EXAMPLE: Edgewater, Inc., has been formed to build and operate a restaurant on the shore of a scenic lake. Chester, a wealthy investor who has been a partner in three major deals with Todd, the president of Edgewater, Inc., is going to invest $75,000 in the new corporation and receive 75,000 shares of stock. Chester's stock purchase is exempt from complex state regulations covering the sale of securities because it falls under the state's exemption for "limited offerings," defined as sales of stock to the following purchasers: an insider (a director, officer, or incorporator of the corporation); someone who has a preexisting business or personal relationship with the corporation or one of its officers; or a sophisticated investor (someone who has enough business or financial experience to protect his or her own interests). Chester qualifies as both a sophisticated investor and one who has a preexisting business relationship with the corporate president. Todd prepares a shareholder representation letter reciting these facts for Chester to sign.

Californians can obtain sample shareholder representation letters and reliable information on how to prepare them for their corporation (as well as blank stock certificates) from *How to Form Your Own California Corporation*, by Anthony Mancuso (Nolo).

Before you issue a stock certificate, make sure that the corporation has actually received payment for the shares. For example, if the shares are being purchased for cash, the corporation should receive the money before issuing the shares. If the corporation is issuing the stock in return for a promise of future payment by the shareholder (a practice allowed in some states but not others), the corporation should have in its possession a promissory note from the shareholder. If property is being transferred to the corporation in exchange for stock, the person transferring the property should sign a bill of sale for the property at the same time the corporate shares are issued.

Step 8. Complete Any Initial Financial Transactions

Tie up any other loose ends relating to the financing of the corporation. As noted earlier, your corporation may borrow some of its start-up money from friends, relatives, or other lenders. The corporation should issue written promissory notes as evidence that loans have been made. In addition, if you're leasing a building or equipment to the corporation, sign a lease.

Step 9. Set Up a Corporate Records Book

You can create a corporate records book in an ordinary loose-leaf binder. A more official looking way to do it is to buy a corporate records book from a local stationer. These usually come with stock certificates and an embossed corporate seal.

The main items that you'll keep in the corporate records book are the articles of incorporation, the bylaws, the minutes of meetings (or consent resolutions), and the stock certificate stubs or ledger sheets showing who received the stock certificates and when. In many small corporations, shareholders prefer the convenience of simply leaving the completed stock certificates in the corporate records book even though each shareholder is, of course, entitled to possession of his or her certificate.

Step 10. Follow Through on State Government Requirements

Your state might require that you file documents in addition to the articles of incorporation. For example, in California, you need to file a notice of stock transaction within 15 days after your first sale of stock and an annual statement of domestic stock corporation within 90 days after you file your articles of incorporation. To learn about requirements in your state, contact your state's corporate filing office.

Step 11. File S Corporation Election

As discussed in detail in Chapter 1, an S corporation is a corporation that decides to be taxed as a partnership. That is, it's not a separate tax entity like a C corporation. Instead, the profits and losses of the corporation flow through to the individual shareholders, who report them on their individual tax returns.

For purposes of incorporating under state law, the procedure is the same whether you're a C corporation or an S corporation. But to become an S corporation, you need to file Form 2553, *Election by a Small Business Corporation,* with the IRS. All of the shareholders must sign the form.

If you want to have S corporation status during the first tax year that your corporation exists, you need to file the election form before the 15th day of the third month of your tax year. In other words, you have a two-and-a-half-month window during which you can file the election. When does your tax year start? For a new corporation, your tax year starts when your corporation has shareholders, acquires assets, or begins doing business, whichever occurs first. If you miss the deadline, you have to wait until the next tax year to file the election form.

After You Incorporate

This chapter concentrates on steps you need to take to form your corporation. What must you do after incorporating? Obviously, you need to comply with federal and state tax filing rules. (See Chapter 8.) Your business might also need to get business licenses and permits. (See Chapter 7.) And it's smart to buy insurance before you begin doing business. (See Chapter 12.)

In addition, corporations must file an annual report with the state's corporate filing office. Typically, this is a form sent to you by the corporate filing office that requires you to update information about corporate officers and your location. Simply fill it out and return it with the necessary fee. If you forget to send the form back, your corporation might face fines and penalties and might even be automatically dissolved.

Safe Business Practices for Your Corporation

Last week you were the sole proprietor of a catering business you called Feasts On The Go. Today you own all the stock of a new corporation, Feasts On The Go, Inc. In addition, you're the corporation's director, president, secretary, and treasurer.

Or maybe last week you and Emily were partners in a used record shop called Around Again. Today you each own 50% of the stock in a new corporation called Second Time Around, Inc., which is running the old partnership business. Emily's the president and you're the secretary-treasurer.

What has changed? On a day-to-day level, not much. You still show up at the same place each day and do the same kind of work you did before you incorporated. In fact, your before- and after-incorporation lives will probably be so similar that it will be easy to forget the fact that you're now working for a corporation that is a separate legal entity.

But forgetting can be risky. If you're careless about maintaining the separation between the corporation and yourself, you can jeopardize your tax benefits or your freedom from personal liability—the main reasons to incorporate in the first place. Though it's rare for a judge to disregard a corporation and impose personal liability on a shareholder, it does happen. When it does, it's almost always in a small corporation where the owners have allowed the line between the corporation and the shareholders to get fuzzy or disappear.

Also, the IRS has the power to decide that a corporation is a sham if you fail to maintain it as a separate legal entity. Consider the following actual case:

- Walter Otto had an export-import business in San Francisco. After 15 years, he decided to incorporate his business and filed articles of incorporation with the California Secretary of State for "Otto Sales Company, Inc." He invested $50 in his new corporation. A few years later, the business became insolvent. A salesman sued for unpaid commissions, naming both the corporation and Walter as defendants. After a trial, the judge ordered Walter, personally, to pay the salesman over $18,000. Doing business through a corporation didn't protect Walter from personal liability.

What did Walter do wrong? Several things:

- He never issued any stock certificates to himself or anyone else.

- He contributed only $50 to the corporation as his equity in the business. (For more on equity and how to structure the financial side of a corporation, see "Financing Your Corporation," above.)

- He continued to use the same sales contracts that he used before he incorporated. These contracts said "W.E. Otto" at the top. At the bottom (for seller's signature), the contracts said: "W.E. Otto, by _____ , Sellers."

In the judge's view, Walter formed the corporation solely for his personal convenience and did not treat it as a real entity. So the judge "pierced the corporate veil" to make Walter personally liable for the debt. (*Shafford v. Otto Sales Company*, 308 P.2d 428 (Cal. App. 1957).)

Here are two more cases in which the owners of small corporations were found personally liable:

- J.C. Chou formed Oriental Fireworks, Inc., a corporation that grossed from $230,000 to $400,000 annually. Its assets, however, never exceeded $13,000, and the company never bought liability insurance. Gregory Rice was seriously injured by fireworks distributed by the corporation. He sued and was awarded $432,000. Because the corporation lacked funds to pay the judgment—and didn't carry insurance—the court ruled that J.C. was personally liable.

J.C.'s Mistake: Failing to provide even minimally adequate funds to the corporation (in legal lingo, failing to adequately capitalize the corporation) or to carry proper insurance. (*Rice v. Oriental Fireworks Co.*, 707 P.2d 1250 (Or. App. 1985).)

- Dusty Schmidt and Terry Ulven were partners in a business called Western Oregon Christmas Trees. At Christmastime, the partnership rented tents from the Salem Tent and Awning Company to display their trees. Later, Dusty and Terry formed a corporation—Western Oregon Christmas Trees, Inc. They continued to rent tents from Salem but didn't sign rental agreements or checks as corporate officers. When several tents were destroyed by a storm, Salem sued the corporation and was awarded a judgment of $12,500. The court ruled that Dusty and Terry also were personally liable for the judgment.

Dusty's and Terry's mistakes: Dusty and Terry made a $2,000 down payment on the tents using a check from their previous partnership—not from the corporation. Also, the pair commingled (mixed together) personal and corporate assets and failed to keep corporate records. (*Salem Tent & Awning v. Schmidt*, 719 P.2d 899 (Or. App. 1986).)

Even though these cases had unhappy endings for the owners of the small corporations, doing business as a corporation isn't all that dangerous. There are simple steps you can take to preserve your corporate status so that you don't have to lie awake nights worrying about personal liability. These steps are not time-consuming and they make good business sense.

Put Adequate Capital Into Your Corporation

Put in enough money and other assets to meet your foreseeable business requirements. The amount, of course, varies from business to business. What's reasonable to start a brick-and-mortar clothing store that requires a considerable inventory, as well as a retail location and several employees, might be vastly different from what's reasonable to start an online clothing shop. See if you can get a recommendation as to what constitutes adequate capital from your accountant or someone in the same business.

Insure Against Obvious Risks

Try to determine whether there's a substantial risk that customers or others might be injured because of your business. If so, it's wise to obtain a reasonable amount of insurance coverage. (See Chapter 12 for more on insurance.) There have been some cases—not many—in which a judge has felt that the failure of a small corporation's owners to buy insurance that was reasonably available was so reckless that it was a factor in disregarding the corporation and holding its owners personally liable.

> EXAMPLE: Elly owns all the stock in a corporation called Roadside Enterprises, Inc. The corporation sells and installs tires. It's obvious that an improperly installed tire can cause a serious accident. What if a Roadside employee forgets to tighten the lugs on a newly installed tire and the tire falls off, causing the driver to swerve into a tree? If the driver is killed, his or her family will probably sue Roadside. And if the corporation doesn't have reasonable insurance coverage (and hasn't set up a reasonable reserve fund), a judge could rule that Elly has some personal liability—even though she wasn't even at the tire store when the employee was inattentive.

Basically, it's a matter of exercising reasonable business judgment. If your business involves the risk of injury and you can buy liability insurance at a reasonable price, you should do so. On the other hand, if affordable insurance isn't available—an unfortunate reality in some industries today—it's highly unlikely that a judge would find fault with the owners of the corporation for not insuring against the risks.

Observe Corporate Formalities

Another way to protect yourself from the possibility that your corporation could be disregarded by a court is to always take it seriously yourself. Issue stock certificates to the shareholders before your corporation starts doing business. Keep a corporate records book containing your articles of incorporation, stock records, bylaws, and minutes of shareholders' and directors' meetings. Comply with state law requirements that you hold annual meetings of shareholders or act by signed consent actions or resolutions. Either way you should document all actions taken, such as election of officers for the next year.

Conference Calls. If it's not convenient for all the directors to meet at the same place, many states allow them to participate through a conference call. Follow up by documenting the telephone meeting in writing as soon as possible and sending a copy to each director.

Keep in mind that the annual meetings are minimum requirements. Although it's not necessary or appropriate to write up minutes or consent actions for every conference you have with your colleagues, if you take significant corporate actions during the year, it's wise to document them through minutes of a special meeting or a consent action form. Keep the minutes and consent actions in your corporate records book.

Here are some types of business activities that you should document with minutes of a directors' meeting or a signed consent action form signed by the directors:

- authorizing corporate bank accounts and designating who is eligible to sign checks and withdraw funds
- determining salaries and bonuses of officers
- contributing to pension and profit-sharing plans
- acquiring another business
- borrowing money
- selling stock
- entering into major contracts

- buying, selling, or leasing real estate
- adopting or amending employee fringe benefits plans, and
- applying for trademark registration.

Separate Your Personal Finances From the Corporation's

The corporation needs its own bank account. Don't use the corporate bank account to pay your personal expenses. Get salary checks on a regular basis from the corporation (deducting employee withholding taxes), deposit the checks in your personal account, and then pay your own bills.

If you use personal funds to pay business expenses—for example, you pick up a ream of printer paper while you're out for lunch—you can have the corporation reimburse you, but be sure the corporation keeps the receipt for the paper to justify the payment as a proper business expense.

To further preserve the distinction between you and the corporation, document all transactions as if you were strangers. If the corporation leases property from you, sign a lease. If the corporation borrows money from you, get a promissory note. If you sell property to the corporation or use your property to buy stock, sign a bill of sale or other legal document formally transferring legal title to the corporation.

Use the Correct Corporate Name

Suppose the name of your corporation is The A.B. Smith Fitness Store, Inc. Use that full business name in all your business dealings—on your stationery, business cards, and signs; in phone book listings and catalogs; and on the Internet. Be careful not to use a different or abbreviated version (such as Smith Fitness Center) unless you file an assumed name certificate or fictitious name certificate as permitted by state law. (For more on corporate names, see "Name Searches," in Chapter 6.)

Sign Documents as a Corporate Officer

In correspondence and on checks, sign your name as William Jones, President, along with the full name of your corporation, rather than just William Jones. This makes it clear to those who deal with you that you're acting as an agent or employee of the corporation and not as an individual. Follow this practice on any other documents you sign, such as contracts, order forms, and promissory notes.

Sample Signature of Corporate Officer

Jones Bakery, Inc.

By: _____
William Jones, President

In some cases, you might have to sign the contract or promissory note personally as a guarantor. For example, banks usually won't lend money to a small corporation without the personal guarantees of the principals, and some extra-cautious landlords might insist on similar guarantees for leases. But even if you have to accept personal liability for some corporate obligations, it's better to do this as a guarantor than as the main signer. The reason: The guarantee provides further evidence that you and the corporation are separate legal entities.

Assign Existing Business Contracts to the Corporation

If you incorporate an existing business (such as a sole proprietorship or partnership), the old business might have contracts, which the corporation will take over, still in effect. For example, maybe the prior business leased space and the lease still has a year to go. Or maybe you're a computer consultant and, as a sole pro-prietor, you'd just gotten started on a contract to design customized billing software for a medical clinic.

It's usually a good idea to formally transfer these contracts to the corporation. Generally, unless the contract expressly prohibits an "assignment," you're free to transfer it to your corporation without getting the consent of the other party.

But bear this in mind: Unless you get that consent and a release of personal liability, or unless your contract already specifically permits you to assign it to a new corporation and be free from personal liability, you're still going to be legally responsible for performance of the contract. This means that the landlord can turn to you if the corporation doesn't pay the rent, and the medical clinic can hold you personally responsible if you don't deliver the software you promised.

SEE AN EXPERT

Important tax note. If your corporation will derive income from passive sources, such as rents, royalties, or dividends, or from the performance of personal services, get professional tax advice before you transfer contracts to the corporation. A transfer could lead to a personal holding company penalty, which could be quite substantial.

To assign a contract, prepare a short document called an "Assignment of Lease" or "Assignment of Contract." A sample is shown below. Have the corporation agree to accept the assignment and to carry out the terms of the contract. From a business and legal standpoint, it makes sense to continue your business through a single entity— the corporation—rather than doing business simultaneously as a sole proprietor and as an employee of your corporation. Putting your eggs in one basket reduces the chances of blurring the distinction between the corporation and your personal business interests.

RESOURCE

The Corporate Records Handbook: Meetings, Minutes & Resolutions, **by Anthony Mancuso (Nolo),** shows how to hold and document necessary corporate meetings and includes all forms.

Sample Assignment of Contract

Assignment of Renovation Contract

In consideration of the sum of $_____ , receipt of which is acknowledged, Cecil Hardwick (d/b/a Hardwick Construction) assigns to Hardwick Building Company (a Nevada Corporation) all of his rights, duties, and obligations under his contract with Plaza Building Associates dated _____ , 20____ , concerning the renovation of the Plaza Building.

Hardwick Building Company accepts this assignment and accepts all of Cecil Hardwick's duties under the assigned contract.

Dated: _____ , 20____

ASSIGNOR:

ASSIGNEE:
Hardwick Building Company,
A Nevada Corporation

By:_____
    Cecil Hardwick d/b/a
    Hardwick Construction

By:_____
    Cecil Hardwick
    President

Creating a Limited Liability Company

Chapter 1 introduced the basic business entities—the sole proprietorship, the partnership, the limited liability company (LLC), and the corporation. This chapter tells you more about setting up an LLC.

As explained in Chapter 1, an LLC is often the best choice if you want to limit your personal liability as the owner of a small business. (Having limited liability means that being a member of an LLC doesn't normally expose you to legal liability for business debts and court judgments against the business.)

Though forming a corporation will also give you and your co-owners (if you have any) limited liability, a corporation's structure is somewhat more complicated than an LLC's. In even the smallest corporation, for example, you have a three-level organizational structure consisting of shareholders, a board of directors, and corporate officers. It's true that the same people can fill all of these roles—in fact, in a one-person corporation, a single individual can do it all. But keeping track of what corporate hat you're wearing can be challenging when you have more pressing business matters to think about.

With an LLC, you might be able to avoid some of the legal and tax paperwork associated with a corporation. For example, an LLC needn't worry about getting signatures on stock subscriptions or issuing stock certificates or drawing up board of directors' resolutions—although an LLC whose members prefer a higher degree of formality are certainly free to issue membership certificates and to document all major company decisions. (See "Record Keeping," below.)

And when it comes to taxes, a one-member LLC that prefers pass-through taxation (as in a sole proprietorship) rather than corporate-style taxation can remain what the IRS calls a "disregarded entity"—which means the LLC itself needn't file any tax documents at all.

In addition to requiring less paperwork, an LLC can be far more streamlined and flexible than a corporation. LLC owners can run their business with much less formality. For instance, the owners of an LLC (known as members) jointly manage the LLC (although they can instead designate one or more managers to manage it if they want to impose a separate level of management). And in most states, LLCs don't have to hold annual meetings of the members (although they can hold them if they choose). Finally, as discussed in Chapter 1, LLCs have the flexibility to choose to be taxed as corporations or as partnerships.

The paperwork requirements and legal rules governing LLCs are based on state laws. Although these laws vary somewhat from state to state, LLCs do enjoy a surprising amount of consistency around the country. This chapter is based on the LLC state laws that are typical in most states. As you go through this chapter, you should keep in mind that the rules and practices for LLCs in your state could have some quirks that aren't covered here. It's your job to make sure that you're following the law in your state for creating an LLC.

RESOURCE

For comprehensive information and guidance on setting up an LLC, consult *Form Your Own Limited Liability Company*, by Anthony Mancuso (Nolo). Among other things, the book contains complete details on preparing your LLC articles of organization and LLC operating agreement. The book also contains forms to help you prepare these documents. You can also create your LLC online at www.nolo.com/products/business-formation/online-business-formation-services. Also, be sure to see the LLCs section in the Business Formation center on www.nolo.com, which includes detailed advice for each state on how to form an LLC.

Number of Members Required

Every state lets you form an LLC that has just one member.

RESOURCE

For information specifically on single-member LLCs, get *Nolo's Guide to Single-Member LLCs*, by David M. Steingold (Nolo).

Management of an LLC

As with any company, at least one person has to be in charge of managing the day-to-day business. In most states, unless you appoint one or more members or nonmembers to manage the LLC, you and all the other members are automatically responsible for managing the business. This is called "member-management." If you choose the other option and do appoint one or more people to manage the LLC, it's called "manager-management."

Chances are that your LLC will choose member-management rather than manager-management. That's because you probably won't want or need a separate level of management.

EXAMPLE: Joyce, Phil, and Nora form Cyber Networking LLC, a small consulting firm. All three members are experienced computer experts who actively work in the business and participate equally in running it. They meet weekly to review new project proposals and to decide whether or not to take on the new work. They are all member managers.

There are situations, however, in which a manager-managed LLC is the better way to go. This is most likely to be the case if you have passive investors who will feel more comfortable if the LLC appoints an active managing member (or perhaps several managing members) whose duties are explicitly defined.

EXAMPLE: Terry, Bill, and Chester form Wheel Wellness LLC, a bicycle repair business, built around Chester's years of experience in repairing exotic bikes. Terry and Bill contribute most of the money but, knowing little about bicycle repair, stay out of the running of the business. Chester contributes a small amount of money to the LLC but his main contribution is his skill. Because Terry and Bill are passive investors, they agree that Chester will manage the company—but they carefully spell out his duties in the operating agreement so that he knows what decisions require input from the investors. All three are happy with their manager-managed LLC, in which the lines of authority are clearly defined.

If your LLC chooses to designate managers, you'll need to specify this choice in either your articles of organization or your operating agreement (see below), depending on your state law.

Financing an LLC

Assets come into an LLC in two forms: equity and debt. Let's look at each.

Capital Contributions (Equity)

Ordinarily, you and the other LLC members will make an initial financial contribution to the business. In return, you'll each get a percentage ("capital interest") in the LLC. Among other things, this capital interest determines the portion of the LLC assets each of you is entitled to receive if the business is dissolved or sold. Also, this percentage is frequently used to determine how profits and losses will be allocated while the business is in operation.

Under most state statutes, your capital contributions can consist of cash, property, or services—or the promise to provide any of these in the future.

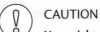

CAUTION

You might need to comply with securities laws. If an LLC membership is considered a "security," you'll need to register it at the federal or state level unless it's exempt from registration. Unfortunately, the rules for when LLC memberships are securities and when they're not haven't been well defined yet. Generally, if a member relies on his or her own efforts to make a profit—that is, the member actively engages in managing or working for the business—the interest probably won't be considered a security. If, however, a member relies on someone else's effort, that member's interest is probably a security and must be registered.

Because the law on whether LLC interests are securities is in flux, you might want to see an experienced business lawyer before you sell membership interests in your LLC to people who won't be active in the day-to-day business. You might want to make sure that the membership interests are not considered securities or, if they are, that they're exempt from government registration.

Normally, a cash capital investment in an LLC is tax free. You and the other members don't pay tax on the membership interests you receive, and the LLC doesn't pay tax on the cash it accepts in exchange. The tax effects of paying capital into an LLC are deferred until a later time; as an LLC member, you'll be taxed on any profit you make when you sell your interest or you dissolve the business.

> **EXAMPLE:** Wendy makes a capital contribution of $10,000 to her new pet supply business, Puppy Love LLC. As the sole member, she receives a 100% capital interest in the business. She pays no tax at this time. Five years later when Wendy sells the business and receives $50,000 after all expenses are paid, she pays tax on the $40,000 profit.

Loans (Debt)

To supplement capital contributions, LLCs often borrow funds from time to time from their members or a member's family or friends. These loans help increase the LLC's cash reserves or cover operational expenses. The money your LLC borrows isn't treated as business income—after all, it has to be paid back. As a result, neither the LLC nor the members pay tax on it.

These insider loans can benefit both the LLC and the lender. A loan payable with interest can result in an immediate investment return to the lender if repayments are made in monthly installments.

> **EXAMPLE:** Phil's mother lends $10,000 to Phil's one-person LLC. The interest rate is 5%—less than Phil would pay to a bank but more than Phil's mother would earn from a government

bond. The loan is repayable in monthly installments of principal and interest over a five-year period. Phil's mother receives a return on her money whether or not the LLC turns a profit in any given month or year.

To avoid IRS problems, your LLC should pay a lending member or other insider a commercially reasonable rate of interest—a rate that's close to what a bank would charge. When the LLC makes payments on the loan to the lending member, that member reports the interest payments received from the LLC on his or her individual income tax return, and pays taxes at the individual income tax rate. Of course, the repayment of principal by the LLC to the lending member is simply a return of loan proceeds, and isn't taxable income.

The LLC deducts the interest payments that it makes to the lending member as a business expense. These deductions reduce the net profit of the LLC, which in turn reduces the profits allocated and taxed to members at the end of its tax year.

Attracting Financing for Your LLC

In the past, corporations sometimes had an edge over other business forms in attracting investment capital because the corporate stock structure easily accommodates the issuance of shares to investors. These days, however, a growing number of venture capitalists are investing in LLCs because LLCs can be taxed as either corporations or partnerships and they offer flexibility in how they're managed.

For example, you can give majority voting power to a venture capital group in return for investing in your LLC. You simply amend your LLC operating agreement and issue voting membership interests to the group. What's more, if your LLC elects to be taxed like a partnership, the profits allocated to the investor-members won't be taxed twice (as corporate dividends are), but will pass through the LLC to the investors. They'll then report and pay taxes on the profits on their individual income tax returns.

Compensating Members

We've looked at how money gets put into an LLC. Now let's get to the fun part and look at how you take money out. We'll assume that your LLC has chosen the usual course and opted for partnership-style rather than corporate-style taxation (discussed in Chapter 1).

LLC management can choose to pay active members a regular salary or a share of LLC profits. (If a member is inactive, the LLC can pay that member only a share of the profits—see directly below). If the LLC does choose to pay an active member a salary, the salary must be reasonable in light of the services the member performed— the IRS has rules on what an LLC can pay to its members as salaries and what must be paid out as profits (see IRS Publication 535, *Business Expenses,* Chapter 2).

A salary paid in return for the performance of services (one that is not tied to net income of the LLC) is classified as a "guaranteed payment." A guaranteed payment is taxed as ordinary income to the member, and the LLC will deduct it as a business expense before computing the net LLC income available for distribution to all members.

> EXAMPLE: Will and Peter each have 50% ownership interests in their home repair business, Fixer Upper LLC. Will works half time in the business and receives guaranteed payments (a salary) of $30,000 annually for his services. Peter works full time and receives guaranteed payments of $60,000 annually. During the year, the LLC earns $100,000 and has no expenses other than Will and Peter's salaries. After paying the salaries to the two members, the LLC is left with a $10,000 profit. That profit is allocated 50-50 between Will and Peter at the end of the year.

Now suppose you don't receive a "salary" for your services in the form of guaranteed payments during the year (or that you're an inactive member). In that case, your earnings are tied entirely to the net income of the LLC. An LLC's profits and losses are allocated to its members at the end of the LLC's tax year, according to the allocations in the LLC operating agreement.

Typically, the share of profits and losses allocated to each member is based on each member's percentage, or capital, interest in the LLC. So, going back to the above example, if Will and Peter didn't receive guaranteed payments for their services, the LLC's $100,000 profit would be allocated equally between them at the end of the tax year. The capital accounts of both Will and Peter would be credited with $50,000.

Self-Employment Taxes for LLC Members

As mentioned in Chapter 1, the IRS collects a self-employment tax. For 2021, that tax is 15.3% of the first $142,800 earned by a self-employed person and 2.9% on earnings above that amount for Medicare alone. Owners of S corporations do not have to pay the self-employment tax on the profits passed through the corporation to them. But according to proposed IRS regulations (which Congress has placed on hold), as an LLC member, you would have to pay self-employment tax on money you receive as compensation for services and in addition on all profits passed through the LLC to you, but only in the following situations:

- you participate in the business for more than 500 hours during the LLC's tax year, or
- you work in an LLC that provides professional services in the fields of health, law, engineering, architecture, accounting, actuarial science, or consulting (no matter how many hours you work).

If you fall into one of the categories listed above, 100% of your income from the LLC will be subject to self-employment tax. Otherwise, you can apply the S corporation rules, described in "Choosing Between an LLC and an S Corporation: Self-Employment Taxes Can Tip the Balance" in Chapter 1.

Sometimes members decide, and state in their operating agreement, that one or more members may receive what's called a "draw"—a periodic payment against future LLC profits. In this case, members do not have to wait until the end of the LLC's tax year to take profits from the LLC. Each member takes a draw each month or quarter; that draw, or distribution of future profit, is subtracted from the member's capital account. When profits are allocated to each member at the end of the LLC tax year, the member's capital account balance goes back up.

In tax lingo, profits that are allocated to an LLC member are known as the member's "distributive share." An LLC member must pay income tax on his or her distributive share whether it's actually distributed to the member or retained in the LLC coffers.

Choosing a Name

Your LLC name will have to comply with state legal requirements. This often means including an LLC designator such as "Limited Liability Company" or "Limited Company" in the LLC name. Many states allow abbreviations such as LLC or LC.

> EXAMPLE: You choose Andover Services as the name of your business. Depending on the state in which you're located, one or more of the following might be appropriate ways to indicate that your business is an LLC:
> - Andover Services Limited Liability Company
> - Andover Services L.L.C.
> - Andover Services LLC
> - Andover Services Limited Liability Co.
> - Andover Services Ltd. Liability Co.
> - Andover Services Limited Company
> - Andover Services Ltd. Co.
> - Andover Services L.C.
> - Andover Services LC.

You'll need to put the name of your LLC in the articles of organization that you'll file with your state's LLC filing office. If you pick a name that's already on file for an LLC in your state, your articles of organization will be rejected. The same thing will occur if your proposed name is simply too close to one that's already on file. Some states will also cross-check your proposed name against names on file for existing corporations or limited partnerships.

By planning ahead, you'll avoid the annoying setback of having to choose another name. In many states, you can check for available names online. In addition, in some states, you can call the LLC filing office, and the clerk will make an instant computer check and let you know if there's a name conflict. A few states will ask you to request the information in writing.

CAUTION

Name availability check is only preliminary. Until you've reserved an LLC name (as explained below) or filed your LLC articles of organization and had your filing accepted, your proposed name isn't yours to use. The information on name availability that you receive online, by phone, or in response to a written request for a name check is just preliminary. Until you definitely have the name reserved or filed and accepted, don't spend money on business stationery, signs, or advertising using the proposed name.

Be aware that even if your name is accepted by the LLC filing office, you might not have the full legal right to use that name to identify your products or services. The LLC filing office looks only at whether the name meets the requirements of the state LLC law and whether it's already in use by another LLC in the state. Some states will cross-check your proposed name against names on file for existing corporations or limited partnerships, but many will not even do that.

And, of course, legal conflicts might arise from other sources. Most important—especially if you'll use your name as a trademark or service mark to identify your goods or services—you'll need to make sure your proposed name isn't the same as or very similar to another well-known business name or trademark—Starbucks or Intel, for example (see Chapter 6). If it is, the owner of the famous name will insist that you drop it; if you don't, the name owner will very likely go to court and win. To avoid this complication, you might want to do a national name search—and perhaps register your name as a trademark or service mark if the name is clear for your use.

 RESOURCE
To learn more about trademark law in general and name searches in particular (including how you can do a simple name search yourself), read *Trademark: Legal Care for Your Business & Product Name*, by Stephen Fishman (Nolo).

Suppose your LLC name is available but you're not quite ready to file your articles of organization. In most states, you can reserve the name for 30 to 120 days by paying a small filing fee. Many states have a preprinted form you can use for this purpose. After reserving a name, if you file your articles of organization within the reservation period, the name will be accepted by the LLC filing office.

 TIP
You're not locked into your business name forever. Your business can use a name that's different from the name used in your articles of organization. You can even use several alternative names. However, to use one or more alternatives with legal safety (in other words, to preserve the benefits of limited liability), you'll have to register each name as an "assumed name" or "fictitious business name" at the state or county level or both. For more on this subject, see Chapter 6. It's also possible to change the name of your LLC by filing amended articles of organization.

Paperwork for Setting Up an LLC

Setting up an LLC is simple. Typically, you must complete just two basic legal documents—the "articles of organization" (also called "articles of formation" or a "certificate of formation" in some states) and the "operating agreement" (called "regulations" in a few states).

 TIP
Additional form for corporate-style taxation. In the somewhat unusual event that you want to have your LLC taxed as a corporation, you'll also need to file a form with the IRS; it's IRS Form 8832, *Entity Classification Election*. See "After You Form Your LLC," below.

 RESOURCE
Form your LLC online. If you're ready to form your LLC, you might be able to do much of the work online—including validating the name of your LLC, preparing and filing your articles of organization, and preparing your statement of information and operating agreement. To get started, go to www.nolo.com/lander/entry/llc/llcname.

Articles of Organization

In most states, preparing your articles of organization is surprisingly simple—especially if your LLC is a typical small business consisting of a handful of owners. Many states provide a printed form for the articles of organization; just fill in the blanks, sign the form, and file it with the LLC filing office. The task is made even easier in the states that allow you to complete the process online.

Other states don't provide the actual articles of organization form but do furnish something almost as convenient: sample articles with instructions. You can prepare your own articles of organization by following the format and contents of the sample.

If your state is one of the few that provides neither fill-in-the-blanks forms nor sample forms with instructions, check your state's LLC statute to learn what to put into the articles of organization.

Typically, your articles of organization will not need to include anything more than the following information:

- **The name of your LLC.** See "Choosing a Name," above, for more on picking a name.
- **The name and address of your LLC's initial registered agent and office.** You'll probably name one of your members as your registered agent—the person who receives official correspondence

relating to the LLC and who gets served with lawsuit papers if someone sues the business. You'll generally use the LLC's business location or the registered agent's home as the registered office address.

- **Statement of purpose.** In most states, you don't need to specifically describe your business activity—a general statement of purpose will suffice. Example: "Purpose: To engage in any lawful business for which limited liability companies may be organized in this state."

- **Type of management.** You usually need to say whether your LLC will be member-managed or manager-managed. (In some states, the type of management is specified in the operating agreement rather than the articles.) The difference between the two is explained in "Management of an LLC," above. In most states, if you don't specify the type of management, your LLC will be managed by all the members (that is, member-managed). Typically, you'll also need to give the names and addresses of your initial members and, for manager-managed LLCs, your initial managers.

- **Principal place of business.** You'll give the address of your main business location. For most small businesses, it's also the only location.

- **Duration of the LLC.** In many states, your articles must specify how long your LLC will be active. You might be able to choose between a "perpetual" (unlimited) duration or a specific number of years. Some states put an upper limit on the number of years you can choose—30 or 50 years, for example. These statutory limits should cause no problem because when the time is up, you or your LLC successors can extend the life of the business for another long term of years.

- **Signatures of people forming the LLC.** Usually, state law allows one person to sign the articles as the organizer of the LLC. But if your LLC is member-managed, you'll probably choose to have all the initial members sign the articles

of organization to give everyone a sense of participation.

After preparing your articles, you file them with your state's LLC filing office—usually the secretary of state, located in your state's capital city. Many states allow you to do this online. In a few states, before or after you file your articles of organization, you might need to put a legal notice in a local newspaper stating your intention to form an LLC.

CAUTION

There might be special requirements for licensed professionals. In many states, if you're a licensed professional, you must comply with additional rules for starting an LLC. For example, you might have to file special articles of organization for a professional LLC and end your LLC name with special words or initials such as "Professional Limited Liability Company," or "PLLC." In a few states, such as California, many types of professionals, such as accountants, doctors, and physical therapists, to name a few, are not allowed to form LLCs.

Operating Agreement

Once you've filed your LLC articles of organization with your state's LLC filing office and the document has been accepted, you're officially in business. But if you have more than one member, don't overlook another important piece of LLC paperwork: the operating agreement.

This document is recommended even for a one-person LLC (see "Ask your tax adviser about allocating goodwill payments in your operating agreement," below), and it's very important to have one if your LLC has two or more members.

 SEE AN EXPERT

Ask your tax adviser about allocating goodwill payments in your operating agreement. If you plan to sell your LLC membership interest in the future, you might want to specifically provide in your LLC operating agreement that part of the buyout price includes a reasonable payment for the selling member's share of the business's goodwill. ("Goodwill" is an intangible factor—often based on brand recognition or business reputation—that makes a business worth more than just the value of its physical assets.) You're probably aware that it's better to have income taxed as a capital gain rather than as ordinary income. By including such a goodwill allocation in an operating agreement, you ensure that the portion of the buyout price attributed to goodwill will be treated as a capital asset. This will save the selling member from having to pay tax on it at the higher, ordinary income tax rates. If you set up a one-person LLC, an operating agreement is important at least for the purpose of making a goodwill allocation. See your tax adviser, as this is a complicated area of business tax law.

The operating agreement serves a function similar to partnership agreements (Chapter 2) and corporate bylaws (Chapter 3). It sets the rules for how the owners will run the business and it defines their rights and responsibilities, such as the members' voting power and right to profits.

A typical operating agreement for a member-managed LLC usually covers at least the following provisions:

- **Capital contributions.** One of the most important parts of an operating agreement sets forth how much money or property each member will contribute to the LLC and what additional contributions might later be required.
- **How a member's percentage interest is determined.** The operating agreement should state how members' percentage (capital) interests are computed. Typically a member's percentage interest will be based on how a member's capital account compares to the total of all members' capital accounts. So if Ed has $25,000 in his capital account and the total of all capital accounts is $100,000, then Ed's percentage interest is 25%.
- **Type of management.** Your agreement might need to specify whether your LLC will be member-managed or manager-managed. (In most states, you can elect the type of management either in your articles or your operating agreement.) Most small LLCs will opt for member-management, and in the majority of states, if you don't specify your choice, the law says that your LLC will be member-managed. Typically, you'll also need to give the names and addresses of your initial members and, for manager-managed LLCs, your initial managers.
- **Membership voting.** Your agreement should also specify how issues will be voted on and decided. In the case of a member-managed LLC, you'll probably want a simple majority (51%) of membership interests to decide most issues, but you can also provide for a larger majority (two-thirds, for example) to decide some matters. You can also provide for per capita voting, where each member is given one vote.
- **Profits and losses.** Explain how profits and losses will be allocated to members. Typically, it will be on the basis of each member's percentage (capital) interest in the LLC.

Capital Accounts Explained

In bookkeeping-speak, a member's capital account represents the current value of that member's percentage of ownership interest.

When an LLC member contributes cash or property to the LLC, the member's capital account is credited with the cash amount or fair market value of the property contributed. Later, when profits are allocated at the end of the LLC tax year, the member's capital account balance goes up (the business owes the member this money); as distributions of profits are made, the capital account balance goes down (the business no longer owes this money to the member).

The capital account balance is also the amount of LLC assets that a member expects to be paid if the company is liquidated and split up among the members (assuming there's sufficient cash or other assets left after all creditors have been paid).

- **Distribution of money.** You may decide to put language in your operating agreement spelling out who will decide if and when LLC profits will be distributed to members. For example, you might provide that all members must agree on a distribution or, perhaps, that a majority of members can make that decision.
- **Tax election.** As noted above, an LLC is taxed as a partnership unless it elects to be taxed as a corporation. It's a good idea to state in your operating agreement how the LLC will be taxed initially.
- **Transfer of a membership interest.** Your operating agreement should say how a member can withdraw from the business and whether a member can transfer his or her interest in the LLC to someone else.
- **Addition of new members.** Explain whether new members will be allowed into the LLC and how—that is, by a simple majority, a larger majority, or a unanimous vote.
- **Buyout provisions.** Chapter 5 covers the important subject of what happens if a member dies, moves away, gets sick, or simply wants to get out of the business. Can the LLC force the departing member to sell his or her interest to them? How will the interest of a departing member be valued? Though you can cover these issues in a separate buyout agreement, it makes better sense for LLC members to deal with them in the operating agreement.
- **Other businesses.** Your operating agreement can provide, for example, that members are free to own interests in or work for other businesses that don't compete with the LLC's business.

As mentioned above, most small businesses that operate as LLCs will prefer to have the business member-managed rather than manager-managed. If your business chooses the less popular manager-managed option, you'll need a special section in your operating agreement dealing with how managers are selected and replaced, and what authority they have.

SEE AN EXPERT

Have a lawyer review your operating agreement. If you prepare your own operating agreement, it's a good idea to have an experienced small business lawyer look it over before you and the other members sign it. That will help ensure that the provisions are internally consistent and that you haven't made any technical errors that can cause legal, tax, or financial problems later. And lawyer's fees for reviewing the operating agreement should be a fraction of what they would be if the lawyer drafted the document from scratch.

RESOURCE

Looking for a lawyer? Asking for a referral to an attorney from someone you trust can be a good way to find legal help. Also, two sites that are part of the Nolo family, Lawyers.com and Avvo.com, provide excellent and free lawyer directories. These directories allow you to search by location and area of law, and list detailed information about and reviews of lawyers.

Whether you're just starting your lawyer search or researching particular attorneys, visit www.lawyers.com/find-a-lawyer and www.avvo.com/find-a-lawyer.

After You Form Your LLC

Once your LLC articles of organization have been accepted by your state's LLC filing office and you've signed an LLC operating agreement dealing with such important issues as managing the business, allocating profits and losses, and transferring membership interests, you're ready to start doing business. However, there are a few additional actions that are either legally required or worth considering to put your new company on a sound footing.

Set Up an LLC Bank Account

Remember, your LLC is a legal entity distinct from its members and managers. For this reason, your LLC needs its own bank account so that its finances can be kept separate.

If you're creating an LLC out of an existing business that already has a bank account—for example, your sole proprietorship or partnership business is now going to be run as an LLC—start fresh by opening a new bank account for the LLC. The bank might ask for a copy of your articles of organization and your Employer ID Number (EIN), which is issued by the IRS. (EINs are discussed in Chapter 8.)

If you decide to simply continue the old account, you'll need to check with your bank to learn their procedures for moving a bank account from a prior business to a new legal entity. Again, the bank will probably want to see your articles of organization and your EIN. You need to keep detailed records showing exactly how much money was in the account when it was changed over to the LLC. Also, keep track of checks that were written by your prior business but haven't cleared yet. These checks should be treated as expenses of the prior business and deducted from the amount considered transferred to the LLC. If you don't prepare and retain these records, you can wind up with one big headache a few years from now when you try to reconstruct exactly what you transferred to the LLC.

Complete Any Initial Financial Transactions

Tie up any other loose ends relating to the financing of the LLC. For example, make sure that the members deposit their initial cash contributions into the LLC bank account. If a member transfers property—computer equipment, for example—to the LLC in exchange for a membership interest, the member should sign a bill of sale confirming the transfer of property to the LLC.

If your LLC is borrowing start-up money from friends, relatives, or its members, be sure to issue promissory notes from the LLC stating the interest rate and other terms of repayment.

Finally, if you or another member will be leasing space to the LLC, prepare a lease as if the landlord were a complete outsider.

Inform the IRS If Your LLC Chooses Corporate Taxation

A single-member LLC is normally taxed as a sole proprietorship. (In IRS lingo, the single-member LLC is a "disregarded entity.") You report your profits (or losses) on your personal Schedule C. The LLC pays no tax on its profit. A multimember LLC, on the other hand, is normally taxed as a partnership. For federal income tax purposes, a multimember LLC itself doesn't pay a tax on its profits. Profits or losses pass through to the individual members, who include their share of LLC profits or deduct their share of LLC losses on their personal tax returns. Most LLC members prefer these arrangements. If that's what you want to do, you don't have to let the IRS know. You'll automatically be treated as a sole proprietorship or partnership for federal income tax purposes.

The other tax option is to have your LLC treated as a corporation for tax purposes. Your tax adviser might recommend this if you expect your LLC profits to be substantial and the members are prepared to leave some of the profits in the business. The funds can be used in a later year, for example, to pay for a new building or the purchase of additional equipment. With corporate tax treatment, the income retained in the LLC is taxed at a favorable corporate tax rate—as of 2018, a flat 21% rate. This rate is lower than all but two of the individual tax rates that might apply to income allocated to members of an LLC that has elected partnership-style taxation.

If your members want to have your LLC taxed as a corporation, the LLC will need to file IRS Form 8832, *Entity Classification Election*, within 75 days of the formation of the company. Otherwise, you'll have to wait until a later tax year to make the change.

For more on complying with federal and state tax filing rules, see Chapter 8.

The Tax Cuts and Jobs Act: New Pass-Through Tax Deduction

The Tax Cuts and Jobs Act created a new tax deduction for people who earn income through pass-through entities, such as LLCs, S Corporations, partnerships, and sole proprietorships. These individuals might now be eligible to deduct up to 20% of their business income from their income taxes. This deduction went into effect in 2018 and is scheduled to last through 2025. You must meet certain requirements to qualify for the deduction, and limitations exist. In addition, if your business provides certain services, such as health care or law, you're not allowed to take the deduction if your income exceeds specific amounts. To learn more, go to the Legal Updates page for this book at www.nolo.com/back-of-book/RUNS.html, as well as the "What's New In Business Taxes?" section of Nolo.com. For specific advice about your situation, talk to a tax professional.

Safe Business Practices for Your LLC

In a small LLC consisting of just one member or a few members, it's sometimes hard to keep in the front of your mind the fact that the LLC is a separate legal entity from you and the other members. You and your business are not the same. In the eyes of the law, you are an agent of the LLC. For example, when you sign contracts and other documents, you're signing them (or should be signing them) on behalf of the LLC and not as an individual.

Remembering this distinction between you and your LLC can seem especially burdensome if you've done business in the past as a sole proprietorship or partnership and have just changed over to an LLC. On the day-to-day level, it's really business as usual and, in many respects, nothing at all has changed. Yet, if you want to get the maximum protection from personal liability for debts of the business, you need to carefully observe the legal distinction between yourself and your LLC. Fortunately, as you'll see shortly, that task isn't as tough as you might think.

The reason it's so important to always treat the LLC as a separate entity is that if you don't, a judge could decide that you're personally liable for a business debt or that you have to pay a lawsuit judgment out of your personal assets. It's becoming clear that in cases involving LLCs, judges will follow the same rules that they apply to corporations and will hold LLC owners personally liable for business debts if the owners haven't respected entity formalities. (See "Safe Business Practices for Your Corporation" in Chapter 3 for some examples of what courts did when owners failed to treat their corporations as separate legal entities.)

So if you ignore the fact that your business is organized as an LLC, and you operate it more like a sole proprietorship or a partnership, you will needlessly face the risk of personal liability. It follows that many of the recommended precautions for protecting corporate shareholders from personal liability, discussed below, should help to shield LLC members.

Put Adequate Capital Into Your LLC

Put enough money and other assets into your business to meet business expenses that are likely to come up. If you don't and there's a lawsuit, a judge might rule that the LLC is a sham—that it really isn't a separate entity from its owners—in which case you and the other members could be personally liable.

Each business has different financial needs. You can often legally fund a small home-based business, such as a computer consulting operation, on a shoestring. But opening a pizza restaurant would require considerably more money, because you'd need to lease space, outfit a kitchen and dining area, and hire employees. Your accountant should be able to recommend a reasonable level of funding for your LLC.

Insure Against Obvious Risks

Think carefully about whether there's a substantial risk that customers or others might be injured because of your business. If so, it's a good idea to buy a reasonable amount of liability insurance coverage. (See Chapter 12 for more on insurance.)

In some cases, you might have to personally sign an LLC document or promissory note as a guarantor. For example, a bank typically won't lend money to a small LLC unless the members personally guarantee repayment, and a supercautious landlord might want you to guarantee the lease. But even if you have to accept personal liability for some LLC obligations, it's better to do this as a guarantor than as the main signer. The reason: The guarantee serves as further evidence that you and the LLC are separate legal entities.

Separate Your Personal Finances From Your LLC's Finances

The LLC needs its own bank account. Don't use that account to pay your personal expenses. If you receive checks from the LLC for salaries or draws, deposit the checks in your personal account and then pay your personal bills from that account.

If you use personal funds to pay business expenses—for example, you pick up a business book on the way home from work—you can have the LLC reimburse you. Be sure the LLC keeps a receipt for your purchase of the book to justify deducting the cost as a proper business expense.

To further separate you and other members from the LLC, document all transactions as if you were strangers. If the LLC leases a building from you, sign a lease. If the LLC borrows money from you, get a promissory note. If you sell equipment to the LLC, sign a bill of sale to formally transfer legal ownership to the LLC.

Use the Official LLC Name

Suppose the name of your LLC is Kitchen & Bath Designers LLC. Use that full business name in all your business dealings—on your stationery, business cards, and signs; in phone book listings and catalogs; and on the Internet. Don't use a different name or abbreviation (such as Kitchen & Bath Designers, without the letters LLC) unless you file an assumed name certificate or fictitious name certificate as permitted by state law. For more on LLC names, see "Choosing a Name," above, and Chapter 6.

Sign Documents as an LLC Member or Manager

In correspondence and on checks, sign your name as Paula Smith, Member (for a member-managed LLC), or Paula Smith, Manager (for a manager-managed LLC), along with the full name of your LLC, rather than just Paula Smith. This makes it clear to those who deal with you that you're acting as an agent or employee of the LLC and not as an individual. Follow this practice on any other documents you sign, such as contracts, order forms, and promissory notes.

Sample Signature of LLC Member or Manager

Whole Grain Bakery LLC

By: _____
Paula Smith, Member

or

Whole Grain Bakery LLC

By: _____
Paula Smith, Manager

In some cases, you might have to personally sign an LLC document or promissory note as a guarantor. For example, a bank typically won't lend money to a small LLC unless the members personally guarantee repayment, and a supercautious landlord might want you to guarantee the lease. But even if you have to accept personal liability for some LLC obligations, it's better to do this as a guarantor than as the main signer. The reason: The guarantee serves as further evidence that you and the LLC are separate legal entities.

File Annual State LLC Reports

In most states, you're required to file a one-page annual report on a form available from the LLC filing office. Usually, the form is automatically mailed to you. You'll have to pay a small filing fee in the range of $10 to $50—although the fee is higher in a few states. To avoid losing your legal status as an LLC and your protection from personal liability, it's important that you complete the form and return it along with the filing fee to the appropriate state office.

Assign Existing Business Contracts to Your LLC

If you've been doing business as a sole proprietorship or partnership and are now switching over to an LLC, you might have some ongoing contracts that you'd like the LLC to take over. For example, maybe your sole proprietorship signed a five-year lease for business space and there are still two years left to go under the lease. Or maybe the partnership you established for your lawn maintenance business has several contracts in force to service the lawns of major businesses in a local research park.

It makes sense to transfer these contracts to your LLC. You usually can do this without getting the consent of the other party to the contract, unless the contract specifically prohibits an assignment. But be aware that if you do assign a contract to your LLC,

you'll still be personally liable for complying with it. There are basically only two situations in which this isn't true. The first is when the other party consents in writing to release you from liability. The second is when the contract contains language allowing you to assign it to a new LLC or corporation and be free from personal liability.

Unless you fall into one of these two exceptions, the landlord in the first example will be able to turn to you for the rent if the LLC doesn't pay it. Or in the second example, the businesses that contracted for your lawn maintenance services will be able to hold you personally responsible if your LLC doesn't perform and the businesses have to pay a higher price to get the work done by someone else.

Sample Assignment of Contract

Assignment of Contract

In consideration of the sum of $_____ , receipt of which is acknowledged, WordSmith Associates (an Indiana partnership) assigns to WordSmith Media Consultants LLC (an Indiana limited liability company) all of its rights and duties under the contract with Smoke Stack Industries, Inc., dated _____ , 20____ , for advertising, marketing, and public relations services.

WordSmith Media Consultants LLC accepts this assignment and accepts all of WordSmith Associates' duties under the assigned contract.

Dated: _____ , 20____

ASSIGNOR:	ASSIGNEE:
	WordSmith Media Consultants LLC,
An Indiana Partnership	An Indiana Limited Liability Company
By:_____	By:_____
Cynthia Cardone Partner	Cynthia Cardone Member

SEE AN EXPERT

Tax rules on passive investments are tricky. If your LLC will receive income from passive sources (rents, royalties, or dividends, for example) or from the performance of personal services, get professional advice before transferring contracts to the LLC. A transfer could lead to a personal holding company penalty—which could be quite substantial.

Record Keeping

If someone goes to court and asks the judge to disregard your LLC and hold you personally liable, you might be able to bolster your position if you can produce a record book that shows you've consistently treated the LLC as a separate legal entity.

This is clearly the case when someone seeks to get behind a corporation and hold the owners (shareholders) personally liable. That's because by law and tradition, corporations are expected to observe a number of formalities such as holding annual meetings and documenting meetings of the board of directors. The paperwork requirements for an LLC are minimal compared with those for a corporation. Still, you might want to hold periodic meetings and document important LLC decisions—especially if you have more than two or three members.

It's a good idea to keep an LLC record book containing important paperwork, such as:

- the articles of organization
- the operating agreement
- a membership register listing the names and addresses of your members
- a membership transfer ledger showing the dates of any transfers of membership interests by a member

- membership certificates and stubs (if your LLC decides to issue certificates to members), and
- minutes of LLC meetings and written consent forms (if your LLC decides to hold formal meetings or to get written membership approvals for certain LLC decisions—see discussion directly below).

Even if your LLC has decided to proceed with a minimum amount of formal paperwork, you should consider documenting the members' approval of the most significant LLC actions, including:

- authorizing LLC bank accounts and designating who's eligible to sign checks and withdraw funds
- borrowing money from a bank or from an LLC member
- amending the articles of organization or the operating agreement
- entering into major contracts
- buying, selling, or leasing real estate
- electing corporate-style taxation or a tax year other than a calendar year
- authorizing distributions of profits to members
- admitting new members, and
- authorizing the LLC purchase of the interest of a departing member.

By staying on top of this simple paperwork, you'll have a paper trail of important LLC decisions that will help satisfy courts, the IRS, and others that you've attended to all the legal and tax niceties and that you've treated the LLC as a separate legal entity.

RESOURCE

Your Limited Liability Company: An Operating Manual, **by Anthony Mancuso (Nolo),** explains ongoing record-keeping requirements and provides minutes, written consent forms, and resolutions for a multitude of business decisions.

Preparing for Ownership Changes With a Buyout Agreement

If you're in business with others, there's a good chance that there will be ownership changes as the years go by. That's true whether you organize your business as a partnership, a limited liability company (LLC), or a corporation. Ownership changes might be the last thing you want to think about when the business is brand new. However, the fact is that many things can happen down the road—or maybe only a few steps away—to affect the ownership of your business. For example, you or a co-owner might:

- decide to move out of state to pursue a new line of work
- become physically or mentally disabled— or even die
- seek to buy out a co-owner's interest in the business, or
- want to sell to an outsider.

What happens then? Will the transition proceed smoothly and fairly? Or will there be discord and, possibly, lawsuits? The answer might depend on how well you've planned for the future. Without careful planning, the business itself may be in jeopardy. In an extreme case, all the time and money that you and the other owners have put into the venture might evaporate as the business falls apart.

Certainly, during the sunny, optimistic days when you're putting the business together, it's hard to focus on disruptive changes that you might face in the future. And it's equally difficult to do so when the business is humming merrily along. But planning ahead can save all involved from a ton of grief.

Most businesses with two or more owners should put together a "buyout agreement"—traditionally, these are known as "buy-sell" agreements. This principle applies regardless of the legal format you've chosen for your business. Partners in a partnership, shareholders in a corporation, and members of an LLC will all benefit from well-drafted buyout provisions.

First, let's get our terms straight. When I use the term buyout agreement, I'm not talking about a contract in which you promise to buy an outsider's business or an outsider promises to buy yours; that's a separate topic, covered in depth in Chapter 10. The buyout agreement we're looking at here is a binding contract among the owners of your business that controls the buying and selling of ownership interests in that business, much like a "premarital" agreement for business owners. A good buyout agreement gives the continuing owners some control over the transaction when a departing member sells or gives away that member's interest in the business. Often the agreement will regulate who can buy the departing owner's interest and at what price or, sometimes, whether the co-owner can sell at all.

Importantly, a buyout agreement helps ensure that you and your co-owners aren't forced to work with strangers or other people you won't get along with. It provides an exit strategy. It can help ensure that if a co-owner leaves the business, that person will receive a reasonable sum in exchange for the ownership interest—or if a co-owner dies, the heirs will be paid fairly.

Typically, a buyout agreement also gives the business and its continuing owners a chance to buy out an owner who's stopped working for the business or has died. This eliminates the possibility that active owners will be forced to share profits with an inactive owner or an unsuitable new owner. Some buyout agreements also say that if an owner dies, the surviving owners can force the deceased owner's estate representative or inheritors to sell back the deceased owner's interest to the company or to its surviving owners. Similar provisions might apply when an owner decides to retire after a certain period of time or becomes disabled and can't actively participate in the business.

RESOURCE

This chapter simply introduces you to the important concept of buyout agreements. For comprehensive coverage of the subject and precise guidance on how to develop your own agreement, consult *Business Buyout Agreements: Plan Now for All Kinds of Business Transitions,* by Bethany K. Laurence and Anthony Mancuso (Nolo). The book comes with forms and worksheets to walk you through the process.

SEE AN EXPERT

Check your agreement with an expert. With the help of the comprehensive book and worksheets recommended above, you should be able to craft a respectable buyout agreement. However, as authors Mancuso and Laurence wisely note, even their book can't provide the depth of advice—especially in the tax and estate-planning realm—that a buyout or financial planner or tax expert can provide. And of course, their book can't customize an agreement for you that suits exactly your company's and each owner's individual needs. So if you do draft your own buyout agreement, be sure to take it to a small business tax or legal adviser before putting your finalized agreement into action.

Major Benefits of Adopting a Buyout Agreement

If you don't have a buyout agreement, here are some things that can happen:

- You might be forced to work with and share control of the company with an inexperienced or untrustworthy stranger who buys the interest of a departing owner.
- You could be forced to work with the spouse or other family member of a deceased or divorced owner. While this might work out just fine, there's also a substantial possibility that the family member will lack the necessary business skills or the right personal qualities for working with you and the other co-owners.
- If you leave the company or die, you or your survivors might be stuck with a small business interest that no outsider wants to buy—and for which no insider will give you a decent price.
- You and your co-owners might argue with a departing co-owner or the inheritors of that co-owner over what price should be paid for the interest that's changing hands. This can cause an angry deadlock that can wreak havoc on your business operations.

Now let's see how a buyout agreement can help your business avoid these situations.

Controlling Who Can Own an Interest in Your Company

An outsider who gains an ownership interest can disrupt the smooth flow of your business—especially in the case of major management decisions that require unanimous approval of the owners. Consider this example.

EXAMPLE: Joe and Cindy form a small corporation. Each receives 50% of the corporate stock. They don't foresee problems down the road so they don't bother with a buyout agreement. A few years later, Joe and Cindy have a serious disagreement over how to expand the business. To avoid further hassles, Joe sells his shares to Andrew, whom Cindy has never met before. The two quickly reach an impasse on management issues and the business comes to a standstill.

A buyout agreement can prevent this from happening by giving the owners the power to prevent outsiders from buying in. Sometimes this is accomplished by giving the remaining owner or owners the opportunity to meet any outsider's offer for an interest in the company. This type of provision is called a "right of first refusal." To better understand its purpose, see what happens if Joe and Cindy had a buyout agreement.

EXAMPLE: Joe and Cindy form a small corporation and they wisely create a buyout agreement to deal with what happens if one of them wants to leave the business. A few years later when they disagree on how to expand, Joe decides to sell his shares. Andrew offers to buy the shares for $10 each. The right of first refusal provision in their buyout agreement requires Joe to offer the shares to Cindy at the same price. Rather than share control of the business with a stranger, Cindy buys Joe's shares. The business continues to run smoothly and prospers.

A buyout agreement can also give the surviving owners the power to purchase the interest of an owner who's died if the surviving owners don't want the inheritors of the deceased owner to become co-owners of the business.

Who Doesn't Need a Buyout Agreement?

Although a buyout agreement can benefit most small businesses, there are situations where one isn't essential.

You're the 100% owner of the business. If you have a one-person business, obviously you won't have much interest in an agreement that controls who may own interests in the company, because you can do that yourself. But consider the possibility that you might want to plan for the future by agreeing to sell the business to a valuable employee who is willing and able to take it over. In that situation, you might decide to sign a buyout agreement with the employee. This will assure the employee of the expectation of taking over some-day, and you'll know that you or your inheritors will receive payment when ownership of the company is transferred to the employee upon your death.

You own the business with your spouse. If you've been married a long time and have a good, solid marriage, you probably won't need a buyout agreement. It's unlikely that either of you will want to leave the company unless you both do. And if one of you dies, the other one probably will inherit the ownership interest. On the other hand, if you haven't been married long, or your future with your spouse is uncertain, a buyout agreement can make sense.

You own the business with one of your children. If you plan to transfer part or all of your business to your child, a buyout agreement isn't required. You can arrange the transfer through a regular contract or your will or a trust. But even here, you may want to sign a buyout agreement. It's always possible, for example, that your child will die or want to leave the business before you do. A buyout agreement can address this and other possibilities.

Providing a Guaranteed Buyer for Your Ownership Interest

As we've seen, a buyout agreement can protect your company by making sure that an outsider does not disrupt the business by becoming an owner without the approval of the existing owners. But a buyout agreement can also help you individually if you ever reach the point where you want or need to sell your ownership interest.

Obviously, it can be quite difficult to sell a less-than-100% share of a small business. There might be no market at all for a minority interest. A person interested in buying into a small business will normally not find it attractive to be in business with strangers and to have very little say in how the business is managed.

This lack of a true market for your interest can be a problem for you and your family. The time might come when you want to leave the business but your co-owners could be unwilling to pay you a fair price for your interest. If that happens, you might be stuck with a share of the company you can't sell. The same thing can happen if your heirs inherit your piece of the company.

> EXAMPLE: Oliver, Sophia, and William form a small corporation, each receiving one-third of the shares. They neglect to sign a buyout agreement. Three years later, Oliver dies unexpectedly. His wife and two children inherit his shares. They'd like to sell the shares to raise money for college and other living expenses but can't find an outside buyer. Knowing this, Sophia and William buy Oliver's shares for a pittance, leaving Oliver's family in dire economic straits.

A good buyout agreement can avoid an unfortunate outcome like this by requiring the company or the remaining owners to pay a fair price if your inheritors want to sell your interest in the business. You accomplish this by putting a "right to force a sale" provision in your buyout agreement, which requires the company or the continuing owners to buy you out if you die, and sometimes under other circumstances. (The agreement can also provide that the company purchase life insurance on its owners to fund the future purchase of a deceased owner's interest.) This can protect you and your inheritors from taking a financial hit if the company or continuing owners refuse to buy your interest at a fair price or from becoming embroiled in bruising negotiations over what will happen to your ownership interest.

Let's see how a buyout agreement could have changed the grim outcome for Oliver's family in the above example.

> EXAMPLE: Oliver, Sophia, and William form a small corporation, each receiving one third of the shares. Wisely, they sign a buyout agreement containing a right to force a sale clause, which kicks in if one of them dies. The clause requires the surviving owners to buy the interest of an owner who has died, assuming the estate representative, trustee, or inheritors want to sell it.
>
> Three years later, Oliver dies unexpectedly. His wife, as representative of his estate, invokes the right to force a sale clause. Because the agreement required the purchase of life insurance policies on each owner, Sophia and William can easily buy out Oliver's shares at the price in the agreement by using the insurance proceeds. Oliver's wife spends the money for college expenses for the children and other living expenses.

A buyout agreement can also require the company or remaining owners to buy your interest in other situations as well. For instance, you might want to retire or stop working, or you might become mentally or physically disabled. If you don't have a buyout agreement in these situations, there's no guarantee that you'll get a fair price for your business interest.

Setting a Fair Price and Providing a Workable Method for a Buyout

A well-prepared buyout agreement can set a price for interests in the business—or a formula for setting a price. This can eliminate lengthy disputes and unpleasant lawsuits about the value of an owner's interest. Equally important, the agreement can provide a mechanism for how the departing owner (or his or her family members) will be paid. Having to come up with a lump-sum payment for a departing owner's interest, for example, might create financial stress for the company or the remaining owners. As a solution, a buyout agreement may provide for payments to be made in installments over a number of years. Or maybe the payments will come from life or disability insurance that the company buys for each owner.

Be forewarned that figuring out a fair price in advance of a buyout scenario is no easy task. You and the other owners will be trying to arrive at a price that, years from now, will represent the true value of the company. You can't know today if your business will prosper in the years ahead or struggle to make a profit. And because there's no public market for small business interests, it's hard to make comparisons with interests in similar businesses—not that such information would be of great help anyway. Each industry and small business is different; comparative data from other companies has limited value. Still, picking a fair price—or a formula for setting the price—is essential if the buyout agreement is to do its job.

There are five basic methods for setting a buyout price—all of which are explained clearly and in great depth in *Business Buyout Agreements: Plan Now for All Kinds of Business Transitions,* by Bethany K. Laurence and Anthony Mancuso (Nolo). Typically, you'll set a price for the business as a whole—or a formula for determining that price—and the interest of an owner will usually be a percentage of that price. For example, if the entire business is worth $500,000, the interest of a 25% owner will be worth $125,000 for buyout purposes. Let's briefly look at the most common methods for valuing a company for purposes of a buyout.

Valuation Method 1—Agreeing on a Fixed Price in Advance

Using this method, you simply agree on a price for the business as a whole and put that number in your buyout agreement. This "agreed value," or "fixed price," method is simple and certain. However, it's hard to pick a price that will reflect the value of the business throughout its life—the price you decide on today can quickly become outdated. So if you use this method, provide that the number will be updated each year.

Valuation Method 2—Book Value

The "book value" of a company is generally its assets minus its liabilities as shown on the company's most recent year-end balance sheet. Because the book value is basically a snapshot of the company's finances on a given day, it doesn't give information about the profitability of the business. Also, book value might not reflect assets, such as customer goodwill, that reflect the profit-making ability of the company. Compared to other formulas for determining value, the book value method usually results in the most conservative (lowest) value for a business.

Valuation Method 3—Multiple of Book Value

If a small business has been up and running for several years, its real value is probably greater than its book value. The "multiple of book value" method takes into account intangible assets that add to the worth of the business—assets such as goodwill, patents, copyrights, brand names, and trade names. You might decide that the price of the business should be, for example, two or three times its book value.

Valuation Method 4—Capitalization of Earnings

This method is best suited to established companies, because it measures a business's value by its past profits. If your company is just starting out or hasn't been around very long, you can't use this method because you have no earnings history.

But after your company has produced a good profit for several years, you might want to shift over to this method. Here's how it works: You first determine the company's annual earnings, or profit, by subtracting the cost of doing business from gross revenues. Next you multiply the earnings by a number called a "multiplier." The number you choose should depend, to some degree, on your company's industry and also on prevailing interest rates. Generally, you'll apply the multiplier to your company's average annual earnings for a base earning period of three years or longer.

Valuation Method 5—Appraisal

Your buyout agreement can simply provide that at the time of a buyout, a professional business appraiser will establish the value of the business. Actually, you might want to provide for two appraisers. Typically, as part of the buyout process, the buyer (usually the company or remaining owners) and the seller (for instance, the departing owner or the representative of a deceased owner's estate) each choose an appraiser to value the company. If they come up with the same price, that value is used. If they come up with close prices, the parties might be able to negotiate and agree on a price. But if the two appraisers are far apart on the price, the agreement may require them to choose a third appraiser who will set the price. A drawback is that the appraisal method can be costly and time-consuming.

Where to Put Your Buyout Provisions

You might be wondering what kind of document should hold your buyout provisions. Basically, you need to choose between putting the provisions in a separate buyout agreement or adding them to another document that may already be in existence—for example, your corporate bylaws, your LLC operating agreement, or your partnership agreement. Here are my recommendations:

Corporations

If you do business as a corporation, you can add your buyout provisions to your organizational documents—either your articles of incorporation or, more likely, your bylaws. Or you can adopt a separate agreement, often called a "shareholders' agreement" in the corporate context. I believe that the latter approach—adopting a distinct agreement—is best. You're emphasizing the importance of these provisions so that an owner can't later claim surprise when another owner asserts the terms.

If you follow this recommendation, it's a very good idea to refer to the separate buyout agreement in the bylaws. This can help head off a legal challenge by someone looking for a legal way to escape from the buyout terms.

Whichever approach you take, make sure your buyout provisions don't conflict with the existing provisions of your articles of incorporation or bylaws. You might want a lawyer to help you with this consistency check.

To make sure that potential buyers of your corporate stock as well as potential creditors know about the buyout agreement, add language to each stock certificate stating that the shares are subject to restrictions on transfer as provided in a shareholders' agreement. This type of statement is called a "stock certificate legend."

LLCs and Partnerships

For a partnership—general or limited—the partnership agreement is the primary (and, usually, only) agreement among the business owners. Similarly, for an LLC, the operating agreement is the primary agreement between owners. So for partnerships and LLCs, I recommend that you place your buyout provisions in the partnership or LLC operating agreement itself. You'll want to

make sure, of course, that the buyout terms mesh well with the other provisions of the agreement. A lawyer can help with this chore.

Perform a Consistency Check on Your Buyout Provisions

Whether you adopt your buyout provisions as part of a separate agreement or add them to your bylaws, partnership agreement (discussed in Chapter 2), or LLC operating agreement (discussed in Chapter 4), make sure they do not conflict with the current provisions of those organizational documents.

Mostly, you want to check to make sure an existing provision in one of those documents does not prohibit, or impose additional rules on, any of the buyout provisions that you're adding. For example, if your partnership agreement prohibits the transfer of ownership interests to outsiders, but the buyout provision you want to use allows an owner to sell to an outside buyer under certain circumstances, you should amend your partnership agreement to delete the restriction on transfers.

CAUTION

Prevent legal termination of partnerships and LLCs. One area that partnerships and LLCs need to cover in their buyout provisions is what happens to the company when an owner leaves (sells out, retires, or dies). Some state laws say that the partnership or LLC automatically dissolves when an owner leaves unless the partnership agreement or LLC operating agreement says otherwise, or unless the remaining owners vote to continue the company within 90 days. If the owners don't vote to continue the company in that period of time, the company is considered dissolved and must file dissolution papers with the state. To avoid risking the future of the partnership or LLC and having to take a vote after an owner leaves, as part of your buyout provisions state that the partnership or LLC continues without a vote of the owners when an owner leaves the company.

When to Create a Buyout Agreement

The key to a successful buyout agreement is coming up with a reasonable plan early on, before anyone knows who will be most affected by it. At the outset, when you're just getting started, your concerns and those of the other owners will be roughly the same because no one knows who will be the first to leave. Because at that early point no one wants to sell out, everyone has the same interest in crafting an agreement that's fair to everyone.

With a brand-new business, you and your co-owners can start by putting together a very simple buyout agreement. You can concentrate on giving your company or continuing owners the right to buy a selling or departing owner's interest at a fair price or a price to be set according to a simple formula, such as the book or appraised value.

After you've been in business a few years, you might want to come up with a more complex agreement. The same holds true if your business's assets have become quite valuable or there's a concern about limiting estate taxes. Though it's always a good idea to have a small business lawyer look over your buyout agreement before it's final, it's especially important to get a lawyer's help in creating a more sophisticated agreement.

Naming Your Business and Products

Naming your business and products might not be as simple as it first appears. For one thing, you need to comply with legal procedures mandated by state law. If you incorporate, for example, or form a limited liability company, you must choose a corporate or LLC name acceptable to your state's business filing office. And all businesses—corporations, LLCs, partnerships, and sole proprietorships—must comply with laws dealing with the registration and possible publication of assumed names or fictitious names.

Other legal procedures having to do with business names are not mandatory, but it nevertheless makes good sense to follow them. For example, before using a cool-sounding name—especially one that will also be used to identify your products and services—it's extremely smart to find out whether someone else already has rights to the name and, as a result, can legally limit how you use it or tell you not to use it at all. This normally involves at least two steps. To avoid a claim of unfair competition, your first step is to do a local name search to make sure that no local business in your field uses a similar name. Don't start Jimmy's French Laundry if there's already a Jenny's French Laundry a few miles away.

Step two involves making sure you gain maximum protection for your trademarks or service marks— names you'll use to identify your products or services. Especially if you're looking for comprehensive protection for a trademark or service mark, you'll want to first carefully check and then register the mark under federal and state trademark laws.

Just how much effort and expense should you sensibly invest in protecting the name of your business, product, or service? The answer depends on many factors, such as the size of your business, the size of the market in which you'll operate, the type of product or service, and your expectations for growth and expansion.

As a general rule, the more customers your business will reach, the more you need to be sure you have the exclusive right to use your chosen

Trademark Terminology

- **Trademark:** A word, phrase, design, or symbol that identifies a product brand—such as Dell computers, Nike shoes, Xerox photocopiers, and Marathon gasoline.

- **Service Mark:** A word, phrase, design, or symbol that identifies the provider of a service—such as Burger King (fast foods), Roto-Rooter (sewer-drain service), or FedEx (shipping).

- **Mark:** Sometimes used to refer to both a trademark and a service mark, because the terms are nearly, but not completely, interchangeable.

- **Corporate Name:** The name of a corporation as registered with one or more states. Examples: Time, Inc., and Sony Corporation. The corporate name refers to the corporation only and not to any products or services it offers.

- **Trade Name or Business Name:** The name used to identify a business, as distinct from the product or service it offers. It might be the same as the product or service name; for example, Sony Corporation sells electronic equipment under the Sony trademark and McDonald's Corporation uses the service mark McDonald's on its fast food service. Or the trade name or business name might be different—for example, Ford Motor Company sells cars under the Lincoln trademark.

- **Assumed Name or Fictitious Name:** A business name different from the owner's name. Example: Laura does business as Coffee Express. Partnerships and (in many states) corporations may also use assumed or fictitious names. In most places, you must register a fictitious name. (See "Assumed and Fictitious Names," below.)

- **Federal Trademark Register:** A list of all trademarks and service marks registered with the federal government. To be accepted, a trademark or service mark must be distinctive and not confusingly similar to an existing mark. All states maintain trademark registers, too, and some maintain service mark registers; preexisting federal trademark rights have priority.

name within your business or product niche. For example, if you're starting a local computer repair service, you won't need as much business name protection as if you were planning to sell a new line of low-fat salad dressings in all 50 states. But be aware that because of the Internet and other electronic communication methods, the number of small businesses that compete with one another is rapidly growing, meaning that the need to do in-depth name searches and to consider the implications of trademark law is also rapidly growing.

RESOURCE

Learn more about trademarks. For a thorough discussion of business names, see *Trademark: Legal Care for Your Business & Product Name*, by Stephen Fishman (Nolo). That book discusses in great depth how to choose a legally protectable name and offers step-by-step instructions on how to file a federal trademark registration. Also check out the Nolo website (www.nolo.com) where you'll find extensive legal information on patents, copyrights, and trademarks.

Business Names: An Overview

Complying with the few mandatory legal procedures for naming your small business is relatively simple. For some very small, local businesses, meeting these requirements and doing nothing more might be adequate.

EXAMPLE: Jeff wants to start a food delivery service called "Speedy Eats for All." He'll be a sole proprietor. Because his is a small, unincorporated, local business, he is probably safe enough if he registers the name as an assumed or fictitious name. In most states, he will register it at the county level, but some states require registration at the state level and also require publishing the name in a newspaper. Jeff probably doesn't need to spend time and money to register the name as a state trademark or service mark. With a descriptive name and a small local business, there's little likelihood that the customers of any other business would be misled, so there's not much to protect. However, Jeff should check to be sure there are no other food delivery services in his area using the same or a very similar name. If there are, Jeff should change his name or risk a claim of unfair competition. If Jeff wants to go the extra legal mile, he should check his state's trademark register and the federal register to see if other "Speedy Eats" businesses are registered. (See "Name Searches," below, for how to do a trademark search.)

In the past, a wide range of local businesses—small retail stores, repair services, and craft studios, for example—didn't need to worry about registering a trademark or service mark. And to avoid possible claims that they were unfairly using another business's name, they could feel relatively secure if they checked for possible name conflicts in state and local business directories and by doing a basic online search with no need to do a more formal state or federal trademark search.

But today, the rules of the game are dramatically different. Because of the Internet, mail order, and rapidly growing national chains, the idea of "local" isn't what it used to be. Today, even modest-sized businesses must consider taking name protection steps that used to be the sole concern of larger, more expansive enterprises. For example, you might think you have no problem if you're choosing a name for a shoe store in a small town. Think again. If you happen to pick a name that's similar to a shoe store that sells on the Internet, you are very likely to be accused of trademark infringement and probably forced to change your business name, even though the online store's headquarters is located 2,500 miles away.

These days, about the only time you might be able to ignore thinking about trademarks and service marks is if you have a tiny, local business that uses your own name—or a very common name—to market goods and services locally. In short, if you plan to sell services using your own name (Harvey Walker Roof Repair) or if yours will be a one-person, home-based business such as a graphic design service (A+ Design), you're not likely to have a trademark problem.

But if your business is just a little bigger, such as a large camping equipment store (Wilderness Outfitters), or sells goods or services beyond a very local or industry-specific niche (Lamps.com Online Lamp Store), you really should take time to understand the basics of trademark law—and conduct a name search to see if someone else in your field is already using your proposed name.

The reason to be absolutely sure you have the legal right to use your chosen business name is simple: You don't want to invest time and money in signs, stationery, and ads for your business and then get a nasty letter from a large company that claims a right to the name you're using and threatens you with a trademark infringement lawsuit. Just defending such a case in federal court can cost you upwards of $100,000, meaning that even if you're sure that you're in the legal right, you'll probably wind up changing your name just to duck the lawsuit—no fun, given the investment you've already made.

Mandatory Name Procedures

As mentioned, there are name-related legal tasks that every business must attend to.

Corporations

Part of the process of creating a corporation is choosing a corporate name. Most states require certain words or abbreviations in your corporate name so the public can recognize that your business is a corporation. This puts them on notice that, in general, you're not personally liable for debts of the corporation. (See Chapter 1 regarding limitations on the liability of corporate shareholders.)

Each state has its own laws dealing with what words you must include in your corporate name, so check your own state's statute. Most secretary of state websites have information on naming corporations as well as blank articles of incorporation forms that you can download.

Typically, the state will require one of the following in your official corporate name:

- Incorporated
- Corporation
- Company
- Limited, or
- the abbreviation Inc., Corp., Co., or Ltd.

If the name doesn't include one of the required terms, the state won't accept your corporate filing.

The law in your state will also likely list some words that can't be included in your corporate name or that can be used by only certain types of businesses.

To learn about the prohibited or limited words in your state, start by calling the office where you file the articles of incorporation. This is usually the secretary of state or the corporate commissioner's office.

Most states will reject a corporation name that's the same as one already on file or that's confusingly similar to the name of an existing corporation. If this happens to you and you've really got your heart set on the name you've picked out, there might be a way to get around the rejection. One approach is to change the name slightly or add something to it. Even a relatively small change could result in approval of the name.

Words That Are Typically Limited or Prohibited

Most states prohibit or limit the use of the following words in corporate names:

bank	banking	cooperative
engineering	trust	national
federal	United States	insurance
acceptance	guaranty	pharmacy
credit union	medical	architect
indemnity	thrift	certified accountant
olympic	surveyor	

This is by no means a complete list, so contact the office (such as the secretary of state) where you'll file your articles of incorporation with questions about your corporate name.

Doing Business on the Web

If you decide to have a website, and you probably should, you'll need to select a domain name—a unique address that computers understand and customers can use to find you. The issues involved in choosing a domain name range from getting your hands on an available one to avoiding trademark lawsuits based on your choice of name.

A good domain name should be memorable, clever, and easily spelled. Unfortunately, many of the best names are already taken. To see if the name you have in mind has been registered, go to https://whois.icann.org/en or the website for any major Web hosting company, such as Network Solutions or GoDaddy. These sites allow you to search for a particular name. For example, if you are starting a food delivery business, you might check "mealdrop.com." If you find that mealdrop.com is already taken, you can search other possibilities. After you enter relevant keywords (such as food, meal, restaurant, and delivery), you'll get a list of related names that are still up for grabs.

Once you've found an available name, you'll need to make sure it doesn't conflict with someone else's trademark. If your choice will cause customer confusion between your company and another, you're safer choosing another name. This is true even if the other business is halfway across the country. Once you've established a Web presence, you are in competition with businesses around the globe and must address trademark issues equally broadly. A generic name such as "coffee.com" will keep you safest from lawsuits but will also leave you unable to argue that other businesses cannot legally use a very similar business or domain name—you'll need to strike a balance.

After you've chosen an appropriate domain name, you can register it online with a Web hosting company or at any of the domain name registrars at www.icann.org. Some businesses register under more than one name or register common misspellings of their names.

For more information on choosing and registering domain names, as well as avoiding domain name conflicts, see *Trademark: Legal Care for Your Business & Product Name*, by Stephen Fishman (Nolo).

Or in some states, you can use a similar (but not identical) name if the prior holder of the name consents in writing. The document in which the other company gives its consent will have to be filed with the office that accepts corporate filings. Obviously, you're most likely to get cooperation from the other corporation if your business involves a completely different product or service.

EXAMPLE: Country Squire, Inc., sells wood-burning stoves in the southern part of the state. It consents in writing to the use of the name "Country Squire Inn, Inc." by a new corporation that will run a bed and breakfast in the northern part of the state. With the consent on file, the state corporations commissioner accepts the Country Squire Inn, Inc., incorporation papers.

To avoid filing your corporate papers and then receiving word three weeks later that your name has been rejected, in many states you can call the government office that receives incorporation papers and ask whether your proposed name is available. They might give you preliminary clearance by phone if the records show that no other corporation in your state is using the same or a similar name.

CAUTION

Watch how you use the name. The fact that the state filing office accepts your corporate name doesn't ensure that you have the exclusive right to use the name in your state. An unincorporated business might already be using it as its trade name in your state. Or another business—whether incorporated in your state or elsewhere—could be using the name as a trademark or service mark. Depending on the situation, the prior use often gives the user the right to legally prevent your use of the name if your use of the name would be likely to confuse customers. It's always prudent to check further to avoid conflicts with other users.

Relying on a State Filing Search Might Not Be Adequate

When you form a corporation or an LLC, the state filing office will check to see whether your proposed business name is the same as or confusingly similar to one already on file. If so, your name will be rejected. But just because your name is accepted by the state filing office doesn't mean your business name is safe to use. That's because these offices don't check state or federal *trademark* registers. In short, even though a name might be available in your state to identify your business, you could run into costly trademark infringement problems if you also use it to identify your products and services.

EXAMPLE: Tony and Lars form a corporation that will design state-of-the-art sound systems for restaurants and jazz clubs. Their name—The Ears Have It, Inc.—has been cleared by the secretary of state for their state. Can they now safely use this name as a service mark to market their services? No. When the secretary of state cleared the corporate name, it simply meant that the name didn't duplicate the name of another corporation in that state. Another company might have already been using the name as a trademark or service mark. This wouldn't show up in the secretary of state's corporate name records.

Because Tony and Lars are hoping to market their services in several states, they (or a name search company they hire) should do a thorough search, including checking federal and state trademark registers. If they don't, they might inadvertently find themselves in conflict with a company that's already using the name. If they find that their proposed name is clear, they should think about registering it as a federal trademark or service mark.

If you expect some delay between the time you choose a name and the time you file your incorporation papers, find out if your state lets you reserve your preferred corporate name. Many states allow you to hold a corporate name for one to four months by simply filing a form and paying a small fee.

Limited Liability Companies

The procedures for LLC names are very similar to the procedures for corporate names. When you prepare the articles of organization for your LLC, you'll need to include its name. If another LLC on file with the LLC filing office is using your proposed name or a similar name, your articles of organization will be sent back to you unfiled. To avoid this inconvenience, it's wise to check the availability of the name before you file the articles.

Your LLC will have to include certain words or abbreviations that let people know its legal status. Examples include:

- Limited Liability Company
- Limited Company
- Ltd. Liability Co.
- L.L.C. or
- LLC.

The list of words and abbreviations varies a bit from state to state, so check the law in your state to learn all the possibilities.

TIP

Here's a shortcut for picking a required LLC designator. Ending your LLC name with the words "Limited Liability Company" will meet the name requirements of all states.

As with a corporation, your state law might prohibit you from using certain words in your LLC name—words, for example, that refer to banking, insurance, trust, or financial services. And again, as with a corporation, your state filing office won't accept your proposed LLC name if it's the same as or very similar to an LLC name that's already on file. Your state might also cross-check the name against the names of nonLLC entities—such as corporations and limited partnerships—that are required to register with the state. Your name will also be rejected if it's too close to one of these.

RESOURCE

For an in-depth discussion of choosing a name for your LLC, see *Form Your Own Limited Liability Company,* by Anthony Mancuso (Nolo).

Assumed and Fictitious Names

Sole proprietors sometimes choose to do business under names that are different from their own names, and partnerships usually select a partnership name other than the full names of all partners. Corporations and limited liability companies may also decide to do business under names that are different from their official corporate names. Depending on state law, these adopted business names will legally be called "assumed names" or "fictitious names." If your business uses such a name, you probably must register it.

Sole Proprietorships and Partnerships

If you're planning to do business as a sole proprietor or partnership under an assumed or fictitious name, in most states you're required to file an assumed name or fictitious name certificate with the designated public office—usually at the county level—before you start doing business. Generally, there's a printed form for you to fill out, and you'll probably have to pay a small filing fee. In some states, the registration is good for a limited period, such as five years, and must be renewed. State law might also require that you publish notice of your business name in a local newspaper.

Terminology

Some people refer to an assumed name or a fictitious name as a "DBA." That's short for "doing business as"—for example, Albert White doing business as Al's Cabinet Shop. On legal documents such as contracts and lawsuits, this may appear as Albert White d/b/a Al's Cabinet Shop.

States require you to file the certificate for a simple reason: It lets members of the public know who is behind the name. If you don't register your assumed or fictitious name, you might encounter both legal and practical problems. For one thing, in many states, you might not be able to sue on a contract made or another transaction done under the business name. And in some states, you might be fined. In a number of states, you can't open a bank account in the name of your business without filing an assumed or fictitious name certificate.

Corporations and LLCs

Most corporations and limited liability companies operate under their corporate or LLC name, which is, of course, on file with their state filing office. If, however, a corporation or an LLC decides to do business under a different name, many states require it to file an assumed or fictitious name registration. This involves completing a simple form and sending it to the state filing office with a modest filing fee.

> EXAMPLE: Miracle Widget Manufacturing Company, a corporation, wants to do parts of its business under the name "Widco" and other parts under the name "Industrial Innovators." In many states, it will have to register both of these names as assumed or fictitious names.

It's important to use your correct corporate or LLC name, because this makes it more difficult for anyone to claim that your business entity is a sham (lawyers call this "piercing the corporate veil") and impose personal liability on you. (See Chapter 3 for more on corporate liability.) If you're going to do business under a name that deviates from the official name on your articles of incorporation or LLC articles of organization, it's essential that you properly register the name. That way, you won't jeopardize your immunity from personal liability that's part of your reason for having a corporation or an LLC.

If your state doesn't allow a corporation or an LLC to register an assumed or fictitious name, there might be an easy way to reach this same end while complying with state rules. You can use a preferred business name in conjunction with your official corporate or LLC name.

> EXAMPLE: Contemporary Home Furnishings LLC is established in a state that doesn't allow registration of assumed or fictitious names. The company wishes to operate a lamp store called "Bright Lights." It does this by calling the lamp store "BRIGHT LIGHTS" and then in smaller print adding "a division of Contemporary Home Furnishings LLC" or by saying "BRIGHT LIGHTS, owned and operated by Contemporary Furnishings LLC."

By always using your official corporate or LLC name along with your preferred business name, you put everyone on notice that your business isn't a sole proprietorship or partnership—and you continue to enjoy the benefits of limited personal liability.

When it comes to products and services, a corporation or an LLC is completely free to use names that are unrelated to its corporate or LLC name (as long as these names don't infringe on someone else's trademark, of course). In fact, this is common. Apple Inc., for example, sells products under the name iPhone, and the Ford Motor Company sells Taurus automobiles.

Trademarks and Service Marks

A trademark or service mark normally consists of a word or words (or another signifier) that identify a product or service as different from all others. Buick automobiles, Volvo automobiles, Blue Shield health plan, and Kaiser health plan are all examples of trademarks.

For most small businesses, a trademark or service mark will consist of words or a logo. Occasionally, a business can obtain trademark or service mark protection for a product shape, color, or scent that's linked exclusively to the source company in consumers' minds. For example, the distinctive "curved and ribbed shape" of the old Coca-Cola bottle is a federally registered trademark. But such protection is not easy to come by.

Trademark law is the main tool that businesses use to protect the symbols and words that identify the origin of services and products. The basic rule is that the first user of a distinctive (that is, creative or unusual) name or symbol gets the exclusive right to use it on relevant goods or services. The twin goals of trademark law are to:

- prevent businesses from getting a free ride off the creativity of others in naming and distinguishing services and products, and
- prevent customers from being confused by names that are misleadingly similar.

If you're the first user of the mark on certain goods or services, you can register the name or symbol with the United States Patent and Trademark Office (USPTO). Registration enhances your rights, particularly your ability to go after infringers, because it places competitors on nationwide notice of your ownership of the mark. And even if you don't get around to registering your rights as soon as you begin using the trademark, you'll probably be able to stop later users of a similar mark, provided that you used it first within a specific region.

Trademark laws are powerful, but not all-encompassing. They don't automatically protect a business name (the name of your company). There are various rules as to what qualifies as a trademark, and not all terms or logos meet the test. Essentially, to be considered a mark, a business name must create an association between consumers' minds and your product or service.

Strong and Weak Trademarks

Trademarks that consist of creative, unusual, or otherwise memorable terms are called "distinctive" and "strong." These marks receive the most protection from federal law—if you're the first to use such a name or symbol, you can usually stop others from using it in most situations. By contrast, trademarks that consist of ordinary descriptive terms are called "weak" and require more effort to protect.

Strong Trademarks

Distinctive trademarks—the ones most amenable to protection—are memorable, evocative, unique, or somehow surprising, such as 7-Up, Lycra, or Google. The words themselves have little or no descriptive function; they simply set the product or service apart from others. For example, Kodak and Exxon are fanciful or "made-up" words and therefore by their nature, they are distinctive. Other distinctive terms are arbitrary; they're real words but they're not used in an expected manner—for example, Arrow for shirts, or Camel for cigarettes. Nearly as good are suggestive trademarks—ones that hint at some aspect of the product. For example, Talon suggests the gripping power of a zipper.

Weak Trademarks

While original and distinctive words (like Buick) can be protected by trademark law, generic terms cannot. The name Buick distinguishes a line of cars from others, but the name means nothing apart from its trademark use. Conversely, Dependable Dry Cleaners merely tells you something about the business; it doesn't help you distinguish it from rivals who might also advertise their services as reliable or efficient. So Dependable Dry Cleaners, unlike Buick, would probably not qualify for trademark or service mark protection unless it has been in use for many years or it has developed a sizable following—that is, a secondary meaning, explained below.

Fortunately, an ordinary name (a weak trademark) can sometimes be protected from someone else using the name in a confusing way, in violation of a state's laws on unfair competition (state law on unfair competition supplements the federal law on trademarks). For instance, even though the name "Giant Salads" might be weak and perhaps not a candidate for federal protection, its owners might get some relief from a rival's use of the identical name on the identical product or service in a competing market.

Trademark law never allows a business to claim the exclusive right to use generic names (like Bicycle for bicycles or bicycle products), because competitors also need these words to describe their products. If you could tie up common, key words for your exclusive use, your competitors would be unduly restricted in describing their goods. Besides, descriptive terms aren't particularly memorable and don't further the purpose of trademarks and service marks. (However, ordinary words will be considered distinctive when they're used for "unexpected" products—for example Bicycle for playing cards.)

Weak Trademarks That Become Strong: Secondary Meaning

Merely descriptive words (such as Easy Clean for a cleanser) or surnames (like Jones or Smith) or geographic terms (such as Atlantic or New York) usually are not legally protectable unless the trademark's owner can demonstrate that consumers associate the mark with its product or service. Such consumer association, known as "secondary meaning," results from substantial advertising, significant sales, or prolonged usage. When a weak mark has secondary meaning, it becomes strong—examples include Liquor Barn, Jiffy Lube, and Stop & Shop. When that happens, the trademark owner is then able to register the trademark with the USPTO, and the trademark is protected under unfair competition law if there's a local conflict with a similar mark.

For example, the ChapStick brand of lip balm was originally a weak trademark. It simply described the condition the product was designed to cure—chapped lips. But it became strong, as advertising and word of mouth helped the public develop a clear association between the name and a specific product. Over time, the name developed distinctiveness based on familiarity rather than any quality inherent in the name.

McDonald's is another good example of a weak mark that developed a secondary meaning over the years and now qualifies for broad protection.

Before the Trademark: Name Searches

You don't want to start work with someone else's trademark. For this reason, it's important to conduct a "name search" before you lock in the name of your business. As explained above, this is especially true if you choose an unusual or unique business name that will also be used to identify your products— Z Pop, Inc., for example, to sell a new carbonated drink called Z Pop. If someone else in your field is already using this name or has registered it as a state or federal trademark or service mark, you will be an infringer if you start to use the name (based on the fact that customers are likely to be confused as to the source of either of the two businesses' services and products). In such circumstances, you will likely be forced to give up the name.

Conducting Your Search

Here are some suggestions for checking to see if others are using a business name similar to the one you have in mind.

Search the Internet. You've probably already done this, but if you haven't, type the potential name and the product or service into a search engine and sift through the results. For some marks—for example, Apple—a search engine might unearth hundreds or thousands of results that are of no value for your trademark searching purposes. For that reason you need to focus your search, using some of the searching tips provided at the Google site. Alternatively, you may choose to use a fee-based trademark search engine, such as SAEGIS on SERION. You should also search domain names to determine if a business has claimed the domain for its product or services. To search domain names, go to https://whois.icann.org/en.

Check state and county records where business names are filed. To avoid a claim that you're unfairly competing with another local business by using its name, check the records of your state's office where corporations and LLCs are registered—usually the secretary of state or corporations commissioner—as well as the state office (if any) that maintains a list of assumed or fictitious names for corporations, LLCs, partnerships, and sole proprietorships. In addition, if assumed or fictitious names are filed at the county or local level, check the lists for the counties or localities in which you plan to do business now or in the future.

Check the federal trademark register. Because goods and services are widely marketed over the Internet, as well as through mail order catalogs, your small business—even though you think it's local—might find itself competing with national companies. It makes sense to confirm you're not infringing on a trademark or service mark that is federally registered. All of the federally registered trademarks (as well as current applications) can be located by searching the trademark records at the United States Patent and Trademark Office website (www.uspto.gov). Click on "Trademarks" and search the database for potential conflicts with your name.

Hire a search firm. If you are investing heavily in promoting your products or services under a certain mark, you might want to pay for a trademark search. A full comprehensive search could cost between $150 and $300 per mark searched. The ranges of rates reflect variations in search coverage, the type of report you get, the experience of the searchers, and economies of scale. Be wary of firms that advertise an unusually low price to draw you in; they might later add on charges, so the overall cost becomes excessive.

Reviewing Your Search Results

So now you've done your search, whether by hiring a search firm or performing the search yourself, and you have the results in hand. What do the results mean? When you read through the names that were found in your search, be on the lookout for the following matches:

An identical match. If your search revealed names that are identical to the one you are using or plan to use (and keep in mind that a sound-alike—for example, "phat" and "fat"—is considered to be identical), this doesn't automatically mean that you must scrap plans to use your proposed name, though it should make you pause. If the identical name is being used for a very different product or service from the one you are producing or plan to produce, then you have good reason to move forward with your plans to use the name and register it as a trademark or service mark. For example, just because a plumbing business in Coos Bay, Oregon, calls itself Z Pop doesn't mean you, in Arizona, can't use Z Pop as the brand name for your new beverage. That plumbing business in Oregon is not your competitor, and your use of Z Pop for your drink will not likely confuse customers into thinking that your product is related to that plumbing business.

On the other hand, if you find an identical name being used on an identical or closely related product or service, such as another carbonated beverage product, then you really should consider choosing a different name. Even if the company using the name seems like a local outfit in a faraway place, you can't assume it will never expand its territory

An identical (or very similar) name that is linked to a very famous company or product. For example, suppose you want to name your dog toys Chewy Vuiton. Alas, this is very similar to the Louis Vuitton trademark. In trademark lingo, using a name that's similar to a famous existing name and that blurs or tarnishes the famous mark—even for an entirely different product—is referred to as "dilution." If it turns out that the mark you've had your eye on is famous and highly marketed, don't touch it. Let it go and find another name.

A name that is very similar to the name you want to use and it is being used to market the same type of product or service that you are planning to create or offer. For example, suppose your proposed name for your pool toy is AquaMate, but you learn that another company sells an inflatable mermaid named AquaCate. In this situation, you should seriously consider choosing a different name. How close is close? That is a very tricky issue and is often a matter of considerable subjectivity on the part of the courts and the USPTO. If you're not sure and really want to use the name, consider hiring an attorney specializing in trademark law to help you decide whether the two names are too close for comfort.

We've given you a few guidelines for evaluating your search results, but there is more to evaluating competing names than what we can provide in this chapter. If you think your situation is more complex, please consult *Trademark: Legal Care for Your Business & Product Name,* by Stephen Fishman (Nolo).

How to Use and Protect Your Trademark

Trademarks need proper care and management. If you improperly use your mark, you might find it harder to register or to stop others from using it. For example, if you use the symbol when you're not entitled, you might be prevented from later federally registering your mark. And if you use your trademark in an improper context, you might set it on a course for "genericide," when trademarks become the nouns they are meant to describe (sad examples include former trademarks such as aspirin, escalator, cellophane, thermos, raisin bran, and shredded wheat). Here are some steps that your business can take to best use and protect your mark:

- **Take prompt legal action if other businesses use your trademark without permission.** A trademark might become weakened or even generic if others use it to describe their products and you do nothing about it. You or your lawyer should send a letter (return receipt requested), demanding that the infringement cease. If your demand is ignored, be prepared to go to court to seek an injunction—but first do a careful cost/benefit analysis to satisfy yourself that it's worth the expense.

- **Use your trademark with a noun that describes your product.** You'll notice that ads refer to a Xerox copier, Jell-O gelatin, and Band-Aid adhesive strips. If people continue to use the words Xerox, Jell-O, and Band-Aid alone, without being challenged, these marks can easily be declared generic and go the way of other trademarks like nylon, mimeograph, and yo-yo.

- **Always capitalize the first letter of your trademark.** And some place on each ad or package, state specifically that the trademark is owned by your company.

- **If your trademark has been placed on the federal trademark register, consistently give notice of that fact by using the ® symbol.** If a trademark isn't federally registered or is registered only by a state, you may use the letters "tm" or "sm" to give notice of your claims. You may not use ® unless your mark is in fact on the federal register.

- **If you discover that a newspaper or TV program has improperly used your trademark, send them a letter.** Keep a copy in your records as proof that you have consistently enforced your trademark rights.

Licenses and Permits

You'll probably need a license or permit—maybe several—for your business. In some locations, every business needs a basic business license. But whether or not that is required, your business might need one or more specialized licenses. This is especially likely if you plan to serve or sell food, liquor, or firearms, work with hazardous materials, or discharge any materials into the air or water.

There are licensing and permit requirements at all levels of government—federal, state, regional, county, and city. It's not always easy to discover exactly what licenses and permits you'll need. But it's very important. You should thoroughly research this issue before you start a business, complete the purchase of a business, change locations, or remodel or expand your operation. If you don't, you might face huge expenses and hassles.

In a worst-case situation, you could be prevented from operating your planned business at a particular location—but still be obligated to pay rent or a mortgage. For example, what if you sign a five-year lease for business space and then discover that the location isn't zoned properly for your business? What if you buy a restaurant and then find out that the liquor license isn't transferable? Or suppose you rent or buy business space thinking that you can afford to remodel or expand it, without realizing that remodeling means you must comply with all current ordinances? You might have to pay for $15,000 worth of improvements to comply with the federal Americans with Disabilities Act (ADA) or $10,000 for a state-of-the-art waste disposal system.

Here are several examples that illustrate the types of licenses and permits many businesses need:

- Misook plans to open a new restaurant. Before doing so, she needs a permit from the department of building and safety for remodeling work and a license from the health department approving the kitchen equipment and ventilation system. She also needs a sign permit and approval of her customer and employee parking facilities from the city planning department. Finally, she has to get a sales tax license; even though in her state sit-down meals are not taxed, she must collect and report sales tax for take-out orders and miscellaneous items such as cookbooks.

- Leisure Time Enterprises, a partnership, buys a liquor store that also sells state lottery tickets. In addition to obtaining a basic business license issued by the city, the partners must have the state-issued alcoholic beverage license transferred to them. They also have to apply to the state lottery bureau for a transfer of the lottery license and to the state treasury department for a sales tax license.

- Electronic Assembly, Inc., a corporation that assembles electronic components for manufacturers of stereo equipment, must obtain a conditional use permit from the planning and zoning board in order to conduct its "light manufacturing operation" in a commercial district. The company also needs clearance from a tri-county environmental agency concerned about possible air pollution and disposal of toxic chemicals. In addition, the new elevator must be inspected and approved by the state department of labor.

- Peaches and Cream, a new nightclub, has to get fire department clearance for its exit system and also must comply with the city's parking ordinance—which, practically speaking, means negotiating with the planning department for the number of off-street parking spaces the nightclub will provide for customers. The club also needs a liquor license from the state liquor control commission, a cabaret license from the city council, and a sales tax license.

- Glenda needs an occupational license from the state department of cosmetology before she can open up her beauty shop. Because she carries a line of shampoos, conditioners, and makeup, she needs a sales tax permit as well. In addition, because she's extending the front of her shop three feet into the front setback area, she needs a variance from the zoning board of appeals. Finally, because she's in a "historic preservation area," her sign must be approved by the local planning board.

If zoning requirements are too restrictive, you might decide to avoid the hassle and move where you don't have to fight City Hall for the right to do business. Similarly, if building codes require extensive—and expensive—remodeling to bring an older building up to current standards, you might want to look for newer space that already complies with building and safety laws.

Each state has its own system of licensing as does each unit of local government. Obviously, it's impossible to provide a comprehensive list of every permit and license in the United States. Fortunately, I can give you some general principles and a positive approach to help you learn about and comply with the licensing requirements that affect your business.

The Purposes of Licenses and Permits

Governments require licenses and permits for two basic reasons. One is to raise money; the whole point behind some licenses or permits is to levy a tax on doing business. In a way, these are the easiest to comply with—you pay your money and get your license.

The other basic purpose behind licenses and permits is to protect public health and safety and, increasingly, aesthetics. A sign ordinance that dictates the size and placement of a business sign or an environmental regulation that prohibits you from releasing sulphur dioxide into the atmosphere are two of many possible examples. Complying with regulatory ordinances can often be far more difficult than complying with those designed simply to raise money.

CAUTION

Double-check license and permit rules. When you investigate the type of licenses and permits you need for your business, check directly with the appropriate governmental agencies. Never rely on the fact that an existing business similar to yours didn't need a license or had to meet only minimal building code requirements. Laws and ordinances are amended frequently—generally to impose more stringent requirements. Often an existing business is allowed to continue under the old rules, but new businesses must meet the higher standards. Similarly, for obvious reasons, don't rely on the advice of real estate agents, business brokers, the seller of a business, or anyone else with a financial interest in having a deal go through.

Federal Registrations and Licenses

Most small businesses don't have to worry about federal permits and licenses, but all businesses must know about federal tax registrations.

Tax Registrations

On the federal level, there are two tax registrations that you should know about. The first is the *Application for an Employer Identification Number* (EIN) (Form SS-4), which every business should file. The form is available online at www.irs.gov. If you're a sole proprietor, you may use your own Social Security number rather than a separate EIN, but I generally recommend that even sole proprietors obtain an EIN—especially if they plan to hire employees or retain independent contractors. It's one good way to keep your business and personal affairs separate. Similarly, if you have a single-member LLC and you haven't elected to have it taxed as a separate entity, you don't need to get an EIN unless you plan to hire employees. Like sole proprietors, you can use your Social Security number. Still, getting an EIN is a good idea. EINs are covered in Chapter 8.

The second federal registration requirement applies if your business is a corporation and you want to elect status as an S corporation. In that case, you need to file Form 2553 (*Election by a Small Business Corporation*; also available at www.irs.gov). S corporations are discussed in Chapters 1 and 3; the requirements for filing Form 2553 are discussed in Chapter 8.

Federal Licenses and Permits

The federal government doesn't require permits from most small businesses, but it does get into the act when certain business activities or products are involved. Below is a list of the business operations most likely to need a federal license or permit, along with the name of the federal agency to contact.

Business	Agency to Contact
Investment advisers	Securities and Exchange Commission (www.sec.gov)
Ground transportation business such as a trucking company operating as a common carrier	Federal Motor Carrier Safety Administration (www.fmcsa.dot.gov)
Preparation of meat products	Food and Drug Administration (www.fda.gov)
Production of drugs	Food and Drug Administration (www.fda.gov)
Making tobacco products or alcohol, or making or dealing in firearms	Bureau of Alcohol, Tobacco, Firearms and Explosives of the U.S. Treasury Department (www.atf.gov)

State Requirements

It might take a little effort to discover which business permits and licenses your state requires. Fortunately, small business assistance agencies set up in every state can help you cut through the bureaucratic thicket. (To find contact information for small business assistance agencies in your area, visit the website of the U.S. Small Business Administration at www.sba.gov.) Most of these agencies offer free or inexpensive publications that list the required state registrations, licenses, and permits. Often the information is available online at the agency website.

Beyond contacting these general-purpose agencies, it's wise to call all state agencies that might regulate your business and ask what they require. In addition, you can often get valuable information from the state chamber of commerce and from trade associations or professional groups serving your business, profession, or industry.

Licensing of Occupations and Professions

It should come as no surprise that states require licensing of people practicing the traditional professions, such as lawyers, physicians, dentists, accountants, psychologists, nurses, pharmacists, architects, and engineers. Most states also require licenses for people engaged in a broad range of other occupations. The list varies from state to state but typically includes such people as barbers, auto mechanics, bill collectors, private investigators, building contractors, cosmetologists, funeral directors, pest control specialists, real estate agents, tax preparers, and insurance agents. Because you can't always guess the occupations for which licenses are needed, you'll need to inquire.

Some licenses are taken out by the business entity (for example, your partnership or corporation), while others must be issued to the individuals who work in the business. For example, licensing laws for professionals—including lawyers, doctors, accountants, and architects—tend to place requirements on the individual rather than the business entity.

The procedures vary, but to get a license for a profession or occupation, you'll probably have to show evidence of training in the field, and you might have to pass a written examination. Sometimes you must practice your trade or profession under the supervision of a more experienced person before you can become fully licensed.

For example, a real estate agent usually must work under the supervision of a licensed broker for several years before the agent is eligible to become a broker. Usually there's a formal application process, which might involve a background check. A license could be good for only a limited period, after which there might be retesting before the license can be renewed. License laws for some occupations and professions require evidence of continuing education, usually in the form of short professional seminars.

Tax Registration

In all but the few states that still assess no taxes on income, chances are you'll have to register under your state's income tax laws in much the same way that you do under the federal laws. The state agency in charge (such as the treasury department or the department of revenue) can tell you what registrations are necessary. In addition, if you're engaging in retail sales, you might need to register for or obtain a sales tax license. There might also be registrations for other business taxes.

Employer-Employee Matters

As an employer, you might have to register with your state's department of labor or with agencies administering the laws on unemployment compensation and workers' compensation. As explained in more detail in Chapter 15, workers' compensation is a method of paying the medical bills and lost wages of employees injured in the course of their employment—regardless of who is at fault. Some state laws allow a business to be self-insured under some circumstances, but for most small businesses this isn't practical, so you'll have to carry workers' compensation insurance.

In addition, if your state has its own version of the federal Occupational Safety and Health Act (OSHA), your business might need to meet certain state-mandated requirements to protect your employees in the workplace.

Finally, a number of tax requirements relate to a business that has employees or works with independent contractors. For example, you'll need to get EINs from both the IRS and state tax authorities. And you'll have to withhold income taxes and Social Security taxes from your employees' paychecks, and report the figures to both the employee and the government.

With independent contractors, you need to report income annually on a Form 1099, which goes to the independent contractor and the federal government.

For more on EINs and taxation, see Chapter 8. For more on employees and independent contractors, see Chapter 15.

Licensing Based on Products Sold

Some licenses for businesses are based on the type of products sold. For example, there often are special licenses for businesses that sell liquor, food, lottery tickets, gasoline, or firearms.

Environmental Regulations

Governmental regulation of environmental concerns continues to expand. As the owner of a small business, you might have to deal with regulators at the state or regional (multicounty) level. It's unlikely that you'll become involved with environmental regulations at the federal level.

Here are several activities that affect the environment and might require a special permit:

- **Emissions into the air for an incinerator, a boiler, or another facility.** For example, if you're going to be venting your dry cleaning equipment into the outside air, you might need a permit.
- **Discharge of wastewater to surface or ground water.** For example, you might need a discharge permit if byproducts from manufacturing are being disposed of in a nearby pond. And you might need a storage permit if materials that you store on your site could contaminate ground or surface water

Handling of hazardous waste. If your business has any connection with hazardous waste, it's likely that the environmental agency will require you to at least maintain accurate records concerning the waste. You might need special disposal permits as well. Environmental regulations might also require you to register underground storage tanks holding gasoline, oil, or other chemicals. And if there's an underground tank on your business site that's no longer being used, you might be required to remove it.

> **(!) CAUTION**
>
> **Permits aren't just for big factories.** At first glance, the above list might suggest that only manufacturers or owners of large businesses need to worry about environmental regulations. Not so. Many small businesses need to obtain permits, or at least become informed about what they must do to avoid contaminating the environment. For example, if you create and sell leaded glass windows, you need to know whether you can dump your lead-laced wastewater down the nearby storm sewer or need a permit for some other means of disposal. Similarly, dry cleaners, photo processors, and others need to know the rules for handling and disposing of the hazardous substances used in their work.

Regional Requirements

Increasingly, some environmental concerns are being addressed by regional (multicounty) agencies rather than by an arm of the state or local government. If so, you might need a permit or license from that regional body.

Environmental Regulations

In many areas, control of air pollution is now handled by a regional (multicounty or state) agency that issues permits and monitors compliance. For example, in Northern California, the Bay Area Air Quality Management District covers nine counties. A regional body with environmental responsibilities might also have jurisdiction over wastewater discharge or the storage or disposal of hazardous materials.

Water Usage

Questions affecting the use of water by a small business are usually dealt with at the local (city or county) level, but some issues could fall within the jurisdiction of a regional authority. For example, if your business is in a semirural area and plans to draw its water from a well rather than the public water supply, a regional health authority may test the purity of the water before you're allowed to use it. In scarce-water areas, a regional water management body might have authority to decide whether or not you may install a well or use an existing one.

Similarly, though regulation of septic systems typically is left to local health departments, in some areas permits might be under the control of a regional body.

Local Requirements

On the local level, begin by asking city and county officials about license and permit requirements for your business. A few larger cities that hope to attract economic growth might have a centralized office that provides this information. Otherwise, the city and county officials most likely to be of help are as follows:

- city or county clerk
- building and safety department
- health department
- planning (zoning) department
- tax offices (for example, tax assessor or treasurer)
- fire department
- police department, and
- public works department.

Nonofficial but often extremely helpful resources include local chambers of commerce, trade associations, contractors who have experience in building or remodeling commercial space, and people who have businesses like yours. You can also consult a lawyer familiar with small businesses similar to yours.

Local Property Taxes

Your city might impose a property tax on the furniture, fixtures, and equipment that your business owns. If so, you might be required by law to file a list of that property with city tax officials, along with cost and depreciation information. You might have to update this information annually. Sometimes there's also a tax on inventory—which leads many retail businesses to run a stock reduction sale a few weeks before the inventory-taking date mandated by the tax law.

Other Local Taxes

Some cities, especially larger ones, tax gross receipts and income. Check with the city treasurer for registration and filing requirements.

Health and Environmental Permits

If your business involves the preparation or sales of food, you'll need a license or permit from the local health department. The health ordinances might require regular inspections as well.

Whether you run a sit-down or fast-food restaurant or a catering establishment, you can expect the health department to take a keen interest in the type of cooking equipment you use, the adequacy of the refrigeration system, and many other features of the business that can affect your customers' health.

You might also run into health department regulations if you receive water from a well rather than a public water supply. In small towns or semirural areas, health departments routinely test well water for purity.

Also, where septic systems are used for sanitary sewer disposal, the health department supervises the installation of new septic systems to make sure that there's no health hazard. (As noted above, in some areas, these matters are handled by regional rather than local authorities.)

Increasingly, local health departments are getting involved in environmental duties, covering such things as radon tests and asbestos removal. Many other environmental problems, however, such as air and water quality, are still dealt with mainly at the state and regional level.

Crowd Control

If your business deals with large numbers of customers, you might need licenses or permits from the fire or police departments. These agencies are concerned about overcrowding and the ability of people to leave the premises in case there's an emergency.

The role of the fire department might overlap with that of the building and safety department in prescribing the number of exit doors, the hardware on those doors, the lighting to be used, and the maintenance of clear paths to the exits. The fire department will also be concerned about combustible materials used or stored on your business premises.

Complying With Rules and Safety Guidelines During the Coronavirus Crisis

During the coronavirus crisis, businesses also must adhere to state and local orders regarding social distancing, face coverings, and capacity. For example, you might have to provide a hand sanitizer station or require customers to wear a face mask while inside your business.

Building Codes

For anything but the most minor renovation (such as putting in track lighting or installing shelves), you're likely to need a permit—maybe several—from the building and safety department that enforces building ordinances and codes. Often, separate permits are issued for separate parts of a construction or remodeling project, including permits for electrical, plumbing, or mechanical (heating and ventilating) work. If you don't have experience in these areas, you might need a licensed contractor to help you discover the requirements for your construction or remodeling project.

Building codes are amended frequently, and each revision seems to put new restrictions and requirements on the building owner. Municipalities often exempt existing businesses from laying out money to retrofit their premises—at least for major items such as elevators, heating and ventilating systems, and overhead sprinkler systems. But not imposing new rules retroactively can create surprises. You might look at space in an older building and figure that you'll have no problems in doing business there because the current business owner or the one who just vacated the premises didn't. But the prior occupant might have had the benefit of language in the building code that didn't require the space to be brought up to the level of the current code. A change in occupancy or ownership might end the benefits of the exemption, and a new occupant or owner might be required to make extensive improvements.

An experienced contractor can help you determine the building and safety requirements that apply to a particular space—for example, a code section mandating that railings on outside stairs be 36 inches high.

Other municipal ordinances might be administered by the building and safety department or by another unit of local government. There's no uniformity in how cities or counties assign the responsibility for administering these other ordinances. A large municipality or county might have several separate departments to act as the enforcing agency. A smaller city or county would probably leave everything to the building and safety department.

Zoning Ordinances

Before you sign a lease, you absolutely need to know that the space is properly zoned for your usage. If it's not, it's best to make the lease contingent on your getting the property rezoned or getting a variance or conditional use permit (for more on variances or conditional use permits, see "Appealing an Adverse Ruling," below)—whatever it takes under the

ordinance to make it possible for you to do business there without being hassled by the city or county.

In some communities, you must get a zoning compliance permit before you start your business at a given location. Other communities simply wait for someone to complain before looking at zoning compliance. Keep in mind that by applying for a construction permit for remodeling or by filing tax information with the municipality, you might trigger an investigation of zoning compliance.

Zoning laws might also regulate off-street parking, water and air quality, waste disposal, and the size, construction, and placement of signs. In some communities, historic district restrictions could keep you from modifying the exterior of a building or even changing the paint color without permission from a board of administrators.

Years ago, people tried to argue in court that such regulation of aesthetics wasn't a proper governmental function—that it wasn't related to the protection of public health and safety. However, a carefully drawn ordinance seeking to preserve the special appeal of a historic district will very likely survive a legal challenge. So if you look at space in one of these protected neighborhoods, be prepared to suspend your freedom of choice and place the destiny of at least the exterior of the building in the hands of a panel of administrators.

In Chapter 14, which deals with home-based businesses, you'll find a discussion of zoning ordinances as they relate to businesses in the home. Take the time to review Chapter 14 because zoning restrictions apply to all businesses.

How to Deal With Local Building and Zoning Officials

Building and zoning officials have a certain amount of administrative discretion under building codes and zoning ordinances—enough, certainly, that it can help greatly to have the administrators on your side. Here are some ideas for accomplishing this.

Seek Support From the Business Community

If you employ local people and will contribute positively to the economy, it might make sense to make contact with city or county business development officials or even the chamber of commerce. If they see your business as an asset and don't want you to locate your business in the next city, they might be helpful in steering you through the building and safety department and could even advocate on your behalf before zoning and planning officials.

Trade associations and merchants' associations might also come to your aid if you need building and safety officials to decide in your favor in areas in which they have some administrative discretion. Finally, contractors, lawyers, and others who are familiar with the system and the personalities often know how to get things done and can be helpful to you.

Appealing an Adverse Ruling

The decision of a zoning or building official isn't necessarily final. If you get an adverse decision from the local planning commission, for example, you might be able to have a board of zoning adjustment or board of appeals interpret the zoning ordinance in a way that's favorable to you. Alternatively, you might be able to obtain a variance (a special exception to a zoning law) if a strict interpretation of the ordinance causes a hardship. In some cases, you can get a conditional use permit, which lets you use the property in question for your kind of business as long as you meet certain conditions the administrative panel requires.

In dealing with administrators and especially with appeals boards, it's important to have the support of neighbors and others in your community. A favorable petition signed by most other businesses in your immediate area or oral expressions of support from half a dozen neighbors can make

the difference between success and failure at an administrative hearing.

Conversely, if objectors are numerous and adamant, you might not get what you're after. So if you sense opposition developing from those living or doing business nearby, try to resolve your differences before you get to a public hearing—even if it means you must make compromises on the details of your proposal.

Law From the Real World

Strategic Planning Pays Off

Shelby, owner of Small Universe Books, is delighted to learn that the drugstore next door is going out of business. He immediately seeks to buy or sign a long-term lease for the building so he can expand his profitable business. The future looks rosy.

Not so fast. Shelby learns that he'll have to supply eight parking spaces to get a permit to expand his business into the new building. Doing this in his desperately crowded neighborhood is totally impossible at anything approaching an affordable price.

Instead of giving up, Shelby asks the city planning commission for a variance to waive the parking spaces rule. A public hearing is scheduled. Shelby knows he has to put on a persuasive case, so he:

- calls hundreds of local writers, publishers, critics, educators, and book lovers to pack the hearing room and testify that an expanded bookstore will be a great community resource
- documents the prohibitive cost of buying or leasing the required parking spaces
- offers to validate parking at a lot four blocks away, just outside the worst of the congested area
- hires an architect who determines that a heavily used, nearby public garage can accommodate 20 more cars if the parking spaces are striped differently, and
- offers to pay for the restriping.

Shelby gets the variance.

Going to Court

Every day, hundreds if not thousands of interpretations and applications of building and zoning laws are worked out through negotiation with administrators and through administrative appeals. But if these channels fail, it's possible in many instances to go to court. This can be very expensive and time-consuming. What good is it if you win your battle for a permit to remodel your premises but you waste two years getting to that point?

Still, there are times when what you're seeking is so valuable and your chances of success are so great that you can afford both the time and money to get a definitive ruling from the courts. And in some instances, you can get a court to consider your dispute fairly quickly.

If, for example, you submitted plans to the city that complied with all building and safety codes, and the building official refused to issue a building permit unless you agreed to put in some additional improvements you believe the ordinance does not require, you could quickly go to court and ask the judge to order the city to issue the building permit. Your argument would be that the administrator wasn't following the law.

Before you consider court action, however, get as much information as you can about the cost of litigation, how long it will take (you can win in the trial court, but the city might decide to appeal), and the likelihood of your ultimate success. This is a specialized corner of the law, so you're going to need someone who's had experience in the field—and there may not be that many to choose from in any given location. Look for a lawyer who's represented a similar business in a dispute with the city, or someone who formerly worked as a city attorney and knows all the ins and outs of the local ordinances.

Tax Basics for the Small Business

No matter whether your business is organized as a sole proprietorship, partnership, corporation, or limited liability company, you've automatically got a silent partner: Uncle Sam. The federal tax laws make this unavoidable. To guard against interest and penalties, you need to know what tax forms to file and when to file them. And to succeed in business, you need at least a basic, working knowledge of the tax system.

On a more positive note, by being aware of the fine points of the tax laws, you can often legally save a bundle of money—not to mention aggravation. For example, having a clear picture of what the IRS regards as a proper business expense will allow you to take deductions that otherwise might not occur to you.

! CAUTION

Get detailed information. The tax laws are vast and complicated, and you'll surely need much more information than you'll find in this chapter. A good starting place is the IRS website at www.irs.gov, especially the Small Business and Self-Employed Tax Center.

In addition to what you learn from books and other publications, you might have to hire a bookkeeper and an accountant. If you're operating a one-person word processing business out of your home, you might be able to keep your books and do your taxes with no professional help at all—or perhaps get help just the first time you file your annual tax return, to make sure you've correctly completed Schedules C (*Profit or Loss From Business*) and SE (*Self-Employment Tax*). On the other hand, if you've formed a corporation that's operating a good-sized dry cleaning shop with eight employees, you might want an accountant to help set up your books and to prepare—or at least review—your business tax returns each year. And you might find that employing a part-time bookkeeper not only results in your records being well kept, but also frees you for more important tasks.

A word of caution about one other possible source of assistance: IRS employees. Most of them are hardworking and well-meaning, but their training and supervision are often inadequate. Unfortunately, it's common to receive poor oral advice in answer to questions. And if the advice proves to be so inaccurate that it results in your being assessed interest and penalties, the fact that you got it from an IRS employee won't get you off the hook. In short, it's often cheaper in the long run to rely on the advice of an experienced small business accountant than on a free oral opinion from the IRS.

State Taxes. In addition to federal taxes, you need to be aware of your state's tax scheme, which might include an income tax structured along the same lines as the federal version or one that has some major differences. Before you begin your business, contact your state's taxing authority to get detailed information. You'll also find helpful links at www.statetaxcentral.com.

Employer Identification Number

You must get an Employer Identification Number (EIN) from the IRS when you start a business that you've set up as:

- a partnership
- an S corporation
- a C corporation
- a limited liability company (LLC) with two or more members, or
- a single-member LLC with employees or that you've chosen to have taxed as a corporation.

Technically, if you're a sole proprietor or the sole member of a limited liability company (LLC) that is not being taxed as a corporation and you have no employees, you can use your personal Social Security number instead of an EIN. But even in those situations, it's good business practice to get an EIN to differentiate cleanly between your personal and business finances.

You'll need your EIN before you file a tax return or make a tax deposit. In some cases, a bank will require you to have an EIN before you can open a business bank account.

How to Apply

To get an EIN, file Form SS-4, *Application for Employer Identification Number.*

The form isn't difficult to fill out if you follow the instructions. Nevertheless, these few pointers might help. (An example of Form SS-4 is included below.)

Space 1. Insert your official corporate name if you're a corporation or your official company name if you're a limited liability company. If you're a partnership, use the partnership name shown in your partnership agreement. If you're a sole proprietor, insert your full name—the name you use on your personal tax return.

Space 12. Here you're asked to state the closing month of your business accounting year. Your answer, however, isn't binding. You make your binding election of a fiscal year-end on the first federal income tax return that you file for the business.

Sole proprietors, partnerships, S corporations, personal service corporations, and limited liability companies are generally required to use a calendar year—that is, a year ending December 31—for tax purposes. Personal service corporations have two basic characteristics:

- the professional employees of the corporation own the stock, and
- the corporation performs its services in the fields of health, law, engineering, architecture, accounting, actuarial science, performing arts, or consulting.

To use a tax year other than a calendar year, an S corporation must demonstrate to the IRS that there is a substantial business reason to do so, such as the seasonal nature of the business. Basically, the IRS wants to make sure that permitting you to claim a tax year other than the calendar year won't substantially distort your income.

RESOURCE

For details about choosing your tax year, see "Business Purpose Tax Year," in IRS Publication 538, *Accounting Periods and Methods.*

A C corporation that's not a personal service corporation is freer to choose a fiscal year. Most small businesses find that where there's a choice, the calendar year is the most convenient way to proceed. Sometimes, however, there are tax planning reasons for a business owner to choose a different tax year for the business.

EXAMPLE 1: Radcraft, Inc., a C corporation, selects the calendar year for its fiscal year. In December 2021 it pays a $30,000 bonus to Jill, the president and sole shareholder. The bonus is included on Jill's 2021 income tax return, and tax on the bonus is due in April 2022.

EXAMPLE 2: Jill selects a fiscal year of February 1 through January 31 for Radcraft, Inc. (On Form SS-4, she lists January in space 12 for the closing month of the corporation's accounting year.) In January 2023, the corporation pays Jill a $30,000 bonus. The bonus is included in Jill's 2023 income tax return. This means that the tax on the bonus isn't due until April 2024—although Jill must keep track of it when computing her quarterly estimates in 2023.

SEE AN EXPERT

An accountant or other experienced tax adviser can help you decide whether or not you and your corporation can realize a tax advantage by using a tax year other than a calendar year.

Space 13. These numbers can be estimated. It's usually best to estimate on the low side.

Space 15. The IRS will send you computer-generated payroll tax forms based on your answer to this question.

Space 18. This question refers to the business, not the owner. Normally, a partnership, corporation, or limited liability company has only one EIN. A sole proprietor might have several businesses, each with a separate number.

Form **SS-4** (Rev. December 2019) Department of the Treasury Internal Revenue Service	**Application for Employer Identification Number** (For use by employers, corporations, partnerships, trusts, estates, churches, government agencies, Indian tribal entities, certain individuals, and others.) ▶ Go to *www.irs.gov/FormSS4* for instructions and the latest information. ▶ See separate instructions for each line. ▶ Keep a copy for your records.	OMB No. 1545-0003 EIN

<table>
<tr><td rowspan="16" style="writing-mode:vertical-rl">Type or print clearly.</td></tr>
<tr><td colspan="4">1   Legal name of entity (or individual) for whom the EIN is being requested</td></tr>
<tr><td colspan="2">2   Trade name of business (if different from name on line 1)</td><td colspan="2">3   Executor, administrator, trustee, "care of" name</td></tr>
<tr><td colspan="2">4a Mailing address (room, apt., suite no. and street, or P.O. box)</td><td colspan="2">5a Street address (if different) (Don't enter a P.O. box.)</td></tr>
<tr><td colspan="2">4b City, state, and ZIP code (if foreign, see instructions)</td><td colspan="2">5b City, state, and ZIP code (if foreign, see instructions)</td></tr>
<tr><td colspan="4">6   County and state where principal business is located</td></tr>
<tr><td colspan="2">7a Name of responsible party</td><td colspan="2">7b SSN, ITIN, or EIN</td></tr>
</table>

8a	Is this application for a limited liability company (LLC) (or a foreign equivalent)? . . . . ☐ Yes ☐ No	8b	If 8a is "Yes," enter the number of LLC members . . . . . . ▶

8c	If 8a is "Yes," was the LLC organized in the United States? . . . . ☐ Yes ☐ No

9a Type of entity (check only one box). **Caution:** If 8a is "Yes," see the instructions for the correct box to check.

☐ Sole proprietor (SSN) _____   ☐ Estate (SSN of decedent) _____
☐ Partnership   ☐ Plan administrator (TIN) _____
☐ Corporation (enter form number to be filed) ▶ _____   ☐ Trust (TIN of grantor) _____
☐ Personal service corporation   ☐ Military/National Guard ☐ State/local government
☐ Church or church-controlled organization   ☐ Farmers' cooperative ☐ Federal government
☐ Other nonprofit organization (specify) ▶ _____   ☐ REMIC ☐ Indian tribal governments/enterprises
☐ Other (specify) ▶   Group Exemption Number (GEN) if any ▶

9b	If a corporation, name the state or foreign country (if applicable) where incorporated	State	Foreign country

10 **Reason for applying** (check only one box)
☐ Started new business (specify type) ▶ _____   ☐ Banking purpose (specify purpose) ▶ _____
_____   ☐ Changed type of organization (specify new type) ▶ _____
☐ Hired employees (Check the box and see line 13.)   ☐ Purchased going business
☐ Compliance with IRS withholding regulations   ☐ Created a trust (specify type) ▶ _____
☐ Other (specify) ▶   ☐ Created a pension plan (specify type) ▶ _____

11	Date business started or acquired (month, day, year). See instructions.	12	Closing month of accounting year
13	Highest number of employees expected in the next 12 months (enter -0- if none). If no employees expected, skip line 14.	14	If you expect your employment tax liability to be $1,000 or less in a full calendar year **and** want to file Form 944 annually instead of Forms 941 quarterly, check here. (Your employment tax liability generally will be $1,000 or less if you expect to pay $5,000 or less in total wages.) If you don't check this box, you must file Form 941 for every quarter. ☐

Agricultural	Household	Other

15	First date wages or annuities were paid (month, day, year). **Note:** If applicant is a withholding agent, enter date income will first be paid to nonresident alien (month, day, year) . . . . ▶

16 Check **one** box that best describes the principal activity of your business. ☐ Health care & social assistance ☐ Wholesale-agent/broker
☐ Construction ☐ Rental & leasing ☐ Transportation & warehousing ☐ Accommodation & food service ☐ Wholesale-other ☐ Retail
☐ Real estate ☐ Manufacturing ☐ Finance & insurance ☐ Other (specify) ▶

17 Indicate principal line of merchandise sold, specific construction work done, products produced, or services provided.

18 Has the applicant entity shown on line 1 ever applied for and received an EIN? ☐ Yes ☐ No
If "Yes," write previous EIN here ▶

Third Party Designee	Complete this section **only** if you want to authorize the named individual to receive the entity's EIN and answer questions about the completion of this form.	
	Designee's name	Designee's telephone number (include area code)
	Address and ZIP code	Designee's fax number (include area code)

Under penalties of perjury, I declare that I have examined this application, and to the best of my knowledge and belief, it is true, correct, and complete.

Name and title (type or print clearly) ▶

	Applicant's telephone number (include area code)
Signature ▶ Date ▶	Applicant's fax number (include area code)

For Privacy Act and Paperwork Reduction Act Notice, see separate instructions.   Cat. No. 16055N   Form **SS-4** (Rev. 12-2019)

After filling out the form, there are three ways to obtain the number:

- **Online.** The IRS has made it a snap to get your EIN online. You'll find full instructions at the IRS site (www.irs.gov) for completing the EIN application form (SS-4)—instructions that will be useful even if you prefer to fill out and file a paper form.
- **By fax.** You can fax your Form SS-4 to 855-641-6935 if you have a principal place of business, office, or agency, or, in the case of an individual, a legal residence located in the United States. If you do not already have any location in the United States, the fax numbers to use are 855-215-1627 from inside the United States and 304-707-9471 from outside the country. Be sure to provide your own fax number so the IRS can fax the EIN back to you—probably in a day or two.
- **By mail.** If you have enough lead time, you can mail Form SS-4 to the IRS and wait for the number to be mailed to you, which will take about four weeks. Mail your completed Form SS-4 to Internal Revenue Service, Attn: EIN Operation, Cincinnati, OH 45999.

Use your EIN on all business tax returns, checks, and other documents you send to the IRS. Your state taxing authority might also require your EIN on state tax forms.

When to Get a New Number

If your S corporation chooses to change to a C corporation—or your C corporation chooses to change to an S corporation—it doesn't need a new EIN; the one you already have is still sufficient. However, you'll need to get a new EIN if any of these changes occur in your business:

- You incorporate your sole proprietorship or partnership.
- You convert your sole proprietorship or partnership to a limited liability company.
- Your sole proprietorship takes in partners and begins operating as a partnership.

- Your partnership is taken over by one of the partners and begins operating as a sole proprietorship.
- Your corporation changes to a partnership or to a sole proprietorship.
- You purchase or inherit an existing business that you'll operate as a sole proprietorship.
- You represent an estate that operates a business after the owner's death.
- You terminate an old partnership and begin a new one.

Filing Form SS-4 for an LLC

If your LLC will have employees, you'll need to get an EIN and use it when depositing employment taxes. You can also get an EIN for nontax reasons (such as a state requirement) or simply as a bookkeeping preference.

For a single-member LLC, check the "Other" box in space 9a of Form SS-4 and write: "Disregarded Entity—Sole Proprietorship." If you have a multi-member LLC, and you plan to run it as if it were a partnership (using Form 1065 to report business income), check the "Partnership" box in space 9a.

However, in the unlikely event that your LLC prefers to be taxed as a corporation, check the "Corporation" box; be sure to also file Form 8832 to elect corporate status, as explained in "After You Form Your LLC," in Chapter 4.

Becoming an S Corporation

Many corporations derive tax benefits from choosing S corporation status. The difference between a C corporation, which is a separate tax entity from its shareholders, and an S corporation, whose income is reported on the owners' tax returns, is described in some detail in Chapter 1. If you're not thoroughly familiar with this material, please reread it before going on.

To become an S corporation, all shareholders must sign and file IRS Form 2553, *Election by a Small Business Corporation*, with the IRS by the 15th day of the third month of the tax year to which the election is to apply.

EXAMPLE: Mia, James, and Evelyn form a corporation, Phoenix Ventures, Inc. They start to do business on September 1, 2023 and, like most businesses, use the calendar year for accounting and tax purposes. Their 2023 tax year will be a short one: September 1 through December 31. To obtain S corporation status for that first tax year, they need to file Form 2553 by November 15, 2023, which is the 15th day of the third month of that tax year. If they miss that deadline, their corporation won't qualify for S corporation status in 2023. But if they file Form 2553 by March 15, 2021, their corporation will get S corporation status for 2024.

A number of technical rules govern which corporations can elect to become S corporations. Your corporation must meet these requirements:

- It must be a domestic corporation—one that's organized under U.S. federal or state law.
- It must have only one class of stock.
- It must have no more than 100 shareholders.
- It must have as shareholders only individuals, estates, and certain trusts. Partnerships and corporations can't be shareholders in an S corporation.
- It can't have any shareholder who is a nonresident alien.

There are other technical rules, but the vast majority of new, small corporations may become S corporations if they choose to do so.

To elect S corporation status, you need the consent of all shareholders. Unless yours is a one-person corporation, you should agree on this election before you form your corporation.

An S corporation election doesn't have to be permanent. You can start out as an S corporation and then, after a few years, revoke your S corporation status and be taxed as a C corporation. If you terminate your status as an S corporation, generally you'll have to wait five years until you can again become an S corporation—although you might be able to get permission from the IRS to shorten this waiting period.

Once the shareholders file Form 2553, the corporation continues to be an S corporation each year until the shareholders revoke that status or it's terminated under IRS rules. What terminates S corporation status? For one thing, ceasing to qualify as an S corporation. For example, your corporation would no longer qualify if it had more than 100 shareholders or if you or another shareholder transferred some of your stock to a partnership.

Business Taxes in General

Three main categories of federal business taxes might apply to your business:

- income tax
- employment tax, and
- self-employment tax.

This section looks briefly at each of these tax categories. Get IRS Publication 509, *Tax Calendars*, to see when to file returns and make tax payments. It's updated annually.

Excise Taxes. In addition to the three main business taxes, the federal government imposes excise taxes on a few specialized transactions and products. These taxes almost never are of concern to small businesses. To see whether your business is affected, see IRS Publication 334, *Tax Guide for Small Business.*

Income Tax

You must file an annual federal tax return reporting your business income. Below is a list of the forms to use.

Business Income Tax Forms	
Type of Legal Entity	**Form**
Sole Proprietorship	Schedule C (Form 1040)
Partnership	Form 1065
C Corporation	Form 1120
Single-Member LLC	Schedule C (Form 1040)
S Corporation	Form 1120-S
Multimember LLC	Form 1065 or 1120

Sole Proprietorship

If you're a sole proprietor, your business itself doesn't pay income tax. You report your business income (or loss) on Schedule C and file it with your Form 1040. Your Schedule C income (or loss) is added to (or subtracted from) the other income you report on your personal Form 1040. If you have more than one business, file a separate Schedule C for each business.

If you and your spouse jointly own and run a business, and you file a joint return, you can treat the business as a sole proprietorship rather than as a partnership. In that case, you'd want to file a separate Schedule C for each of you, listing your respective income and expenses. This will let you each get your own credit for Social Security and Medicare purposes. For more information, check the section on qualified joint ventures in IRS Publication 334, *Tax Guide for Small Business* (available at irs.gov).

Partnership

A partnership Form 1065 is an informational tax return telling the IRS how much each partner earned. The partnership doesn't pay tax on this income. Each partner reports his or her share of income (or loss) on Schedule E, *Supplemental Income and Loss*, and files it with Form 1040.

This Schedule E amount is added to (or subtracted from) the other income the partner reports on his or her personal Form 1040. In other words, a partner's income is treated like a sole proprietor's income on Form 1040: It's listed in a separate schedule and then blended with other income listed on the first page of the 1040.

> **CAUTION**
>
> **Passive losses.** Losses from passive partnership activities—such as real estate investments or royalties—in which the partnership plays the role of a passive investor, can usually be taken as a credit only against income from other passive activities. This is explained in greater detail in IRS Publication 925.

S Corporation

The S corporation itself doesn't pay income tax. Form 1120-S filed by an S corporation is an informational return telling the IRS how much each shareholder earned. As a shareholder, you report your portion of income or loss on Schedule E and file it with your personal Form 1040. Then you add that income to (or subtract a loss from) your other 1040 income.

C Corporation

A C corporation reports its income or loss on Form 1120 and pays a tax if there is income. But in many small corporations, the shareholders are employees who receive all business profits in the form of salaries and bonuses, which are tax deductible by the corporation as a business expense. In that situation, the corporation would have no taxable income.

Not all small corporations, however, are able to pay out their income in the form of salaries and bonuses. If they don't, they must pay a corporate income tax.

> **EXAMPLE:** Jenny and her twin sister Janet are the sole shareholders in Neptune Corporation, which manufactures swimming pool supplies. In the second year of their corporate existence, to encourage growth, Jenny and Janet decide to pay themselves minimal salaries and to plow most of the corporate income into inventory and the purchase of rehabilitated but serviceable equipment. The money that the corporation puts into inventory and equipment isn't available for distribution to Jenny and Janet. In addition, most of that money isn't a currently deductible business expense, so it is taxed at the corporate income tax rate of 21% as of 2018. (The equipment will be capitalized; depreciation deductions will be spread over several years.)

If you have a C corporation that expects to have taxable income, your corporation needs to make periodic deposits of its estimated income taxes. And if you're an employee of your C corporation (as is almost always the case with an owner of a small business corporation), taxes and Social Security payments must be withheld from your paychecks.

Limited Liability Company

A single-member LLC is normally taxed as a sole proprietorship, meaning that you'll report the income (or loss) on Schedule C and file it with your Form 1040. The bottom line will be added to (or subtracted from) the other income you report on Form 1040.

An LLC that has two or more members, unless the owners choose to have the business taxed as a corporation, will be taxed as a partnership (tax liability passes through to the LLC members) and will use Form 1065—an informational return that tells the IRS how much each member earned. The LLC doesn't pay tax on its income but, as with a partnership, each member reports his or her share of income (or loss) on Schedule E, *Supplemental Income and Loss*, which is filed with personal Form 1040. This Schedule E amount is added to (or subtracted from) the other income the member reports on Form 1040.

An LLC that chooses to be taxed as a corporation will use Form 1120.

Federal Payroll Taxes

There are several types of employment-related taxes the federal government exacts from businesses.

Federal Income Tax Withholding (FIT)

You must withhold income taxes from employees' paychecks based on:
- the employee's filing status (single, married, or married but withholding at the higher single rate)
- the number of dependents (withholding allowances) declared by the employee, and
- the size of the employee's salary.

Each employee should give you a signed Form W-4 stating his or her withholding allowance. Save these forms. You needn't send them to the IRS unless the IRS requests them.

Use the tables in IRS Publication 15, Circular E (referenced below) to figure out how much income tax to withhold.

 RESOURCE

Want to learn more about taxes? Here are some excellent resources:
- IRS Publication 15, Circular E, *Employer's Tax Guide*, explains employment-related taxes clearly and in great detail. Updated whenever the tax rates change, Circular E is available at www.irs.gov and is mailed automatically to all businesses with an EIN.
- IRS Publication 334, *Tax Guide for Small Business*, and if you're just getting started, IRS Publication 583, *Starting a Business and Keeping Records*, are well worth reading. You can read or download these publications at www.irs.gov.
- *Tax Savvy for Small Business*, by Frederick W. Daily (Nolo). An excellent guide to all the tax problems small businesses face, including the complicated area of deductions and depreciations. The audit material alone is well worth the price of the book.
- *Small-Time Operator*, by Bernard B. Kamoroff (Taylor Trade Publishing), is a clearly written book that covers not only taxes but also many other practical aspects of doing business, including bookkeeping.
- *U.S. Master Tax Guide* (CCH, Inc.) is updated annually and available in law libraries, business school libraries, and the reference departments of major public libraries and is for sale online. It features in-depth explanations of tax complexities.
- *The Kiplinger Tax Letter*, published by Kiplinger Washington Editors Inc., is a biweekly newsletter that does an excellent job of keeping you up to date on what's happening in the tax field. The breezy— some would say breathless—style is fun to read. Go to www.kiplinger.com.

Also, there is software that handles payroll, including tax computations.

Withholding From an Owner's Paycheck

If you perform substantial services for your corporation and you receive a salary or bonuses for those services, you're considered an employee for tax purposes. This means you must complete and submit a Form W-4 to the corporation the same as any other employee, and the corporation must withhold income taxes and your share of Social Security and Medicare taxes from your paychecks.

These requirements might seem burdensome, but if you're an employee of a C corporation the time you spend completing the paperwork is well worth it because the money you take out as an employee is taxed only once rather than twice. (See "C Corporations," in Chapter 1.)

Social Security Tax (FICA)

You must withhold the employee's share of Social Security tax and Medicare tax from the employee's pay. And you must also pay the employer's share. The amounts to be withheld are listed in the most current edition of Circular E. In 2020, for example, the employee was required to pay 7.65% on the first $137,700 of his or her annual wages; the 7.65% is the sum of the 6.2% Social Security tax and the 1.45% Medicare tax. The employer is required to pay 7.65% on the first $137,700 of the employee's annual wages; the 7.65% is the sum of the 6.2% Social Security tax and the 1.45% Medicare tax.

There is no Social Security tax on the portion of the employee's annual wages that exceeds $137,700—only the Medicare tax; the employer and the employee each pay the 1.45% Medicare tax on the excess amount. The rates and the cutoff point for the Social Security tax change annually.

In 2020, there was a Medicare surtax of 0.9% on the wages and self-employment income of high earners. This surtax applies when a single person's earnings exceed $200,000 and when a married couple's earnings exceed $250,000. On earnings above those amounts, the Medicare tax rate becomes 3.8% rather than 2.9%. This surtax doesn't affect the employer's share, however. The employer still pays the Medicare tax at the 1.45% rate, regardless of how much the employee earns.

Delayed Payment of Self-Employment Taxes under the Coronavirus Aid, Relief, and Economic Security (CARES) Act

If you're self-employed, you have to pay a 12.4% Social Security tax on up to $137,700 in net self-employment income for 2020. Normally, you pay this tax as part of your quarterly estimated tax payments to the IRS. The federal Coronavirus Aid, Relief, and Economic Security (CARES) Act allows you to defer 50% of your Social Security taxes. Of that deferred 50%, half is due on December 31, 2021, and the other half is due on December 31, 2022.

Federal Unemployment Tax (FUTA)

Under the Federal Unemployment Tax Act (FUTA), you must report and pay the FUTA tax for each of your employees; the amount of the tax is not withheld from the employee's pay. In 2020, the FUTA tax rate was 6% of the first $7,000 of the employee's wages for the year. Employers, however, received a credit for participating in state unemployment programs. The credit was generally 5.4%. This yielded a net tax rate of 0.6% (6% – 5.4% = 0.6%), which translated to $42 for an employee earning $7,000 a year or more. But because many states owed money to the federal government for loans taken by them from the federal unemployment fund, the credit in those states was less than 5.4%. This meant that in the states that owed money to the federal government, the net FUTA tax rate was higher than 0.6%; the employer paid more than $42 per employee. To find out what the FUTA tax rate currently is in your state, contact your state unemployment agency. (You can find contact information for your state unemployment agency by visiting the U.S. Department of Labor's website, www.dol.gov, and clicking "Unemployment Insurance," "State Unemployment Insurance," then "contact the State Unemployment Insurance agency.")

Use Form 940 to report federal unemployment tax. Sole proprietorships and partnerships don't pay the FUTA on owner compensation.

Periodic Payments

You must periodically pay to the IRS the withheld income tax and employer's and employee's shares of Social Security and Medicare taxes. In most cases, the IRS requires you to do this electronically through its Electronic Federal Tax Payment System. For complete information on using this system, go to www.eftps.gov/eftps. The frequency of your payments is based on the size of your payroll and amounts due. A typical small business makes monthly payments.

In January of each year, you must give each employee a completed Form W-2, *Wage and Tax Statement*, listing the employee's total earnings for the prior year and the amount of employment taxes withheld. Also, in the Form W-2, you must state the value of any health care coverage you provided to the employee that was not part of the employee's gross income.

In the past, you needed to file W-2s with the federal government either by the end of February (for paper returns) or the end of March (for electronic filings). However, as of 2017, all W-2s must be filed with the federal government by the end of January.

> **CAUTION**
> **Remit taxes on time.** Be sure to withhold taxes as the tax laws require—and to remit those taxes on time. There are substantial penalties if you don't. And if you're an owner of a small business and personally involved in its management, you can be held personally liable for these taxes and the additional penalties, even if the business has the funds to pay them. If your business suddenly runs into financial trouble, put the withheld taxes at the top of the list for payment. If that means not paying suppliers and

others, so be it. The amounts you owe to other creditors can be wiped out in bankruptcy if the business continues to go downhill. Not so with the withheld taxes. You can remain personally liable for these amounts even if the business goes through bankruptcy. However, passive investors—for example, those who merely own corporate shares and play no role in making business decisions—face very little risk of being personally liable for payroll taxes.

> **RESOURCE**
> **Filing returns and making tax payments.** Get a copy of IRS Publication 509, *Tax Calendars*, to see when to file returns and make tax payments. It's available at www.irs.gov. The publication is updated annually.

> **TIP**
> **Consider using a payroll service.** If you're overwhelmed by the requirements for calculating payroll taxes and the fine points of when to pay them, you can pay a payroll service to do the work for you. A payroll service can prepare paychecks, compute payroll taxes, and help you remit the taxes at the proper time. Using a payroll service can be cost effective—even for a very small business—when compared to the hours it will take to handle your own tax reporting.

Self-Employment Tax

The self-employment tax applies to income you receive from actively working in your business—but not as an employee of that business. Technically, it's not an employment tax, but it's so closely related that you should be aware of it to fully understand employment taxes.

If you're a sole proprietor or a partner (or an LLC member, probably—see note below), you must pay the federal self-employment tax in addition to regular income tax. The self-employment tax is equal to the employer's and employee's portion of the Social Security and Medicare taxes that you and your employer would pay on your compensation if you received it as an employee.

You compute this tax each year on Schedule SE, which you then attach to your personal Form 1040. The self-employment tax is added to the income tax that you owe. For example, in 2021 the self-employment tax was set at 15.3% on earnings up to $142,800 and 2.9% on earnings over $142,800. The tax law lightens the burden of the self-employment tax somewhat by allowing you to deduct one-half of this tax in computing your adjusted gross income.

You take the deduction on the first page of your federal tax return.

You might not owe the full self-employment tax on all of your business earnings. If you have income from another job that's subject to withholding— common for people just getting started in business —the income from your other job will reduce the tax base for your self-employment tax. So in computing your self-employment tax for 2021, for example, you'd reduce the $142,800 figure to reflect any of your job earnings that were subject to employer withholding.

> **EXAMPLE:** Max works part-time as a chemistry instructor at a local college where he receives an annual salary of $80,000. He also does consulting for several chemical companies for which he earns an additional $100,000 a year after expenses. The $80,000 salary at the college—which is subject to withholding by the employer—is used to reduce the $142,800 cap on income that's subject to the 15.3% self-employment tax. So Max computes the tax at the rate of 15.3% on $62,800 of his consulting business income ($142,800 − $80,000 = $62,800). On the remaining portion—$37,200 ($100,000 − $62,800 = $37,200)—he computes the tax at the rate of 2.9%.

RESOURCE

LLC members might have to pay self-employment tax. As explained in Chapters 1 and 4, LLC members might have to pay self-employment tax on all income they receive from the LLC, whether in the form of a salary or allocations of profit.

Business Deductions

Of all the federal taxes that can affect a small business, income tax is the one that business owners are most concerned about. The general formula is that you first figure out your gross profit—your gross receipts or sales less returns, allowances, and the cost of goods sold. Then you subtract your other business expenses to find the net income or loss of your business. For an in-depth analysis of what business expenses can be deducted, see IRS Publication 535, *Business Expenses.*

In this section, we'll look at common categories of deductible business expenses.

 RESOURCE
If you have a home-based business, you'll find special tax pointers in Chapter 14.

IRS Guidelines for Business Deductions

The IRS has broad, general guidelines for what constitutes deductible expenses. For example, to be deductible, a business expense must be "ordinary and necessary"—something that's common in your type of business, trade, or profession. If you have an expense that's partly for business and partly personal, you must separate the personal part from the business part. Only the business part is deductible.

So much for generalities. Here's a partial list of the kinds of expenses that your business can normally deduct:

- advertising
- bad debts
- car and truck expenses
- commissions and fees
- conventions and trade shows
- depreciation on property owned by the business
- employee benefit programs
- insurance
- interest
- legal, accounting, and other professional services
- office expenses
- pension and profit-sharing plans
- rent
- repairs to and maintenance of business premises and equipment
- supplies
- taxes and licenses

- trade publications
- travel and meals
- utilities, and
- wages.

This list isn't all inclusive. You can also deduct any other expenses that you believe—and can convince the IRS—are ordinary and necessary business expenses.

Now let's look at the rules affecting a number of specific expenses and deductions in more depth.

Depreciation

If you buy equipment or machinery that has a useful life longer than one year, the IRS generally won't let you deduct the full cost in the year you buy it. Instead, you deduct a portion each year over the term of the item's useful life by using depreciation.

"Depreciation" is the loss in the property's value over the time the property is used—including wear and tear, age, and obsolescence. IRS tables list the useful life of various types of equipment and machinery for depreciation purposes.

 TIP
You don't need to depreciate inexpensive items. The IRS makes exceptions for inexpensive items for which the cost of detailed record keeping would be prohibitive. For example, your $75 back-up drive for your computer might last for five years, but you'd undoubtedly be allowed to deduct its entire cost in the year you buy it. You'd probably treat it as part of your office supplies.

You may choose one of two methods for figuring depreciation—straight-line or accelerated.

Straight-Line Depreciation

The "straight-line depreciation method" means that you deduct an equal amount each year over the projected life of the asset. Actually, that's a bit of an oversimplification; something called the half-year convention makes things slightly more complicated. That rule allows only a half-year's worth of depreciation to be deducted in the first year.

EXAMPLE: Norbert buys a $1,000 computer that can be depreciated over five years according to the IRS table. Under a strict application of the straight-line depreciation method, he'd deduct $200 each year for five years. But the half-year convention allows him to deduct only a half year's worth of depreciation—$100—the first year. So Norbert would deduct $100 the first year; $200 a year for the next four years; and the final $100 in the sixth year.

(Exceptions to the half-year rule are explained in IRS Publication 946, *How to Depreciate Property*.)

Accelerated Depreciation

Another method of depreciating assets—"accelerated depreciation"—is also available. Most small businesses will want to use the accelerated depreciation tables instead of the straight-line method. It allows them to write off a large amount of the purchase price in the years immediately following a machinery or equipment purchase. That, of course, makes the tax savings available sooner.

Immediate Write-Offs

Another tax rule lets you get around the depreciation rules to some extent. As of 2018, you can write off up to $1,000,000 of depreciable assets you purchase during the year. Here's how the write-off works:

EXAMPLE: Bella buys $8,000 worth of computer equipment in 2020. Ordinarily, she'd have to use IRS depreciation tables and spread the cost over several years. But she has the option of deducting the cost all at once in the year 2020. This is known as a Section 179 capital expense election.

There is an important limitation to this deduction—though it doesn't affect most businesses that are just starting out. In 2020, if you bought more than $2,500,000 in depreciable assets during the year, the amount you could deduct as a Section 179 capital expense deduction was reduced. The $2,500,000 cap may be adjusted in future years.

To Take Business Deductions, You Need a Business

The tax laws don't allow you to take business deductions for a hobby. Sometimes, however, the line between a business and a hobby can get fuzzy. This can happen if your small business is more a labor of love than a dependable source of income. Let's say you're a chiropractor but your real passion is growing orchids. Occasionally, you sell your orchids to friends and neighbors. You can't possibly get rich doing this, but you are intrigued by the possibility of deducting the cost of your plant materials, gardening equipment, fertilizer, plant-related magazine subscriptions, and the expenses of attending an orchid-growers convention. Can you legitimately deduct these items? Maybe—or maybe not.

The answer lies in whether you're motivated by profit. To test for a profit motive, the IRS relies mainly on a simple "3-of-5" test. If your business makes a profit in any three out of five consecutive years, you're presumed to have a profit motive. That's true even if during the profitable year the profit was only $1. If you don't pass the "3-of-5" test, you might still be able to convince the IRS that you have a profit motive—but the going will be tougher. You'll have to use your ingenuity to establish that you have a real business. Some things that might help: business cards, letterhead, well-kept books, a separate bank account, a separate phone line, business licenses and permits, and expenses for marketing.

EXAMPLE: Susan, an artist, succeeded in having her part-time art efforts treated as a business—even though she lost money in 18 out of 20 years. Susan was a full-time art professor but, on her own time, created hundreds of works of art. In establishing that her art production was really a business and not a hobby, Susan had proof that she kept records of her inventory, retained a gallery to market her creations, and attended networking events with other artists. The Tax Court ruled that Susan was in business, and could deduct appropriate expenses.

Second, the amount you write off can't exceed the total taxable income that your business received in that year. You may, however, carry forward any disallowed part of this write-off so that you get some tax benefit in future years.

Any depreciable assets that you don't write off under Section 179 can be depreciated and written off under the straight-line or accelerated methods of depreciation, discussed above.

Employees' Pay

You can deduct salaries, wages, and other forms of pay that you give to employees as long as you meet certain IRS tests listed below. If you're an employee and a shareholder of your business, your own salary must meet the same tests for deductibility as salaries paid to any other executive or employee.

For a salary to be deductible, you must show that all of the following are true:

- The payments are ordinary and necessary expenses directly connected with your business.
- The payments are reasonable. Fortunately, you have broad discretion to decide what's reasonable. Short of a scam—such as paying a huge salary to a spouse or relative who does little or no work—the IRS will almost always accept your notion of what's reasonable pay.
- The payments are for services actually performed.

If you use the "cash method of accounting" (very common among small businesses), you can deduct salaries and wages only for the year in which they were paid. However, you can deduct employee taxes your business withheld in the year your business withheld them; you can't deduct (until paid to the government) the employer's matching portion of these taxes. Businesses using the accrual method have more latitude as to when they can deduct salaries and payroll taxes.

You can also deduct bonuses you pay to employees if they're intended as additional payment for services and not as gifts; most bonuses qualify for deduction. If your business distributes cash, gift certificates, or similar items of easily convertible cash value, the value of these items is considered additional wages or salary regardless of the amount. If a bonus is considered part of an employee's wages or salary, it's subject to employment taxes and withholding rules.

Certain noncash bonuses that are, in fact, intended as gifts are deductible if they are less than $25 per person per year.

> EXAMPLE: To promote employee goodwill, Pebblestone Partnership distributes turkeys, hams, and other items of nominal value at holidays. The value of these items isn't considered salaries or wages, but the partnership can deduct their cost as a business expense.

Employee Benefits

A number of employee benefits can be deducted, including:

- health and dental insurance
- group term life insurance
- moving expenses
- qualified employee benefit plans, including profit-sharing plans, stock bonus plans, and money purchase pension plans, and
- employee benefit plans that allow employees to choose among two or more benefits consisting of cash and qualified benefits.

These benefits are not only tax deductible by your business, they also are not taxed to the employee.

Though these benefits sound attractive, there are two serious drawbacks. First, many small businesses—particularly those just starting out—can't afford them. Second, plans that mainly benefit the owners of the business are not tax deductible. (See "Corporations," in Chapter 1, for a more thorough discussion. Also, consult IRS Publication 15-B, *Employer's Tax Guide to Fringe Benefits*.)

TIP
Your business might qualify for a health care tax credit. First, be aware that if your business has fewer than 50 "full-time equivalent" employees, you face no penalty under the Affordable Care Act if you don't furnish or contribute to health care insurance. (In applying this rule, two half-time employees are treated as one full-time equivalent.)

And if you have fewer than 25 full-time equivalent employees, your business will qualify for a tax credit of up to 50% of the premiums you pay at the single (employee only) rate, if the following conditions are met:

- the average yearly wage of your employees is about $55,000 a year or less (a 2019 figure that will be adjusted for inflation)
- the insurance is part of a plan offered through a Small Business Health Options Program (SHOP) Marketplace, and
- you pay at least 50% of the insurance premiums.

You claim the credit using IRS Form 8941, *Credit for Small Employer Health Insurance Premiums.*

For details on the Small Business Health Options Program Marketplace and tax credits, see www.healthcare.gov.

Meals and Travel

To be treated as a business deduction, travel expenses must be ordinary and necessary in your type of business. Basically, these are any reasonable expenses you incur while traveling for business. You (or your business) can't deduct expenses for personal vacations or any business expense that is lavish or extravagant. (If you're on a tight budget like most small business owners, you won't have to worry about this last restriction.)

Here are examples of travel expenses you would typically be able to deduct if you incurred them while traveling on business:

- airplane, train, and bus tickets
- taxis to your hotel or to a client's office
- shipping sample and display materials
- meals and lodging

- dry cleaning and laundry
- telephone, and
- tips incidental to any of these expenses.

You cannot deduct expenses for transportation while you're not traveling. The IRS says that you're traveling away from home if (1) your duties require you to be away from the general area of your "tax home" for a period of time substantially longer than an ordinary day's work, and (2) you need to get sleep or rest to meet the demands of your work. (Napping in your car doesn't count.) Generally, your "tax home" is your main place of business regardless of where your family home is.

If a trip is entirely for business, you can deduct all of your ordinary and necessary travel expenses. If your trip was primarily personal, you can't deduct any travel expenses—even if you did some business at your destination.

Meal expenses have special rules and restrictions. You can generally deduct only 50% of your business-related meal expenses. In addition, the IRS may disallow extravagant and excessive expenses.

But short of fraud or obvious gross excess, the IRS doesn't monitor where you go for your business meals. So in practice, for most small business owners, 50% of all business-related meal expenses are deductible. As an employer, this 50% limit applies to your business even if you reimburse your employees for 100% of their meal expenses.

If you're a sole proprietor, deduct the allowable portion of your own business travel and meal expenses on Schedule C of your Form 1040. Use Schedule C to also report the expenses that you reimburse or directly pay your employees. (Consult IRS Publication 463 for an in-depth treatment of this subject.)

If you're a partner or a shareholder of a corporation in which you play an active management role, it's usually best to have your partnership or corporation reimburse you for your business-related travel expenses. The business can then deduct these amounts to the extent allowed by law.

CAUTION
Excessive expenses might trigger an audit.
Your overall travel budget might result in a tax audit if these expenses are out of proportion to what the IRS thinks is reasonable, given your type of business and income. For most honest small businesspeople, this isn't usually a problem unless they have some extraordinary need to travel.

EXAMPLE: Ben starts a marble importing business and spends his first year visiting 200 prominent architects and interior designers from coast to coast to introduce his business. His high travel expenses trigger an audit, but Ben is able to show that these trips were necessary to get his business off the ground.

If you are audited, you'll need to show the IRS complete and accurate records of your travel and meal expenses, including actual receipts. Also, because you need to tie each trip and meal to a specific business purpose, it makes good sense to keep a log stating the purpose. Otherwise, if challenged, you might have trouble recalling the details.

Automobile Expenses

If you use your car for business, you might be able to deduct some or all of your car expenses. Deductible items include:

- costs related to maintaining and repairing your car, such as oil changes and new tires
- costs related to operating your car, such as licenses, gas, tolls, and parking, and
- the cost of the car itself, whether it be to rent, lease, or purchase the car (the purchase cost must be deducted over several years, however; see the discussion of depreciation, below).

The following discussion assumes you use your car more than 50% for business. Special rules apply if you use your car 50% or less for business. For complete information about deductions for your car, see IRS Publication 463.

If you use your car for both business and personal purposes, you must divide your expenses between business and personal use. (This rule applies to all items you use for both business and personal use.) The miles you put on your car driving from your home to your main place of business are considered to be commuting miles—a personal use and not deductible. The same thing applies to fees you pay to park your car at your place of business.

EXAMPLE: Tricia has a catering business that requires her to call on customers. She drives 20,000 miles during the year: 12,000 for business and 8,000 for personal use (including her daily trips from home to her shop). She can claim only 60% of the cost of operating her car as a business expense (12,000 ÷ 20,000). The coins she fed the parking meter in front of her shop each day would be a personal (commuting) expense and not deductible; fees paid for parking while calling on customers would, however, be deductible.

What about depreciation? As with other business assets, you can deduct the cost of a car (but only the portion used for business), but you must spread the deductions over several years. IRS depreciation tables have special schedules for cars. These schedules are updated periodically.

Depreciation for Employees' Cars. If your employees use their cars in their work, they can't take a depreciation deduction unless this use is for your convenience as their employer and you require it as a condition of employment.

If you don't want to keep track of your car expenses and you want to avoid the complexity of the depreciation rules, the IRS offers a second method for deducting car expenses. You can use the standard mileage rate for your business usage. Beginning January 2020, the rate was 57.5 cents per mile. The rate changes periodically, so check IRS publications for the latest figure.

If you're going to use the standard mileage rate, you must start using it in the year you begin using the car for business. If you don't use the standard mileage rate that first year, you can't use it for that car later on; you'll have to continue keeping track of your actual car expenses and following the IRS's rules on depreciation. If you use the standard mileage rate, you can also deduct tolls and parking fees that were paid while on business.

If you take a deduction for car expenses, you must file Form 4562 with your tax return. If you give an employee a car for business and personal use, the employee must report as income the value of the personal usage. For example, an employee who keeps a company car at home and drives to and from work must report that commuting usage—and any other personal usage—as income.

If you lease rather than own your car, you can deduct the part of each lease payment that's for your business use of the car. If you use your leased car 60% for business, you can deduct 60% of each lease payment. You can't deduct any payments you make to buy the car even if the payments are called lease payments. A lease with an option to buy may be a lease or a purchase contract, depending on its wording.

Keep accurate records of your car usage so that if you're challenged by the IRS, you can demonstrate the extent of your business use. The best procedure is to keep a daily log in your glove compartment to record the following about each business trip:

- date
- destination
- mileage, and
- business purpose.

Tax Audits

As a small business owner, you're three times more likely to be audited by the IRS than a regular employee-taxpayer would be. If you're audited, you have the burden of proving that your tax return is accurate. In over 80% of audits, the taxpayer winds up owing more taxes—usually because of poor record keeping rather than dishonesty.

RESOURCE

If your business is facing an audit, you'll get excellent guidance from *Tax Savvy for Small Business*, by Frederick W. Daily (Nolo)—which is the source of much of the material in this section. The *Tax Savvy* book goes through the audit process step by step and in great depth. And if, as commonly happens, the business audit turns into a personal audit as well, refer to *Stand Up to the IRS*, by Frederick W. Daily and Erica Pless (Nolo).

How the IRS Audits a Small Business

The IRS conducts two kinds of audits of small businesses and their owners: "office audits" and "field audits." There's a difference not only in where the audit is held, but also in the intensity of the process.

If you're a sole proprietor and gross less than $100,000 per year, the IRS is likely to ask you to come to their office for the audit. Usually an office audit lasts from two to four hours, and a typical business taxpayer is hit for additional taxes averaging about $4,000.

If you have a partnership or corporation, or a sole proprietorship that grosses over $100,000 a year, the IRS will probably order a field audit. The process will be much more intensive than an office audit. Field auditors—called revenue agents—are much better trained in accounting than are IRS office tax auditors. The average amount owed by a business after going through a field audit is over $20,000, including additional taxes, penalties, and interest.

An IRS field audit may be conducted at your business place, but doesn't have to be. If your business premises are very small, you might point out that having the audit conducted there would interfere with your operations. Ask that the audit be held elsewhere—at the IRS office, for example. Or if you plan to be represented by a tax professional—a lawyer or an accountant with tax experience—you can request that the audit be conducted at the professional's office.

Even though you have the right to have an audit conducted elsewhere, an auditor has the power to enter your business if it's open to the public. But an auditor can't go into a private area—such as a storeroom or your private office—unless you consent. But if you have nothing to hide, there's no reason to raise suspicions by denying access. Offer the IRS auditor a complete tour.

If you have a home office, you don't have to let an auditor into your home unless there's a court order. But if you refuse entry, your home office depreciation or rental expense will probably be disallowed because you did not prove you had a home office.

The IRS Inquiry

Wherever the audit is conducted, the auditor will want to see the business records you used to prepare the tax returns. This can include check registers, bank statements, canceled checks, receipts, invoices, and a formal set of books.

To get still more financial information about you and your business, an auditor can require records from your tax preparer, banks, suppliers, customers, and others.

Hiring a Tax Professional

Many small business owners can handle a run of the mill IRS office audit without professional representation. Often it's sensible to do this, because the cost of hiring professional help might be more than the IRS is likely to bill you. However, if you fear that some serious irregularity could come to light—perhaps you've taken a huge deduction and can't produce a receipt or canceled check to verify it—consult with a tax professional before the audit.

When it comes to a field audit, where more money will almost surely be at stake, it's usually wise to bring in a tax professional from the outset. The IRS uses experienced auditors to conduct field audits, so you might be overmatched if questions come up about your documents or interpretations of the tax law.

Preparing for Your Audit

Thoroughly review the tax return that's going to be audited.

Make sure you can explain how you came up with the figures. Identify problem areas, such as how you reported particular items of income or expense.

Then find all the records you need to substantiate your tax return and organize them logically and clearly for the auditor. Among the items to gather up for the audit are:

- bank statements, canceled checks, and receipts
- electronic records—for example, charge card statements
- books and records—which can range from a formal set of books to cash register tapes
- appointment books, logs, and diaries
- car records, and
- travel and meal records.

If records are missing, you might still be able to prove a deduction by offering an oral explanation or by reconstructing records in writing. Business-related expenses of less than $25 each don't require substantiation.

 RESOURCE

Neatness counts. It can be tempting to dump a pile of receipts on the table and require the auditor to search through them. This is one temptation you'll want to avoid. Neatness helps build credibility with the auditor who, when presented with well-maintained records, might even give you the benefit of the doubt on questionable items.

What Auditors Look For

In auditing your business, the IRS will try to determine if you:

- failed to report all of your business sales or receipts (income)
- skimmed cash from the business
- wrote off personal living costs—family travel, for example—as business expenses
- failed to file payroll tax returns on time or to make the required deposits, or
- improperly classified some workers as independent contractors rather than employees.

This isn't a complete list—just the things the IRS auditor will most likely scrutinize.

Be prepared for the auditor to analyze your bank accounts. Office auditors don't always take the time to do this, but field auditors do. This consists of adding up all the deposits in all of your business bank accounts to see if the total is more than your reported income. The auditor will also want to see all of your personal account records to learn if the amounts deposited are consistent with your business cash flow.

It's smart to review your bank accounts in advance to try to spot and be able to explain deposits that weren't income and therefore weren't reported on your tax return—loan proceeds, for example, or proceeds from the sale of assets (other than the capital gain portion), transfers from other accounts, inheritances, gifts, or money held for relatives.

After confirming that your income figures are accurate, turn to your business expenses. The tax law makes you prove that your deductions were legitimate; the IRS doesn't have to disprove them. Be especially careful to have good documentation for deductions you took for travel and entertainment, a home office, thefts, bad debts, depreciation, and car expenses—all prime targets during an IRS probe.

If you can't produce thorough records to back up your deductions, don't despair. You might be able to reconstruct the missing documents. For guidance on how to do this, see *Tax Savvy for Small Business,* by Frederick W. Daily (Nolo).

How to Behave at an Audit

Keep small talk to a minimum. An auditor is trained to listen for clues about your lifestyle—which might not seem affordable on your reported income. Raising suspicions in an auditor's mind can prolong the agony of an audit.

If you're asked a direct question, try to answer "yes" or "no." Don't overexplain or answer questions that weren't asked. If you don't have a ready answer, it's okay to say, "I don't know," "I'll get back to you on that," or "I'll have to check with my accountant." Often the auditor will let it go. At the very least, you've bought some time, which can work to your advantage.

Most auditors are businesslike, but now and then you run into one who's impolite, hostile, or maybe is just having a bad day. You're entitled to courteous treatment from IRS auditors. If your auditor gets out of line, mention your right to courteous treatment and politely ask the auditor to lighten up. If that doesn't work, ask to speak to the auditor's manager and describe the unfair treatment you're receiving.

TIP

It's all right to ask for a time out. You can stop or recess an audit for just about any good reason—for a few minutes to go to the bathroom or eat lunch, or for the day because you feel ill or need to confer with a tax professional. If you ask for a recess, the auditor might find it more convenient to resume the audit in a week or two—giving you time to regroup or get professional advice.

How to Negotiate With an Auditor

As Fred Daily explains in much greater depth in *Tax Savvy for Small Business* (Nolo), there's often room to bargain during the audit process—despite the official line that IRS auditors don't negotiate.

One approach is to suggest that a disputed item be resolved by applying a percentage figure.

Suppose you claimed the costs of a trip as a business deduction. The auditor, believing it was a personal trip, wants to disallow the deduction. You might say: "Perhaps, in fairness, the trip can be seen as being both for business and pleasure. How about agreeing that 70% of the expenses were for business and 30% for pleasure?" This might work. On the other hand, IRS auditors are instructed not to talk about compromising the dollars—so you might not get as far by using a more direct approach and proposing, for example, to pay $5,000 to settle a $10,000 IRS claim.

Another tactic in negotiating is to take the offensive. An audit isn't a one-way street. Auditors must make adjustments in your favor when you're legally entitled to one. Maybe you missed a deduction or were overly conservative on your return. When the auditor's review has been completed, bring up the items that entitle you to an adjustment in your favor. This can help offset the amounts the auditor claims you owe.

Raising Money for Your Business

To succeed in business, you'll need money to get started and keep afloat until you become profitable—and, assuming you're successful, you'll probably need more money to expand than you can generate internally. How much you'll need and when you'll need it will depend on the nature of the business. However, unless you have a good-sized nest egg put aside or are starting a tiny, home-based business on a shoestring, finding money to finance your new enterprise is likely to be a major concern.

Fortunately, there are many places to look for start-up funds. If one source doesn't pan out, you can try another and then another.

And there's no requirement that you get all your money from a single source. Often, you can tap a combination of sources—for example, savings, loans, and equity investments—to provide the needed funds. In this chapter, we'll look at all of these sources—and the legal rules that apply. But first we'll discuss how you can use a business plan to figure out how much money you'll need and to convince others to invest in your business.

> **CAUTION**
>
> **Watch your pennies.** Although you may be chomping at the bit to get your new business going, it can be a mistake to pour in too much money at the beginning. You need time to learn whether the business is viable. Because a fair number of small businesses fail, raising and spending a pile of money for an untested business idea can lead to much grief—especially if you're personally on the hook for borrowed funds. Although some small businesses require a great deal of cash or credit up front, my experience is that many others don't. Consider starting as small and cheaply as possible. If your concept works, more funds will become available. If not, you can move on and take advantage of the lessons you've learned—and you won't be burdened with a ton of debts.

Consider Writing a Business Plan

Before you start searching for money, it might be helpful to write a "business plan"—a statement that analyzes your proposed business and explains how it will become profitable. Putting numbers on paper forces you to focus on where the money will be coming from and how it will flow through your business. This is a valuable reality test for you and—equally important—it's something that lenders and investors will want to look at before shelling out money.

Many excellent books are available to guide you, including *How to Write a Business Plan,* by Mike McKeever (Nolo), and *Successful Business Plan: Secrets and Strategies,* by Rhonda Abrams (The Planning Shop). For software, *Business Plan Pro,* by Palo Alto Software, comes very highly rated. Also, several websites offer practical suggestions and provide sample plans. You might start with the U.S. Small Business Administration site at www.sba.gov, where you'll find advice and dozens of real business plans.

But whatever source you turn to for ideas for writing a business plan, keep in mind that a short, simple plan is usually better than a long, complex one—especially for a small business that's just starting out. Formality can get in the way, and it's all too easy to let the details of a complicated plan hinder your progress.

One good approach to the task is to imagine that you're sitting across a table from a friend and want to take a few minutes to explain your business idea. What are the key things you'd say? What kind of language would you use? Try to capture that clear, conversational tone in your written plan.

There are many ways to organize your business plan. But however you decide you do it, you'll probably want to cover four main areas.

A Description of Your Business

Start with the business name and your Internet domain name, if you already have one. Then specify the products and services you plan to sell, and describe how your business will meet the needs of customers and clients. You can also explain where your business will be physically located—in rented, downtown space, for example, or in your home. It's also important to analyze the competition you'll face and why you think your business will survive and thrive despite it. This part of the plan is also the place to describe any demographic, economic, and industry trends that you believe will help the business get off to a good start.

Your Marketing Program

Here, you can set down your thoughts on who your customers and clients will be, and how they'll learn about your new business and be motivated to give it a try. First, you'll need to develop a profile of your typical customer. For example, if you're planning to start a self-storage facility, your customers might be apartment dwellers from nearby apartment complexes who lack sufficient closet space. Or, if you're starting a landscaping service, your target clients might be people who are buying homes in new, suburban subdivisions. Once you have a good notion of the kind of customers you'd like to reach, think about the methods you'll use.

It's said that word of mouth is the best way for a business to build a loyal following, but that takes time. With a brand-new business, you'll have to prime the pump. There are lots of ways you might do this. Traditional advertising in newspapers and on radio or television is just the tip of the iceberg.

Among other things, you might consider newsletters; direct mail; a website linked to high-traffic sites; trade show exhibits; billboards; discount coupons; event sponsorship; free classes; telemarketing; and favorable press reports. Many businesses use the sides of their vans and trucks to capture people's attention. (For more on advertising and marketing, see Chapters 16 and 17.)

How You'll Operate the Business

A key concern here is the competence of those who will be running the business. Be sure to include your own qualifications and those of any co-owners and managers in any plan that you'll be showing to others. List past business experience and any employment or training that's relevant to your new business. If a small business is organized as a corporation, then most likely the owners will be the board of directors. But if you'll have some outsiders serving on the board, you can name them here and give their qualifications. And consider naming your professional team—a lawyer and an accountant whom you may consult from time to time.

You might also mention the number of employees —full time and part time—you expect to hire at the beginning, and give some idea of what their jobs will consist of. If you'll rely on independent contractors for some work, you can spell out their duties.

In addition to describing the business's workforce, it's often worth describing other aspects of your business operations, such as any special equipment you'll be using and your arrangements with suppliers. You might also describe any improvements you'll be making to the premises the business will occupy—usually rented space for a new business. If you already have some contracts lined up with customers or clients, that's great because you have a running head start. It makes sense to mention these in your business plan.

For many businesses, order fulfillment and customer service play a major role. Your business plan can explain how your business intends to handle these functions—hopefully in a way that will keep customers happy and coming back for more.

The Financial Highlights

Here, you should list your fixed costs and your estimates for other costs, and how much you'll need in start-up funds—that is, funds to buy needed equipment, supplies, and inventory, with enough cash left in the till to cover other bills until adequate money starts rolling in (which could take several months). Explain where the start-up funds will come from: your own funds on hand, or loans or cash from investors. Be sure to include your break-even analysis, too (see "Do a Break-Even Analysis," below).

Do a Break-Even Analysis

No one can tell for sure whether a particular business idea will be profitable. You can, however, make an informed judgment by doing what's called a "break-even analysis." This shows you how much money you'll need to bring in to cover your expenses, even before you make a dime of profit. You don't want to start or buy a business unless you're reasonably sure that sales will far exceed your costs of doing business.

To perform a break-even analysis, you'll have to make educated guesses about your expenses and revenues. This requires some preliminary research. To make the job easier, take advantage of business planning books and software, as well as the free Web resources listed below.

Here are the most important facts and figures you'll need to assemble for your break-even analysis:

- **Fixed costs.** These costs—sometimes called "overhead"—stay pretty much the same from month to month. They include rent, insurance, utilities, and other expenses that must be paid regardless of how much you produce or sell. Be sure to add another 10% to cover unexpected fluctuations in these costs, such as a boost in insurance premiums or the price of natural gas to heat your business premises.
- **Sales revenue.** This is the total amount the business brings in each month or year. Be realistic in figuring the volume of business you can expect. You'll need to specifically identify your customer base, then do some demographic research to find out how many people who fit that profile you can expect to reach and attract.

- **Average gross profit for each sale.** This is how much you earn from each sale after paying the direct costs of the sale. For example, if you pay an average of $200 for each bicycle that you sell at an average price tag of $300, your average gross profit per sale is $100.
- **Average gross profit percentage.** This tells you how much of each dollar of sales income is gross profit. You divide your average gross profit (from above) by the average selling price. In the bicycle example, the gross profit percentage is 33.3% ($100 ÷ $300).

Now you're ready to figure out the break-even point. Divide your estimated fixed costs total by your gross profit percentage. This tells you the amount of sales revenue you'll need to bring in just to break even. For example, if your fixed costs are $6,000 a month and your expected profit margin is 33.3%, your break-even point is about $18,000 in sales revenue per month ($6,000 ÷ 0.333). This means you must take in $18,000 each month just to pay your fixed costs and your direct (product) costs. Stated another way, you must sell 60 bicycles a month at $300 each. At the break-even point, there's no salary or profit for you.

If you can work out a realistic break-even point that gives you reasonable assurance of earning a decent profit, you can move ahead with a more detailed business plan. Otherwise, you'll need to come up with a different business idea.

Want more information on researching and developing your break-even analysis? Check the following websites:

- www.businessknowhow.com/startup/break-even.htm, and
- https://businesstown.com/articles/create-a-break-even-analysis-for-your-small-business.

Probably the most difficult part of the financial highlights portion of your business plan will be your projections for gross income for the first three years. When you start a business from scratch, this is a largely unknown number. At best you'll be making a rough approximation. It's better to estimate on the low side and be pleasantly surprised if the income exceeds your expectations. If you estimate too high and it turns out there's not enough income to meet expenses, the business will struggle to stay alive and might ultimately fail. To be as accurate as possible in projecting revenues, you'll need to rely on your business acumen, information from multiple industry sources, and perhaps input from an accountant or other business consultant. With careful preparation, you can significantly reduce the risk that your income forecast will be far too high.

Just Do It

Finally, try not to get stuck on the small details of your plan. Experts have found that there's no clear correlation between writing a complex business plan and a business's success. Spending months and months formulating a long complicated plan might not be worth the time or effort, especially if there are competitive advantages to starting the business quickly. Investors want to see smart, well-formulated ideas, so focus on putting together a clear and simple plan that covers the key issues well.

Two Types of Outside Financing

If you're starting a small business, chances are that at least part of the initial funding will come from your own pocket—savings, an inheritance, or a severance check you received for taking early retirement. But you might also need to seek money from outside sources, so it's important to understand the two main categories of such funding and the differences between them. One category is loans and the other is equity investments.

Loans

As you know, a loan is based on a simple idea: Someone gives you money and you promise to pay it back—usually with interest. Because you must pay back the lender whether your business is a fabulous success or a miserable failure, the entire risk of your new enterprise is placed squarely on your shoulders.

Of course, nothing in business—or in life, for that matter—is without risk. Nevertheless, a commercial lender will be unwilling to lend you money if the odds of your repaying the money look low. And to help keep the risk down, a lender will very likely ask for "security" for the loan—for example, a mortgage on your house so that the lender can take and sell your house if you don't keep up your loan payments.

But as compared to selling a portion of your business to investors, there's an obvious plus side to borrowing money: If your business succeeds as you hope and you pay back the lender as promised, you reap all future profits. There's no need to share them.

In short, if you're confident about your business's prospects and you have the opportunity to borrow money, a loan is a more attractive source of money than getting it from an equity investor who will own a piece of your business and receive a share of the profits. Again, the downside is that if the business fails and you've personally guaranteed the loan, you'll have to repay it. By contrast, you don't have to repay equity investors if the business goes under.

Loans are so common that you probably are familiar with the mechanics, but nevertheless it makes sense to review the basics.

The Promissory Note

A lender will almost always want you to sign a written "promissory note"—a paper that says, in effect, "I promise to pay you $XXX plus interest of XX%" and then describes how and when payments are to be made. Sample promissory notes are included later in this chapter. A bank or another commercial lender will use a form with a lot more wording than in our forms, but the basic idea of all promissory notes is the same.

A friend or relative might be willing to lend you money on a handshake. This is a poor idea for both of you. It's always a better business practice to put the loan in writing—and to state a specific interest rate and repayment plan. Otherwise, you open the door to unfortunate misunderstandings that can unnecessarily harm a great relationship.

Sign only the original of the promissory note. When it's paid off, you're entitled to get it back. You don't want several signed copies floating around that can cast doubt on whether the debt has been fully paid. But you should keep a photocopy of the signed note—marked "COPY"—for your business records.

For sample promissory notes, see "Document All of the Money You Receive," below.

Repayment Plans

As long as the interest rate on the loan doesn't exceed the maximum rate allowed by your state's usury law, you and the lender are free to work out the terms of repayment.

Typically, a state's usury law will allow a lender to charge a higher rate when lending money for business purposes than for personal reasons—in fact, in several states, there's no limit at all on the interest rate that can be charged on business loans, as long as the business borrower agrees to the rate in writing.

In a few states, the higher limit or absence of any limit applies only when the business borrower is organized as a corporation. In other states, the higher rates permitted for business borrowers are legal even if the borrower is a sole proprietorship, partnership, or limited liability company.

> **CAUTION**
> **Check your state usury law.** As a general rule, if your business is a corporation and the terms of repayment are in a promissory note, the lender can safely charge interest of up to 10% per year and not have to worry about the usury law. But because there's so much variation in usury laws from state to state, you or the lender should

check the law in your state. Look under "interest" or "usury" in the index to your state's statutes. (For more on doing your own legal research, get Nolo's *Legal Research: How to Find & Understand the Law*, by Stephen Elias (Nolo).)

Assuming there are no usury law problems, you and the lender can agree on any number of repayment plans. Let's say you borrow $10,000 with interest at the rate of 10% a year. Here are just a few of the repayment possibilities:

- **Lump sum repayment.** You agree, for example, to pay principal and interest in one lump sum at the end of one year. Under this plan, 12 months later you'd pay the lender $10,000 in "principal"—the borrowed amount—plus $1,000 in interest.

- **Periodic interest and lump sum repayment of principal.** You agree, for example, to pay interest only for two years and then interest and principal at the end of the third year. With this type of loan plan—often called a "balloon" loan because of the big payment at the end—you'd pay $1,000 in interest at the end of the first and second years, and then $10,000 in principal and $1,000 in interest at the end of the third year.

- **Periodic payments of principal and interest.** You agree, for example, to repay $2,500 of the principal each year for four years, plus interest at the end of each year. Under this plan, your payments would look like this:
  - End of year one:
    $2,500 principal + $1,000 interest
  - End of year two:
    $2,500 principal + $750 interest
  - End of year three:
    $2,500 principal + $500 interest, and
  - End of year four:
    $2,500 principal + $250 interest.

- **Amortized payments.** You agree, for example, to make equal monthly payments so that principal and interest are fully paid in five years. Under this plan, you'd consult an amortization table in a book, on computer software, or on the Internet to figure out how much must be paid each month for five years to fully pay off a $10,000 loan plus the 10% interest. The table would say you'd have to pay $212.48 a month. Each of your payments would consist of both principal and interest. At the beginning of the repayment period, the interest portion of each payment would be large; at the end, it would be small.

- **Amortized payments with a balloon.** You agree, for example, to make equal monthly payments based on a five-year amortization schedule, but to pay off the remaining principal at the end of the third year. Under this plan, you'd pay $212.48 each month for three years. At the end of the third year, after making the normal monthly payment, there'd still be $4,604.42 in unpaid principal. So along with your normal payment of $212.48, you'd make a balloon payment to cover the remaining principal.

CAUTION

Avoid loans with prepayment penalties.
Whenever you borrow money, you'd like to be free to reduce or pay off the principal faster than called for in the promissory note if you have the wherewithal to do so, because this reduces or stops the running of interest. In other words, if you have a three-year loan but are able to pay it off by the end of year two, you don't want to pay interest for year three. By law, some states always allow such early repayment and you pay interest only for the time you have the use of the borrowed money. In other states, however, the law allows a lender to charge a penalty (amounting to a portion of the future interest) when a borrower reduces the balance or pays back a loan sooner than called for. Because it seems unfair to have to pay anything for the use of borrowed money except interest for the time the principal is actually in your hands, try to make sure any promissory note you sign says you can prepay any or all of the principal without penalty. If the lender doesn't agree, see if you can negotiate a compromise under which you'll owe a prepayment penalty only if you pay back the loan during a relatively short period, such as six months from the time you borrow the money.

Security

Lenders, with the possible exception of friends or relatives, will probably require you to provide some valuable property—called "security" or "collateral"—that they can grab and sell to collect their money if you can't keep up with the loan repayment plan. For example, the lender may seek a second mortgage or deed of trust on your house, or might ask for a security interest or lien on your mutual funds or the equipment, inventory, and accounts receivable of your business. Again, the reason for doing this is if you don't make your payments, the lender can sell the pledged assets (the security) to pay off the loan.

But it's important to realize that a lender isn't limited to using the pledged assets to satisfy the loan. If you don't make good on your repayment commitment, a lender also has the right to sue you.

Typically, a lender will seize pledged assets first and then sue you only if the funds realized from those assets are insufficient to pay off the loan—but that's not a legal requirement. A lender might decide to sue you before using up the pledged assets. If the lender wins the lawsuit and gets a judgment against you, assets you haven't specifically pledged as security are at risk—as is a portion of your future earnings.

In short, before you borrow money—under either a secured or an unsecured promissory note—think about what will happen if you run into financial problems.

Cosigners and Guarantors

If you lack sufficient assets to pledge as security for a loan, a lender might try other methods to attempt to guarantee that the loan will be repaid. One is to ask you to get someone who is richer than you to cosign or guarantee the loan. That means the lender will have two people rather than one to collect from if you don't make your payments.

When asking friends or relatives to cosign or guarantee a promissory note, be sure they understand that they're risking their personal assets if you don't repay it.

If you're married, the lender might insist that your spouse cosign the promissory note. Be aware that if your spouse signs, not only are your personal assets at risk, but also those assets that the two of you jointly own—a house, for example, or a bank account. What's more, if your spouse has a job, your spouse's earnings will be subject to garnishment if the lender sues and gets a judgment against the two of you because the loan isn't repaid as promised.

Community Property States

If you live in a community property state—Arizona, California, Idaho, Louisiana, Nevada, New Mexico, Texas, Washington, or Wisconsin—you'll need to do a bit of research or consult briefly with a business lawyer to learn the legal effect of your spouse cosigning a promissory note. (For tips on how to do your own legal research, get Nolo's *Legal Research: How to Find & Understand the Law*, by Stephen Elias (Nolo).) In researching Wisconsin law, you'd look under "marital property," but the concept is the same as community property for all practical purposes.

In a community property state, debts incurred by one spouse are usually the legal responsibility of both—meaning that a couple's community property is at risk if the debt isn't paid.

In addition to community property, you or your spouse may have separate property—which, depending on the law of the particular state, is usually property owned by a spouse prior to marriage or acquired after marriage by gift or inheritance. If you live in a community property state and your spouse cosigns a promissory note for your business loan, the lender may go after your spouse's property if you fail to repay the loan.

! CAUTION

Forming a corporation or LLC might not protect you from personal liability on a loan. As explained in Chapter 1, a virtue of doing business as a corporation or an LLC is that corporate shareholders and LLC members aren't personally liable for paying business debts, including loans taken out by the corporation or LLC. But a small corporation or LLC—especially one just starting up—will find it impossible to borrow money from a bank or other sophisticated lender unless the shareholders or members personally guarantee repayment. And if this guarantee is made, the shareholders or members are just as obligated to repay the loan as if they signed as personal borrowers in the first place. Typically, lenders will continue to require that shareholders or LLC members guarantee repayment of a corporate or LLC loan—at least until the business is well established and has a long record of being profitable.

Equity Investments

"Equity investors" buy a piece of your business. They become co-owners and share in the fortunes and misfortunes of your business. Like you, they can make or lose a bundle. Generally, if your business does badly or flops, you're under no obligation to pay them back their money.

However, some equity investors would like to have their cake and eat it too; they want you to guarantee some return on their investment even if the business does poorly. Unless you're really desperate for the cash, avoid an investor who wants a guarantee. It's simply too risky a proposition for someone starting or running a small business.

Limiting Risk

Because equity investors are co-owners of the business, they might be exposed to personal liability for all business debts unless your business is a corporation, limited partnership, or limited liability company. If you recruit equity investors for what has been your sole proprietorship, your business will now be treated as a general partnership. This means your equity investors will be considered to be general partners, whether or not they take part in running the business. And, as explained in Chapter 1, as far as people outside of the business are concerned—people who are owed money or who have a judgment against the business—general partners are all personally liable for the debts of the partnership.

Equity investors often want to limit their losses to what they put into the business. An investor who puts $10,000 into a business might be prepared to lose the $10,000—but no more. In short, the investor doesn't want to put the rest of his or her assets at risk. The investor will want to avoid being—or being treated as—a general partner.

Fortunately, there are three common ways to organize your business so that you can offer an investor protection from losses beyond the money being invested:

- **Corporation.** Form a corporation and issue stock to the investor. A shareholder who doesn't participate in corporate activities and decision making is virtually free from liability beyond his or her original investment. A shareholder who does help run the company is liable to outsiders for his or her own actions—for example, making slanderous statements or negligently operating a piece of equipment—but isn't liable for corporate debts or the actions of corporate employees.
- **Limited Partnership.** Form a limited partnership and make the investor a limited partner. A limited partner's freedom from liability is similar to that of a shareholder, as long as the limited partner doesn't become actively involved in running the business.
- **Limited Liability Company.** Form a limited liability company and make the investor a member. The investor will be protected in much the same manner as a shareholder or limited partner.

Each of these business formats is described in much greater detail in Chapter 1. See the end of this chapter for more on equity investors.

CAUTION

Encourage investors to determine their own degree of risk. As mentioned, an investor in a business organized as a corporation, limited partnership, or limited liability company usually stands to lose no more than his or her investment. However, state laws must be followed carefully to achieve this result. To avoid having investors accuse you of giving misleading assurances, recommend that they check with their own financial and legal advisers to evaluate whether their investment exposes them to the possibility of incurring additional losses.

Return on Investment

Someone who invests in your business might be willing to face the loss of the entire investment and not insist that you guarantee repayment. But to offset the risk of losing the invested money, the investor might want to receive substantial benefits if the business is successful.

For example, an investor could insist on a generous percentage of the business profits and, to help ensure that there are such profits, might seek to put a cap on your salary. The terms are always negotiable—there's no formula for figuring out what's fair to both you and the investor.

Here are just a few possibilities:

- John, a former police detective, decides to start a business to offer security training seminars to midsized manufacturing companies. He forms STS Limited Liability Company and invests $10,000, which is only part of his $20,000 start-up budget. His aunt Paula, recently widowed, invests $10,000 of her inheritance in the company. The STS operating agreement states that John will be in full control of day-to-day operations. John and Paula agree in writing that John will receive a salary of no more than $4,000 a month from STS for the first four years, and that Paula will receive 60% of STS profits during that period. After that, John's salary will be tied to gross receipts, and John and Paula will share profits equally.
- Stella wants to start a travel agency. She approaches Edgar, a friend from college days, who has just sold a screenplay to a major studio and is looking for investment opportunities. They agree that Stella will form a limited partnership and act as the general partner. Edgar will invest $60,000 in the business and

become a limited partner. Stella will work for $3,000 a month and use the first profits of the travel agency to pay back Edgar's $60,000 investment. After that, the profits will be split 50–50.

- Larry, an experienced carpenter, wants to become a general contractor so he can build custom homes and do major remodeling jobs. He's able to invest his savings of $30,000 in his new venture, but needs another $20,000 to get started. Larry forms a corporation, Prestige Homes, Inc., and invites his friend Brook, who owns a building supply business, to invest $20,000 in return for a 40% interest in Prestige Homes. Brook agrees, on the condition that the new corporation will buy all its lumber and other building materials from Brook's company—and, in addition, pay Brook $5,000 for each home that's built by Prestige Homes. They sign a shareholders' agreement containing those terms.

Compliance With Securities Regulations

The law treats corporate shares and limited partnership interests as securities. Issuing these securities to investors is regulated by federal and state law. In some cases, an investor's interest in a limited liability company might also come under these laws.

This means that before selling an investor an interest in your business, you'll need to learn more about the requirements of the securities laws. Fortunately, there are generous exemptions that normally allow a small business to provide a limited number of investors an interest in a business without complicated paperwork. Chances are good that your business will be able to qualify for these exemptions.

In the rare cases in which the exemptions won't work for your small business and you have to meet the complex requirements of the securities laws— such as distributing an approved prospectus to potential investors—it's probably too much trouble to do the deal unless a great deal of money is involved.

 RESOURCE

For a first-rate introduction to securities laws and the exemptions for small businesses, see *Incorporate Your Business: A Step-by-Step Guide to Forming a Corporation in Any State* or *How to Form Your Own California Corporation*, both by Anthony Mancuso (Nolo).

Thirteen Common Sources of Money

Though there are many sources of money for a small business, some are more accessible than others. There are 13 that entrepreneurs tend to rely on most frequently.

Salary

"Don't give up your day job." That's the advice commonly given to aspiring actors and musicians —but it's equally applicable to many entrepreneurs who are testing the waters. If you start small enough, you might be able to stay afloat for many months by continuing your full-time job or cutting back to part time. This steady source of income can reduce your need for turning to others for start-up funds and can help keep you solvent if the business doesn't succeed.

Personal Savings

Putting your own money into your business is the simplest way to get started or to expand your business. You avoid entanglements with others, keep your business affairs private, and steer clear of possible legal complications.

If your business takes off, you'll own business assets—such as inventory, equipment, and furniture —free of debt, making it easier to borrow money later or bring equity investors into the business.

Your money may come from savings that you've carefully accumulated over the years. Or it may come from a lump sum of money that's available all at once. For example, you might have received an inheritance from a relative or an attractive severance package from a job you've just left. Or perhaps you've sold your house and will be living in a less expensive one or in rented quarters. Investing this money in your own business might yield a bigger return than you could ever expect to receive by investing it in someone else's business.

If You're the Beneficiary of a Trust Fund

Another possible source of funds can be a trust fund established on your behalf at the death of a parent, a grandparent, or another relative. Often these funds provide the beneficiary with income for a number of years before the trust ends and all remaining funds are turned over to the beneficiary in a lump sum. However, in the meantime, the trustee often has the discretionary power to take additional money out of the trust for a good reason, such as education, health needs, and possibly starting a business.

Because the trustee's discretion will be tied to the specific wording of the trust document, you'll want to read it carefully. But assuming that distributing money for a business venture would qualify as a proper purpose under the trust, you should present your business plan to the trustee. If the trustee agrees that your plan has merit, this can magically free up the cash you're looking for.

CAUTION
Try to keep some cash in reserve. Because no business is risk free and cash flow is usually unpredictable, it makes sense not to commit every last dollar to your business. Yes, this can be extremely hard to do. But if you can plan well enough to keep a reasonable amount of cash on hand to cover several months' worth of living expenses and possible medical emergencies, you'll improve your odds of succeeding in business. And you'll receive an added bonus of not having to worry constantly about how to pay personal bills.

Equity in Your Home

If you own a home, you might be able to tap into a portion of the equity to raise cash. As you know, "equity" is the difference between what the home is worth and how much is left on the mortgage. Let's say you bought your home several years ago for $150,000 by paying $30,000 down and getting a $120,000 mortgage. Today, the house would sell for $200,000 and the mortgage balance is down to $100,000. You have $100,000 in equity—some of which you can use to help finance your business.

There are two ways to get your hands on a portion of the equity. One is to get a new, larger mortgage that will pay off the earlier one and still yield some cash. For example, if you get a new mortgage for $160,000—which is 80% of the home's current value and likely to be approved by a conservative lender—you'll have $60,000 after the earlier mortgage balance of $100,000 is paid off.

Unfortunately, the actual amount you'll end up with will be significantly less because the bank will require you to pay some hefty costs for processing the mortgage. These transaction costs typically include an application fee, document preparation fees, closing costs known as points, fees for a personal credit check, an appraisal of the home, and mortgage title insurance.

CAUTION
Plan carefully before applying for a new mortgage. If your purpose in getting a new mortgage is to raise a relatively small amount of money for your business, make sure you understand all of the costs involved. Obviously, unless it's your only way to raise money, you don't want to plunk down $2,000 in expenses to get your hands on $10,000 that, of course, will also require you to pay interest. Before applying for a mortgage, ask the lender to itemize the costs involved. Also, if you're planning to quit your job or cut back to half-time to run the business, it might be wise to wait until after the mortgage loan has been made—especially if you don't have a spouse or significant other earning a decent income. This is because before approving the

new mortgage, the lender will be looking at your ability to repay. Having a steady source of income from a job when you apply for and receive a mortgage loan can help convince the lender to approve the loan.

The second approach is to apply for a line of credit based on your home equity. The bank will have a second mortgage on your home. Using the assumptions in the example, you might be able to obtain a line of credit for $60,000. Typically, the bank will give you a checkbook that you can use to write checks against the line of credit. Your monthly payment to the bank will depend on how much of the credit line you've used.

Deciding which method to use can be difficult. A line of credit will likely cost less to set up—perhaps there will simply be a $250 up-front fee rather than a few thousand dollars in closing costs for a mortgage—but the interest rate will likely be higher or, if the loan has a variable interest rate, the bank will have the right to increase the interest rate if interest rates in the overall economy rise.

 TIP

Don't overdo borrowing against your house. Whichever method you use to borrow against your house, you put your home at risk if you can't meet the repayment schedule. You don't want to lose your house to the lender or be forced to sell under pressure of an imminent foreclosure to save a portion of the equity. So don't borrow more than you absolutely need. Also, take time to figure out how you'll make the mortgage payments if your business is slow to get off the ground or you end up closing it. One good approach is to look for a loan with a long repayment window and, hence, lower monthly payments. If your business does well, you can always repay the loan sooner.

Retirement Savings

If you have money in a retirement savings plan where you work, you might be able to borrow some of that money. As you know, income tax on the money you contribute to an IRS-qualified plan—such as a 401(k) plan—is deferred, allowing your retirement to grow faster.

Check the plan language to see whether loans are allowed for business purposes. If so, you should be able to borrow up to one-half of what you have in the plan—but no more than $50,000. Also check other conditions, such as the maximum term allowed for a loan (typically, five years), the interest rate, and the loan fees. You will have to pay interest on the money you borrow from your plan, but that's not all bad. Because the money you're borrowing is yours, the interest goes back into your plan.

Generally, unless you've reached the age of 59½, you wouldn't be wise to simply take rather than borrow money from the tax-deferred plan. Early withdrawals are subject to a penalty tax. After age 59½, however, IRS rules allow you to withdraw funds without paying a penalty tax.

 CAUTION

Don't borrow from an IRA. Unfortunately, if you borrow money from an Individual Retirement Account (IRA), it will be treated as a withdrawal and you'll have to pay a penalty tax if you're not yet 59½ years old.

Credit Cards

You can use your credit cards to help finance your business. Plastic can quickly get you a computer, other business equipment, and furniture. And for expenses such as rent, phone bills, or money to pay employees, you can usually get a cash advance.

Credit cards are a convenient way to arrange for short-term financing because they're so easy to use. Over the long haul, however, they're less attractive—mainly because the interest charges are relatively high, often as much as 20% or more per year. If you're going to succeed in business, you shouldn't need me to tell you not to borrow very much for very long at those rates.

Buying on Credit

The companies from which you're buying goods or services might offer favorable credit terms to capture your business. Often this will mean you don't have to pay your bill for 30, 60, or more days. Or you might be able to spread payments for a purchase over a period of several months with no finance charges as long as you pay each installment on time. And the interest rate that's charged could be substantially lower than that charged by a credit card company.

Don't be discouraged by the fact that the best credit terms usually go to established businesses and that new businesses typically have to pay up front. Credit decisions are somewhat subjective, leaving you room to convince the seller that your new business deserves special consideration.

Especially if you'll need starting inventory, as in the case of a retail store, call suppliers and ask for help. Show them a copy of your credit history and business plan. If they look good and you're persuasive, you might be able to get a fair amount of your inventory on favorable terms.

Leasing

If you need equipment—anything from computers and copiers to forklifts and trucks—consider leasing it. Leasing doesn't put money directly in your hands but, almost as good from a cash flow point of view, the amount of cash you have to come up with to lease is much less than the cost of buying the same equipment. And many leases offer you the option to acquire the equipment for a nominal amount when the lease period is over.

Over the long term, leasing usually costs more than buying—but if the cash flow from your business will be tight for a few years, leasing can be an effective way to get the equipment you need now.

Friends, Relatives, and Business Associates

Those close to you can often lend you money or invest in your business. This helps you avoid the hassle of pleading your case to outsiders and enduring extra paperwork and bureaucratic delays—and can be especially valuable if you've been

through bankruptcy or had other credit problems that would make borrowing from a commercial lender difficult or impossible.

Some advantages of borrowing money from people you know well are that you might be charged a lower interest rate; you could be able to delay paying back money until you're more established; and you might get more flexibility if you get into a jam. But once the loan terms are agreed upon, there's one thing that borrowing from friends, relatives, or business associates doesn't do: It doesn't legally diminish your obligation to meet those terms.

In addition, borrowing money from relatives and friends can have a big downside. There's always the possibility that if your business does poorly and those close to you end up losing money, you'll damage a good personal relationship. So in dealing with friends, relatives, and business associates, be extra careful to not only clearly establish the terms of the deal and put it in writing, but also make an extra effort to explain the risks. In short, it's your job to make sure your helpful friend or relative won't suffer a true hardship if you're unable to meet your financial commitments.

CAUTION

Don't borrow from people on fixed incomes. Don't borrow or accept investment money from folks who can't afford to lose money. It's fine to borrow needed money from your mom if she's well enough off that lending you $20,000 won't put her in the poorhouse if things go wrong and you can't repay the loan. But if your mom lives on Social Security, don't borrow her last $10,000 no matter how badly you need it.

TIP

How to promote family harmony. If your parents give you money for your business, it might make sense for them to make equal gifts to their other children. Or if your parents aren't financially able to do this, they can even things out by leaving your siblings more in a will or trust. If this is done, the reason for the discrepancy can be explained in the will or trust itself, or in a separate letter.

Gifts Can Save Taxes

If you're likely to inherit money from a parent or grandparent in the future, it can make sense for them to make a gift now. Why? Because if a family member's estate exceeds a certain amount ($11.7 million in 2021), the excess will be heavily taxed by the federal government when that person dies.

By contrast, up to fairly generous limits, there will be no estate or gift tax on the money the relative gives away while alive. Specifically, for 2021, an individual can make a gift of up to $15,000 per year per person free of any federal gift or estate tax—and a couple can give twice that amount.

For example, your mother and father can each give $15,000 to you and $15,000 to your spouse—a total of $60,000—in one year. This has the effect of removing this money from their estates with neither a federal estate nor gift tax. Obviously, gifts of that size can be a big boost to any small business because there is no worry about the need to repay. The $11.18 million estate tax exemption and the $15,000 annual gift amount are the figures for 2018. These numbers are subject to change in future years. For updates, check the Legal Updates for the Wills, Trusts & Estates section of www.nolo.com.

Supporters

As Mike McKeever points out in *How to Write a Business Plan* (Nolo), many types of businesses have loyal and devoted followers—people who care as much about the business as the owners do. A health food restaurant, a women's bookstore, an imported car repair shop, or an art studio, for example, might attract people who are enthusiastic about lending money to or investing in the business because it fits in with their lifestyle or beliefs.

Their decision to participate is driven to some extent by their feelings and is not strictly a business proposition. These people can also be a source of great ideas—ideas that can be as valuable as money —and they'll probably be happy to share them with you at no charge.

The rules for borrowing from friends and relatives apply here as well. Put repayment terms in writing—and don't accept money from people who can't afford the risk.

Banks

Banks are in the money business, so it's natural to look to them for start-up funds. It's hard to predict, however, whether the banks you approach will be willing to lend you money on reasonable terms.

Historically, banks were reluctant to lend a substantial sum to a new business, even if the owner was willing to pledge a house or other valuable asset as security for repayment (for example, by giving the bank a second mortgage). Often this reluctance to lend was because loan officers were looking for an established record of business profitability, which, of course, a new business couldn't provide.

Consider a Line of Credit

A line of credit is often better than an outright loan. You can draw against a line of credit as you need funds and not have to pay interest on sums you don't currently need. Be aware, however, that a line of credit can take one of two forms:

- **Contractual line of credit.** Here, you pay a fee up front to the bank, and the bank reserves money for you up to the full amount of the credit line. The bank makes a commitment to have the money available if and when you ask for it.
- **Guidance line of credit.** There's no up-front fee. The bank simply sends you a "guidance letter" saying that you have a line of credit and that the bank will review the credit line from time to time. You might feel good about getting such a letter, but there's no assurance that the money will be available when you really need it.

Fortunately, that standoffish attitude is starting to crumble. Many banks, in fact, have departments geared especially to the needs of small businesses—and some are even eager to establish a banking relationship with those just getting started. With a little luck, you might be able to locate such an enlightened, small-business-oriented bank in your community. As you might imagine, banks offer their best terms to businesses that appear the least risky and that are likely to maintain sizable deposits as the business grows.

The Five C's of Credit

Bankers like to speak of the five C's of credit analysis—factors they look at when they evaluate a loan request. When applying to a bank for a loan, be prepared to address these points:

- **Character.** Bankers lend money to borrowers who appear honest and who have a good credit history. Before you apply for a loan, obtain a copy of your credit report and clean up any problems.
- **Capacity.** This is a prediction of the borrower's ability to repay the loan. For a new business, bankers look at the business plan. For an existing business, bankers consider financial statements and industry trends.
- **Collateral.** Bankers generally want a borrower to pledge an asset that can be sold to pay off the loan if the borrower lacks funds.
- **Capital.** The borrower's net worth—the amount by which assets exceed debts—is scrutinized.
- **Conditions.** The current economic climate can influence whether a loan is given and the amount of the loan.

Banks tend to respond more favorably to loan applications when the requested loan has been guaranteed by the Small Business Administration (SBA). Two SBA loan programs are particularly worth a look:

- **Basic 7(a) Loan Program.** If you qualify, the SBA can guarantee up to 85% of a loan; the loan can't exceed $5 million. You can use the loan proceeds for most sound business purposes, such as working capital, equipment, and buying or renovating a building. You get the loan from a commercial lender, and the SBA supplies the guarantee.
- **Microloans.** These are short-term loans to let you buy inventory, supplies, furniture, fixtures, and equipment. You can borrow up to $50,000, but the average loan is about $13,000. You apply through a local intermediary lender—a nonprofit organization with experience in lending and in giving technical assistance. The SBA provides the funds.

Other Commercial Lenders

If you can't get a bank loan, consider applying to other commercial lenders. More than one-third of the money loaned to small businesses comes from non-bank sources. They're often less tightfisted than banks and might give more weight to intangible factors like your business vision and personal integrity. You'll be in an especially good position to borrow from a non-bank lender if your loan qualifies for SBA backing.

Venture Capitalists

There are companies and individuals looking to invest in extraordinary companies that will reward them with large profits. See if your city has a venture capital club that helps introduce new businesses to venture capitalists. If so, get in contact and find out how you can meet potential investors.

Often, you'll be afforded a chance to make a short presentation that can make an impression on someone with deep pockets. Your local or state chamber of commerce should be able to direct you to the closest club, or you can check with the instructor of a business school that offers courses in entrepreneurship.

The Seller of an Existing Business

If you're buying an existing business, you might be able to negotiate favorable payment terms—which can reduce the amount of cash you have to come up with. You have a number of variables to work with. Try to keep the down payment low and see if the seller will agree to below-market interest rates or will even charge no interest for the first year or two.

Try, too, to extend the payments over as many years as possible. As with a bank loan, you can always pay the debt off early if your business prospers. (For more on buying a business, see Chapter 10.)

Document All of the Money You Receive

In raising money for your business, you should be familiar with the related basic paperwork and other legal requirements, a number of which I've already mentioned in this chapter.

Gifts

If a family member gives you money for your business, it's smart to put it in writing. Strictly speaking, this isn't a legal requirement, but nevertheless I highly recommend that you do so. For one thing, it can help with taxes. An individual can make a gift each year of up to $15,000 (as of 2021) to any number of people. These gifts won't be subject to either the federal estate or gift tax. (See "Gifts Can Save Taxes," above.) The $15,000 figure is in effect for 2021 and is subject to change in future years. If the giver states in writing that the money is a gift and not a loan, it will be clear to the IRS that no tax is owed.

A second reason to document the gift is to avoid possible future misunderstandings with other people who eventually inherit from the giver. Incredible as it might seem, brothers and sisters have sometimes gone to court to argue that a sum of money that a parent advanced to one child should be treated

not as a gift but as a loan to be repaid to the estate. And even where siblings haven't resorted to such drastic action, doubts about a parent's intentions can simmer beneath the surface for years, hurting relationships.

Loans Without Security

The way to document a loan is through a promissory note.

Banks and other commercial lenders will have their own forms for you to sign. The following forms can be used if you borrow money from a relative or friend.

Sample Promissory Note for Installment Payments That Include Principal and Interest

September 1, 20xx

For value received, I promise to pay to Leo Lender $10,000 and interest at the rate of 10% per annum on the unpaid balance as follows:

1. I will pay 60 monthly installments of $212.48 each.

2. I will pay the first installment on October 1, 20xx, and a similar installment on the first day of each month after that until principal and interest have been paid in full.

3. Payments will be applied first on interest and then on principal.

4. I will pay the entire amount of principal and interest within five years from the date of this note.

5. I may prepay all or any part of the principal without penalty.

6. If I am more than ten days late in making any payment, Leo Lender may declare that the entire balance of the unpaid principal is due immediately, together with the interest that has accrued.

_____

Bob Borrower

RESOURCE

Where to find promissory notes. Nolo offers promissory notes for various types of business loans, such as ones with interest-only payments or with amortized payments. For the complete list of online promissory notes, see www.nolo.com/products/promissory-notes. Promissory notes are also included in *Legal Forms for Starting & Running a Small Business*, by Fred S. Steingold (Nolo).

Sample Promissory Note for Annual Interest Payments and Balloon Payment of Principal

---

September 1, 20xx

For value received, I promise to pay to Leo Lender $10,000 and interest at the rate of 10% per annum on the unpaid balance as follows:

1. I will pay interest on September 1 each year for five years beginning in 20xx.

2. I will pay the principal five years from the date of this note.

3. I may prepay all or any part of the principal without penalty.

4. If I am more than 10 days late in making any payment, Leo Lender may declare that the principal is due immediately, together with the interest that has accrued.

_____

Bob Borrower

Sample Promissory Note for Lump Sum Repayment

September 1, 20xx

For value received, I promise to pay to Leo Lender $10,000 and interest at the rate of 10% per annum on the unpaid balance on [*insert date when the entire $10,000 plus interest is due*]. I may prepay all or any part of the principal without penalty.

_____

Bob Borrower

Loans With Security

If you're pledging property as security for a loan, you can start with one of the sample forms shown above—but the promissory note should also state that it's a secured loan and that additional documents have been prepared and are being signed to fully protect the lender.

Commercial lenders will generally prepare these additional documents. When you're borrowing from a friend or family member, however, and pledging security for the loan, you and the lender will need to follow through on these details.

Note Secured by Personal Property

Personal property is property that's not real estate —equipment and inventory, for example. If you're pledging personal property as security, here is sample language to include in a promissory note.

Secured Interest Provision

I agree that until the principal and interest owed under this note are paid in full, the note will be secured by a security agreement signed today giving (*lender's name*) a security interest in the equipment, fixtures, inventory, and accounts receivable of the business known as (*name of borrower's business*).

You should prepare and sign a separate security agreement that gives the lender the right to take the specified assets if you don't repay your loan as agreed. Also, if you do grant a security interest, the lender may complete a *Uniform Commercial Code Financing Statement*—sometimes called Form UCC-1. The form is typically available online at the website of a state government office, such as a secretary of state's office.

The lender should file the completed form with the appropriate state office. In addition, in many states, the lender should also file a copy at the county office that keeps records of liens on personal property. The form notifies future creditors that the lender is a secured creditor and holds a lien on the listed assets. When you pay off the loan, the lender should release the lien—and, as with real estate liens, the release should be filed at the same public office where the Form UCC-1 was filed.

If you pledge a car or truck, check with the office in your state that handles motor vehicle titles to learn how to record the fact that the lender is obtaining a security interest in the car or truck.

Note Secured by Real Estate

Here is sample language to include in a note secured by real estate.

Secured Interest Provision

I agree that until the principal and interest owed under this note are paid in full, the note will be secured by a mortgage [*or deed of trust*] to real estate commonly known as (*address or other description*) , owned by (*name*) signed on (*date*), and recorded at (*place recorded*).

You'll probably need professional help in preparing the mortgage or deed of trust. This is routine stuff for an experienced real estate lawyer, so you should be able to get it done by paying for about an hour of a lawyer's time.

The mortgage or deed of trust will have to be witnessed and notarized, and then get recorded for a small fee at a government office that handles real estate registrations. To learn the name and location of the correct government office, call the county clerk or inquire at a title insurance company.

 CAUTION

Be sure the security interest gets canceled. You don't want to face problems ten years from now when you sell the real estate. So, when you pay off the loan, don't forget to get a paper signed by the lender that releases or discharges the mortgage or deed of trust. The document, which will need to be witnessed and notarized, must be filed at the same place where the mortgage or deed of trust was filed. Again, you'd be wise to consult briefly with a lawyer or check with a local title insurance company to make sure you're doing this correctly.

Equity Investments

Equity investments in a limited partnership, corporation, or limited liability company are usually treated as securities, which are regulated by federal and state laws. It's unlikely that this will be a problem for a small business with just a few owners and investors. Investments in these businesses are usually exempt from the regulations. If that's so in your case, you won't have to deal with the sometimes burdensome paperwork.

If, however, you decide to "go public"—offer interests in your company for sale to the public—then you definitely need to seek detailed legal advice.

Whether or not you must meet special requirements under federal or state laws regulating securities, you should always have a written agreement with an equity investor. The mechanics will depend on the legal structure of your business:

- **Sole Proprietorship.** By definition, a sole proprietorship is owned by just one person. Anyone else who invests in your business and acquires equity in it becomes a co-owner—which means that, legally, your sole proprietorship is converted into a partnership. It makes sense to sign a partnership agreement outlining your responsibilities and those of the investor (see Chapter 2).
- **Partnership.** An equity investor in a partnership is a partner, so you should amend your partnership agreement to include your new partner and specify the financial relationships. All partners—old and new—should sign it. (Again, see Chapter 2 for help on partnership agreements and consult *Form a Partnership: The Complete Legal Guide,* by Denis Clifford and Ralph Warner (Nolo).)
- **Limited Partnership.** Any investor who will play a passive role and won't be actively involved in running the business will be a limited partner. Your limited partnership agreement will define how the limited partner gets money from the business. You will give the limited partner a certificate recognizing his or her interest in the limited partnership.

- **Corporation.** The equity investor will be a shareholder. You, the equity investor, and all other shareholders should sign a shareholders' agreement—or amend the existing agreement if there is one—to spell out the corporation's obligations to the new investor. The corporation should issue a stock certificate in the investor's name.

- **Limited Liability Company.** The equity investor will be a member. You, the equity investor, and all other members of the LLC should sign an operating agreement—or amend the existing operating agreement, if there is one.

Buying a Business

For those who would like to own their own business, buying an existing business might be a better approach than starting from scratch. After all, there's something attractive about letting someone else find a location and sign a lease; test the market and develop a customer base; buy furniture, fixtures, equipment, and inventory; hire employees; and perform the countless other chores that go with starting a business. In short, someone else will prove for you that the business works.

If you find yourself looking for an existing business to buy, keep an open mind. It's not always possible to buy a business you'll be happy with at a price you can afford. Many people who buy existing businesses do very well, but others, having explored the opportunities and finding nothing to their liking, return to the idea of starting their own business. And some people pay too much money for a poor business or one they might never really enjoy operating.

This chapter first looks at how to find a business to buy. Then it turns to the nuts and bolts of actually buying a business, including how to structure the purchase, what to investigate before closing the deal, and the legal documents needed for a business to change hands.

This chapter focuses on buying a business, but a seller's concerns are also discussed briefly under "Selling a Business," below.

RESOURCE

For in-depth guidance, and a full set of forms, on how to buy a business, see *The Complete Guide to Buying a Business,* by Fred S. Steingold (Nolo).

Finding a Business to Buy

Before you look for a business to buy, narrow your field of possible choices. First, decide whether you want to be in a service, manufacturing, wholesale, retail, or food service business. Once you make this choice, consider the specific type of business you're interested in—perhaps a desktop publishing center, a management consulting business, a direct-mail processing business, a dance studio, a flower shop, or a used bookstore.

Your choice of business should be motivated by the type of work you've done in the past, courses you've taken, special skills you've developed through a hobby, or perhaps just a strong yearning to work in a particular field. It's almost always a mistake to consider buying a business you know little about, no matter how good it looks. For example, if you're confused by mechanical and electronic equipment, buying an auto tune-up shop or a business that installs security systems makes little sense even if the business looks like a bargain.

If you're currently employed by a small business you like, what are the chances of that business becoming available to you? Maybe the current owner wants to retire, is in bad health, is moving out of the city, or is just getting bored. If you know the inner workings of the business and are sure that it's doing well—or at least that it has the potential to flower under your able leadership—that would be an ideal place to start. Failing that, perhaps business associates or friends could provide you with leads to similar businesses that could be available.

Here are some other time-tested ways to search for an available business:

- **Newspaper and online ads.** This is a traditional starting point and can quickly put you in touch with people who are actively seeking a buyer for their business. Check websites such as www.bizbuysell.com, www.businessesforsale.com, www.bizquest.com, and even www.craigslist.org. Unfortunately, ads are only the tip of the iceberg. Many of the best business opportunities never get published but surface by word of mouth.

- **Professionals who advise small businesses.** Bankers, lawyers, accountants, insurance agents, and real estate brokers who regularly work with small businesses often know about available businesses before they go on the market. Think about who you know who is plugged into this network and get on the phone. A few well-placed phone calls might be enough to identify likely candidates in your area.

- **Business suppliers.** Another great way to tap into the grapevine is to contact the network of suppliers for that business. For example, if you're thinking of opening a flower shop, a floral wholesaler in your area will probably know who is thinking of retiring or selling out for other reasons.
- **Trade associations.** Almost every business has a local or regional trade association—for example, the Northern California Independent Booksellers Association or the Michigan Pest Management Association. An employee or associate of such a group might have heard about a business owner who's thinking of retiring.
- **The direct approach.** If there's a business that you've admired from afar, simply drop in and politely ask if the owner has ever thought about selling. Who knows? Maybe that person has been thinking about moving to another part of the country or changing to a different type of business. Once in a while, you'll be in the right place at the right time. A long shot? Probably—but you have nothing to lose by trying it.
- **Business brokers.** Finally, there are business brokers—people who earn commissions from business owners who need help finding buyers. As is true in all endeavors, not all business brokers are created equal. A few are honest, ingenious, and hardworking. Many more are adequate but nothing special when it comes to competence, energy, and integrity. More than a few are sleazy, incompetent, and interested almost exclusively in earning a commission. In short, before working with a broker, it pays to carefully check out his or her reputation. Several glowing recommendations from a banker, accountant, or fellow small business person should raise your confidence level. On the other hand, if the feedback you get is lukewarm, look for someone else.

It's foolish to rely on a broker—who gets paid only if the deal goes through—for advice about the quality of the business or the fairness of its price. If you do, the picture painted will almost surely be an unrealistically rosy one. Also, because the seller typically pays the broker, the broker's loyalty will be to the seller—not to you. Use a broker only to find a business, not to negotiate the purchase price and other terms. See "The Sales Agreement," below, on drafting the documents involved, particularly the purchase agreement.

What's the Structure of the Business You Want to Buy?

If you find a business you're interested in, one important question is: What kind of legal entity owns the business—a sole proprietorship, partnership, corporation, or limited liability company?

Buying From a Sole Proprietor or Partnership

When you buy a business from a sole proprietor or a partnership, you never acquire the old legal structure of the business, only its assets (and possibly its liabilities, depending on how your deal with the seller is structured).

Legally, it's simplest to buy a business from a sole proprietor, because one person owns the business and the assets are in his or her name. Buying from a partnership is almost as simple, although a partnership agreement typically requires the consent of all owners before the business can be sold. If you're dealing with only one partner in a partnership, to avoid disappointment, promptly ask to see the partnership agreement. Then make sure that the person negotiating the deal has received proper authority from the other owners. Beyond that, get a clear understanding early on about whether you'll be buying only the assets of the business, or whether the seller is also trying to get you to assume responsibility for all liabilities. (Entity sales of a partnership are rare.)

CAUTION
It's best to avoid assuming business liabilities. You'll avoid many potential legal and debt entanglements if you insist on buying the business's assets only (even if this means a higher price). But whatever you and the seller decide, it's vital that you clearly record your understanding in the purchase documents.

TIP
Changing a business's structure. A new owner is free to change the legal form of a business. For example, you can buy a business from a sole proprietor and then operate it through a partnership or corporation.

Buying From a Corporation

When you buy a business owned by a corporation, you run into a special problem: figuring out the best way to structure your purchase. You can buy the corporate entity itself (the stock) or you can buy only its assets, leaving the seller still owning the corporation minus the assets you purchased.

In almost any purchase of a business, you'll be much better off buying the assets rather than the corporate stock. Buying assets has four distinct advantages:

- It helps you avoid the liabilities of the existing business.
- It gives you significant tax advantages.
- You can avoid acquiring unwanted assets from the corporation.
- You generally can get a higher tax basis for depreciable assets, which means there's less taxable gain to report if you later sell the assets.

EXAMPLE OF STOCK PURCHASE: Brown Manufacturing, Inc., is a small corporation owned by Joseph Brown and his two sons. The company, which makes specialized computer circuit boards, owns a small factory, several machines, raw materials, an inventory of completed items, office furniture and equipment, and two delivery trucks. The corporation owns all of the assets of the business. In a stock purchase, you'd buy 100% of the corporation's stock from Joseph Brown and his sons. As the new owner, you'd elect yourself (and anyone else you choose) to the board of directors; the board would then typically appoint you to the office of president.

Get the Consent of Shareholders When You Purchase Corporate Assets

Remember that a corporation is a separate legal entity from its owners—the shareholders. When you purchase a small corporation's assets, you want to avoid the possibility of dealing with disgruntled minority owners. Even though the corporation's bylaws or shareholders' agreement might permit the corporation to sell its assets with the consent of the holders of a majority of the shares, it's far safer for you legally to insist that all shareholders agree to the asset sale. Get this consent in writing by:

- requiring that all shareholders sign the purchase contract, and
- asking that all of the corporation's shareholders and directors sign and give you a copy of an official corporate resolution authorizing the sale of assets.

A big bonus that comes with insisting that all shareholders sign the purchase contract is that they then become personally liable for the warranties and representations in the contract. Without their signatures, should things go wrong, your only recourse would be against the corporation, which by that time would probably be without funds. You can also include language committing each shareholder to any noncompetition clause in the agreement—but as with other noncompete covenants, you must pay the signer something to make the covenant legally binding.

EXAMPLE OF ASSET PURCHASE: You want to buy the business operated by Brown Manufacturing, Inc., but instead of buying the corporate stock, the corporation sells you all or most of its assets, such as the factory, the machines, the trucks, and several patents and trade secrets associated with circuit board assembly. The seller would continue to own Brown Manufacturing, Inc., minus its assets. You would use these assets to run the manufacturing business as a sole proprietorship or partnership (if you have one or more business associates), or perhaps you would choose to place the assets in your newly formed corporation or LLC.

Corporate Liabilities

If you buy the stock of a corporation, you're buying not only its assets but any liabilities as well. This is fine if there aren't any liabilities, but this can be difficult to determine. Maybe the corporation owes federal income taxes that you don't know about or has a huge balance to pay on a bank loan. Or maybe a customer slipped in the entryway of the business three months ago, broke his leg, and is right now visiting a lawyer to prepare a million-dollar lawsuit. Or maybe there's an underground storage tank quietly leaking into the earth below the corporation's main office. Hidden liabilities can surface for injuries caused by defective products, discrimination against employees, or environmental or safety violations, to name but a few.

In addition, the business might have contracts that you don't want to assume. For example, the corporation might have a five-year maintenance contract for service on the computers it owns—and there could be four more years to go, at a rate you consider exorbitant.

You can protect yourself against some unknown liabilities. A good investigation will uncover many (though not all) potential liabilities. And personal warranties from the seller guaranteeing payment of any liabilities not disclosed can give you someone to turn to if unknown or undisclosed liabilities suddenly surface. Insurance might cover some of these risks, such as claims for injuries caused by defective products. But the point remains—if you buy a corporation, it's almost impossible to get 100% protection from its obligations.

In contrast, by buying the assets of the corporation rather than the corporate stock, you can avoid virtually all of these liability problems as long as you don't lead creditors to believe that you're picking up the liabilities of the corporation.

It's important to realize, however, that under some circumstances, if you continue the business of the prior corporation, you or your new corporation might still be subject to some liabilities incurred by the old corporation even if you purchase only assets. Known in legal lingo as "successor liability," the most common area of concern is product liability—liability to a person injured by a defective product.

This is particularly likely to arise if you buy the assets of a corporation that manufactured a potentially hazardous consumer product and you directly continue the business. Each state has its own legal rules governing what constitutes a sufficient link (often called continuity) between the first manufacturer and the second to hold the second liable. One court ruled that there might be such a link if:

- there is a continuation of the management, personnel, physical location, assets, and general business operations of the selling corporation
- the selling corporation quickly ceased its ordinary business operations and then liquidated and dissolved, and
- the purchasing company assumed the liabilities and obligations of the seller ordinarily necessary for continuing the business operations of the selling corporation.

In addition, depending on state law, a company that's just a continuation of an earlier corporation might be liable for other legal problems of the earlier corporation—for example, a wrongful discharge case brought by an ex-employee—or even for contractual obligations such as a union contract.

The good news is that if you're fully informed about the law in your state, you can usually anticipate any successor liability problems and structure your purchase to avoid them. Or you might be able to buy insurance—often called "tail coverage"—to protect you from the long tail of the old corporation's liabilities.

Tax Advantages

You might be able to get several kinds of tax advantages in an asset purchase because you can allocate the purchase price among various assets you buy. As long as this allocation is based on an arm's-length negotiation between you and the seller, it's likely to be upheld by the IRS.

You want to allocate the greater portion of the purchase price to assets you can quickly write off or depreciate on your tax returns. These include things like the inventory of the business, supplies, machinery, equipment and vehicles, furniture, and fixtures.

On the other hand, you'll want to assign minimally reasonable values to assets that can't be deducted as current expenses, depreciated, or amortized. This includes such assets as goodwill, trademarks, customer lists, and trade names. (How to allocate purchase price to different assets you're buying is discussed under "The Sales Agreement," below.)

In addition, by buying assets rather than corporate stock, you can depreciate assets that the seller has already fully depreciated.

> **EXAMPLE:** Arthur is buying a dry cleaning business. The business has dry cleaning equipment that's ten years old but in excellent condition. The owner has fully depreciated it. Arthur and the seller allocate $30,000 of the purchase price to the equipment. That way, Arthur can start to depreciate it a second time. If Arthur bought the corporate stock, he wouldn't be able to take any depreciation for this equipment.

Exceptions: When You Must or Should Purchase Stock

In some situations, you might not be able to swing a deal in which you buy only corporate assets. This can occur, for example, if the seller insists on a stock sale—perhaps believing there's a tax advantage in going this route. If you agree to this, see "How to Protect Yourself If You Buy Corporate Stock," below.

In some limited circumstances where the corporation has a uniquely valuable asset that can't be transferred, it could actually be better to buy the stock of the corporation rather than its assets. For example, the corporation might have tax benefits such as a net operating loss (NOL) carryover that you want to take advantage of. The NOL carryover would be lost if you purchased the assets rather than the corporate stock. Also, if a store had a favorable five-year lease with a five-year option to renew that isn't freely assignable, that can provide an incentive to you to buy the corporate stock. Or suppose a ski shop has a hard-to-get distributorship for a popular brand of skis. If the distributorship contract can't be assigned to you and you're not sure you can qualify for a similar contract yourself, you might consider buying the corporate stock because the corporation will likely continue to have the rights to be a distributor.

> ⚠ **CAUTION**
>
> **Investigating distributorships.** Even in a stock purchase, you will want to read all contracts carefully and check with the other party to confirm that the other party didn't reserve the right to cancel the contract if the corporate stock changes hands.

How to Protect Yourself If You Buy Corporate Stock

If you do decide to purchase a corporation's stock instead of its assets, protect yourself to the maximum extent possible. Conduct an in-depth investigation of the corporation's financial affairs. Try to get a strong personal guarantee from the shareholders that things are as stated.

You can also get a warranty from the seller to pay for certain types of problems such as tax liabilities, obligations to former employees, or damage claims by the landlord. Then arrange to pay for the business in installments spread over a number of years. Most liabilities will come to light in the first few years after you purchase the business. If the seller fails to make good on his or her warranty, you can pay for these liabilities and then withhold the amounts from the balance you owe the seller.

Also, as mentioned earlier, insurance might be in place or obtainable to protect against product liability and other personal injury claims.

Buying From an LLC

In buying a business from an LLC, you'll have to start by making the same decision as when buying from a corporation: Should you purchase the whole entity (the LLC) or just its assets? In my opinion, you're much better off buying the assets rather than the entity, for the reasons I listed above, in "Buying From a Corporation."

Buying the Entity. If you buy the LLC entity, you won't be buying shares of stock as you would with a corporation. An LLC doesn't issue stock. Instead, you'll purchase the membership interests of all the LLC members. By doing so, you'll wind up owning the LLC, which in turn owns the company's assets.

Buying the Assets. If you simply buy the business's assets, the LLC will transfer the assets to you, leaving the current LLC members with ownership of the LLC shell. (The shell is a company without any assets, except possibly your promissory note for the balance of the purchase price.) To avoid possible problems with dissatisfied LLC members, you should require all members to sign the sales agreement.

Gathering Information About a Business

Buying a business takes weeks or months. During that time you'll need to diligently gather information—lots of information—about the business so that you don't get stung on the purchase price or have surprises later about income, expenses, or undisclosed liabilities. Eventually, this information will help you structure a sound sales agreement.

In most small business purchases, the buyer learns everything possible about the business before signing the sales agreement. By contrast, business brokers sometimes advise making a quick formal offer to purchase with a number of contingencies that allow you to terminate the deal if all the facts don't turn out as represented by the seller. I recommend against this latter approach.

Better to request early access to financial records that will help you decide whether you're really interested in the business. Then if you're satisfied with the finances you can sign a sales agreement with appropriate contingency clauses or wait until closing (legal lingo for the transfer of the business) to sign.

If you and the seller are strangers to one another, however, the seller might be reluctant to turn over sensitive business information until becoming confident that you're a serious buyer. The seller could suspect you have some secret plan in mind, like using the information in a competitive business. To allay these fears, consider giving the seller a confidentiality letter like the one below.

That kind of letter will satisfy many sellers. But a few sellers prefer a longer, more formal confidentiality agreement drafted by a lawyer. That's okay, but you (and perhaps your lawyer as well) should make sure that the proposed document contains no binding commitment to buy the business. It should be limited to your agreement to treat the information as strictly confidential and use it only to investigate the purchase of the business. If the proposed agreement goes further than that, find out why and get legal advice.

Don't be surprised if the seller wants to learn about your own financial status, job, or business history. Remember that most purchases of a small business are done on an installment basis where the seller receives a down payment and other payments over a period of time. The seller is interested in your financial stability, your reputation for integrity, and your general business savvy because the seller, in effect, will be extending credit to you.

Sample Confidentiality Letter

Carlos Mendez, President
Mendez Furniture Company, Inc.
Dear Mr. Mendez:

As you know, I am looking into the purchase of your furniture business. Our conversations have been helpful but I'm now at the stage where I would like to see your company's financial records, including your tax returns, for the past five years.

I know that the information that I'm requesting is confidential and that improper use of the information could damage your business. Consequently, I will use this confidential information only to help me decide whether I want to purchase your business and what the terms of that purchase will be. I will disclose this confidential information only to my coinvestors, my lawyer, and my accountant. I'll make sure that each of these people knows that this information is confidential, and I'll ask them to sign confidentiality agreements before I release the information to them.

If I don't buy your business, I will return all of the confidential information, including any copies, to you and will continue to treat in confidence the information you have disclosed to me.

I look forward to receiving this information.

Sincerely yours,
Suzanne Gerstein
Suzanne Gerstein

Valuing the Business

Does it sound impossibly demanding to determine a fair purchase price for a business? It's really not—especially if you take the sales price with a grain of salt. Most sellers ask for way too much, and far too many inexperienced buyers don't bargain aggressively enough. Lots of little businesses are worth no more than the fair current value of inventory and equipment. Goodwill, over and above the value of the continuing hard work of the owner, is commonly a myth.

What Are You Buying?

Generally, the assets of a business consist of inventory, fixed assets (furniture, fixtures, and equipment), and intangible assets (such as a lease, a trade name, customer lists, and goodwill). The most important factor in establishing the fair market value of these assets is this: Given the realities of the business and the industry in which it operates, what kind of return would a buyer reasonably expect on his or her investment? To arrive at this number, an appraiser will look both at the business's earnings and what similar businesses typically earn.

Goodwill Can Be a Myth

Be very careful about what you pay for goodwill—the portion of the purchase price attributed to such intangible factors as the reputation of the business, its location, and the loyalty of its customers. Despite what sellers will almost surely tell you, many small businesses have little or no value beyond the value of the hard assets such as furniture, fixtures, and equipment.

How can this be if a business earns a good yearly profit? Easy. Most of the profit is commonly attributable to the hard work, clear vision, and good judgment of the owner, not to the inherent value of the business. Think of it this way: Most rug cleaning businesses, hardware stores, print shops, and restaurants don't make a substantial profit. Those that do are usually run by uniquely talented people. When these people move on, many of those businesses quickly lose their luster.

> **EXAMPLE:** Joe and Monte own Caretti Brothers, a highly successful produce store that they've operated for 20 years. They sell the business to Anna Marie, who pays $200,000, including $100,000 for goodwill. Anna Marie continues

to run the business as Caretti Brothers and does her best to preserve the store's distinctive atmosphere. Nevertheless, in her first year she earns only one-third the profits generated by the former owners.

Unhappily, she realizes that Joe and Monte succeeded because customers valued their extroverted personalities and their rare ability to select only the freshest and tastiest tomatoes and grapefruit. Too late, she understands that she should have paid little or nothing for goodwill, which was largely personal to the Carettis and couldn't be transferred to her.

Goodwill isn't always a myth. Some profitable businesses—usually those that have been established for years and have strong name recognition—are worth significantly more than the value of their tangible assets, because they have a good reputation. Even if the owner retires or sells out, this reputation will continue to bring in business.

Unfortunately, deciding that a business has goodwill is easier than deciding how much. One approach is for buyer and seller to try to agree on a multiplier—the number by which earnings (or sometimes sales) must be multiplied to determine the value of the business.

Where does the multiplier come from? In some industries, there are rough norms. For example, certain types of businesses typically sell for five times earnings, while others often sell for ten or more. Construction companies, retail stores, and restaurants are examples of businesses where you can often obtain standard multipliers from business evaluators or appraisers who specialize in that industry.

> CAUTION
>
> **Be critical of all multipliers.** Never accept a multiplier without loads of caution. The facts of a particular business, the state of the local economy, and industry trends change so quickly that last year's sensible multiplier can be completely off base this year.

Evaluating the Business's Financial Health

To properly evaluate the business, ask for access to the following documents:

- tax returns, profit and loss statements, and balance sheets for the last five years
- loan documents, if you're going to assume any obligations of the business
- papers relating to specific assets; for example, the lease if you're taking over the seller's space or title documents if you're purchasing the seller's building
- patents, trademarks, copyrights, and licenses
- documents that relate to lawsuits, administrative proceedings, and claims against the business, and
- all accountants' reports, including compilation reports, reviews, and audit reports. (See "Types of Accountants' Reports," below.) A full-fledged audit report is the best, but not all small businesses have one available. Whatever type of report the business has, specifically ask for a list of all assets and their depreciation schedules.

In addition, if you're purchasing corporate stock, ask for:

- corporate contracts with major suppliers, as well as contracts obligating the corporation to deliver goods or services, and
- employment agreements, union contracts, and any other documents concerning wage levels and fringe benefit obligations.

Once the books are in your hands, have an experienced small business accountant study them. You and your accountant should look especially hard at the years before the last one. It's relatively easy for a business owner to pump up earnings and depress expenses for a year or two, so assume that the results for the last year at least have been manipulated.

Types of Accountants' Reports

Reports from certified public accountants come in three basic varieties.

Compiled. The CPA compiles the balance sheet of the company and the related statements of income, retained earnings, and cash flows for a specified year. The compilation simply presents, in the form of a financial statement, the information gathered by the owners of the company. The accountant doesn't audit or review the information or offer an opinion about it.

Reviewed. The CPA goes a step further by asking questions of company personnel and analyzing the financial data presented by the owners. Short of a full-scale audit, the CPA certifies only that the review hasn't revealed any material modifications that should be made to the financial statements to conform to generally accepted accounting principles.

Audited. Here, the CPA examines, on a test basis, evidence supporting the amounts and disclosures in the financial statements. For example, the CPA might visit the warehouse to see if it really contains the inventory that's claimed. Also, the accountant assesses the accounting principles used by the owners and evaluates the overall financial statement. If everything is in order, the CPA signs an opinion that the financial statements are accurate and maintained in conformity with generally accepted accounting principles.

TIP

Tips for spotting exaggerated earnings. One way to see if earnings have been exaggerated is to see if there are fewer employees now than previously—almost any business can operate shorthanded for a limited time. Also, check to see whether equipment maintenance or replacement has been deferred by comparing maintenance and replacement costs for the last year with those of the years before.

Expert Help

Consider hiring an experienced appraiser to appraise the business as a whole as well as the individual assets. Check references and be sure the person you pick understands the business field you are entering.

For example, if you're thinking about buying an office supply store, work with someone who thoroughly understands that you'll be competing against national chains such as Office Max, Staples, and Office Depot—companies that maintain huge inventories, and sell online as well as from their big-box stores. Appraisals do cost money, but it's money well spent if it saves you from overpaying for the business.

Where can you turn for an accurate assessment of the value of a business? Here are three suggestions:

- Consult a member of the American Society of Appraisers who specializes in business valuations. For a list of such appraisers visit www.appraisers.org.
- Check with a respected firm of certified public accountants. Many CPA firms offer business valuation services.
- Seek guidance from an experienced business broker. But use caution. Brokers are best at making deals. They often lack the technical training needed for placing a value on a business.

Other Items to Investigate

Now let's look at some other items that are worth investigating before you close on the purchase of a business.

Title to Assets

If real estate is included in the sale, ask to see the deed and the title insurance policy. The title should be rechecked to make sure no new encumbrances appear, and the title insurance policy will need to be updated. Also ask to see ownership documents for any cars and trucks.

It's a good idea to check with the appropriate county or state offices to see if there are liens on any of the vehicles or other equipment or merchandise. Lenders who have taken a security interest in the business or suppliers who have extended credit might have filed a UCC (Uniform Commercial Code) financing statement with the appropriate state agency to record that fact.

Any bank lending officer, small business lawyer, or accountant should be able to tell you where and how to check in your state.

Litigation

Ask to see copies of any lawsuit papers and letters from any people threatening lawsuits. Also check with the court clerk in the main counties in which business is conducted. What you're looking for are actual or threatened lawsuits involving injuries or claimed breaches of contract.

This type of investigation is particularly important when you're buying corporate stock or LLC membership interests—and buying the liabilities of the corporation or LLC along with its assets—but you might also turn up information that will be valuable to an asset purchase. For example, if the business manufactures or distributes aluminum stepladders, finding pending product liability lawsuits will help you determine whether the ladders are safe or need to be redesigned. Also, remember that in a few circumstances even those who purchase assets of a corporation rather than its stock might be held liable for the existing business's liabilities.

Warranties and Guarantees

If you buy corporate stock or LLC membership interests, you want to know what types of warranties the business has extended to its customers so you can anticipate claims. For example, if you buy a business that writes customized computer software, you'll want to know what promises have been made should bugs be discovered in already installed programs.

Workers' Compensation Claims and Unemployment Claims

Check with the business's workers' compensation insurance carrier to learn the claims history of the business and current insurance rates. Also check with the state office handling unemployment affairs to learn what rate is currently applied to the payroll of the business. These facts will be primarily of concern if you're planning to purchase a corporate or LLC entity, because they'll indicate how much you'll probably have to pay for workers' compensation insurance or unemployment coverage. But in some states, even purchasers of an entity's assets may have their future workers' compensation or unemployment rates affected if it looks like the new business is simply a continuation of the old one.

Employee Contracts and Benefits

This is a concern primarily if you'll be buying an entity and will be subject to its contracts. However, if you intend to keep the same employees, you need this information for other types of business purchases as well so that you'll know the employees' expectations when they come to work for your new business entity. They won't be happy campers if you offer them less pay or fewer benefits than they're currently getting.

If it's a concern, ask the seller for permission to talk to key employees to see if they'll stick with you after you buy the business. (Strictly speaking, permission isn't required, but being polite helps bring about a smooth transition.)

Maintenance of Trade Secrets

Not every business has trade secrets, but if the one you're purchasing does—and those secrets are a valuable asset for which you're paying—you want to be sure they've been properly safeguarded. Ask what the business has done to protect its trade secrets and other proprietary information such as customer lists. Has this information been disclosed only to key employees? Have those employees signed confidentiality agreements and covenants not to compete? If not, and key employees leave and set up a competing business, you might be buying a lot less than you bargained for.

Taxes

Taxes are a concern primarily for a purchase of a corporate or LLC entity, because you want to know what tax liabilities are hanging over the head of the entity. But whatever kind of business purchase you're making, you can gain valuable information about the income and expenses of the business, including the kinds of items that have been tax deductible in the past. Check on state and local property taxes and sales taxes, federal and state income taxes, and any special taxes levied by federal and state governments.

Leases

Look carefully at all space and equipment leases. How long does the lease have to run? Is it renewable? And, most important, if you're purchasing the assets of the business, is it transferable? If the lease isn't clearly assignable, check with the landlord or equipment lessor about taking over the lease. If they respond favorably, get a commitment in writing. (For more on real estate leases, see Chapter 13.)

Other Contracts

If the business has contracts with suppliers or customers, become familiar with their terms. In the case of an asset sale, the important question is whether or not the contracts are assignable by the seller. Often, you need the consent of the supplier or customer. For example, if you're buying a gas station, does the oil company have to approve your taking over the contract for that brand of gasoline? Where a contract is freely transferable if all the conditions have been met, make sure the seller isn't in default or otherwise in noncompliance. If there is such noncompliance, you might not be able to enforce the contract.

Patents and Copyrights

Many small businesses don't own patents or copyrights. However, as information becomes a more valuable part of many businesses, patent and copyright issues are cropping up more frequently. Of course, if you're interested in buying a book, software, or music publishing company, you can be pretty sure that the business's most valuable assets will be its intellectual property.

If patents or copyrights are involved, get hold of the basic registration documents and any contracts that give the business the right to exploit these rights. If you're not fully familiar with these matters, have the documents and contracts reviewed by a lawyer who specializes in patent and trademark law.

RESOURCE

Looking for a lawyer? Asking for a referral to an attorney from someone you trust can be a good way to find legal help. Also, two sites that are part of the Nolo family, Lawyers.com and Avvo.com, provide excellent and free lawyer directories. These directories allow you to search by location and area of law, and list detailed information about and reviews of lawyers.

Whether you're just starting your lawyer search or researching particular attorneys, visit www.lawyers.com/find-a-lawyer and www.avvo.com/find-a-lawyer.

Trademarks and Product Names

Trademarks, service marks, business names, and product names might be important assets of the business you're thinking of buying. If so, make sure that you'll have the continuing right to use them. Ask about the extent of any searches for conflicting marks and names, and what has been done to register or otherwise protect the marks and names you'll be taking over. (See Chapter 6 for more on business and product names.)

Licenses and Transferability

Check into any special licenses that you'll need to continue the business. For example, if you're buying a restaurant with a liquor license, is the license transferable? Has the existing business obtained an environmental permit for disposal of its wastes? If so, what about transferability of that permit? (If not, look into your potential liability.) The same goes for other special permits the existing business has, such as a health department license, or a federal license for trucking or broadcasting. (For more on licenses and permits, see Chapter 7.)

Zoning

The existing business might be operating under a temporary zoning variance or a conditional use permit that has important limitations. Learn exactly what the requirements and conditions are and whether you can continue operating under the variance or conditional use permit.

Also, if you buy the business assets rather than corporate stock or LLC membership interests, you could find that you're no longer covered by prior zoning or building preferences; you might, for example, need more parking, better access, and different signs. (See Chapters 7 and 14 for more on zoning and related requirements.)

Toxic Waste

If the business must dispose of toxic waste, or if its activities have any possible adverse impact on the purity of water and air, look into what licenses or permits are needed. Also, if your purchase involves real property, check carefully to see how toxic waste has been handled in the past. Otherwise, you could find yourself stuck with liability for past improprieties.

Franchisor Approval

If you're looking at a business that's operating under a franchise, the seller undoubtedly will need the approval of the franchisor before assigning the franchise to you. Look at the franchise agreement to see exactly what's involved in obtaining the franchisor's approval and then speak directly to the franchisor to see how the approval process can be expedited. (For more on franchises, see Chapter 11.)

Availability of Credit

Find out whether banks and major suppliers will be willing to extend credit to you. Credit might mean the difference between success and failure.

Scuttlebutt

Never rely entirely on documents and public records. You can learn a lot simply by talking to people who have had contact with the existing business—bankers, key customers, suppliers, neighboring businesses, and former employees. When talking to key people, take your time and pay attention to subtleties. Many people are reluctant to talk frankly until they've sized you up, and others will have ties of friendship to the seller or be worried about their own possible legal liability if they divulge unfavorable information about the business.

Letter of Intent to Purchase

If all goes well, you and the seller will eventually agree on most major aspects of the purchase. But you still might not be quite ready to put together a formal sales agreement. Perhaps you need time for additional investigation, or maybe your lawyer, business adviser, or key lender is out of town for a week or two.

One device that can be helpful to keep up the momentum is a nonbinding letter of intent to purchase. The same objective can be accomplished through a more formal "memorandum of intent to purchase"—but a memorandum usually turns out to be more legalistic and, therefore, more threatening to a seller.

Giving the seller a modest, earnest money deposit along with the letter of intent is also helpful, because it shows you're sincerely interested in pursuing the

Sample Letter of Intent to Purchase

Robert Tower, President
The Tower Mart, Inc.
25 Glen Blvd.
Arlington Heights, IL

Dear Robert:

Thanks for meeting with me again last week. I continue to be interested in purchasing the assets of The Tower Mart, Inc. If we reach an agreement regarding my purchase, I plan to transfer these assets to a new corporation that I'm forming. My new company would then run a convenience store similar to what you're currently operating.

I'm interested in purchasing the following assets: the inventory, fixtures, equipment, leasehold improvements, and business name. In addition, I will need all necessary licenses and permits transferred to me. I will expect you to give me a covenant not to compete stating that for three years, you won't open a similar store in our city. The purchase price for all of the assets as well as the goodwill and your covenant not to compete would be $150,000, as we have already discussed.

As an indication of my good faith in pursuing this matter, I am enclosing a check for $1,000 as earnest money. I would pay an additional $49,000 in cash at closing. The balance of $100,000 would be amortized in equal monthly installments over a period of ten years with interest at the rate of 10% per annum.

We will review the inventory at the time of closing. If the inventory is valued at less than $45,000, the purchase price would be reduced accordingly. Also, as you and I discussed, your corporation would remain responsible for all liabilities of the present business. My new corporation would not assume any such liabilities.

Before I have my lawyer draft a sales agreement, there are some things I need to investigate:

1. I want to meet with your landlord to make sure that I can assume the existing lease and that I can get an option to extend it for another five years.
2. I need to have my accountant review all of your tax returns and business records for the past five years so that I can satisfy myself regarding the financial condition of your business.
3. I want to make sure that the state liquor board will approve a transfer of the beer and wine retail license to my new corporation.

Assuming that I'm satisfied with these items and all other aspects of the proposed purchase, I will have my lawyer draft a sales agreement and then we can close approximately 45 days from now.

This letter states my intent but it is not a legally binding contract or commitment on either my part or yours. Upon further investigation I may change my mind. If the deal doesn't go through for any reason, I'll be entitled to my earnest money back.

If my letter has captured the essence of what we talked about and you're still interested in pursuing the sale, please let me know. I believe that we are moving toward a transaction that can be advantageous to both of us.

Sincerely,

Madison Beyer

Madison Beyer

purchase and are not wasting the seller's time. But because details of the purchase have not solidified at this point, be sure to provide that the deposit is to be refunded if the purchase falls through.

A sample nonbinding letter of intent is shown above.

CAUTION

Don't commit yourself. Make it clear in a letter of intent that it is not meant to be a binding contract. You might or might not need your lawyer's assistance in writing a letter of intent, but I do recommend that you call your lawyer to at least check on the adequacy of the language you use to describe the nonbinding nature of the letter.

The Sales Agreement

The sales agreement is the key legal document in buying business assets or an entire corporation or LLC. You should create a written outline of the terms that you and the seller have agreed on. Next, you might want to have your lawyer review it and help draft the next version. Once you and your lawyer are satisfied, present the agreement to the seller.

Why take on the document drafting yourself, rather than letting the seller do it? Because even though it's more time-consuming, this approach will almost surely give you more control over the overall shape of the transaction. By seizing the initiative, you could well wind up with 95% or more of what you want.

This section briefly reviews the principal types of clauses in a business sales agreement. Remember, as discussed earlier, it's almost always better to buy the assets from the corporation than to buy its stock. Accordingly, these clauses are geared primarily to an asset purchase. If for some reason you decide to buy corporate stock, make corresponding changes in your sales agreement.

Names of Seller, Buyer, and Business

Your sales agreement will start with the name and address of the seller and the buyer. It will also identify the business by its current name:

- **Purchase from or by a sole proprietor.** Name the sole proprietor, adding the business name if it's different from the individual's. Example: Michelle Perfect doing business as Perfect Word Processing Service.
- **Purchase from or by a partnership.** Use the partnership's legal name and the names of all partners. Example: Ortega Associates, a Colorado partnership of William Ortega and Henry Cruz.
- **Purchase from or by a corporation.** Simply use the corporate name and identify it by the state where it's registered. Example: XYZ Enterprises, Inc., a Massachusetts corporation.
- **Purchase from or by an LLC.** Just use the LLC name and the state where it's registered. Example: ABC Associates LLC, an Illinois limited liability company.

If you're going to operate the business you're purchasing as a new corporation or LLC, I recommend one of two procedures: Set up the new corporation or LLC before signing the purchase agreement and name the new entity as the purchaser. Or list the purchaser as yourself as the agent of a corporation or LLC to be formed. Using either of these methods, the assets can go directly into your new corporation or LLC rather than having a two-stage process in which you receive the assets and then transfer them to the new entity.

If you're going to be putting the assets into a corporation or an LLC, the seller undoubtedly will want you (and probably your spouse as well) to personally guarantee the payment of any part of the purchase price that's being paid on an installment basis.

Background Information

Often, before a sales agreement gets into the terms of the transaction, it outlines some background facts. For example, the sales agreement might state that "Miranda Johnson currently owns a business in Cincinnati that produces ice cream, sorbet, and other dessert products" and that the sales agreement "applies only to the portion of the business operated at seller's west side location at 123 Maple Street."

You can also include some statements about the buyer; for example, "The buyer is a building contractor licensed under the laws of the state of Maine." These statements aren't usually a key section of a purchase agreement, but if they are included, it's important to be accurate.

Assets Being Sold

This is where you list what you're purchasing. You can put the details, such as lists of equipment, on a separate page, which is sometimes referred to in the body of the agreement as a schedule or an exhibit and specifically made part of the contract. Here's an example of how a sales agreement might list assets being sold:

> 1. All furniture, trade fixtures, equipment, and miscellaneous items of tangible personal property owned by seller and used in the business, listed and described in Exhibit A, which is hereby made a part of this agreement.
>
> 2. Customer lists and all other files and records of the business.
>
> 3. Assignment of the seller's interest (as tenant) in the lease dated March 1, 20xx for the building located at 123 Main Street owned by Central Property Associates (landlord).
>
> 4. Assignment of the seller's interest (as lessee) in the computer equipment lease with CompuLease dated March 1, 20xx.
>
> 5. All telephone numbers of the business and the right to use the business name, "The Tower Mart." Seller will cease using that name on the day of closing.

If you have so agreed, also include a statement that you're not acquiring any of the liabilities of the business or that you're acquiring only those that are specified.

> Except as otherwise specified in this agreement, buyer is not assuming responsibility for any liabilities of the business. Seller will remain responsible for all liabilities of the business not specified in this agreement, and will indemnify buyer and save buyer harmless from and against all such liabilities.

Purchase Price and Allocation of Assets

After stating the purchase price, allocate the price among the different categories of assets. Some typical allocations are shown below.

Allocation for a Retail Business

Merchandise on hand	$ 75,000
Tangible personal property	30,000
Assignment of lease agreement	4,000
Trade name and goodwill	8,000

Allocation for a Small Computer Company

Inventory (computers and software)	$ 100,000
Trade name and goodwill	20,000
Patents and copyrights	5,000
Building owned by seller	100,000
Land	30,000

For tax reasons, as a buyer, you want most of the price assigned to the assets that give you the fastest recovery of your investment. You want the least amount to be allocated to items such as goodwill (which must be amortized over 15 years), or land (which can't be depreciated at all). Here's a summary of the write-off rules:

Type of Asset	Normal Write-Off Period
Inventory	As sold
Furniture, fixtures, and equipment	5 to 7 years
Trade name and goodwill	15 years
Buildings	39 years
Patents and copyrights	Remaining term of patent or copyright
Lease assignment	Remaining term of lease
Land	No write-off

Because you and the seller will have differing tax priorities, you might have to negotiate the allocation of the purchase price. The seller will want the bulk of the purchase price to be assigned to categories that are taxed at lower long-term capital gains rates—for example, buildings and goodwill—rather than ordinary income rates. You'll be more interested in tilting the allocation toward items you can start to write off or depreciate—like equipment. If you wind up allocating the price in a way that saves you a ton of taxes but costs the seller a fair bit of change, you might need to raise the purchase price a little to help even things up. Similarly, if the allocation favors the seller, it's reasonable to work out a modest price reduction. A tax pro can help you crunch the numbers.

In the first example above, "Allocation for a Retail Business," let's say that the merchandise on hand could reasonably be given a value between $50,000 and $75,000. As the buyer of the business, you would want the merchandise on hand to be given as high a value as can be reasonably supported ($75,000) so that you would be able to write off that amount immediately. In the second example, "Allocation for a Small Computer Company," let's say the seller's building and land could reasonably be valued anywhere from $130,000 to $160,000, depending on the appraisal used. As a buyer, you would want the lowest reasonable value assigned to building and land because, under IRS guidelines, the building must be depreciated over a period of 39 years and the cost of the land can't be depreciated at all.

If the seller is going to provide consulting services to you for a year or so, consider assigning a portion of the purchase price to those services so that you can write off that amount quickly as a business expense. Better yet, remove an appropriate amount from the purchase price and put it in a separate agreement for consulting services.

Covenant Not to Compete

Especially if the seller is well known and would be a threat to your business by subsequently opening a rival business, you want a "covenant" (promise) not to compete. In such a covenant, the seller agrees not to compete directly or indirectly with you in the operation of the type of business that you've purchased. If the seller violates the covenant, a judge or an arbitrator will usually enforce it unless it unreasonably limits the seller's ability to earn a living.

To increase chances that your agreement will be enforced, it's wise to place a reasonable geographic limitation on the seller's right to run a similar business (for example, within 25 miles of your business) and also a reasonable time limit (for example, three years). If you're purchasing a business from a corporation or an LLC, have the individual operators of the business sign their own personal promises not to compete.

Obviously, whatever geographic limitations you and the seller agree on should fit the area. In New York City, a 25-mile zone would take in a huge chunk of New Jersey and some 15 to 20 million people—probably an unreasonable restraint on the seller's future ability to earn a living. In drafting a covenant not to compete, get help from a savvy lawyer who knows what the state courts enforce.

An example of a covenant not to compete is shown below.

Covenant Not to Compete

Seller shall not establish, engage in, or become interested in, directly or indirectly, as an employee, owner, partner, agent, shareholder, or otherwise, within a radius of ten miles from the city of
_____ , any business, trade, or occupation similar to the business covered by this sales agreement for a period of three years. At the closing, the seller agrees to sign an agreement on this subject in the form set forth in Exhibit B, which is hereby made a part of this agreement.

Law From the Real World

Why You Need a Covenant Not to Compete

Sydney is buying a travel agency from Mariah Jones, who has been in the travel business for 25 years and is well known in the community. Part of the reason Sydney is buying the business is the excellent reputation and following that business has earned.

Two months after Sydney takes over the business, Mariah—who quickly tired of retirement—opens a new travel agency four blocks away. Inevitably, some, perhaps many, of her old customers will abandon Sydney and patronize Mariah's business. Sydney should have included a covenant not to compete in the sales agreement to protect herself against this possibility.

Adjustments

You'll probably need to adjust the sales price slightly at closing. For example, you should reimburse the seller for payments the seller has made for such items as rent, utilities, or insurance for periods after you take over. On the other hand, if salaries and wages are paid every two weeks and you take over the business halfway through that period, the purchase price should be reduced at closing to reflect the fact that you'll be paying salaries for a period when the seller still owned the business.

Adjustments may also be made for license fees, maintenance contracts, equipment leases, and property taxes. Your sales agreement should contain a clause spelling out what items will need to be adjusted at closing and the method for making the adjustments.

Terms of Payment

Nearly 80% of small business purchases are handled on an installment basis, with the seller extending all or most of the credit. Typically, a buyer puts down about one-third of the purchase price and pays the balance over four or five years. For example, in the purchase of a $250,000 business, you may negotiate a contract that requires you to make a $50,000 down payment at closing with the balance paid in five annual installments of $40,000 each plus interest at 10% per year.

Tax and Usury: Charge Reasonable Interest

The IRS will accept the interest rate agreed to by the seller and buyer if it is reasonable in terms of the current financing market and the risk involved in extending credit. If the interest rate is outside the reasonable range, the buyer might not be able to deduct the excess interest paid. To avoid this, stick close to prevailing interest rates.

Also be aware that state usury laws limit the rate of interest that can be charged. Here, it's the seller rather than the buyer who runs the risk of running afoul of the law. In addition to being unable to collect excessive interest, the seller might also face criminal penalties.

It's a good idea to attach the proposed promissory note as well as the proposed security agreement as exhibits to the sales agreement.

At the closing, you'll sign a promissory note for the unpaid portion of the purchase price. The seller generally will want to retain an ownership (security) interest in the equipment and other assets of the business until the purchase price has been paid. Sometimes called a "lien," this is akin to a mortgage on your home. Just as the bank could sell your home to pay off your loan if you fell behind in your payments, the seller of a business who retains a lien on or security interest in your business assets could, if you were delinquent in making payments, take possession of those assets and sell them to cover the balance owing.

Here's a sample terms of payment clause:

Purchaser will pay seller $_____ at closing and will pay the balance of $_____ according to the terms of a promissory note purchaser will sign at the closing, in the form set forth in Exhibit_____ , which is hereby made a part of this agreement. The promissory note will provide for monthly payments of $_____ each. The payments will include interest on the unpaid balance at the rate of _____% per annum from and after the date of closing. The first installment will be due on the first day of the month following the closing and the remaining installments will be due on the first of each month after that until the principal and interest are fully paid. Payments will be applied first on interest and then on principal. The unpaid principal and interest shall be fully paid no later than _____ years from the date of the note. There will be no penalty for prepayment.

Until purchaser has paid the full balance of principal and interest on the debt, seller will retain a security interest in the business assets being purchased. As evidence of such security interest, purchaser, at closing, will sign a security agreement in the form set forth in attached Exhibit _____ , which is hereby made a part of this agreement. Purchaser agrees that the note will be further secured by a Uniform Commercial Code Financing Statement. Purchaser will sign any other documents that seller reasonably requests to protect seller's security interest in the secured property.

Inventory

Because the inventory of salable merchandise is likely to fluctuate between the time you sign the sales agreement and the closing, consider putting a provision in the sales agreement that allows for adjustment. For example, you might say that you'll pay up to $75,000 for merchandise on hand at the closing based on the seller's invoice cost. You might also provide that if there's more than $75,000 worth of merchandise on hand when you close, you have the right to purchase the excess at the seller's cost, or to choose $75,000 worth and leave the rest in the hands of the seller.

Here's another way to handle this problem. Simply provide that a physical count of all merchandise will be made on the day of the sale or another mutually agreeable date. You might define the word merchandise to include only unopened and undamaged merchandise. In a retail business, you can agree to value the merchandise at its current wholesale cost, or at the seller's current retail price less a certain percentage.

If you don't have experience doing an inventory, you might also put in the sales agreement that you and the seller will split the cost of hiring an inventory service company to determine the purchase price of the merchandise.

In a manufacturing or service business, you might have the analogous problem of placing a value on work in progress.

Accounts Receivable

The business you're buying might have sold goods to or performed services for customers who haven't yet paid. These unpaid sums are called "accounts receivable." Usually the accounts receivable of an existing business remain the property of the seller and aren't transferred to the buyer. But a seller who prefers to be free of collection problems might want to include them.

Be very careful. When a business changes hands, accounts can be hard to collect. A considerable percentage will probably never be collected, so you should get a substantial discount. How much depends on how collectable these accounts are. By now you should know this through your close examination of the seller's books and, if most of the money is owed by only a few accounts, by checking with them personally.

Seller's Representation and Warranties

In the sales agreement, the seller should guarantee the basic facts of your transaction. An example of the guarantees when the seller is a corporation is shown below.

In addition, if the seller made specific statements to you about the business and these influenced your decision to buy it, have the seller reiterate these statements in writing in this section of the agreement.

> CAUTION
> **Don't rely on the seller's promises.** Never use the seller's warranties and representations as an excuse for not thoroughly checking all important facts yourself. Enforcing a warranty against the seller or suing for a misrepresentation can involve a long and expensive lawsuit.

If you're buying a business or the assets from a corporation, have the principal owners sign the warranties as individuals in addition to signing them as officers of the corporation. That way, you'll be able to go after their personal assets if they've misrepresented facts or if their warranties are violated.

The contract should also say that the warranties survive the closing. This gives you the right to sue if you discover some unpleasant facts about the business several years after you purchase it. Here's some wording to consider:

> The representations and warranties of the parties to this agreement and those of the seller's shareholders shall survive the closing. The act of closing shall not bar either party from bringing an action based on a representation or warranty of the other party.

Seller and seller's shareholders represent and warrant that:

1. Andover Corporation is in good standing under the laws of Wisconsin.

2. Andover Corporation's board of directors has authorized (through board resolutions to be delivered to buyer at closing) the signing of this sales contract and all of the transactions called for in the contract.

3. Andover Corporation has good and marketable title to the assets that are being sold and will convey them to buyer free and clear of all encumbrances, except that the assets listed in Exhibit A, which is hereby made a part of this agreement, will remain subject to the encumbrances listed in Exhibit A.

4. The balance sheet that Andover Corporation gave buyer correctly reflects the assets, liabilities, and net worth of the business as of October 31, 20xx, and there will be no material changes between the balance sheet date and the closing.

5. The income statement that Andover Corporation gave buyer accurately reflects the income and expenses of the company during the period covered, and no significant changes in the level of income or expenses will occur between the contract date and the closing.

6. The lease under which Andover Corporation occupies space at 789 Oak Avenue is in full effect and is assignable to buyer. Andover Corporation will take all necessary steps to assign the lease to buyer.

7. Between the contract date and the closing, Andover Corporation will operate the business as usual and will take no action out of the ordinary.

8. Andover Corporation has complied with all applicable laws and regulations of the federal, state, and local governments.

9. There are no lawsuits or claims pending or threatened against Andover Corporation other than those listed in Exhibit B, which is hereby made a part of this agreement, and Andover Corporation does not know of any basis for any other lawsuit or claim against the business.

10. Andover Corporation has disclosed to buyer all material facts that would reasonably affect a prudent investor's decision to purchase the assets covered by this agreement.

Buyer's Representations and Warranties

The seller might expect the buyer to sign representations and warranties as well. For example:

Buyer represents and warrants that:

1. Buyer is a corporation in good standing under the laws of Wisconsin.

2. Buyer has the authority to enter into and perform the buyer's obligations under the sales agreement.

3. Buyer has had an opportunity to inspect the assets of the business and agrees to accept the assets as is, except for the items listed in Exhibit C, which is hereby made a part of this agreement.

The first representation in this example assumes you've established a corporation. You wouldn't include this statement if you were buying as a sole proprietor or signing on behalf of a partnership.

In the second representation, a corporate buyer would agree to furnish the seller with a board of directors' resolution approving the terms of the sales agreement and authorizing a corporate officer (such as the president or CEO) to sign the purchase documents.

The third representation says that you're accepting the assets "as is." If it turns out that some of the assets are defective, that will be your problem and not the seller's—unless the seller knew about and failed to disclose some hidden defect that you couldn't be expected to discover through an inspection. Before signing a sales agreement, make sure you have actually inspected all the assets. If there are some that you haven't looked at carefully or which you're *not* willing to take as is, list them in an exhibit that specifically excludes them from the as-is clause.

Access to Information

By the time you sign the sales agreement, you should have seen a lot of financial information involving the business, but you might still want to

see more to verify that everything is as promised. So it's a good idea to include a paragraph or two in the sales agreement covering your right to get full information. In exchange, the seller will probably want to include language ensuring that you'll deal with the information in a responsible manner—that is, that you won't make unnecessary disclosures.

Here's some language you might place in the sales agreement:

Before the closing, seller will provide to buyer and buyer's agents, during normal business hours, access to all of the company's properties, books, contracts, and records, and will furnish to buyer all the information concerning the company's affairs that buyer reasonably requests.

Buyer acknowledges that the company's books, records, and other documents contain confidential information, and that communication of such confidential information to third parties could injure the company's business if this transaction is not completed. Buyer agrees to take reasonable steps to assure that such information about the company remains confidential and is not revealed to outside sources. Buyer further agrees not to solicit any customers of the company disclosed from such confidential information.

The confidential information that may become known to buyer includes customer lists, trade secrets, channels of distribution, pricing policy and records, inventory records, and other information normally understood to be confidential or designated as such by seller.

Conduct of Business Pending Closing

Unless the sales agreement is signed at the closing, be sure that the seller doesn't make any detrimental changes in the business between the time you sign the sales agreement and the time you close. We considered some commitments along this line above, in discussing the seller's representations and warranties.

In addition, if you're purchasing the stock of a corporation, get a commitment that no change will be made in the articles of incorporation or in the authorized or issued shares of the corporation. Also, if you're dealing with a corporation, get a commitment that no contract will be entered into by or on behalf of the corporation extending beyond the closing date, except those made in the ordinary course of business.

Similarly, if you're purchasing the membership interests of an LLC, get a commitment that the owners won't change the number of membership interests issued. You also want assurance that the LLC won't sign a new contract that will carry on beyond the closing date.

Finally, have the corporation or LLC agree that it won't increase the compensation paid to any officer or employee and won't make any new arrangements for bonuses.

Contingencies

A "contingency clause" is a safety valve that lets you walk away from the transaction if certain things don't pan out. For example, if the location of the business is a crucial part of your decision to buy, you'll want to reserve the right to cancel the deal if you find out that the lease can't be assigned to you. The same thing might be true of a required license; if you're buying a bar, you would make the deal contingent on the state transferring the liquor license to you. If you plan to expand the business or move to a new location, make the deal contingent on your being able to get approval from the local zoning and building officials.

Here's a sample contingency clause:

> This agreement is contingent upon buyer receiving approval, by _____ , 20_____ from the landlord and the city's building and safety department for a remodeling of the premises leased by the business as shown in the plans and specifications attached as Exhibit _____, which is hereby made a part of this agreement.

Seller to Be a Consultant

Sometimes it pays to have the seller stay on for a few months as a consultant or employee to help ease your transition into the business and reassure longtime customers and suppliers that the business is in good hands. If you make these kinds of arrangements with the seller, be sure to capture them in the sales agreement, using language such as the following:

> _____ , as an independent contractor engaged by buyer, will provide consultation, customer relations, general assistance, and information to buyer pertaining to the company for up to 20 hours per week as requested by buyer for a period of eight weeks following closing. For such services, buyer will pay seller $_____ per week.

The consulting fees are tax deductible as current business expenses.

Broker Fees

If a business broker is involved, specify who is responsible for paying the fee, unless you independently hired the broker to help you locate the business. Normally, the seller is responsible.

Notices

It's customary to state addresses for both the seller and the purchaser where any notices and demands can be sent—for example, if a payment is late or another contract term is not met. Typically, sales agreements provide that notices can be given by first-class mail, but it is appropriate to require notice by registered mail with a return receipt requested.

Closing Date

Include a date for the closing. That's when you'll make your down payment, and both parties will sign any documents that are necessary to transfer the business to you.

The Closing

Finally, the big day has arrived—you're about to become the owner of a business. In an ideal world, you'd simply give the seller a check and the seller would give you the keys. Unfortunately, there's a lot of additional paperwork involved. There's also a certain amount of stress and pressure at a closing (after all, it's not every day that you buy a business).

Working with your lawyer or other adviser, make a checklist in advance listing all documents to be signed and other actions to be taken at the closing. Review this carefully a couple of days before the closing and be sure you have all your paperwork ready to go. If anything is unclear or doesn't make sense to you, ask your lawyer to redraft the language in plain English so that you and everyone else can understand it.

Checklist for a Typical Closing

☐ **Adjust purchase price** for prorated items, such as rent payments or utilities, or changes in the value of inventory.

☐ **Review documents promised by seller**—for example, a corporate board resolution authorizing the sale or an opinion of the seller's lawyer stating that the corporation is in good legal standing and that the sale has been properly approved by the shareholders and directors.

☐ **Sign promissory note** if you're not paying all cash for the business. The seller might require your spouse's signature as well, so that your joint bank account will be a source of repayment if the business doesn't produce enough income.

☐ **Sign security agreement** giving the seller a lien on the business assets if you don't pay the full price in cash at closing. (If you fail to keep up your payments as promised, the seller can take back the assets subject to the security agreement.)

☐ **Sign assignment of lease** if you're taking over an existing lease. If the landlord's approval is required, be sure it has been obtained before the closing.

☐ **Transfer vehicle titles** if cars or trucks are among the business assets.

☐ **Sign bill of sale** transferring ownership of other tangible business assets.

☐ **Sign transfer of patents, trademarks, and copyrights** if included in the sale.

☐ **Sign franchise transfer documents** if you're buying a business from a franchisee. This should include the signed approval of the franchisor. (Franchises are covered in Chapter 11.)

☐ **Sign closing or settlement statement** listing all financial aspects of the transaction. Ideally, everything in the closing or settlement statement should be based on clear language in the sales agreement so that nothing need be negotiated at the closing table.

☐ **Sign covenant not to compete** if seller agreed to one.

☐ **Sign consultation or employment agreement** if the seller has agreed to stay on as a consultant or an employee.

☐ **Complete IRS Form 8594,** *Asset Acquisition Statement,* indicating how the purchase was allocated among the various assets. You and the seller will attach a copy of the form to your respective income tax returns.

Selling a Business

Obviously, when you're just starting out in business, selling it isn't at the forefront of your mind. But there's a good chance that, sooner or later, you'll need to or want to sell. The reasons can vary widely—from not liking working for yourself, to a need to relocate, to one spouse selling to the other as part of a divorce, to retirement.

Let's look at some things you can do to get a good price for your business and protect your legal position.

 RESOURCE
For in-depth guidance and a full set of forms on how to sell a business, see *The Complete Guide to Selling a Business,* by Fred S. Steingold (Nolo).

Valuing Your Business

When you contemplate selling all of a business or only part (which might occur if you take in a partner or sell out to your co-owner spouse as part of a divorce), your first task is to determine the value of your business.

> EXAMPLE: Pauline has built a thriving retail business with three locations and 24 employees. Now she's getting divorced. She and her husband have agreed that she'll keep the business rather than liquidate it. Pauline must put a value on the business so that she and her husband can arrive at a reasonable property settlement.

You can get help valuing your business from an appraiser or a business broker. A business broker can also help you sell your business. If you do use a broker to sell your business, carefully read the listing agreement. Consider these issues:

- Does the broker have the exclusive right to sell your business or can you sell it directly to a buyer you found on your own without paying a commission?
- Do you have the right to reject a proposed purchaser because of the purchaser's credit history or for other reasons without having to pay the broker's commission?
- If there's an installment sale, will the broker receive a lump sum commission out of the down payment or in installments as you're paid?

The timing of a sale can be critical to getting the best price. Suppose your company has had earnings of $400,000 per year for the past three years. And suppose, too, that you have good reason to believe you'll jump to $600,000 next year. You can, of course, tell a prospective buyer why you expect an increase in profits. But there's often a better tactic: Hang on to the business for another year so that you have actual numbers to point to—not just a theory.

Would-be buyers will have much more confidence in your figures if you can show them several years' worth of financial statements audited or reviewed by a CPA. Also, keep detailed schedules of expenses so that buyers can compare your business with others in your industry.

Getting a Good Price for Your Business

Here are some tips for increasing your business's sale price:

- **Show steadily increasing profits at or above the industry average.** Plan ahead. To show strong profits, you might need to give up some hidden perks. Don't fret; you'll be handsomely rewarded at sale time.
- **Put your business in good general condition.** Everything should be neat, tidy, and in good working order. Machinery should be in good repair; your inventory should be well balanced and current.
- **Maintain adequate personnel.** A buyer will be put off—and discount the price—if the first chore in running the business is to recruit and train new employees.
- **Get a written appraisal supporting your sales price.** This can help persuade the buyer that the price is right.

These suggestions are from *Valuing Small Businesses and Professional Practices*, by Shannon P. Pratt, Robert F. Reilly, and Robert P. Schweihs (McGraw-Hill).

Read Your Lease

Your lease may say that a new business owner can't take over your space without the landlord's consent. If so, such consent will be needed if you signed the lease as a sole proprietor or partner. It will also be needed if the purchaser is buying the assets of your corporation or LLC rather than its stock or membership interests. Find out early whether your landlord will be an obstacle to selling the business and, if so, how you can get his or her support.

Protect Your Privacy

A prospective purchaser will want to investigate your business thoroughly before signing a purchase agreement. To protect your privacy, use a confidentiality or nondisclosure agreement in which the potential purchaser promises not to use or disclose confidential information about your business—unless, of course, that person decides to buy it. (A sample confidentiality letter agreement is shown earlier in this chapter.) A prospective purchaser who violates this agreement can be sued for damages and injunctive relief.

Sign a Letter of Intent

Earlier, we looked at the nonbinding letter of intent to purchase from a buyer's standpoint. A seller can also draft such a letter in order to summarize the terms of the proposed transaction to see whether a potential buyer is serious.

Draft a Sales Agreement

To understand the elements of a sales agreement, read "The Sales Agreement" earlier in this chapter. Here are some additional points to consider from the seller's viewpoint.

Structure of the Sale

The sales agreement structures the sale. If you're doing business as a sole proprietor or partnership, the structure of the sale is a foregone conclusion: You'll sell the assets of the business to the buyer. But if you're doing business as a corporation or an LLC, the matter is more complicated. It's almost always better for you to sell your corporate stock or LLC membership interests than to have your business sell its assets. By selling your corporate stock or LLC membership interests, your profit will be taxed at the lower long-term capital gain rate, and the buyer will assume all of your business liabilities. In asset sales, part of your tax bill will be computed at the higher ordinary income rate, and your liabilities will

most likely remain with you. For the same reasons, buyers prefer to purchase assets rather than stock or membership interests.

Excluded Assets

If you're selling the assets of the business or the business itself—whether it be a sole proprietorship, a partnership, a corporation, or an LLC—the purchase agreement lists the assets being transferred. Typically, this includes furniture, fixtures, equipment, inventory, vehicles, and the business name. It's equally important to specify any items excluded from the sale, for example: cash, accounts receivable, life insurance policies, or your personal desk or computer.

Allocation of the Purchase Price

For tax purposes, the buyer typically wants to assign a relatively high value to items that can be quickly written off or depreciated. The seller generally prefers to place a high value on assets that will provide long-term capital gain treatment; the tax on such gain is lower than the tax on ordinary income. A tax pro can help size up your particular sale and recommend how to allocate the purchase price. Also, a tax pro can suggest ways to adjust the purchase price up or down to reflect whoever takes the tax hit.

Adequate Security for Installment Sales

When a small business is sold on an installment payment basis, the buyer typically makes a down payment of 20% to 40% of the purchase price and pays the balance in monthly installments over three to five years. Plan ahead in case the buyer doesn't keep up the payments as promised. Insist that the buyer's spouse sign all closing documents jointly with the buyer. That way, if you need to sue the buyer because of nonpayment, you have a chance of collecting the judgment out of a house owned jointly by the buyer and spouse, or from bank accounts in their joint names. If the couple's credit is weak, insist that an outside guarantor also sign the documents.

The purchase agreement should require the buyer to give you a security interest (also called a lien) in the business assets. A financing statement that's filed with county or state officials will give public notice that you have a claim on the business assets.

If you're doing business as a corporation and are selling your stock, consider placing the stock certificates in escrow. That way, the buyer won't receive the certificates until the purchase price has been paid in full.

Looking to the Future

The buyer might want to hire you for several months or years as a consultant or an employee. If so, spell this out in the sales agreement or in a separate document signed at the same time. Be specific about the types of services you'll be expected to render, the amount of time you're committing, and the amount you'll be paid. Sometimes, compensation for a seller's post-sale services is simply folded into the purchase price and the seller receives no additional payment.

If you've agreed not to compete with the buyer, the terms should be specified in a covenant not to compete. Cover matters such as the precise business or activities you won't engage in, being careful not to burn all of your bridges. Think carefully about how long you're willing to refrain from working in a competing enterprise and how large a geographical area should be barred during the noncompetition period.

Warranties

Sales agreements typically contain numerous warranties and representations by the seller and a few by the buyer. Read your warranties and representations carefully to make sure they don't go too far.

For example, suppose the proposed warranty language says: "Seller warrants that the business name does not conflict with the name of any other business." What happens if, the day after the sale, a business that you didn't know about surfaces and complains that it had the name first? With the warranty wording given here, you could be liable for damages whether or not you knew about the other company.

If you see a warranty that's too far-reaching, have it rewritten. In the above example, you might say something like, "Seller warrants that, to the best of seller's knowledge, the business name does not conflict with the name of any other business." Or perhaps you could say, "Seller warrants that it has received no notice that its business name conflicts with that of any other business."

Franchises: How Not to Get Burned

America's landscape is dotted with franchises: Take the first exit off any freeway, and you're likely to spot familiar ones offering fast food, gasoline, groceries, lodgings, and more. So, you might conclude, they must be making money, or they'd pack up and disappear. And why shouldn't you buy into an established chain to get a jump on the learning curve and tap into an existing customer base?

Not so fast. For most people hoping to own a small business, buying a franchise is a poor idea. Most of the franchises you see on the road—or on Main Street or at the mall—are just barely eking out a profit beyond the percentage they must pay to the franchise vendor (the "franchisor"). Worse yet, some of their owners would like to sell, but can't. Because of the legal and economic rules exerted by the franchisor, you might end up feeling more like an indentured servant than an entrepreneur. In my view, you'll be happier and farther ahead financially if you start a business from scratch or buy an existing one.

In this chapter, I'll explain how franchises work, and delve deeper into their pitfalls. Then I'll introduce you to the two most important legal documents that are involved in the purchase of a franchise: the Franchise Disclosure Document (FDD) and the franchise agreement.

RESOURCE

For more information and insight into franchise ownership, visit the websites of two organizations dedicated to promoting the rights of franchisees: The American Franchisee Association (www.franchisee.org) and The American Association of Franchisees and Dealers (www.aafd.org). Both contain valuable information to help you protect your legal and financial interests. Also, go to the Federal Trade Commission's website (www.ftc.gov), and search for "franchise."

 SEE AN EXPERT

Get professional advice before you plunge in. Don't wait until you find yourself trapped in a costly and frustrating relationship with a franchisor—at which time you might have little legal recourse. It's worth paying for some sound legal and financial advice before you get locked into a contract or pay the franchisor a cent.

What Is a Franchise?

The most convenient analysis and definition of a franchise comes from the Federal Trade Commission (FTC)—the one government agency that has nationwide regulatory power in this field. The FTC recognizes two types of business relationships that qualify for regulation as franchises:

- **The package franchise.** The franchisor licenses you to do business under a business format it has established. The business is closely identified with the franchisor's trademark or trade name. Examples include car washes, fast-food outlets, motels, transmission centers, tax preparation services, and quick copy shops.
- **The product franchise.** You distribute goods produced by the franchisor or under the franchisor's control or direction. The business or goods bear the franchisor's trademark or trade name. Examples include gasoline stations and car dealerships.

This chapter deals primarily with package franchises, which are more common.

The FTC definition is broad. It covers all of the businesses that you and I would ordinarily think of as franchises. Generally, the FTC (and many state agencies that regulate franchises) will classify your business relationship as a franchise if three conditions exist:

- You have the right to distribute goods or services that bear the franchisor's trademark, service mark, trade name, or logo.
- The franchisor significantly assists you in operating your business or significantly controls what you do. For example, your

franchisor might assist in site selection, train you and your employees, or furnish you with a detailed instructional manual. A franchisor might exercise control by telling you where your business must be located and how your shop must be designed, or by dictating your hours, accounting and personnel practices, and advertising program.

- You pay a fee to the franchisor of more than $500 for the first six months of operations. (In the real world, you're going to be paying a franchisor much more—probably anywhere from $10,000 to $1 million.)

All of this can add up to a complex and expensive relationship between you and the franchisor.

> EXAMPLE: Lila loves the idea of selling doughnuts and buys a franchise from Munchin Donuts International. She pays Munchin Donuts $50,000 as a franchise fee plus an additional $5,000 for training for herself and an assistant. Lila and her assistant must travel to the Munchin Donuts headquarters in another state for the training. Munchin Donuts helps her find a suitable location for a doughnut shop, then prescribes the store layout and décor. Lila makes the necessary improvements, but can't use her favorite contractor—she must use one on Munchin Donuts' approved list. She buys the doughnut-making equipment and shop furnishings directly from Munchin Donuts, as required by her franchise contract. Munchin Donuts provides Lila with a 500-page operating manual called *Making Donuts the Munchin Way.* Lila is also given the right to use the Munchin Donuts logo in her signage and advertising. Lila must buy all of the doughnut mixes directly from Munchin Donuts, and each month she must pay Munchin 8% of her gross sales, plus a hefty fee for participation in Munchin's co-op advertising program. She must keep the shop open from 7 a.m. to 9 p.m., six days a week, as required by the Munchin Donuts operating manual.

The Downsides of Franchise Ownership

During your negotiations to buy a franchise, while everyone is still smiling, the franchisor is likely to assure you that you won't be in business all by yourself, but will be part of a team selling a recognized product or service. Franchisors typically also tout three other supposed benefits:

- **A proven plan for running the business.** The franchisor will furnish an operations manual that can serve as a roadmap to get you started.
- **Help from the franchisor if you run into problems.** The franchisor promises to make people available who are experienced in real estate, personnel policies, accounting, and day-to-day operations.
- **A national or regional marketing program to attract customers.** The franchisor promises to advertise in print and on radio and TV so that the brand will become famous and customers will flock to your door.

Even if the franchisor makes good on all of these commitments—and many won't—the price you'll pay to get these benefits might be backbreakingly high. Do you really need to pay a company month after month, year after year, in order to master the fundamentals of making pizza or cleaning houses? As for business help from the franchisor, can't you simply hire advisers on an as-needed basis to help you with real estate, marketing, or accounting issues? (As a matter of fact, you can probably learn the basic management skills you'll need by taking a course or two at a nearby community college.) And will the franchisor really invest enough money to build the kind of brand recognition that translates into huge profits for you? It's highly unlikely.

It's true that some small business owners have signed on for a franchise and found prosperity and happiness, but many more have lost their shirts and feel bitter about their franchise experiences.

So before you're seduced by the glitter of the franchisor's glib promises, take a hard look at the downsides of investing in a franchise.

TIP

It takes money to make money. Some franchises might have a high profit potential—but the better ones tend to be well beyond the reach of the small operator. National hotel and motel groups might offer fine franchise opportunities, because they provide a real service through their 800 phone numbers and reservation booking services. Ditto for auto rental franchises because they, too, offer something of value. And franchises with famous and respected brands such as McDonald's and Pizza Hut might be worth the high cost. But these blue-chip opportunities are expensive to buy into. If you're an ordinary entrepreneur with possibly $50,000 or $75,000 to invest, you'll probably be looking at lesser-known franchises for which the prospects are not nearly so bright.

Let's look at some reasons why franchises are usually a worse option than starting your own business or buying an existing one.

The Franchisor Gets a Huge Chunk of the Pie

The franchisor will almost certainly insist on getting a thick slice of your financial action—often the lion's share. Franchisors have figured out many ways to make money on your business, including:

- **Franchise fees.** You must always pay up front for the right to be a franchisee. These buy-in fees can verge on the astronomical, especially for a successful, nationally established franchise.
- **Royalties.** Commonly, the franchisor gets a percentage of the income your franchise earns. Income usually means gross sales, not profits. If your franchise takes in $200,000 from gross sales and your contract calls for a 10% royalty, the franchisor will be entitled to receive

$20,000 whether or not your business earns a profit. Other operating expenses can easily eat up the remaining $180,000 of gross income, leaving nothing—or even less.

- **Markups on equipment, goods, and supplies.** The franchisor might add dollars to the cost of equipment, goods, and supplies that the franchisor furnishes. Many franchise agreements require you to buy certain items from the franchisor rather than from outside suppliers; others let you buy through outside sources if the items meet the franchisor's specifications. If, for example, you're required to purchase cooking equipment from the franchisor, you might pay a bundle more than you'd pay a restaurant supply store.
- **Training fees.** Often you must pay the franchisor to train you and your employees—whether or not you need the training.
- **Co-op ad fees.** These fees cover advertising for the entire group of franchises or a regional group. For example, you might have to contribute to a fund for national advertising or for advertising for all the franchisees in your metropolitan area—whether or not any of your customers are likely to see the ads.
- **Interest on financing.** You might have to pay for deferring payment of a portion of the franchise fee, the cost of improving your business premises, or buying equipment.
- **Leases.** Your franchisor might charge you rent on real estate or equipment. Typically, the franchisor does not lease real estate or equipment to you at the franchisor's cost but adds on a profit factor. But because relatively few franchisors own the premises where their franchisees do business, real estate lease charges are relatively uncommon.

If it appears that I'm painting a grim picture, I am. After you've made all the required payments to the franchisor, there might be very little left for you.

Law From the Real World

Going It Alone

Parker, a real estate broker, wanted to open his own shop. He first considered going it alone, but then decided he might do better by purchasing a franchise from one of the national organizations. He contacted several and was amazed to find that he couldn't buy a one-office franchise directly from them. Instead he was told that in his region a "master" franchise had already been sold and that he would have to contact this company to purchase a subfranchise.

When he did, he learned that his region had been divided into hundreds of subregions or territories, each of which was for sale through a local real estate office. All training, quality control, and recruiting was done by the master franchise holder, not the national organization.

Eventually, Parker decided not to purchase any of the local franchises he was offered, concluding that the territories had been divided too narrowly. In the meantime, he has opened his own office and is doing fairly well. He might still affiliate with a franchise organization, but only if he can find one that sells good-sized territories at a reasonable price.

The Franchisor Can Tell You What to Do

If you're like many entrepreneurs, part of the attraction of owning a business is that you're free to make your own business decisions, test new ideas, and change and improve the products and services you offer. Unfortunately, when you're a franchisee, you give up a great deal of that freedom. The franchisor typically prescribes a formula for running the business and, for the most part, you're locked into using it. Don't be surprised if you soon become frustrated and bored.

But the consequences of signing on as a franchisee can go much farther than just stifled creativity.

There's a real chance that your bottom line will be affected. Small businesses normally enjoy a huge advantage over multistate giants: They're nimble enough to respond quickly to local conditions.

By contrast, large organizations can't react nearly as fast, meaning that opportunities for adding profits—or avoiding losses—can be missed. For example, if you own a pizza franchise and notice that everyone in town is going crazy for fresh shiitake mushrooms, you could wait years before your franchisor lets you put any mushroom atop your pizza that isn't straight from a can. You're just a cog in a huge machine.

The Franchise Contract Will Favor the Franchisor

When you buy a franchise, you'll need to sign a contract with the franchisor. Contracts aren't bad in and of themselves—they're useful tools for spelling out all the terms and conditions of the relationship. However, the contract that you'll be handed will have been drafted by a team of skilled lawyers hired by the franchisor and will most likely contain dozens of clauses aimed at giving the franchisor every conceivable advantage. And you'll probably be told to "take it or leave it," with no opportunity to negotiate any of the contract terms.

To give you an idea of how one-sided these contracts can be, here are some clauses you're likely to find in the typical franchise contract:

- **Competition.** The franchisor will usually protect its freedom to grant additional franchises without restriction. This means that if your operation is successful, the franchisor might decide to sell a franchise to someone else right down the street, cutting into your market share. By contrast, you'll be required to agree that after the franchise relationship ends, you won't compete with the franchisor—either directly or indirectly. This stops you from working or investing in a similar business.

Although it's reasonable for the franchisor to want to protect its trademarks and trade secrets, the franchisor already has plenty of legal protection in this area. The franchisor has no solid justification for interfering with your ability to earn a living doing similar work after you've stopped being a franchisee—but it has superior bargaining power. It can usually force even unreasonable restrictions on you as part of the price of buying the franchise.

- **Selling your franchise.** When you own your own business, you're free to sell it to whomever you wish. Not so with a franchise. Typically, you can't sell your franchise unless the franchisor approves of the buyer. This means that if you want to retire or move to another state or shift to a different line of work, you're at the mercy of the franchisor. If the franchisor is picky, you might be left with few—if any—prospective buyers, and you could have to settle for a fraction of what the business is worth. Worse yet, the buyer will have to sign a new franchise contract, which might call for even higher royalty charges than you've been paying, making it all the more difficult to sell the business.
- **Disputes.** The contract might require you to resolve any disputes with the franchisor in the courts of the franchisor's home state. If you do business in Oregon and the franchisor's headquarters are in New Jersey, that's a long and expensive trip.
- **Goods and services.** The contract could force you to buy all your goods and services from the franchisor. If you have to buy your milkshake mix as well as your marketing services from the franchisor, you'll probably end up paying much more than if you were free to buy from vendors of your choice.

For more on franchise agreements, see "The Franchise Agreement," below.

The Government Won't Protect You

Franchisors become very adept at selling franchises—but aren't known for following through on what they promise in the sales presentations. Some franchisors are notorious for misrepresenting key facts about their organization. Many deftly inflate your expectations of the profits you'll bring in. And some are fly-by-night outfits operating entirely by smoke and mirrors.

Don't assume you can go running to the government for help if the franchisor's promises turn out to be puffery. Neither the state nor the federal government is going to thoroughly investigate the accuracy of information in the disclosure document or bail you out if things go wrong. True, you might get limited help from a government agency to close down or even prosecute an operator whose actions constitute outright fraud. But even in the case of blatant dishonesty by the franchisor, you'll be pretty much on your own in trying to get back your money.

The time to be cautious is at the beginning, while you listen to the sales banter from the franchisor. Remember that you're almost surely not receiving a balanced, objective point of view. No matter what they say about peace, brotherhood, and all prospering together, most franchisors look at their job as simply to sell as many franchises as possible, as fast as possible, at the highest price possible.

Investigating a Franchise

If you've done your research and have identified a few businesses in which you believe you could be successful as a franchisee, investigate the franchisors. A good track record counts. Find out how many franchises each franchisor has in actual operation—information that's readily available in the Franchise Disclosure Document. (See Item 20 in "The Franchise Disclosure Document," below.)

Next, carefully evaluate whether the specific franchise operation you're thinking about makes economic sense. Is there really a demand out there for the product or service that you'll be selling? Can you make a decent profit given how much you can charge and your cost of doing business?

Don't forget to count all those franchise fees. The franchisor might give you actual or hypothetical projections of how much money a typical franchisee can earn. Distrust these. Chances are they're full of hype. Ask for financial details about individual franchise operations that are geographically and demographically similar to the one that you're considering.

Most important, speak to a number of other franchisees. The names and addresses of those in your state will be listed in the Franchise Disclosure Document. Be aware, however, that some franchisees might have signed confidentiality agreements that prohibit them from responding to your inquiries.

The more you know about the franchisor, the better. Visit the home office, even if it's in another city or state. Get to know the people you'll be dealing with if you buy. What's the background of the owners, officers, and management staff of the franchisor? Do they have the experience and competence to give you the promised technical support?

Be especially suspicious of franchises that promise big profits for little work and offer a money-back guarantee. Rarely do you get something for nothing in this world and almost never do you get your money back when business deals go awry.

Learn how much help you can expect from the franchisor in:

- selecting a site
- negotiating a lease
- writing and placing help wanted ads for employees
- interviewing prospective employees
- getting the necessary business licenses, and
- ordering equipment.

Make sure all key promises are in writing. Oral statements don't count: Often they're not legally enforceable, but even when they are, proving in court what someone said years before could be impossible. One good way to get things in writing is to take notes when you talk to the franchisor. Then write up your notes, review them with the franchisor, and ask for the signature of someone in authority.

With a larger franchisor, many of your contacts will be with a district or regional manager. Meet these people and find out what they're like.

Ask about whether any franchise operations have closed. Obviously, this is a sensitive topic for a franchisor. Ideally, the franchisor will be honest in discussing failures with you, but you can't count on this. If the franchisor seems to be stonewalling, try to get the names of franchisees whose operations failed from existing franchisees and talk to them directly.

Investigate the area where your franchise will be located. Talk to people who work or live nearby to learn more about the behavior and tastes of potential customers. What do other business owners have to say about your customer base? How do they think your franchise will fit into the community?

The Franchise Disclosure Document

The Federal Trade Commission requires franchisors to give prospective franchisees a disclosure document containing details about the franchise. In addition, the franchisor must give you a copy of the proposed franchise agreement and related documents. But FTC rules don't dictate the terms of the deal you and the franchisor agree to. As long as there's full disclosure, the deal can be very one-sided in favor of the franchisor and still be legal.

The FTC lists the items that a franchisor must include in its Franchise Disclosure Document, and provides a format for the franchisor to follow. Some states require a franchisor to make additional disclosures.

Although the FTC requires the disclosure, it doesn't verify or vouch for the information the franchisor discloses. It's up to you to check out anything you don't understand or that sounds too good to be true.

Under FTC rules, if you're a prospective franchisee, the franchisor must give you the disclosure document at least 14 days before you:

- sign a binding agreement with the franchisor, or
- make any payment connected to the proposed franchise sale.

The franchisor can furnish the disclosure document by:

- hand-delivering, faxing, or emailing a copy to you by the required date
- telling you how to view the document on the Internet by the required date, or
- sending you a paper or tangible electronic copy, such as a CD-ROM, by first-class mail at least three days before the required date.

If a franchisor violates these or other FTC rules, it might face heavy civil penalties. Also, the FTC may sue the franchisor, on your behalf, for damages or other relief, including cancellation of a franchise contract and refunds.

State laws often provide other avenues of relief for a violation of disclosure and other requirements. For example, in some states, you might have the right to sue a franchisor who fails to make disclosures properly. In other words, you won't have to rely on the state to make your case for you.

Knowing that these legal avenues are open to you might give you some peace of mind—but don't relax your guard too much. If the franchisor becomes insolvent or goes into bankruptcy, chances are you'll recover only a minuscule part of your loss, or maybe nothing at all.

Here are the 23 items included in the Franchise Disclosure Document and brief comments about how to think about each.

Item 1: The Franchisor, and Any Parents, Predecessors, and Affiliates

Here you'll learn the name of the franchisor and its predecessors, affiliates, and parent companies, as well as the names under which the franchisor does

business. You'll also find out if the franchisor is a corporation, a partnership, or some other type of business.

The franchisor then describes its businesses and the franchises being offered, and lists the business experience of the franchisor and its predecessors and affiliates. You can find out how long the franchisor has operated the type of business you'd be franchising. You can also learn whether the franchisor has offered franchises in other lines of business and the number of franchises sold.

Finally, the franchisor must describe any regulations that are specific to the industry in which the franchisee operates.

Item 2: Business Experience

The franchisor must list its principal officers and disclose each officer's job for the past five years.

Item 3: Litigation

This is where you learn the legal history of the franchisor. If the franchisor or its directors or officers have a history of legal problems, watch out. If the franchisor follows the FTC rule, you'll discover, for example, whether or not there are administrative, criminal, or civil cases alleging:

- violation of any franchise, antitrust, or securities law
- fraud
- unfair or deceptive trade practices, or
- comparable misconduct.

If any such actions are pending, the disclosure document must provide full information, as well as information about instances in which the franchisor sued its own franchisees.

Furthermore, the franchisor must disclose whether, in the past ten years, the franchisor or its directors or officers have been convicted of a felony, pleaded no contest to a felony charge, or have been held liable in a civil action involving any of the offenses listed above.

And there's more: If the franchisor or any of its directors or officers is subject to an injunction (court order) relating to a franchise or involving any laws on securities, antitrust, trade regulation, or trade practice, the franchisor must disclose this information. This can provide an early warning of potential problems.

Don't rely on the franchisor's explanations of lawsuits involving the company. You can look at the court files, which are open to the public and will name all of the participants on both sides. Call the people on the other side and get their version of events.

Item 4: Bankruptcy

The franchisor must state whether the franchisor or its officers have gone through bankruptcy or been reorganized due to insolvency during the past ten years. The information required is far-reaching. The franchisor must disclose if any officer or general partner was a principal officer of any company or a general partner of any partnership that went bankrupt or was reorganized due to insolvency within one year after the officer or general partner was associated with the company or partnership.

Item 5: Initial Fees

Read this section carefully to learn how much you'll be charged before you open for business and whether you'll have to pay it in a lump sum or installments. The franchisor must also explain under what conditions your money will be refunded.

If the franchisor doesn't charge identical initial fees to each franchisee, the franchisor must tell how fees are determined, or state the range of fees charged in the past year.

Item 6: Other Fees

Here's where you get details about any additional required fees. Using a simple chart, the franchisor must tell you the formula used to compute fees and the conditions for refunds.

When any fees are set by the vote of a cooperative organization of franchisees—for advertising, for example—the franchisor must disclose the voting power of franchisor-owned outlets and a range for the fees.

Item 7: Estimated Initial Investment

These are estimates (or a high–low range) of expenses you'll be responsible for. You'll be told who the payments must be made to, when the payments are due, and the conditions for refunds. If part of your initial investment may be financed, you'll learn the details, including interest rates.

Listed expenses include those for:
- real estate, whether it's bought or leased
- equipment, fixtures, other fixed assets, construction, remodeling, leasehold improvements, and decorating costs
- inventory required to begin operation
- security deposits, utility deposits, business licenses, other prepaid expenses, and working capital required to begin operation, and
- any other payments you must make to start operations.

> CAUTION
> **Don't invest everything in a franchise.** These fees can add up to far more than you first expected and dangerously stretch your budget. Never put every last cent into a franchise. Even with an honest franchisor, there's a good chance you won't make any money the first year. Keep enough money in reserve to live on during the start-up phase. And always be wary about pledging your house for a loan needed to buy a franchise. It's one thing to risk your savings; it's quite another to risk the roof over your family's head.

Item 8: Restrictions on Sources of Products and Services

Here the franchisor states whether you're required to purchase or lease from the franchisor—or from companies designated by the franchisor—any of the following: goods, services, supplies, fixtures, equipment, inventory, computer hardware and software, or real estate.

The franchisor also must say if and how it may earn income from these required purchases or leases. As mentioned in "The Downsides of Franchise Ownership," above, many franchisors mark up the products they require their franchisees to buy from them.

Item 9: Franchisee's Obligations

In a simple table, the franchisor lists each of your obligations and tells you where each is spelled out in the franchise agreement and disclosure document.

Item 10: Financing

Look for the terms and conditions of any financing arrangements offered to help franchisees afford the purchase. Also review the statement of your liability if you can't make the payments.

As you review these, bear in mind that after signing on to a promissory note or financing contract requiring you to make payments to the franchisor, you might find that some other company has acquired the right to collect the debt from you. This can happen if the franchisor sells or assigns (transfers) the promissory note or financing contract to the other company.

In the disclosure document, the franchisor should state whether or not it plans to handle the financing arrangement this way. It might seem like a minor detail, but it can affect you down the road. Here's why: If you're dealing directly with the franchisor in making your payments, you might be able to withhold payment if the franchisor isn't meeting its obligations to you. By contrast, if the note or financing contract has been transferred to somebody else, you'll probably be obligated to pay regardless of how poorly the franchisor is performing.

 CAUTION
Beware of finance charges. Paying finance charges and interest on notes held by the franchisor is a real financial burden. If you can't afford to pay all of the franchise fees up front, maybe you shouldn't buy the franchise. Think long and hard before you pledge your house as security for these obligations—and before you ask your spouse or a relative to be a cosigner or guarantor of the debt.

Item 11: Franchisor's Assistance, Advertising, Computer Systems, and Training

What are the franchisor's obligations to you before you open your franchise business? For example, will the franchisor select a location for your business? Will the franchisor help you:

- Negotiate the purchase or lease of the site?
- Make sure the building you'll occupy conforms to local codes?
- Obtain required building permits?
- Construct, remodel, or decorate the premises?
- Purchase or lease equipment, signs, and supplies?
- Hire and train employees?
- Set up and operate any required cash register or computer systems?

And what kind of assistance will the franchisor give you once your business is operating?

Look for detailed answers to these questions as well as a description of the training program the franchisor will provide, including the location, length, and content of the training program; when the training program will be conducted; the experience that instructors have had with the franchisor; any charges for the training; the extent to which you'll be responsible for travel and living expenses while enrolled in the training program; and whether any additional training programs or refresher courses are available or required.

Item 12: Territory

Here the franchisor describes whether or not you have any territorial protection. Check to see whether the franchisor has established another franchisee or company-owned outlet in your territory or has the right to do so in the future. Obviously, your business will be in trouble if the franchisor defines your exclusive territory very narrowly and then floods the market with outlets offering similar products or services.

Even if you have exclusive rights within a territory, you might not be safe from direct competition. Some franchisors require you to achieve a certain sales volume or market penetration to keep those exclusive rights. Make sure you understand under what conditions your area or territory can be altered.

Item 13: Trademarks

Most likely your franchise will require you to use the franchisor's trademarks, service marks, trade names, logos, or other commercial symbols. Fine. In many ways, these represent much of the value of a franchise. In fact, you'll want to research whether the franchisor itself has an ongoing right to use these marks and symbols.

For starters, the franchisor must tell you in the disclosure document whether or not the franchisor's trademarks and symbols are registered with the U.S. Patent and Trademark Office. The franchisor must also describe any agreements, administrative proceedings, or court cases that might affect your right to use these trademarks and symbols.

Franchisors should stand behind their trade names and trademarks. Even if a trademark is properly registered, it can still be challenged in court by a company that used it before the franchisor used it or registered it. Make sure that your franchisor is obligated in writing to defend any challenges against its names and trademarks and to indemnify you against any damage awards for using them. The

franchisor should also agree to reimburse you for out-of-pocket expenses if you have to replace signs and print new supplies because of an adverse court ruling regarding names or trademarks.

Item 14: Patents, Copyrights, and Proprietary Information

The franchisor must give full details about any patents or copyrights that relate to the franchise and the terms and conditions under which you can use them. Let's say, for example, that you're interested in purchasing a tire store franchise and the franchisor has published an excellent copyrighted booklet telling consumers how to choose the right tires for their cars. The franchisor needs to disclose whether there have been any administrative or other claims filed that might affect the continued use of the booklet. And the franchisor needs to state whether it can require its franchisees to discontinue use of the booklet in running their franchisees.

Also, the franchisor must state if it claims proprietary rights in confidential information or trade secrets.

Item 15: Obligation to Participate in the Actual Operation of the Franchise Business

Some franchisors permit someone to own a franchise without actively participating in the operation of the business. Other franchisors want the owner to be fully involved. The franchisor must state whether or not it will obligate you to participate personally in operating the franchise business. It must also state whether or not it recommends that you participate.

If the franchisor doesn't require you, as a franchise owner, to personally be present and run the business, it could require that you employ an on-site manager who has successfully completed the franchisor's training program.

Item 16: Restrictions on What the Franchisee May Sell

If you're going to be restricted in the goods or services you can offer or the customers you can sell to, this must be spelled out in the disclosure document. Find out if you'll be required to carry the full range of the franchisor's products. For example, with a food franchise, do you have to offer the full menu? Can you add items to the menu?

Also, check whether the franchisor has the right to change the types of goods and services you're authorized to sell.

Item 17: Renewal, Termination, Transfer, and Dispute Resolution

You're entitled to know the conditions under which you may renew, extend, or terminate your franchise and also the conditions under which the franchisor may refuse to deal with you. (See below for more on termination.)

Look, too, for information on whether disputes must be submitted to mediation or arbitration in place of going to court.

 TIP

Mediation or arbitration is usually a plus. Fighting a franchisor in court can be prohibitively expensive for a franchisee. The franchisor usually has very deep pockets and can better afford to finance—or even drag out—the litigation. If a legal dispute can't be settled through negotiation, it's almost always better for you to submit the matter to mediation or arbitration rather than go to court. Mediation and arbitration proceedings are much less expensive than lawsuits—and speedier to boot. There's a trade-off, however: In a lawsuit you can compel the franchisor to show you key documents and to answer questions under oath (in what's called a pretrial deposition). Mediation and arbitration offer only very limited opportunities for this type of information gathering. For more information on mediation and arbitration, see Nolo's Mediation, Arbitration & Collaborative Law section at www.nolo.com/legal-encyclopedia/mediation.

Item 18: Public Figures

Some franchisors use celebrities to promote franchise operations. The franchisor must disclose any compensation or other benefit given or promised to any public figures for using their names or endorsements. You also need to be told the extent to which celebrities are involved in the actual management or control of the franchisor and how much—if anything—they have invested in the franchise operation.

Item 19: Financial Performance Representations

The franchisor has a choice. It can disclose the actual or potential sales, profits, or earnings of its franchisees. Or it can say nothing on the subject—which is what most franchisors choose to do. If the franchisor does make any earnings claims, the disclosure document must describe the factual basis and material assumptions that underlie these claims.

For earnings claims to make sense, you need to know the franchise locations that the numbers are based on and the number of years that they have been in operation. Actual figures are, of course, more helpful than hypothetical projections. Before you buy a franchise, have your accountant go over the numbers with a fine-tooth comb. Also check with a number of existing franchisees to see how they're doing.

Item 20: Outlets and Franchisee Information

The information in this part of the disclosure document can be a gold mine if you take advantage of it. The franchisor must list the total number of franchise locations and state how many of them were in operation when the disclosure document was prepared, as well as how many are covered by franchise agreements but are not yet in operation. The franchisor must also list the names, addresses, and telephone numbers of all its franchises in your state. If there are fewer than 100 franchises in your state, the franchisor must list those in nearby states, until at least 100 are disclosed.

A company with a hundred franchises up and running has had a chance to test its business formula and has experience in helping franchisees get started. A company with only eight or ten units in operation is relatively young and still has a lot to learn. But be leery of a franchise that's merely on the drawing board and isn't yet in actual operation. It might never open and, even if it does, might not prosper. Obviously, a franchise that's not yet open can't give you hard information about sales or profitability.

The franchisor must also tell you how many franchises it has canceled or terminated in the last three years, how many it has not renewed, and how many the franchisor has reacquired.

Contact franchisees in your state or in nearby states. Ask questions: "How's it working out? Was it a good deal? Would you do it again? Are you making a profit? How much?" Franchisees sometimes feel locked in and are reluctant to admit that they made a mistake in buying a franchise, but they might level with you if you ask, "Would you feel comfortable recommending that I put my life savings into this deal?"

Ask franchisees whether they get help and support from the home office and how often they see someone from headquarters. Spend a day or two at a few franchises. Picture yourself in that setting. How does the system seem to be working? If there's a franchisee organization, see if you can attend meetings and get old newsletters. Don't rely on what one or two franchisees tell you—they could have unrevealed ties to the franchisor or be unrealistically positive because they're trying to unload their own franchise or will be paid a commission if they help reel you in.

As noted above, some franchisees might have signed agreements with the franchisor containing gag clauses. If so, these franchisees won't be free to discuss their franchise operations with you.

Item 21: Financial Statements

The franchisor must file audited financial statements showing the condition of the company. Unless you have experience in interpreting financial statements, get an accountant with franchise experience to interpret the figures and help you develop tough questions. You want a franchisor to be financially strong enough to follow through on training commitments, trademark protection, and support services. If a franchisor is financially weak—many are—and folds overnight, your franchise might not be worth much.

To find an accountant with the right experience, seek recommendations from owners of successful local franchises who have been in business for a while.

Item 22: Contracts

The franchisor must attach to the disclosure document a copy of all agreements that you'll sign if you purchase the franchise. This includes lease agreements, option agreements, and purchase agreements. Read them carefully and don't sign until you understand everything.

Item 23: Receipt

The last page of the disclosure document is a detachable receipt, which you sign as evidence that you received the disclosure document.

The Franchise Agreement

If you buy a franchise, you and the franchisor will sign a long document called a franchise agreement. There probably will be other documents to sign at the same time, but the franchise agreement is far and away the most important. Whether or not any terms of the agreement are negotiable depends on whether the franchisor is new or long established and on prevailing market conditions. A new franchisor eager to penetrate the market might be more flexible and willing to make concessions than an established franchisor whose franchises are in high demand.

Again, if the franchisor has made any promises to you, make sure that they're in the franchise agreement. Otherwise, chances are you won't be able to enforce them.

Let's look at a few sensitive areas of a franchise deal that you must be aware of before you plunk down your money and sign an agreement.

Franchise Fee

The extent of your personal liability for the franchise fee and other franchise obligations is a crucial consideration for you in making this deal.

Does the franchise agreement allow you to avoid personal liability for franchise-related debts by forming a corporation to serve as the franchisee? Or does the franchisor require you (and perhaps your spouse as well) to be personally responsible for all franchise obligations?

At the risk of being repetitive, I strongly recommend against pledging your house or other assets as security for payment of the franchise fee. (See "Initial Fees," above, for how the franchise fee is dealt with in the disclosure document.)

Advertising Fees

If the franchise agreement requires you to pay an advertising fee to the franchisor, make sure that part of that fee is earmarked for local advertising over which you'll have some control. Perhaps the franchisor will agree to match any money you spend on local advertising. This is especially important if your franchise will be in an area where there are only a few other franchise locations. Otherwise, the franchisor might spend all the advertising money one thousand miles away where there are more franchisees—and you'll essentially be paying to support someone else's business.

Law From the Real World

Talk to Someone Who's Been There

Jenna, a legal assistant, inherited $200,000. To achieve her goal of financial independence, she decided to start a business. Drawing on the experience of her cousin Max, who had done very well running several franchised taco stores, Jenna decided to look at franchise opportunities.

Because she couldn't afford a major franchise, she narrowed her search to small outfits. One, a Belgian waffle shop, particularly intrigued her. When she expressed interest and her solvency was documented, she was quickly:

- flown to corporate headquarters
- assigned to two enthusiastic "vice presidents"
- shown an exciting video featuring a waffle shop overflowing with happy customers
- taken on a tour of a "typical" waffle franchise outlet, and
- told there were only a few franchises left and she had to decide quickly.

It almost worked. But at literally the last minute before signing she decided she had better call her cousin Max. He yelled "stop" so loudly that she told the franchise she wanted a few days to investigate, even if it meant losing out on the deal.

The investigation showed that the franchise was almost broke, three lawsuits from disappointed franchisees were pending, and the supposedly successful franchise was owned by the parent company and looked successful because prices were kept artificially low to bring in customers. And, oh yes, the "vice presidents" who dealt with Jenna were really sales reps working on commission.

Be alert for arrangements that allow the franchisor to reap profits from the advertising fees it charges you. In one case, a federal court said it was legal for Meineke Mufflers to set up its own in-house ad agency and hire it to handle franchise system advertising—a scheme that profited Meineke to the tune of millions of dollars in fees. (*Broussard v. Meineke Discount Muffler Shops*, 155 F.3d 331 (4th Cir. 1998).)

Royalty Fees

Typically, the royalty fees you pay the franchisor are a percentage of your gross sales. (See "The Downsides of Franchise Ownership," above.) They might, however, be a flat weekly or monthly charge. Be cautious about a franchisor who charges a small initial franchise fee but then charges you a high percentage of monthly sales.

> **EXAMPLE:** Compare two fast food operations. Franchisor A charges Franchisee A an initial fee of $5,000 and monthly royalties of 8% (in addition to advertising fees). Franchisor B charges Franchisee B a franchise fee of $20,000 and monthly royalties of 5% (not including advertising). Let's say that each franchise has annual sales of $500,000. In the first year, each franchisee will pay $45,000 to the franchisor. But look at succeeding years. Franchisee A will pay $40,000 each year to its franchisor, while Franchisee B pays only $25,000.

> **CAUTION**
>
> **Franchise royalties are costly.** Remember that many franchises simply are bad business deals. In a world where it's very hard for any small business to make a 10% profit, giving a huge chunk of money to the franchisor as a royalty rarely makes sense.

Hidden Costs

Read the franchise agreement carefully to uncover any hidden costs—many of which are mentioned earlier in this chapter. It's to your advantage if the income received by the franchisor is primarily based on royalties. That way, the franchisor has a direct interest in making your business profitable. The franchisor's incentive to promote your profitability is somewhat reduced if the franchisor begins to see itself as primarily your landlord or supplier rather than as a business partner.

If you must buy equipment, supplies, or inventory from the franchisor, make sure that the prices you'll pay are competitive with those charged by outside sources. You don't want to sign up with a franchisor that plans to gouge you on these items—especially if they're of iffy quality.

Yes, the franchisor has a legitimate interest in seeing that all franchisees run standardized operations, and this can require that certain items, such as food supplies, be exactly the same. But this need for specialization should be balanced against your need to make a decent profit. Franchisors often allow you to buy equipment and goods through an approved supplier, as long as the franchisor's specifications are met.

Quotas

Some franchise agreements require you to meet sales quotas. For example, your agreement might state that if you don't maintain a certain volume of business, you'll no longer have the right to an exclusive territory. In some cases, the franchisor might also reserve the right to terminate your franchise if quotas aren't met.

Watch out for this one. If the quotas aren't realistic or if it takes you longer than you expected to master the business, you face the horrible prospect of losing some or all of your investment.

The Franchise Term

Typically, a franchise agreement provides for a term of five to 15 years. Beware of an agreement that states that the franchise can be terminated "at will" by the franchisor upon written notice. See below for a further discussion of termination provisions.

Also carefully study your renewal rights. Is renewal entirely in the hands of the franchisor? If you do renew, will a renewal fee be charged? Will you have to sign a new franchise agreement containing whatever terms are in effect when you renew? This could change the whole ball game, because ten years from now when you go to renew, a new franchise agreement could have higher royalties or advertising fees.

Under some franchise agreements, the franchisor can require a franchisee to install expensive improvements in the business premises—even beyond the start-up installations. If the franchise agreement doesn't grant you the automatic right to renew your franchise on the same terms, seek language limiting the franchisor's right to force you to put expensive improvements into the business beyond the initial alterations. You want to be sure that if you're forced to put more money into the premises, you have enough time to recover that investment.

Assignment

Usually, a franchise agreement says that you must get the franchisor's written approval before you transfer or assign your franchise agreement to someone else. But what happens if you have a serious health problem that prevents you from running the franchise? Could you transfer the franchise to a family member? Or, if you were to die, would your spouse automatically be able to continue the business for you?

And if you die, is there a deadline (such as 90 days or six months) during which the franchise must be transferred to a new owner to avoid termination of the franchise by the franchisor? Find out how long it takes, if someone wants to buy your franchise, to learn whether the franchisor approves or disapproves of the sale.

One way of dealing with your possible death as an owner of a franchise is a clause allowing your survivors a period of time to elect to keep and operate the business, as long as they meet the franchisor's training requirements.

Assuming you remain hale and hearty, but want to be able to get out of the franchise, some franchisors might be willing to give you the right to sell, subject to the franchisor's right to match any bona fide offer (called a right of first refusal). For example, if someone comes to you with an offer to buy your franchise, you would have to give the franchisor 30 or 60 days to meet the terms of the purchase.

Termination

Study carefully what the franchise agreement says about the franchisor's right to terminate the franchise. If the franchisor can terminate your franchise because you have supposedly defaulted upon or breached the agreement, you want to be notified in writing of the franchisor's intent and given at least 30 days in which to clear the defaults or correct the breaches. On the other side of the coin, you might want to have the right to terminate the agreement yourself if the franchisor is in default.

Commonly, the franchisor has the right to terminate the franchise if you either fail to operate the business, understate your gross revenues, don't pay royalties when due, or participate in a competing business.

 CAUTION
Termination without good cause. Watch out for franchise agreements that give the franchisor the right to terminate the franchise whether it has a good reason or not. Such clauses are harsh and unfair—so much so that several states have enacted statutes limiting the right of a franchisor to unilaterally terminate a franchisee. Typically, under such statutes, the franchisor would have to show good cause before terminating you.

Competition

It's critical to know where you stand in terms of competition with other franchisees. Typically, the franchisor grants you a protected territory for your franchise operations. Within your territory, your franchisor agrees not to grant another franchise or to operate its own competing business. If you don't have a protected territory, will the franchisor at least give you first crack at buying any proposed new location near yours?

A franchise agreement also usually restricts you from competing in a similar business during the term of the franchise and for several years after its termination. Generally, courts enforce these restrictive covenants if they're reasonable as to time and geographic scope. Franchisors want to make sure their trade secrets aren't misused. You, on the other hand, don't want to give up your right to earn a living in the field that you know best. So take a close look at the noncompetition language and make sure that it doesn't restrict you too severely. Maybe you can live with a provision that says that you won't go into a competing business in the same county as your franchise for two years after a termination; but maybe you can't.

Resolving Disputes With Your Franchisor

If you do opt for a franchise, try to keep the lines of communication with your franchisor open. Talk about problems as soon as they begin to emerge. If you wait until a lawsuit is your only option, you'll discover how expensive, time-consuming, and often frustrating or even hopeless litigating with a franchisor can be.

A better option could be for you to band together with other franchisees to try to work out your mutual grievances with the franchisor. You'll gain negotiating power by presenting your concerns as a group.

Some franchisees even form a separate franchisee's organization to negotiate on their behalf. If such negotiation doesn't work, look into whether the FTC—or perhaps the attorney general who enforces the franchise laws in your state—will take up the cudgels for you.

As a final resort, hire a lawyer familiar with franchisee rights to evaluate your prospects of winning a lawsuit. Be aware that franchise law is a relatively specialized area; not all business lawyers are experienced in this field.

Insuring Your Business

A well-designed insurance program can protect your business from many types of perils. Consider the following:

- A fire destroys all the furniture, fixtures, and equipment in your restaurant.
- Burglars steal $75,000 worth of computer equipment you use in your book publishing business.
- A customer visiting your yogurt store slips on the just-washed floor and shatters her elbow.
- On the way to an office supply store to pick up some printer paper, one of your employees runs a stop sign and injures a child.
- A house painter has a severe allergic reaction to a solvent that your company manufactures and distributes.
- One of your employees is hospitalized for four weeks with a severe back injury she received while trying to lift a heavy package.
- The building where you're located is severely damaged by a windstorm. You're forced to close your doors for two months while repairs are made. In addition to having to pay $35,000 for continuing business expenses, you lose the $25,000 of profit you expected for that period—a total loss of $60,000.
- A client installs a lawn sprinkling system based on specifications you recommended as a landscape architect. Because you hadn't checked soil conditions carefully, the system malfunctions, flooding your client's basement and ruining the antique furniture stored there. Your client sues you for professional negligence.

Maybe none of these will happen to your business—but unless you consider yourself permanently exempt from Murphy's Law ("If anything can go wrong, it will"), don't bet on it. Fortunately, insurance is available to cover each of these events and for many of these risks, if not most, coverage is reasonably cost effective.

Not every small business needs every type of coverage. In fact, a business that tries to buy insurance to cover all insurable risks probably wouldn't have money left over to do anything else. Deciding on insurance coverage usually involves some difficult choices. Here are some general rules to start with:

- Get enough property and liability coverage to protect yourself from common claims. These are the most important kinds of insurance for a small business.
- Buy insurance against serious risks where the insurance is reasonably priced.
- Keep costs down by selecting high deductibles.
- Self-insure if insurance is prohibitively expensive or the particular risk is highly unlikely.
- Adopt aggressive policies to reduce the likelihood of insurance claims, particularly in areas where you're self-insured.

The sections below look at the standard types of insurance available to small businesses and how you can put together a reasonable insurance program.

Working With an Insurance Agent

Find and work with a knowledgeable insurance agent—one who takes the time to analyze your business operations and to come up with a sensible program for your company.

Generally, it's best to work with a single insurance agent for all your business needs so that coverages can be coordinated. But be sure to find out whether any agent you're speaking to is locked into one insurance company. If so, it might be wise to look elsewhere. The agent you choose should be willing to obtain quotes from several companies so that you don't pay more than is necessary.

To find a competent insurance agent or broker, talk to local businesspeople, particularly those in your line of work. Other people in the same field should be able to give you good leads on insurance agents. Working with an agent who knows your business is advantageous because that person is already a fair way along the learning curve when it comes to helping you select an affordable and appropriate package.

EXAMPLE: Louisa, who owns a plant nursery, wants insurance coverage for risks associated with bugs and toxic substances. She finds an insurance agent who already works with similar businesses. The agent knows what insurance is available for a plant nursery and how to tailor the coverage to Louisa's business so that it will be affordable.

Insurance Terminology

In some parts of the country, the term "insurance agent" refers to a person who represents a specific company, and "insurance broker" refers to a person who is free to sell insurance offered by various companies. Elsewhere, the term "insurance agent" is used more broadly to cover both types of representatives —and that's how it's used in this chapter.

Steer clear of an agent who, without learning the specifics of your business, whips out a package policy and claims it will solve all your problems. Yes, the insurance industry has developed some excellent packages that cover the basic needs of various businesses. For example, there are packages offered for offices, retail sales operations, service businesses, hotels, industrial and processing companies, and contractors. One of these might meet your needs, but neither you nor your insurance agent will know for sure until the agent asks you a lot of questions and thoroughly understands your business. If the agent is unable or unwilling to tailor your coverage to your particular business, find someone else.

Be frank with your agent when discussing your business. Reveal all areas of unusual risk. If you fail to disclose all the facts, you might not get the coverage you need or, in some circumstances, the insurance company could later take the position that you misrepresented the nature of your operation and, for that reason, deny you coverage for exceptional risks.

Make sure you have a clear understanding of what your insurance policy covers and what's excluded. Does the policy exclude damage from a leaking sprinkler system? From a boiler explosion? From an earthquake? If so, and these are risks you face, find out if they can be covered by paying a small extra premium.

Also ask how much the agent will help in processing claims if you do have a loss. Ideally, the insurance company should have a local or regional office that's readily accessible to you. That's normally a better arrangement and more personal than dealing with an insurance company that hires an independent claim service to investigate and deal with claims.

It's a good idea to talk to several agents before making a final selection. Ask for written recommendations on comparable coverage and what the cost will be. There should be no charge for providing this information, because the agents will be eager to get your business.

Is the Company Solvent?

In recent years, many insurance companies have become insolvent. If you wind up with a company that goes broke and you have a loss covered by a policy, you might receive only a paltry portion of the coverage that you paid for or none at all. The best way to minimize this risk is to work with a company that appears in good financial shape.

There are organizations that rate the financial health of insurance companies. Before ordering insurance, ask your insurance broker or agent to obtain and give you a report on the financial solvency of any insurance company you are considering.

Property Coverage

In considering property coverage, there are four main issues to think about:

- What business property should you insure?
- What perils will the property be insured against? In other words, under what conditions will you be entitled to receive payment from the insurance company?
- What dollar amount of insurance should you carry? (Obviously, the higher the amount, the higher the premiums. You don't want to waste money on insurance but you do want to carry enough so that a loss wouldn't jeopardize your business.)
- Should you buy coverage for replacement cost or for the present value of the property?

 SKIP AHEAD

"Tenant's Insurance," below, outlines property insurance from a renter's point of view. Renters might want to skip ahead, then return here and read the general information on how property insurance works.

Property Covered

Your insurance policy will contain a section called "building and personal property coverage form," which lists exactly what property is covered. If you own the building you're occupying, be sure the building is covered, including:

- completed additions
- permanently installed fixtures, machinery, and equipment
- outdoor fixtures (such as pole lights), and
- property used to maintain or service the building (such as fire extinguishing equipment).

The policy may also cover additions under construction as well as materials, equipment, supplies, and temporary structures on or within 100 feet of the main building.

Be sure that your business personal property is also covered. A typical policy covers the following items located on the business premises:

- furniture and fixtures
- machinery and equipment
- inventory
- all other personal property used in the business (such as technical books and software)
- leased personal property, if you're contractually obligated to insure it, and
- personal property of others that's in your custody.

> **CAUTION**
>
> **Be sure that everything is covered.** Check carefully to be sure the policy covers all the types of personal property that you own or expect to own: furniture, equipment, goods that you sell, products that you manufacture, and raw materials used in the manufacturing process.

Typically, various items are excluded, such as accounting records, currency, deeds, and vehicles held for sale. If you need coverage on excluded items, you can usually arrange it for an additional premium.

Perils Covered

More than 90% of the time, property insurance for small businesses is written in one of three "forms," or types of coverage (explained just below): "basic form," "broad form," and "special form." Special form coverage is the most common and affords the best protection.

Whichever policy you choose, read it carefully before you pay for it—not just when you've suffered a loss. You might discover that some coverage is narrower than it first seemed. For example, smoke loss could refer only to loss caused by a faulty heating or cooking unit; it might not cover smoke damage from industrial equipment. Similarly, an explosion might not include a burst steam boiler.

Fortunately, most insurance policies today are written in plain English so you should have little problem in understanding what's covered and what isn't. If you need coverage not provided in the policy, talk to your agent about how to add it on.

Basic form coverage includes losses caused by fire, lightning, explosion, windstorm or hail, smoke, aircraft or vehicles (but not loss or damage caused by vehicles you own or operate in the course of your business), riot, vandalism, sprinkler leaks, sinkholes, and volcanoes. The policy defines these perils—and also lists some exclusions, such as nuclear hazards, power failures, or mudslides.

Broad form coverage contains everything that's in the basic form and adds protection from a few more perils, including breakage of glass (that is part of a building or structure), falling objects, weight of snow or ice, and water damage. Again, these terms are defined in the policy and, again, exclusions are listed.

Special form policies are constructed differently than basic and broad form policies and offer wider and slightly more expensive coverage. Instead of listing specific covered perils such as fire and lightning, special form policies simply say that your business property is covered against all risks of physical loss unless the policy specifically excludes or limits the loss. This type of policy offers the most protection. For example, it's a convenient way to insure against loss by theft, which isn't covered by basic and broad form policies. ("Crime Coverage," below, discusses theft insurance.)

 CAUTION

If you need additional coverage. If you're concerned about property loss caused by perils not covered or, in the case of a special form policy, excluded from an insurance policy, you can often get the additional coverage through an endorsement (an add-on page) to the policy by paying an additional premium. For example, such coverage is usually available for losses due to earthquakes and floods.

 TIP

Consider getting insurance coverage for damage caused by terrorists. Congress has reauthorized the Terrorism Risk Insurance Act of 2002 several times, most recently in 2019. Barring additional extensions, the Act now is set to expire at the end of 2027. So, at least until 2027, you can add terrorism coverage to your insurance policy for a small additional premium.

Earthquake and Flood Insurance

Earthquake insurance can be handled through a separate policy or an endorsement to basic, broad, or special form coverage. Insurance companies typically state deductibles in an earthquake endorsement as a percentage—such as 10%—rather than as a dollar amount. This means that the higher your policy limit, the bigger the deductible. As a result, some businesspeople choose a $200,000 policy with a $20,000 deductible rather than a $400,000 policy with a $40,000 deductible. They reason that the deductible on the latter policy is so high they're unlikely to ever collect anything.

Flood insurance, by contrast, is usually handled through a separate policy called "difference in conditions."

 TIP

Combining property and liability insurance in one policy. You can purchase property insurance as a stand-alone and buy a separate stand-alone policy for liability coverage (discussed in "Liability Insurance," below), or you can buy a policy that combines both coverages. It's often—but not always —cheaper to buy a combination policy. Here's where comparison shopping definitely pays off.

Amount of Coverage

Be sure to carry enough insurance on the building to rebuild it. But there's no need to insure the total value of your real property (the legal term that includes land and buildings), because land doesn't burn. Especially if you're in an area where land is very valuable, this is a big consideration.

If you're in doubt as to how much it would cost you to rebuild, have an appraisal made so you know that your idea of value is realistic. Because the value of the building and other property might increase, it's wise to get a new appraisal every few years. Your insurance agent should be able to help you do this.

Usually it's best to insure your property for 100% of its value. If doing this is prohibitively expensive, consider a policy with a higher deductible rather than underinsuring.

Underinsuring to get a reduced premium is a false economy for several reasons. Not only are you not covered if you suffer a total loss, but it might also reduce your ability to recover for a smaller loss. This is because most insurance policies carry a coinsurance clause, which states that to recover the full policy amount, you have to carry insurance to cover at least 80% (this percentage may vary) of the property's replacement cost or actual cash value. If you don't, you become a coinsurer if there's a loss, even if it's less than the policy maximum; the policy will only pay off a percentage of its face value.

> **EXAMPLE 1:** Fluoro Corporation owns a $1 million building. If Fluoro carries $800,000 worth of insurance or more, the insurance company will pay Fluoro for the full amount of any loss up to the policy limit. For example, if the loss is $500,000 Fluoro will get the full $500,000. If the loss is $900,000, Fluoro will receive only $800,000, the policy limit.

> **EXAMPLE 2:** Pluto Associates owns a similar $1 million building. To get a reduced premium, the partners decide to carry only $400,000 worth of insurance. If there's a fire and Pluto has a loss of $200,000, its insurance company will pay only $100,000. Because Pluto carried only half of the 80% figure mentioned in the policy, it's entitled to only a proportional payment.

Replacement Cost vs. Current Value

Historically, in case of a loss, a basic fire insurance contract covered the actual current value of the property, not its full replacement value. Today, policies are routinely available with replacement cost coverage. This is the coverage you want.

> **EXAMPLE:** Sure-Lock Corporation owns a 20-year-old building. The current cash value of the building (the amount someone would pay to buy it) is $1.5 million. But if the building burned down, Sure-Lock would have to pay $2 million to replace it. If Sure-Lock buys insurance based on the building's cash value and the policy has an 80% coinsurance clause, the company will need to insure the building for $1.2 million. If Sure-Lock buys insurance based on replacement cost, it will need to insure for $1.6 million, which is 80% of $2 million.

The real cost of insurance is reduced when you consider that insurance premiums for a business are a recognized business expense—which means they are tax deductible.

Ordinance or Law Coverage

If you're purchasing insurance for an older building—either because you own it or your lease requires it—understand that a normal basic form, broad form, or special form policy designed to replace your existing building should it be destroyed probably won't be adequate. The problem is that legal requirements adopted since the building was constructed will normally require that a stronger, safer, more fire-resistant building be constructed. Doing this can cost far more than simply replacing the old building. To cope with this possibility, you want a policy that will not only replace the building but pay for all legally required upgrades. This coverage is called "ordinance or law coverage."

EXAMPLE: Time Warp, Inc., sells antique furniture and building materials removed from old homes. In keeping with its image of days gone by, Time Warp does business in a 100-year-old building in a historic part of town. Time Warp carries insurance for the full replacement cost, $300,000. One day a fire destroys 50% of the building. The insurance pays $150,000 toward reconstruction, but the Time Warp owners learn to their dismay that rebuilding will cost much more and that their insurance policy doesn't cover the additional costs.

The value of ordinance or law coverage is apparent when you realize that a typical property insurance policy usually excludes the following:

- **The cost of meeting current health and safety codes.** The old building in the example above was of wood frame construction and lacked an elevator and sprinkler system. That was okay before the fire. The building predated the health and safety ordinances and was "grandfathered"—specifically exempted from the new construction requirements. After the fire, it's a whole new ball game. In rebuilding, Time Warp must spend an additional $200,000 for the masonry construction, elevator, and sprinkler system current health and safety codes require.
- **The cost of rebuilding the undamaged portion of the building.** The local ordinance requires that if a building built before current codes is destroyed by fire to the extent of 50% or more, the entire building must be replaced. The cost of replacing the undamaged 50% of the building is another $250,000.
- **The cost of demolition.** The local ordinance requires that, because of the extent of damage, the entire building—both the damaged and undamaged portions—must be torn down before reconstruction begins. That will cost another $50,000.

Ordinance or law coverage would pay for all of these items.

Tenant's Insurance

If you're a tenant, read the insurance portion of your lease. You might have agreed to insure the building and protect the landlord against any liability suits based on your activities, in which case you'll need the type of coverage an owner would carry. This is available through a renter's commercial package policy, which provides routine product liability coverage for businesses not involved in hazardous activities and allows you to name your landlord as an additional insured.

Even if you haven't agreed to provide insurance coverage in your lease, a renter's commercial policy can make excellent sense. Not only will it cover any of your "leasehold improvements," such as paneling and partitions, but it will also cover damage to the premises caused by your negligence.

For example, if the building you rent suffers fire or water damage as a result of an employee's negligence (a fire in an area where food is prepared spreads and damages the walls and ceiling), you might be liable. This is true even if the building owner is insured and recovers from his or her insurance company, because the owner's insurer has the right to try to recover.

What the insurer will pay you for loss to leasehold improvements is based not on replacement value but on what's called the "use interest" in the improvements. Basically, the insurance company looks at how long you would have had the use of the improvements and reimburses you for the use you lose.

EXAMPLE: Court Reporting Associates (CRA) installs $20,000 worth of paneling in their rented offices. They have a five-year lease with an option to renew for five more years—which, for insurance purposes, is treated as a ten-year lease. Two years into the lease, a fire destroys the paneling. Because CRA used up 20% of the lease before the fire, it will receive payment for only 80% of value of the paneling.

Insurance clauses in leases vary widely. (See Chapter 13 for more on such clauses.)

Liability Insurance

The second major category of insurance coverage for a small business is liability insurance. Your business can be legally liable to people injured and for property damaged because you or your employees didn't use reasonable care. For example, if a customer falls on a slippery floor and then sues you, you might be liable if you negligently failed to provide safe premises.

As you probably know, when it comes to personal injuries, judges are broadening the scope of what people can sue for—and juries are increasingly generous in awarding damages. Because an injured person can collect not only for lost wages and medical bills but also for such intangibles as pain, suffering, and mental anguish, a single personal injury verdict against your business has the potential to wipe it out. For that reason, unless you have a very unusual business that has no personal contact with customers, suppliers, or anyone else, your insurance program should include liability coverage.

Some intentional acts not involving bodily injuries are also usually covered under the liability portions of an insurance policy. Examples are libel, slander, defamation, false imprisonment, and false arrest.

General Liability Policies

Liability policies are designed to protect you against lawsuit judgments up to the amount of the policy limit plus the cost of defending the lawsuit. They provide coverage for a host of common perils, including customers and guests falling, getting mangled by your front door, or otherwise getting injured.

Liability policies usually state a dollar limit per occurrence and an aggregate dollar limit for the policy year. For example, your policy might say that it will pay $500,000 per occurrence for personal injury or a total of $1 million in any one policy year.

Toxic Waste Cleanup

Suppose the government orders your company to clean up a toxic waste problem on your property. This can and regularly does occur even if the pollution occurred years before you bought the property. Will your liability insurance policy cover the cleanup costs (called the "response costs")?

Most courts that have considered this question ruled that response costs are covered by a liability insurance policy, but a significant minority have ruled otherwise. If you have a business or own property that by any stretch of the imagination could become involved in a toxic waste or pollution problem, try to find out exactly how far your liability coverage extends in environmental situations. You might need to buy supplementary coverage (if available and affordable) to cover this risk.

Keep yourself informed on this subject. It's likely that, faced with court decisions saying that general liability coverage requires insurance companies to pay for response costs under cleanup orders, insurance companies will tighten up their policy language to exclude these expenses. You might need to buy special coverage if your business faces the possibility of a cleanup order.

 CAUTION

Excluded claims. The typical general liability policy doesn't cover punitive damages—damages intended to punish your business for willful or malicious behavior rather than compensate the injured person. And liability coverage won't protect your business if an employee intentionally assaults a customer. In addition, a general liability policy doesn't cover injuries caused by defective products or motor vehicles, or by an employer's liability for injuries received by workers on the job. Special coverage for these types of liabilities is discussed in the next three subsections.

As noted, both building owners and tenants may purchase liability coverage separately or as part of a package policy that also provides a number of other types of insurance, including fire insurance for the building itself.

 TIP

Check your coverage for employees who telecommute. If you allow employees to work from home, your business might be liable if a delivery person or another business visitor is injured at the employee's home. This will depend on the law in your state. To be safe, check with your insurance agent to make sure your liability insurance covers this situation. If it doesn't, you can add the coverage at a minimal cost.

Product Liability Insurance

Product liability insurance covers liability for injuries caused by products you design, manufacture, or sell. You might be liable to a person injured by a defective product or one that came without adequate instructions or warnings.

Product liability insurance can be very expensive, but if your business manufactures, distributes, or sells a product that might injure people, you should seriously consider buying it. For example, if you manufacture medical instruments or chemicals, you'll probably want this coverage. If you're a retailer and sell products in their original packages and provide no product assembly, service, or advice, your exposure is drastically reduced; the manufacturer is primarily liable and the product liability coverage provided by standard renter's commercial policies should be adequate.

The amount of product liability insurance that you need depends on the nature of your product and not on your gross sales. Obviously, a company that sells $2 million worth of paper clips a year will need less coverage than a firm that manufactures and sells $2 million worth of gauges critical to the safe operation of heaters.

Vehicle Insurance

Make sure your business carries liability insurance not only on its own cars and trucks but also on employees' cars and trucks when those vehicles are used for business purposes. This coverage is known as "employer's nonowned automobile liability" and is relatively inexpensive—a premium of $65 to $100 might buy you coverage of $1 million for one year. Vehicle insurance isn't provided under general liability policies.

It wouldn't hurt to check your employees' driving records before you entrust company vehicles to them or send them on business errands using their own cars, but failure to check won't be a problem under most vehicle policies unless the insurance company has listed that employee as an excluded driver. To do this, insurance companies periodically ask businesses for the names of employees who are driving on company business. They then check the names against state driving records. If this results in the discovery of a poor driving record for a particular employee, the insurer will likely exclude that driver from coverage and notify you.

You can also add coverage for injury or property damage while using a leased vehicle to either your motor vehicle policy or your general liability policy—which is what a company would do if it owned no vehicles. This is known as "hired vehicle" coverage.

Most vehicle policies also cover physical damage to the car or truck caused by collision, fire, or theft.

Workers' Compensation Insurance

As the name implies, workers' compensation insurance covers your liability for injuries received by employees on the job. All businesses with employees are required to provide for some kind of workers' compensation coverage.

Usually, an injured worker covered by workers' comp can't sue your business for negligence. But as a trade-off, that worker can collect specified benefits from your business for work-related injuries whether or not the business was negligent. All the worker must prove is that the injury came about in the course of employment—a concept that has a very broad definition in many states. For example, an employee injured at a company picnic might have a valid workers' compensation claim.

The amount of money that the employee can recover is limited. The worker can recover for medical treatment and lost wages and, in serious cases, for impaired future earning capacity. But there are no awards for pain and suffering or mental anguish. A growing portion of workers' compensation claims, however, result from mental or emotional stress.

As a sole proprietor, you usually can't be personally covered by workers' compensation insurance for any work-related injuries you sustain; only your employees can be covered. Workers' comp coverage of a partner or of an officer of a small corporation usually isn't required but can be obtained if you choose.

Each state has a law setting out what an employer must do to provide for workers' compensation benefits. Sometimes an employer can self-insure. Usually, that isn't practical for small businesses because they can't afford the type of cash reserve required by state law. Most small businesses buy insurance through a state fund or from a private insurance carrier. Insurance rates are based on the industry and occupation, as well as the size of the payroll. Your business's safety record can also influence the rate; if you have more accidents than are usually anticipated, your rate is likely to be increased.

Although workers' compensation laws cover virtually all injury claims by an employee against an employer, in a few instances employees can still sue an employer for pain and suffering resulting from a work-related injury. For example, in some states, an employer whose gross negligence or intentional conduct caused an injury can be sued. A second part of a workers' compensation policy (sometimes called "coverage B" or "employer's liability") insures the employer against liability for these types of claims. Most businesses should consider policy limits of $500,000 for this coverage.

The Expanding Boundaries of Workers' Comp

Premiums for workers' compensation insurance are on the rise—partly because judges are extending the types of claims for which workers can receive payment. A key factor in many cases is stressful working conditions. Money has been awarded to:

- a worker who suffered a heart attack after an argument with his boss
- a truck driver who blacked out while driving and was then unable to drive because of anxiety that he might black out again, and
- a worker who fainted, fell, and suffered a head injury after his supervisor told him he would be transferred to a new department and had to take a pay cut.

Judges have also expanded the right to receive workers' comp in other situations. For example, benefits were awarded to the family of a convenience store clerk who died after getting into a fistfight with a disorderly customer. And a woman who bought a cold tablet from her employer received payments when the tablet caused her to have tremors due to a congenital condition.

In another case, a cocktail waitress at a resort was on her way home when she stopped to help a resort guest who was having car trouble. The guest sexually assaulted her. The waitress was awarded workers' comp for injuries she received in the assault. The court's reasoning: The waitress had been told to be "very cordial and nice to guests." Therefore, her offer of assistance on the road was related to her employment.

Workers' compensation insurance is required only for employees—not for independent contractors. (Independent contractors are covered in greater detail in Chapter 15.) Small businesses sometimes buy services from independent contractors to save money on workers' compensation insurance, as well as taxes and other expenses normally associated with employees. That's fine as long as you correctly label people as independent contractors rather than employees. But if you make a mistake, and a person improperly labeled as an independent contractor is injured while doing work for your business, you might have to pay large sums to cover medical bills and lost wages that should have been covered by workers' compensation insurance.

In addition, you can sometimes have a problem with a properly classified independent contractor who hires employees to perform some work for you. If you hire an independent contractor who has employees, insist on seeing a certificate of insurance establishing that the employees are covered by workers' compensation insurance.

> EXAMPLE: You hire Sharon, who is doing business as Superior Painters, to paint your store. Sharon will be doing the work along with two of her employees. If Sharon doesn't carry workers' compensation insurance for her employees, and any of them are injured on the job, they might be treated as your employees, which would increase your own workers' compensation premiums. Also, have Sharon show you that she has general liability coverage; if she or one of her employees injures one of your customers while painting your store, your own insurance might not cover these injuries.

Other Insurance to Consider

There are many forms of business insurance on the market today. You won't need them all, but some specialized coverage might make sense for your business.

Bonds Covering Employee Theft

If you're seriously concerned that employees might embezzle money from the business, look into bonds that cover all workers, including those hired after the bond goes into effect. Then, if an employee steals from you, the bonding company reimburses you for the loss.

Crime Coverage

Crime insurance covers losses when the criminal isn't connected with your business. Your policy should cover not only burglary and robbery, but also other thefts and loss or disappearance of property. Depending on the kind of business and the part of the country you're in, you might be more concerned about losses by theft than from fire. Computers and other high-tech equipment are relatively light-weight and easy to carry away. A midsized publisher, for example, could easily suffer a $100,000 loss in a night if its computers were stolen.

Usually, your company's business insurance covers only property the company owns, not your personal property.

> EXAMPLE: Management Concepts, Inc., a small consulting firm, is using an expensive computer that's the personal property of Patricia, the corporation's president. If the computer is stolen from the corporate offices, the corporation's insurance policy normally won't cover it. To protect against this kind of problem, Patricia should sign a bill of sale formally transferring legal title to the computer to the corporation. Or she should make sure that the corporation has an insurance policy that specifically protects property of officers or employees that's used in the business.

Probably the most convenient way to insure your business against loss by theft is to purchase the special form of property insurance, which includes such coverage. (See "Property Coverage," above.)

If property is stolen from your business, you will, of course, have to document the loss. Keep a computerized list of your business property, updated periodically. And keep a copy at home or in a fireproof box in case the computer and your records get stolen or destroyed.

Business Interruption Insurance

If your business property is damaged or destroyed and you can't use it, your business losses will far exceed the cost of repairing or replacing the damaged property. Your business might be unable to function until you can find a new location and purchase more goods. For example, if you're in California and an earthquake levels your retail warehouse, or if your business is in Indiana and a tornado rips the roof off your store, or a fire burns you out, you might be out of business for weeks or months while you replace your inventory and locate a new building.

Business interruption insurance—a valuable but often overlooked kind of insurance—covers your lost income while your business is closed, as well as the expenses you incur in keeping your business going while the lost property is repaired or replaced. This insurance coverage also pays the cost of renting temporary quarters. It's also possible to guard against losses if your business is interrupted because disaster strikes someone else.

> EXAMPLE: Tom operates a small bakery. Half of his income comes from supplying bread, rolls, and pastry to a large restaurant. If the restaurant burns down, Tom's income will be drastically reduced. He might sensibly look into business interruption insurance that covers not only losses that would occur should his property be damaged but also those that would result if a major supplier or customer were suddenly forced to stop or curtail operation.

Before you buy business interruption insurance, run through a contingency plan of what you'd do in case of a disaster. Let's say that your warehouse was destroyed by fire. Assuming the contents of the warehouse were covered by your fire or multiperil insurance, you need worry only about how much it will cost you to be out of business until you can set up a temporary warehouse and get more merchandise. Could you replace key merchandise quickly and take other steps to minimize the harm? If it's reasonable to believe that you'll be partially back in business in a couple of weeks and be in fairly good shape within 30 days, business interruption insurance might not really be worth the cost.

 CAUTION

Business interruption coverage is site specific. If, for example, you have two retail stores and a warehouse, you need to make sure that each location is covered.

Will Your Customers Come Through?

Ben runs a successful bookstore. A multiperil contract covers his inventory from loss from most hazards. But he worries that if he is burned out of his historic building, it might take a year or more to get repairs approved and made. Ben asks his insurance broker whether business interruption insurance makes sense.

After establishing that Ben could get new merchandise within a couple of weeks because book wholesalers and publishers would be anxious to help (Ben's credit is good), the broker recommends against it, pointing out that within a mile of Ben's building there are a dozen empty stores that Ben could rent very reasonably and be back in business almost immediately. The fact that Ben's loyal customers would likely support him after a disaster might even mean that sales would go up.

Industry-Specific Insurance

Supplementary insurance policy packages are often available for retail or manufacturing businesses, or even for specific types of businesses—a bookstore, barber shop, or restaurant—and can be well worth looking into. For example, a manufacturing policy might have broader coverage for losses caused by malfunctioning equipment and machinery than a standard special form policy.

 RESOURCE

Useful insurance resource: The Insurance Information Institute offers several publications online at www.iii.org.

Saving Money on Insurance

This chapter is based on the sensible premise that few businesses can really afford to adequately insure themselves against every possible risk. You need to decide what types of insurance are really essential and how much coverage to buy. Though this is no easy task, here are some guidelines that should help.

Set Priorities

Start by looking at what coverage state law requires. For example, there might be minimum requirements for coverage on business related vehicles, and you will almost surely be required to carry workers' compensation insurance if you have employees.

Next, if you rent, you'll need to purchase any insurance required by your lease. See "Tenant's Insurance," above, and "Required Insurance," in Chapter 13, for a discussion of insurance language in a lease.

Beyond the required coverages for your business, ask these questions: What types of property losses would threaten the viability of my business? What kinds of liability lawsuits might wipe me out? Use your answers to tailor your coverage to protect against these potentially disastrous losses.

Be less concerned about insuring against smaller losses. For example, if you're in the self-help publishing business, consider a package especially tailored to printers and publishers that includes liability coverage for errors and omissions (such as leaving some vital information out of an instruction booklet you publish), but be less concerned about protecting yourself against claims of libel—after all, your material never comments on personalities.

Increase the Amount of Your Deductibles

Deductibles are used primarily for real and personal property insurance, including motor vehicle collision coverage. The difference between the cost of a policy with a $250 deductible and one with a $500 or $1,000 or even higher deductible is significant—particularly if you add up the premium savings for five or ten years.

For example, the difference between a $250 and a $500 deductible might be 10% in premium costs, and the difference between a $500 and $1,000 deductible might save you an additional 3% to 5%. Most businesses can afford to be out of pocket $500 or even $1,000—especially if taking this risk means you pay significantly lower premiums.

Consider using money saved with a higher deductible to buy other types of insurance where it's really needed. For example, the amount you save by having a higher deductible might pay for business interruption coverage.

Initiate Loss Prevention and Risk Reduction Measures

Good safety and security measures might eliminate the need for some types of insurance or lead to lower insurance rates. Ask your insurance agent what you can do to get a better rate. Sometimes something simple like installing deadbolt locks or buying two more fire extinguishers will qualify you for a lower premium. Here are some other ideas to cut losses and premiums:

- Install a fire alarm system, if one can be found at a reasonable cost.
- Install fireproofing materials to minimize fire damage in susceptible areas of the premises.
- Isolate and safely store flammable chemicals and other products.
- Provide adequate smoke detectors.
- Install a sprinkler system.

Ideas for preventing theft include:

- Install tamper-proof locks.
- Purchase a secure safe.
- Install an alarm system.
- Install better lighting.
- Hire a security service to patrol your property at night.

Also consider placing bars on doors or windows. This might create a negative impression; an innovative architect or contractor could be able to help you design and install these security devices in ways that are not unsightly.

To prevent injuries to customers, employees, or members of the public, you might:

- Check each applicant's driving record and not hire people to drive who have poor records.
- Give additional training to drivers you do hire.
- Set up a system for safer operation of machinery.
- Conduct fire drills.
- Give your employees protective clothing and goggles if necessary.

How to protect against some types of risks might be obvious to you, but how to protect against many others won't be. Get help from people who are experienced in identifying and dealing with risks. One excellent resource is your insurance company's safety inspector; your insurance agent can tell you whom to contact.

Another good approach is to ask your employees to identify all safety risks, no matter how small. Also ask them to propose cost-effective ways to eliminate or minimize them—they might have cheaper and more practical ideas than you do.

EXAMPLE: Adventure Apparel Corporation sells recreational and travel clothing by mail order from its well-stocked warehouse. The company's 25 employees all take turns serving on the safety committee, which meets regularly to discuss safety issues ranging from the best way to operate computer terminals to reduce the possibility of repetitive motion injuries to making sure that the electric pallet lifters are run only by trained people. The system works because the employees are in a unique position to monitor safety hazards and to suggest practical solutions.

In the long run, a safety program will reduce your losses and, in turn, lower your insurance rates. In the short term, simply putting these practices into effect and letting insurance companies know about them could put you in a lower rate category. And of course, your employees will appreciate the care you show for their well-being—a significant plus in a world where keeping good employees is a real business asset.

Comparison Shop

No two companies charge exactly the same rates; you might be able to save a significant amount by shopping around. But be wary of unusually low prices—they could be a sign of an unstable company (see "Is the Company Solvent?" at the beginning of this chapter for information on how to check out an insurance company). Or it might be that you're unfairly comparing policies that provide very different types of coverage. Make sure you know what you're buying.

Review your coverage and rates periodically. The insurance industry is cyclical, with alternating phases of low prices and high prices. When competition for insurance customers increases in a particular field, you really can achieve savings. But don't dump a loyal agent for a few cents. Ask your agent to look around and meet or come close to meeting the competition.

You can make the cyclical nature of the insurance industry work for you. If you're shopping for insurance during a time when prices are low, try locking in a low rate by signing up for a contract for three or more years.

Transfer Some Risks to Someone Else

Here are some possibilities:

- **Indemnification by manufacturer.** Suppose you run a store that sells exercise equipment primarily from one manufacturer. If you're buying a significant amount of equipment, the manufacturer could be willing to provide insurance that indemnifies your business from any claim by a customer injured by the equipment.

- **Leasing employees.** Some businesses lease employees at least in part because the leasing company takes care of carrying workers' compensation and liability insurance on the employees (among other things). But be cautious—the overall cost of leasing employees might be greater than if you hire directly. You could also to be able to transfer some risks by simply engaging independent contractors to handle the more hazardous aspects of your business operations. (For more on independent contractors, see Chapter 15.)

Find a Comprehensive Package

Look for a small business package that includes a full range of coverage. This is often much cheaper than buying coverage piecemeal from several different companies. Group plans often offer these packages (see "Seek Out Group Plans," below).

Seek Out Group Plans

Is there a trade association in your industry? If so, it might be a source of good insurance coverage. Trade associations often get good affordable insurance rates for their members because they have superior bargaining power.

Self-Insure

To self-insure, you simply don't buy insurance and hope to maintain your own reserve fund to cover likely losses or liabilities. There are two drawbacks. First, despite good intentions, most small businesses don't have enough funds to set aside for this purpose. Second, unlike insurance premiums, money put into a reserve fund isn't tax deductible until or unless you spend it.

Making a Claim

As soon as a loss occurs, gather and preserve evidence to help prove your claim if it becomes necessary. (If you followed my suggestion and have a comprehensive list of your property, get it out now.) Take pictures of any damaged property. Collect documents such as receipts showing what you paid for the lost property. If you can, secure the damaged property in a safe place so that it will be available for inspection later and for possible use in a lawsuit. Gather names of any witnesses who can help substantiate how the loss occurred and the extent of the damage.

Your next step is to request a claim form from your insurance agent. For small, routine losses you or someone else in your company can probably complete the form, with a little help from your agent. If more money is at stake, a lawyer can help you structure and justify your claim.

 RESOURCE

Looking for a lawyer? Asking for a referral to an attorney from someone you trust can be a good way to find legal help. Also, two sites that are part of the Nolo family, Lawyers.com and Avvo.com, provide excellent and free lawyer directories. These directories allow you to search by location and area of law, and list detailed information about and reviews of lawyers.

Whether you're just starting your lawyer search or researching particular attorneys, visit www.lawyers.com/find-a-lawyer and www.avvo.com/find-a-lawyer.

Damage to Rented Space. If you're renting the space your business occupies, start by figuring out whose insurance policy covers the loss—yours or the building owner's. For example, if a pipe breaks, you'll have to look at both insurance policies to see which one covers this risk.

Ideally, your insurance company will pay you for damage to your inventory and equipment, and the owner's insurance company will pay for damage to the building. To make this happen and avoid squabbles, it helps to have a "mutual waiver of subrogation" in your lease. Without it, you can get caught in the crossfire between two insurance companies. (For more on mutual waiver of subrogation clauses in leases, see "Required Insurance" in Chapter 13.)

Often there's a time limit on filing your claim, but you might need more time to analyze all of your damages. Don't feel rushed. Simply file the claim form within the required time limit, listing the losses you're sure of at that time. Indicate that the list of losses is partial and that you're still gathering information.

If you're served with a lawsuit or are informed that an injured person is going to make a claim against your business, get the lawsuit papers and related information to your insurance company as soon as possible. Contact your agent promptly.

Negotiating a Favorable Lease

Many small businesses start out in leased premises and prefer to use leased space throughout their business lives. By leasing rather than owning, you avoid tying up valuable working capital. Also, it's easier to move to new quarters if your space needs change. This chapter looks at how to find the right place for your business and how to negotiate your lease.

RESOURCE

For more information on commercial leases, see *Negotiate the Best Lease for Your Business,* by Janet Portman and Fred S. Steingold (Nolo).

Finding a Place

Your first step is to find the right space. Begin by analyzing the specific needs of your business. Real estate professionals are fond of saying that the three most important factors in choosing a business space are location, location, and location. For certain types of retail stores and restaurants, this might be true. For example, a sandwich shop requires a location with a high volume of foot traffic. Or maybe you'll benefit if you're near other businesses that are similar to yours; restaurants often like to locate in a restaurant district.

But for many other businesses, where you're located doesn't matter much. For example, if you repair bathroom tile, run a computer-based information search business, import jewelry from Bali, or do any one of ten thousand other things, it won't help you to be in a high-visibility, high-rent district. Chances are your business can efficiently operate in a less pricey area, where you can negotiate a lower rent and the landlord is likely to be far more flexible on other lease terms as well.

After you've analyzed what you need, it's time to begin searching for the right spot. Go to the neighborhoods where you might like to locate; spend a day or two driving or walking the streets to see what might be available. Don't just look for vacant space. A store, office, studio, or workshop that's good for your business might be occupied by a tenant who is going out of business—or moving to larger quarters in a few months. There's a lot of turnover among small businesses, and you might get lucky.

Because some of the best opportunities come to light through word of mouth, ask friends, associates, and other businesspeople if they know of available space. Business owners—particularly those in the part of town that you're interested in—might know of businesses that are moving or going out of business long before these vacancies are announced. And if you get there early, the landlord, relieved to avoid a period of vacancy and uncertainty, could offer you a favorable lease.

Adjusting Your Way of Communicating During the COVID-19 Emergency

In this chapter and throughout the book, we recommend various tactics and strategies that might involve dealing with people in person. While the coronavirus pandemic continues, use appropriate precautions such as wearing a mask and practicing social distancing. You might also consider whether you can accomplish your goal using an alternate communication method, like phone, email, text, or videoconferencing.

For-rent ads in newspapers and online are an obvious place to look. If the selection there is limited, call a real estate office that deals primarily with business space. The agent's fee—usually, a percentage of the rent that you'll be paying—is generally paid by the landlord. If your space needs are special, consider hiring an agent to search the market for you. But if you follow this somewhat unusual approach, you'll probably have to pay the agent's commission.

Leases and Rental Agreements: An Overview

A lease is a contract between you and the landlord. A lease can be for a short term (as little as one month) or long term, and it can be written or oral—although a lease for more than a year must be in writing to be legally enforceable past the first year. Some people use the phrase "rental agreement" to describe a short or oral lease for which rent is typically paid once a month and the tenancy can be terminated on a 30-day written notice. (See "Short-Term Leases (Month-to-Month Rentals)," below, for more on short-term leases.) To avoid confusion, I'll stick to the word "lease."

Terminology

Sometimes a written lease talks about the "Lessor" and the "Lessee." The lessor is the landlord; the lessee is the tenant. If you have a choice in terminology, go with the plain English "landlord" and "tenant"; you'll reduce the risk of typos!

In theory, all terms of a lease are negotiable. Just how far you can negotiate, however, depends on economic conditions. If desirable properties are close to full occupancy in your city, landlords might not be willing to negotiate with you over price or other major lease terms.

On the other hand, in many parts of the country where commercial space has been overbuilt or where employees have transitioned to remote workspaces, landlords are eager to bargain with small businesses to fill empty units. Even in a tight market you might come across some acceptable space that, for one reason or another, the landlord is anxious to fill, giving you greater bargaining power. This is often true with a new building or one under construction and the landlord needs cash. Also, if you're one of the first tenants in the building, you might get an especially attractive deal, because your presence could help the landlord attract other tenants.

If you find a landlord willing to negotiate, what should you ask for? After you read "Written Long-Term Leases," below, you'll have a good understanding of the kinds of terms that usually go into a lease. Because you're not likely to get everything you want, it's important to get your priorities straight in your own mind and concentrate on achieving what's most important. What do you really care about? What would be nice to have but not essential? What benefits can you offer the landlord for things you really need?

A lower rent is likely to be high on everybody's bargaining list. But how about physical changes in the building? Would you want the landlord to redesign the entryway? Add some office space at the back of the warehouse? Customize the interior for your needs? More or better parking for your customers might be worth more than slightly lowered rent. Your priorities might be unique to your business, so think them through carefully before making proposals and counterproposals to the landlord.

Let's look at how you might approach the matter of rent. A landlord who is reluctant to lower the basic rent might be willing to make other adjustments—which could be even more valuable. The landlord might do this in order to be able to truthfully tell other prospective tenants that you're paying a high dollar amount per square foot.

(It might sound silly, but some landlords do play this game.) For example, in a slack market, the landlord might be willing to give you a move-in allowance that you can use to fix up the space. Also, check out what the landlord is willing to do in paying for improvements (often called build-outs) to the space. (See "Improvements by the Landlord," below.)

Short-Term Leases (Month-to-Month Rentals)

Once you've found the space you want, the next step, usually, is to sign a lease. Occasionally, a small business that's just starting out prefers an oral lease permitting the tenant to occupy the space from month to month. This might seem attractive if you just want to test the waters, have great uncertainty about the prospects for your business, and wouldn't mind leaving on short notice if the landlord terminated the lease. But even if you want to make only a very short-term commitment, it almost always makes far more sense to negotiate a written month-to-month lease or rental agreement. A written lease clarifies what's been agreed to and helps avoid disputes.

Whether oral or written, the key feature of a month-to-month lease is that you can move—or the landlord can require you to move—on short notice. You can negotiate how notice is required, but if you don't, the law in your state will dictate the amount of time.

In many states, the law requires 30 days' notice, although states don't always compute the time period in the same way. Some, such as California, allow either the landlord or tenant to give notice at any date during a month; the 30 days runs from the notice date. Other states require that the notice be given at least 30 days before the first day of the next monthly rental period; furthermore, the termination date must coincide with the beginning of a new period.

CAUTION

Notice requirements vary from state to state. For information about what's required in your state, you'll need to check the statutes or case law. To learn how to do your own legal research, get Nolo's *Legal Research: How to Find & Understand the Law*, by Stephen Elias (Nolo).

The clauses in a month-to-month lease, other than those dealing with the length of the tenancy, are much the same as those in any other written lease, so be sure to consult the following sections of this chapter.

Written Long-Term Leases

Many small businesses and landlords prefer the protection of a written lease that lasts a year or more. But when you talk to the landlord, you'll probably be presented with a typed or printed lease prepared by the landlord or the landlord's lawyer. Because the terms typically favor the landlord, consider it as no more than the starting point. Chances are excellent that you'll be able to negotiate at least some significant improvements.

Keep in mind that you have two sometimes conflicting goals: to get a favorable lease and to have a good long-term relationship with your landlord. In the interest of long-term harmony, there are times when it makes sense not to fight for the last scrap of a concession as if you were a starving pit bull.

To eliminate a proposed lease's one-sidedness, ask for equal treatment for you and the landlord for all clauses where this is relevant. For example, if the lease requires you to cure your lease defaults within ten days after you receive notice from the landlord, it should also require the landlord to cure his or her defaults within ten days after you give notice. Similarly, if you're required to pay for your landlord's attorneys' fees in enforcing the lease, the landlord should be required to pay for your attorneys' fees if you have to enforce the lease.

Now let's look at some common lease terms and how you might approach them.

FORM

Legal Forms for Starting & Running a Small Business, **by Fred S. Steingold (Nolo),** includes various commercial lease forms, as does the Leases & Rental Agreements section of the store at www.nolo.com.

Who Should Sign the Lease?

Leases begin by naming the landlord and the tenant. Make sure that the person, partnership, or corporation named as landlord is the owner of the property. A husband might not have legal authority to sign leases for space in a building owned solely by his wife. A management company or on-site manager might have only day-to-day management powers that fall short of the right to approve new leases. Or if they can sign a lease, they might be able to offer only specific terms and concessions. If you have any doubts about whom you're dealing with and what authority they have, ask to see a deed or title insurance policy to verify that the named landlord really owns the building. Here are the rules about who's authorized to sign a binding lease on behalf of the landlord:

- If a building is owned by an individual, that person (or an authorized agent) should sign the lease.
- If a building is owned by a general partnership, insist on the signature of one of the partners.
- If a building is owned by a limited partnership (not uncommon for rental properties), require the signature of a general (managing) partner; a limited partner usually lacks the power to bind the partnership.
- If a building is owned by a corporation, get the signature of a corporate officer or an executive with authority to sign leases.
- If a building is owned by a limited liability company, ask that the lease be signed by a member or manager of the LLC.
- If you're dealing with a rental agent who will be negotiating the lease and signing it on behalf of the owner, ask for written

confirmation from the owner that the agent has that authority. Obviously, you need to worry less about this step if the rental agent is part of an established and respected real estate management company, but it never hurts to request documentation.

Who should be named as the tenant? Before you sign a lease as an individual or a partner, be aware that you'll be personally liable for the rent if your business runs into financial problems. If your business fails, the landlord can (and probably will) go after your personal assets such as your car, home, and bank account. To avoid this exposure, consider incorporating or forming an LLC. Then you can sign the lease as President of XYZ, Inc., or XYZ, LLC—and you're personally off the hook. (Personal liability for business debts is discussed in Chapter 1.)

 CAUTION

Beware of personal guarantees. In addition to signing in your corporate capacity, you might be asked to personally guarantee the lease. Doing this makes you personally responsible for the rent and means that the corporation doesn't shield your personal assets. One approach is to offer to guarantee the lease only up to a maximum amount—say, three months' worth of rent. For even greater protection, see if the landlord is willing to release you from your personal guarantee if all rent is paid on time during the first year.

Defining the Space You're Leasing

The lease should identify the space that you'll be occupying. If you're leasing the whole building, that's easy: simply give the street address. If you're leasing less than the whole building, specify your space more precisely. One way is to refer to building or floor plan drawings. For example, you might say "Suite 2 of the Commerce Building as shown on the attached drawing" or "The south half of the first floor of the Entrepreneur Plaza."

In describing the space you'll be occupying, don't overlook the common areas—space you'll be sharing with other tenants. This often includes hallways, restrooms, elevators, storage space, and parking. Spell out in your lease that your business and your customers have the right to use these additional spaces and facilities.

If your business keeps unusual hours, remember to define when you have access to your space and the common spaces. You don't want to find yourself locked out some evening or weekend.

Because commercial space is often priced by the square foot, find out what method is used to compute square footage. Sometimes it's measured from the exterior of the walls or from the middle of the walls' thickness. If this is the case, you'll be paying for some space that's not really usable. This isn't necessarily bad. But you need to find out about it in advance, because it affects rent negotiations.

The square footage rate is usually stated in annual terms—$20 a square foot means $20 per square foot per year. However, it's sometimes stated by the month—$0.60 a square foot means 60 cents per square foot per month. Obviously you need to know exactly what any numbers you're quoted mean.

Also find out if the quoted figure applies only to the space occupied by your business or whether you're expected to pay for a proportionate share of the common areas. If your rent is computed on the basis of dollars per square foot, and if you're asked to pay for a share of the common areas, it's reasonable to seek a lower square-footage rate for common areas.

If your landlord has agreed to set aside some parking spaces for your business or to let you use a storage building or another outbuilding, get it in writing in the lease. Also specify whether indoor storage space will be shared or is reserved exclusively for your use.

Starting Date of the Lease

Your lease should clearly state its starting date. This can sometimes be a problem, especially if you're renting space in a building that's still under construction or space currently occupied. If you sign a lease

before ground has been broken or if the building is only partially complete, what happens if your space isn't ready by the time you need it? This, too, should be addressed in your lease. Otherwise, there might be little pressure on the landlord to meet deadlines.

One possibility is to negotiate a cutoff date by which you have the right to cancel the lease if the building (or your unit) isn't ready for occupancy. You might also be able to collect damages from the landlord if you suffer losses because your space isn't ready on time. But in negotiating such a clause, remember it's always hard to prove lost profits—particularly if you're just starting out in business—so it's better to negotiate a preset amount for your damages.

Also, with a building to be constructed or under construction, state in your lease that until local building officials have issued a certificate of occupancy for the building, no rent will be due. You might think that this is so obvious it doesn't need to be spelled out in your lease, but some landlords have actually tried to collect rent even before building officials have approved the building for occupancy.

In a slight variation on this problem, some leases call for the landlord to erect a shell building. Then you, the tenant, finish off your own space. Obviously, you want to avoid having to install improvements in a partially constructed building that might not be completed for many months. One good solution: a lease clause saying you don't have to start work on your space until the building is enclosed and the common areas—such as hallways and restrooms—are done.

The lease could also require the landlord to have the building and safety department make a preliminary inspection of your space before you start making improvements. The inspection would make sure the landlord has correctly installed the electrical and plumbing lines, and heating, ventilating, and air-conditioning facilities within your leased space. You don't want to risk the possibility that you'll have to rip out and redo your interior work because the landlord's contractor made a mistake.

With space that's currently vacant, ask the landlord to agree to let you have immediate access to decorate and install equipment. That way, you'll be ready to do business when you start paying rent. Spell this out in the lease.

Ending Date of the Lease

The lease should state its termination date, although you might have an option to renew. (See "An Option to Renew a Lease," below.) Some leases state that if the tenant remains in possession after the termination without exercising an option to renew, the tenancy is from month to month during the holdover period. (See the discussion above for information on month-to-month tenancies.)

An Option to Renew a Lease

When you first negotiate a lease, you can often bargain for a clause that gives you the right to renew or extend your lease when its term ends. Let's say you're negotiating a new two-year lease. You like the location, the rent is favorable, and you'd like the right to stay for an extended period if your business is doing well. But at the same time, you're nervous about signing a four-year lease in case your business doesn't prosper.

A two-year lease that includes an option to renew for two more years might be ideal. Typically, you exercise an option to stay by notifying your landlord in writing a set number of days or months before the lease expires. The amount of notice required is negotiable.

Getting the landlord to include an option in your lease might not be easy. Put yourself in the landlord's shoes. You might well go for a firm commitment from the tenant for eight years with adequate rent increases built in. You'd find it less attractive to grant a series of successive two-year options, which introduce an element of uncertainty—they allow the tenant the right to stay if the location turns out to be profitable but to leave if it's a dud. Not surprisingly, as a landlord, you'd look for some economic incentive to make the deal more attractive.

Now that you understand the landlord's point of view, you won't be too surprised if you find that the rent rate for a short lease with an option to renew is more than the rate you can lock in with a long-term lease. Also, the landlord will likely want a higher rent for the renewal period, either in a fixed amount or an increase tied to a cost-of-living index.

 Law From the Real World

Know the Fine Print

Charlie bought a coffee shop in a high-traffic location. There was only one year left on the three-year lease, but the lease contained an option to renew for an additional three years at a slightly higher—though still favorable—rent. The landlord consented to an assignment of the lease and Charlie took over the business. Things went well. Charlie decided to stay at the location.

Nine months after Charlie took over the business, the landlord came by for a casual chat. Charlie mentioned his plans for the coming year, including some marketing ideas. "Sounds good," the landlord said, "but you'll have a new address. I'm planning to move you to a spot around the corner on the second floor." Charlie was stunned. The new space would be much less visible to the public—and Charlie's business depended on walk-in customers.

Fortunately, Charlie had the presence of mind to dig out his lease. There, nestled in the fine print, was an option to renew clause. All that Charlie had to do was to notify the landlord in writing, at least 60 days before the original lease expired, that he was exercising his option to stay on in the same space. A quick look at the calendar confirmed that Charlie had more than enough time to give the written notice. To be on the safe side, he quickly sent his notice to the landlord by certified mail (return receipt requested)—and thereby averted a financial disaster. For Charlie, the option clause meant the difference between success and failure.

CAUTION

Drawbacks of options to renew. An option to renew isn't always a good idea. If your business isn't particularly sensitive as to its location (maybe you publish a newsletter on how to raise fish, or sell advertising for trade shows), think twice before you waste bargaining clout or pay extra for an option to renew. Sure, you might have to move, but in a high-vacancy climate, you might even find space with a lower rent.

The Right to Expand

If future expansion is a good possibility, you might want the lease to give you the right to add adjacent space or to move to larger quarters in the building. Sometimes this is done through a right of first refusal—the landlord promises in the lease that before any other vacant space is rented to someone else, the landlord must offer it to you on the same terms and conditions.

Rent

Leases usually state the rent on a monthly basis and indicate when payment is due—typically the first of the month, in advance. The lease might also say that the rent for your two-year lease is $24,000 payable in monthly installments of $1,000 per month on the first of the month. Sometimes there's a late charge if you're more than a few days late.

This isn't the only way to compute rent. Depending on the type of building and local custom, here are the main ways that the rental amount is set:

- **Gross leases.** These require the tenant to pay a flat monthly amount. The landlord pays for all operating costs for the building—taxes, insurance, repairs, and utilities. Under one common variation, the tenant pays for its own electricity, heat, and air-conditioning; if your lease uses this method and you are in a building with other tenants, see if there are separate meters available so that you can control these costs. If not, ask to see copies of the bills—you don't want to agree to pay for utilities if someone else in the building runs up huge bills.
- **Net leases.** The tenant must pay a monthly base rent plus some or all of the real estate taxes. If you sign this kind of lease and you're leasing just a portion of the building, make sure that the portion of the real estate taxes allocated to your space is fair.
- **Net-net leases.** This type goes further and requires the tenant to pay the base rental amount plus real estate taxes and the landlord's insurance on the space you occupy (which is different from your own liability insurance, discussed in Chapter 12). In a standard lease, the landlord insures the entire building against property damage caused by fire, flooding, and the weather, as well as negligence and vandalism. The landlord's insurance also covers claims against the landlord brought by people injured on the property. In a net-net lease, the cost of this insurance is allocated among the tenants, usually on the basis of the proportion of space each one occupies.
- **Net-net-net ("triple net") leases.** The tenant pays the base rental amount plus the landlord's operating costs, including taxes, insurance, repairs, and maintenance. Such leases are not often used for space rented by a small business, but there are exceptions, such as storefronts in popular areas of large cities.
- **Percentage leases.** These leases are used most commonly for retailers in a shopping mall. The tenant pays base rent plus a percentage of gross income. (See "Shopping Center Leases," below, for a discussion of shopping center leases.)

If the lease is for more than one year, the landlord might want to build in a rent increase for future years. For example, a three-year lease might provide for rent of $1,000 per month in year one, $1,100 in year two, and $1,200 per month in year three. Sometimes the increase is tied to some external measure, such as the Consumer Price Index (CPI). If the CPI increases 5% during the base year, so does your rent in year two.

Some landlords want the rent to be increased if their taxes or maintenance costs go up. If you're moving into a new building and the landlord proposes this last kind of formula, be particularly careful. No one really knows what operating costs will be in this situation—they might jump 50%. You'll at least want to negotiate a cap on how much the rent can go up because of increased operating costs.

As emphasized throughout this chapter, leases are normally negotiable. For example, depending on market conditions, you might be able to convince the landlord to turn a triple net lease into a gross lease. Or the landlord might be willing to put a cap on the amount of taxes, insurance, and maintenance costs you'll have to pay. If vacancy rates are high, the landlord might be willing to give you a few months of free rent in return for your agreeing to take the space on a triple net basis.

Security Deposit

Landlords commonly request a security deposit in the amount of the last month's rent plus an additional amount equal to a half month's or full month's rent. So if your rent is $1,000 per month, you might have to cough up $2,500 to $3,000 before you take possession—$1,000 for the first month and $1,500 to $2,000 for the security deposit. This is all negotiable.

Ask the landlord to hold the security deposit in an interest-bearing bank account for your benefit. If you're concerned about the landlord's solvency, you might go further and suggest that the security deposit be held in escrow by a third party—but don't be surprised if the landlord balks at either suggestion.

The security deposit is intended to cover unpaid rent if you move out early and any damage you cause during your occupancy over and above normal wear and tear. Usually, your right to be free from liability for normal wear and tear is recognized under state law; you don't have to worry about this unless the lease or the landlord tries to make you

responsible for it. So if your lease obligates you to return your space "in tip-top condition," you'll want to ask for a change. Similarly, it's normally considered unreasonable for the landlord to require you to pay to repaint the space before you move out or install new carpeting—unless, of course, you caused an unusual amount of damage.

Improvements by the Landlord

Unless you rent a recently remodeled space designed for a business such as yours, the space will often need to be fixed up or modified before it's suitable for your use. At the inexpensive end of the spectrum, you might need only a few coats of paint on the walls, or perhaps to have the carpet cleaned. At the more costly end of the spectrum, you might need hundreds of thousands of dollars' worth of improvements, like a new air filtration system, up-to-date kitchen equipment, and an appealing décor, before you could open an elegant new restaurant. Or you might need pollution control equipment and a loading dock before opening a small manufacturing facility.

In between these two extremes, your business might need more lighting and electrical outlets, air-conditioning, or perhaps a partitioned office or work area. Who's going to pay for these things—you or the landlord? It's all negotiable.

Your lease should specify the improvements the landlord will make. Ideally, the landlord should agree to complete all improvements before your move-in date. The next best thing is a stated deadline within the first months of your lease.

Try to get the landlord to agree to pay for all or most of these improvements. But be forewarned that the landlord's willingness to pick up the tab will depend on a number of factors, including the condition of the building, your type of business, the extent and cost of the improvements, whether the improvements would be useful to a future tenant, the length of your lease, and—very important—how much rent you'll pay. For example, if you're starting a fancy restaurant, the landlord isn't likely to make $200,000 of improvements—but this might change if you're a famous chef whom the landlord is counting on as an anchor tenant. But if you're opening a bookstore, the landlord might agree to install shelving for you. If the building is in bad repair, you can probably convince the landlord to put it in decent shape for you and maybe to make needed modifications in the process. If you're paying a hefty rent for five years, you can expect more than if you're signing up for one year at a low rent.

Improvements to leased space usually become the property of the landlord. (See the discussion of fixtures, below.) This means that after you move out, future tenants will continue to use the space in its improved condition, and the landlord will continue to collect rent for the improved space. In other words, if your improvements are sensible, the economic benefits to the landlord will outlast your lease. This is a good negotiating point; you shouldn't be expected to bear the major financial burden for improvements that have a long useful life.

On the other hand, if you have specialized needs—for example, you're running a dance studio—and your specialized hardwood floor would be of limited value to most future tenants, don't expect the landlord to willingly pay for the improvements. The landlord might even want to charge you something to cover the cost of remodeling the space after you leave.

After you agree with the landlord on improvements, make sure the lease clearly describes what's being done. Attach drawings and specifications so later there can be no doubt about what was promised. If extensive improvements are to be made, insist on drawings and specs prepared by an architect or a construction specialist. Think about all your needs: partitions, special lighting, soundproofing, special floor coverings, painting, wall coverings, woodwork, cabinetry, and so on. Many landlords can be very flexible and open to making improvements if you approach them before the lease is signed.

Here is some language you might include in the lease:

> Before the beginning of the lease term, Landlord, at its expense, will make improvements to the premises as set forth in Exhibit A (Plans and Specifications for Improvements). These improvements will be completed in a workmanlike manner and comply with all applicable laws, ordinances, rules, and regulations of governmental authorities.

Improvements to raw space—particularly in a new building—are often called a "build-out." Sometimes the landlord offers a standard build-out to every tenant. For example, the build-out might include a certain grade of carpeting or vinyl floor covering; a particular type of drop-ceiling; a certain number of fluorescent lighting panels per square feet of floor space; and a specified number of feet of drywall partitions, with two coats of paint. Once you understand the landlord's standard build-out, see if you can get some upgrades or extras thrown in. You might wind up with better carpeting, more lighting, or fancier woodwork.

If the landlord offers a build-out allowance based on the cost of the improvements (for example, up to $30 per square foot of rented space), see if you can negotiate a higher figure. Generally, the longer the lease, the better the deal you can negotiate on the build-out. This makes sense. With a lease of three or five years, the landlord has an incentive to do far more for you than if you sign up for only 12 months.

Making Improvements Yourself

You might want to make improvements or alterations that go beyond what the landlord is willing to provide. The lease proposed by the landlord might require the landlord's permission before you can make improvements or alterations to the premises. Meet this clause head on by submitting your plans to the landlord before you sign the lease—and don't sign unless you get approval.

Also, provide that the landlord won't unreasonably withhold consent to future improvements you might want to make.

At the end of the lease, you might want to remove some of the items you've installed and take them to a new location. Leases sometimes prohibit the removal of improvements. The landlord has a legitimate concern in preventing you from removing items in a way that damages the space or impedes renting to a new tenant. If your lease doesn't spell out your rights, the state law on "fixtures" will normally say that anything you've attached has become part of the real estate and is therefore the landlord's property. This can lead to arguments. For example, who owns the window air conditioner that you attached with metal brackets?

The best way to avoid argument is to specify what you can remove and what belongs to the landlord. List all items you'll want to remove—either in the lease itself (if there's room) or on an extra sheet attached to the lease. (See "How to Modify a Lease," below, for how to do this.)

Even if you have permission to remove specific items, make sure that you install them so they can be removed later without damage to the building. It might cost a little more to install easy-to-remove shelves, cabinets, light fixtures, and air-conditioning units. In the long run, however, it will be well worth it, because you can keep these items without having to make extensive repairs to the landlord's property.

Compliance With the ADA

The federal Americans with Disabilities Act (ADA) makes both you and your landlord responsible for making the premises accessible to disabled people. You can work out the details in your lease. Here are some suggestions on how to proceed:

- Ask the landlord to state (lawyers say "warrant") that the building complies with the ADA, based on an ADA survey or audit performed by an engineer or architect.
- If the landlord will be making improvements, see if the landlord will agree to pay for fully complying with the ADA.

- Make sure that the costs of bringing common areas into compliance aren't passed along to you as part of the "CAM" (common area maintenance) charges.

To comply with the ADA, you or the landlord might need to provide accessible parking and install ramps, wide-entry doors, and specially designed restrooms. Because some of these improvements might be costly, you'd like the landlord to foot as much of the bill as possible.

TIP
Your obligations don't end with access to the building. To meet ADA requirements, you might have to redesign your business's interior space to improve access for disabled customers and employees. For example, you could need to widen aisles so that people using wheelchairs, walkers, and electric scooters have ample room to maneuver, and you might need to lower service counters for ease of access. Be sure to budget enough to cover these improvements—your landlord isn't likely to cover these costs. For more information on ADA compliance for business premises, check the U.S. Department of Justice's ADA home page, www.ada.gov, where you can view or download several helpful publications.

Zoning Laws, Permits, and Restrictions on Use of the Space

If the lease says nothing about the use of the space, you can use it for any lawful purpose. However, leases are often quite specific about what you can and can't do. For example, if your business sells and repairs bicycles, the landlord might insist that the lease limit you to these activities. This could seem okay now, but what if you want to do other things in the future? Define the permitted uses broadly enough to encompass any needs you anticipate. A poster business, for example, might want to provide that the space can also be used for classes on making and framing posters. A private post office might want to be free to do photocopying and the retail sale of greeting cards.

No lease or landlord can give you the right to do something that's prohibited under the zoning laws. So it's an excellent idea to check with your local building or zoning department to be sure your anticipated uses are permitted under the local zoning ordinance. A bicycle shop might not be permitted in an office zone, for example.

In addition to zoning ordinances, other planning, building, safety, and health ordinances can affect your intended use. An ordinance might require a specific number of off-street parking spaces for some types of businesses, an entrance accessible to handicapped people, or a restroom for customers—a common requirement for a restaurant. (For more on this subject, see "Zoning Ordinances" in Chapter 7.)

Required Insurance

Most landlords want their tenants to carry insurance to cover damage the tenant does to the building and injuries suffered by customers and other visitors on the premises. This is something that any business would be wise to do even if it weren't required by a lease. (Chapter 12 covers the types of insurance you should consider.) But when you get down to specifics, it can be one of the most complicated parts of the lease.

Look carefully at the policy limits the landlord wants you to carry. Is a $2 million liability policy reasonable for your business? Some landlords want you to buy a policy to cover the landlord's liability for injuries as well as your own. This is often considered unreasonable; bargain to eliminate such a requirement, if you can.

At the very least, your landlord should agree to pay for casualty insurance on the building so that funds are available to repair it if it's destroyed or damaged by a fire or windstorm. And if you're in an area where floods or earthquakes are common, insist that the landlord also include these nonstandard coverages.

With both you and your landlord buying insurance, there's always the possibility of unnecessary duplication of coverage. Ask for a copy of your landlord's policy and review it with your agent.

When a landlord and tenant each carry property insurance, you can run into complications because of the legal concept of "subrogation." Ordinarily, if an insurance company pays an insured business for damaged property, the company has the right to turn around and sue any third party that caused the damage. The insurance is said to be subrogated to the rights of the insured business to collect damages—in other words, the insurance company steps into the shoes of the insured business.

EXAMPLE: Pericles Corporation is a tenant in a building owned by Town Development Associates. Pericles carries insurance on its property and Town Development carries insurance on the building. One evening, employees of Pericles forget to turn off the coffeemaker before leaving. The coffee boils away, the machine overheats, and a fire breaks out, seriously damaging the building, furniture, and equipment of Pericles. Pericles' insurance company pays for replacement of the damaged furniture and equipment, and Town Development's insurance company pays for repair of the building. However, because the negligence of a Pericles employee caused the fire, Town Development's insurance company steps into the shoes of Town Development and sues Pericles to collect the money paid out to repair the building. In doing so, the insurance company is exercising its right of subrogation.

You can head off this kind of headache by including a clause such as the following in your lease:

Mutual Waiver of Subrogation

Landlord and Tenant release each other from any and all liability to each other for any loss or damage to property, including loss of income and demolition or construction expenses due to the enforcement of ordinance or law, caused by fire or any of the Extended Coverage or Special Coverage perils, even if such fire or other peril has been caused by the fault or negligence of the other party or anyone for whom such party might be responsible.

If you don't have such a clause in your lease and try to waive subrogation rights after a loss occurs, you might be out of luck. Most insurance policies provide that a waiver of rights is effective only if it is made in writing before a loss.

Subletting Your Space or Assigning the Lease

Someday you might want to share your space with another business. For example, if you run a toy store, you might want to rent a portion of your floor space to someone who sells children's books. You'd do this by subletting the space. When you sublet, you're still responsible to the landlord for paying the entire rent and honoring all other provisions of the lease. Obviously, subletting is of more concern with a long lease than with a short one.

Another possibility is that you'll want to move out of the space during the term of the lease, because you've found a better space or you've decided to go out of business. If you found another tenant to take over your space, you could sublease the whole space to the new tenant; in that case, you'd still be responsible to the landlord under the lease. But ideally, you'd want to assign your lease to the new tenant. Assigning your lease takes you out of the picture entirely. The new tenant pays the landlord directly and you have no further liability under the lease.

Landlords often are reluctant to give tenants an unlimited right to assign their lease or sublet their space. They're afraid of winding up with an occupant who is a deadbeat or who might damage the property or who runs a business that will adversely affect the image of the building, making it harder to attract good tenants. A typical provision drafted by a landlord looks like this:

> Tenant agrees not to assign or transfer this lease or sublet the premises or any part of the premises without the written consent of Landlord.

In my opinion, such a clause is unfair from a tenant's point of view. To make it fairer, ask to add the following wording:

> Consent of Landlord will not be unreasonably withheld.

With this additional wording in your lease, if you find a reasonable occupant to sublet to, and the landlord refuses to let you sublet, courts will generally rule that you're off the hook for rent after you move out.

 Law From the Real World

When Corporate Status Comes in Handy

Elena formed a corporation called Elena's Mediterranean Deli, Inc. As president of her new corporation, she signed a five-year lease for space in a popular food court. Buried in the lease's small print was a sentence that said the lease couldn't be assigned and the space couldn't be sublet without the landlord's permission.

A few years later, Elena wanted to sell her business to Andrew for a handsome profit. Andrew planned to continue running the business at the same location. Elena told the landlord about her plans to sell and sublet. The landlord, who wanted to install his nephew in Elena's space, objected, saying he wouldn't let Elena assign the lease or sublet the space. The landlord was willing to excuse Elena from the rest of the lease—but this wouldn't allow her to reap the profit from a sale of her business.

What to do? Fortunately, because the corporation rather than Elena was the tenant, the lease was legally a corporate asset. Elena realized that she didn't need to sublet or assign her lease. She sold the corporation to Andrew, which meant that the corporation—although owned by a new shareholder—was still the tenant. Elena used the profits to go to grad school.

> **CAUTION**
> **Uncooperative landlords.** If you find yourself with a landlord who objects to a subtenant you've found, check with your lawyer or do some research to learn your legal rights in your state.

The Landlord's Right to Enter Your Space

Some leases give the landlord a broad right to enter your premises at all times to make inspections or repairs. This is an unnecessary invasion of your privacy, and most landlords will settle for a more limited right of entry. It's reasonable to provide that the landlord can enter your leased space only during normal business hours, unless there's a genuine emergency, such as a burst pipe or an electrical hazard.

Because repairs can be disruptive, you might also require the landlord to consult you before making repairs and schedule them for a mutually convenient time. For many businesses, this won't be a problem. But if repairs could be disastrous—for example, you're a doctor renting space for your allergy practice or the owner of a shop that assembles delicate electronic components—you'll want to tightly control when the landlord can repaint or install new carpeting.

A related issue comes up near the end of a lease. Does the landlord have an unlimited right to enter your place to show it to prospective tenants? Depending on the type of business you have, this can be disruptive and annoying. It's a good idea for your lease to limit this type of intrusion to a slow period (say, 9 a.m. to 11 a.m., Monday through Friday) and to require 24 hours' notice.

Signs

Many types of businesses need one or more external signs. Check the lease to see if it gives your landlord the right to disapprove signs before they go up. One way to be sure the landlord won't be unreasonable is to have your signs approved when you sign the lease. If you do, attach a drawing or photo of the signs to the lease so that there can't be any argument later about what you agreed on.

> **CAUTION**
> **Don't forget municipal sign ordinances.** In some communities, signs are heavily regulated by ordinances that restrict their size, number, color, and location. In a few communities, there are even limitations on the content of signs—for example, in a few places in Southern California, there are limits on the number of non-English words you can use. So besides providing for your signs in your lease, check with local building and planning officials to see what ordinances and regulations might affect you.

Canceling Your Lease

In general, you can't cancel your lease before it runs out without pointing to a specific reason stated in the document itself—unless, of course, your landlord agrees to end the lease early. The right to end your lease early is definitely something you should think about during your negotiations. The future of your business might look positive, but especially with a new business, no one knows for sure.

One approach for a new business is to propose a provision that allows you to cancel your lease if your gross income projections haven't reached a stated level by a certain time—say, six months after you take occupancy. Although this would be a somewhat unusual clause, a landlord with vacant space and no other tenants in prospect might accept it.

An even more compelling reason for ending your lease early would be if the building has been damaged by a fire or flooding and you can't conduct your business there. In most states, if you rent space in just a portion of a building, the law provides that you can terminate your lease if the building is destroyed.

But what if it's only heavily damaged? If the landlord doesn't make repairs promptly, state law might allow you to terminate based on "constructive eviction"; the landlord's inaction, you would argue, constitutes an eviction. But if the landlord disputes this, you'll be stuck with what a judge rules. A better approach is to provide in your lease that if you can't run your business in your space for 30 days because of damage that you didn't cause, you can cancel the lease. Also, if relevant, make sure your 30-day provision covers the possibility that you and your customers can't get access to your space because of damage to another part of the building.

For more information on getting out of a lease, see "Getting Out of a Lease," below.

Mediation or Arbitration

I recommend that all small business leases have a clause requiring mediation or arbitration of landlord–tenant disputes. With mediation, an outside party helps the disputants arrive at their own settlement, which can then be recorded as a legally binding agreement. Arbitration is more like a private court action with the arbitrator in the role of a judge listening to the dispute and rendering a decision. But because no court is involved, it tends to be far faster and cheaper than a full-blown lawsuit. (For more information on mediation and arbitration, see Nolo's Mediation, Arbitration & Collaborative Law section at www.nolo.com/legal-encyclopedia/mediation.)

The Fine Print

Study the lease thoroughly so that you're sure your responsibilities and those of the landlord are clear and reasonable. In addition to the major items already discussed, make sure the lease deals with all possible costs, including any of the following that concern you:

- **Real estate taxes.** If nothing is mentioned in the lease, this is normally the landlord's responsibility.

- **Utilities—water, electricity, natural gas, heating oil, and so on.** These are usually the tenant's responsibility if not specifically mentioned in the lease.

- **Maintenance of the building and of your premises.** Without a lease provision to the contrary, the landlord must pay for maintaining the building; you pay for maintaining your own space. If you're leasing an entire building, you are normally responsible for all maintenance unless the lease specifies otherwise.

- **Repair and maintenance of the interior walls, ceiling, and floors in your space.** This is normally the tenant's problem in the absence of a lease provision.

- **Repair of malfunctioning plumbing, electrical, and mechanical systems (heating, ventilation, and air-conditioning—commonly called HVAC).** Without a lease provision, payment responsibilities are debatable. Generally, the landlord is responsible for systems that affect the entire building—although the opposite is usually true if you lease the entire building. When you rent less than an entire building, the responsibility for mechanical or electrical facilities within the four walls of your space isn't always clear; if the lease doesn't cover it, you could find yourself arguing over who must pay for replacing a defective light fixture or a thermostat that goes haywire.

- **Janitorial services.** These are normally the tenant's responsibility unless the lease says otherwise. Landlords usually provide janitorial services for bathrooms and other areas used in common by several tenants.

- **Window washing.** Without specific lease language, the landlord normally doesn't have to wash windows. In smaller buildings, leases usually leave window washing to the tenant, with the possible exception of windows serving common areas such as hallways, entryways, and storage areas. In larger, multistoried buildings, the landlord usually accepts responsibility—at least for the exterior of the windows.

- **Trash removal.** Without lease language to the contrary, this is the tenant's chore.
- **Landscape care and snow removal.** This is generally the landlord's duty unless you lease the entire building, in which case the burden shifts to you. It's always wise to address this issue in the lease—particularly if you're a tenant in a professional or other building where projecting the right image is important.
- **Parking lot maintenance.** This is something the landlord usually must pay for unless the whole parking lot is under your control, in which case it's usually your job unless the lease provides otherwise. In addition to maintenance, be sure the lease is clear regarding the landlord's duty to make a certain number of spaces available, keep the lot or garage open during normal business hours, and provide security.

On service items such as janitorial services and window washing, specify how often this will be done. If the landlord is responsible for heating and air-conditioning, will these services be available weekends and at night? If your business keeps long hours, you want your space to be comfortable at all times.

Regarding repairs, you and your landlord might find it convenient to allow you to make certain minor repairs not exceeding a fixed sum (say $300) and to deduct those outlays from your next month's rent.

Additional Clauses to Consider

Most of the above lease clauses are relatively common. Here are a few more, which are seen less often but can also be valuable to you as a tenant.

Option to Purchase the Building

If the situation warrants, consider a clause giving you an option to buy the building someday. It gives you the right to buy at a specified future time at a specified price. Or consider a right of first refusal—if your landlord receives an offer from someone else to purchase the building, you'll be given a chance to match that offer. Many landlords will give you this

right because it doesn't cost them anything. If you decide not to exercise your right of first refusal, the landlord simply sells the property to the person who made the offer.

The Right to Withhold Rent

Suppose your landlord violates the lease by not furnishing air-conditioning for a sweltering July—or heat for a frigid January. Can you withhold rent? The traditional legal view is that your obligation to pay rent is independent of the landlord's obligation to perform under the lease. In other words, tenants are expected to quietly pay their rent except in the most extreme circumstances.

But in the last 35 years, a tenants' rights revolution has taken place—mainly in the area of residential leases. For example, in the case of housing, almost all states recognize an "implied warranty of habitability." This means that regardless of what the lease obligates the landlord to do, the landlord must put dwelling units in a habitable condition—and keep them that way throughout the lease. If the landlord fails to do so, in many of these states, the tenant can withhold all or part of the rent without fearing eviction. Unless the parties come to an accommodation, a judge will ultimately decide how much of a rent reduction (the technical term is "abatement") the tenant is entitled to.

Commercial tenants, however, have not fared as well. The courts in most states still say that a commercial tenant must continue to pay rent despite the landlord's failure to meet implied or expressed duties. But courts in several states have shown concern for the rights of commercial tenants. For example, a Texas court ruled that there is an implied warranty by a commercial landlord that leased premises are suitable for their intended purpose. The ruling came in a case where the landlord didn't provide adequate air-conditioning, electricity, hot water, janitorial services, or security to a business tenant. The tenant stopped paying rent and moved out. The court upheld the action of the business tenant. (*Davidow v. Inwood North Professional Group–Phase I*, 747 S.W.2d 373 (Tex. 1988).)

How far the courts will go to protect your rights as a commercial tenant is still uncertain. Certainly a one-day failure to provide air-conditioning wouldn't be enough to let you withhold rent or move out. But what if you and your customers have to sweat it out for two weeks? Or six weeks? That might be enough in some states, assuming you've given the landlord prompt notice of the problem and a chance to make repairs.

I recommend that you deal with all this legal uncertainty by requesting a lease clause giving you the right to withhold rent if, after reasonable notice, the landlord violates the lease in a way that seriously interferes with your ability to do business. Here's a sample clause:

> If, within ten days after notice from Tenant, Landlord fails to cure a default by Landlord that materially affects Tenant's ability to conduct its business, Tenant shall be entitled to a reasonable abatement of rent for the period of default and may withhold all rent until Landlord has cured the default.

Shopping Center Leases

Leases for space in a shopping center are a special breed of animal. They often charge a percentage of sales as part of the rent and restrict competing businesses, to mention just two major differences.

It can be hard to read a shopping center lease and decide whether it offers a square deal or not. So, in addition to reading the lease language carefully, one of your first steps should be to check whether the shopping center has a tenants' association; many shopping centers have them, and they can be a source of invaluable information. If there's no formal association, drop in on some current tenants. Either way, learn as much as you can about the center's management and how tenants are really treated. Also, try to find out which lease clauses the owner considers negotiable. This sort of information as to problems and opportunities will give you a definite advantage in your lease negotiations.

Now let's look at a typical shopping center lease. Many of the lease clauses discussed earlier in this chapter also appear in a shopping center lease, but there are likely to be a number of different wrinkles you should know about.

Percentage Rent

Retail businesses moving into a shopping center often find that the landlord expects to receive a percentage of gross sales in addition to a fixed "base rent." For example, the lease might provide:

1. The landlord will receive $2,000 a month as base rent.
2. In addition, if your gross sales exceed $200,000 a year, the landlord will receive 5% of the amount of your gross sales over the $200,000 figure.
3. The amount received by the landlord under the percentage rent clause won't exceed $25,000 a year.

In addition to trying to negotiate more favorable terms, be specific in how you define gross sales. Depending on your type of business, certain items should be deducted from gross sales before the percentage rent is determined. Here are some possibilities:

- returned merchandise
- charges you make for delivery and installation
- sales from vending machines
- refundable deposits
- catalog, Internet, or mail-order sales, and
- sales tax.

In short, make sure your lease excludes all items that overstate your sales from the location you're renting.

Anchor Tenants

You might be attracted to a specific shopping center because one of the tenants is a major department store or supermarket. These superstars, known as anchor tenants, attract customers to the shopping center. Insist on a provision letting you out of the lease if an anchor tenant closes or, with a new shopping center, if the anchor never opens.

Also seek the right to cancel your lease if center occupancy falls below a certain percentage. There's nothing worse than having a store in a half-empty mall.

Competing Businesses

How many nutritional supplement stores can a mall support? You might want to negotiate a limit on the number of competing businesses allowed in the mall. Similarly, the landlord might want you to agree not to open a second store within a two-mile radius of the mall; the fear is that a second store too close might decrease gross sales from your mall location—thereby reducing the money the landlord gets under the percentage rent clause. At any rate, remember that these issues are usually negotiable. Many shopping centers (especially older ones) can no longer afford to dictate coercive terms to small businesses, and you might find much more landlord flexibility than you expect.

Duty to Remain Open

Your lease might compel you to remain open for business during all mall hours—typically 10 a.m. to 9 p.m. Monday through Saturday, and noon to 5 p.m. on Sunday. With a small business, think about whether you can afford to run your business during all of those hours or if it's appropriate to do so. For example, not many people buy vitamins at 8:45 on Tuesday evening, but there might be a line on Saturday morning that justifies opening at 8:30 or 9 a.m. instead of 10, when the rest of the mall opens. If you need reasonable changes, ask for them.

How to Modify a Lease

As discussed in this chapter, there are a number of constructive ways to modify the lease presented by the landlord. The most important thing is to put the changes in writing. Never rely on oral understandings. The simplest method for making changes will be to have the landlord or landlord's lawyer print out a revised version of the lease—or you can make small changes on the lease itself by crossing out unacceptable wording and adding new language. You and the landlord should initial each of these changes.

If changes are extensive and it's not practical for the landlord to include them in a fresh draft, it's best to prepare an addition to the lease—in legal parlance, an "addendum." The addendum should refer to the main lease and state that in case of any conflict, the terms of the addendum supersede the original lease. You and the landlord should sign and date the addendum. A sample addendum is shown below.

Keep in mind that a lease can be modified even after it's been signed. For example, if six months into your lease your landlord agrees to install some partitions for $2,000, you can sign an addendum then.

Sample Lease Addendum

Addendum

This is an Addendum to the Lease dated _____, 20____ between _____ (Landlord) and _____ (Tenant) for commercial space at _____
_____ .

The parties agree to the following changes and additions to the Lease:

[Insert changes and additions]

In all other respects, the terms of the original Lease remain in full effect. However, if there is a conflict between this Addendum and the original Lease, the terms of this Addendum will prevail.

Landlord-Tenant Disputes

There's almost no limit to the kinds of disputes that landlords and tenants can have. Your landlord might claim that you're damaging the building or that you're consistently late paying rent or that you or your customers or visitors park in other tenants' spaces. You might feel that your landlord hasn't been furnishing services that were promised, such as security, janitorial, or landscaping, or that your landlord is failing to attend to the leaky roof or having the windows washed frequently enough.

No matter what the cause, it's usually best to compromise a landlord-tenant dispute through negotiation. Sometimes a frank discussion and a little give and take by each side can resolve what seems like an impossible problem.

If the dispute is serious and not amenable to face-to-face negotiations, have your lawyer help you analyze your legal rights. They might be stronger than you think. Legal trends in many parts of the country have improved the tenant's position.

If your lease has a mediation or arbitration clause, this is the obvious next step. But even if it doesn't, you might want to suggest one or both of these approaches. Going to court can be expensive and time-consuming—something the landlord probably wants to avoid. In short, a sensible landlord has good reason to listen to your complaints and to mediate or arbitrate disputes. (For more information on mediation and arbitration, see Nolo's Mediation, Arbitration & Collaborative Law section at www.nolo.com/legal-encyclopedia/mediation.)

Put Your Complaints in Writing

If you think your landlord has violated the lease, put your concern in writing in a straightforward, nonhostile way. State specifically what the violation is and what part of the lease it involves. Deliver your notice or letter to the landlord either in person or by certified mail (return receipt requested). Putting a landlord on early notice can help bolster your legal position if the dispute ever goes to court.

Sample Letter to Landlord

August 5, 20xx

Aaron Ace
Ace Real Estate Associates
1234 Main Street
Anytown, U.S.A. 12345

Dear Mr. Ace:

I am writing to you about some problems we are having with our store space at 567 Enterprise Drive.

As you know, paragraph 12 of our lease specifically says that Ace Real Estate Associates will maintain the heating and air-conditioning system and keep it in good repair. I have called your office twice this week and left word that the air-conditioning is not working. No one has come to fix it or given us a date by which the work will be done. Our customers have complained, and on Tuesday we had to close early.

Also, under paragraph 14 of our lease, the landlord agreed to replace the broken floor tiles in the entry area within two weeks after we took possession. We have been here for six weeks now and nothing has been done about the tiles. The broken tiles are hazardous.

These are serious violations of our lease. I am requesting that you immediately repair the air-conditioning and promptly replace the broken floor tiles. We cannot operate without the air-conditioning during this hot weather. Its lack has already caused us to lose substantial revenues and has damaged customer relationships.

If you do not take care of these matters within five days, I plan to have the work done myself and to deduct the cost from next month's rent.

If the cost of fixing the air-conditioning is excessive, I may choose to terminate the lease and to sue your company for damages caused by your breaching the lease, including moving expenses and lost profits.

I hope that this will not be necessary. Please proceed at once to make the repairs as required by the lease.

Very truly yours,

Peter Olsen

Peter Olsen

If rent withholding is allowed in your state or by a specific clause in your lease (see the discussion above), you might want to write a letter or two to the landlord before you hold back on the rent. An example of such a letter is shown below.

Coping With the Threat of Eviction

Many leases contain stern language that appears to give the landlord the right to enter your space and regain possession if you don't pay your rent on time or fail to live up to some other lease obligation. Don't be intimidated. No matter what the lease says, in most states a landlord can't evict you without going to court and getting a court order first. This process requires that you be given notice and an opportunity to present your side of the dispute.

A hearing by a judge—or, if your lease so provides, by a mediator or an arbitrator—gives you a chance to explain any legal defenses you have. For example, perhaps the reason you didn't pay your rent by the first of the month was that the landlord failed to repair the air-conditioning as required by the lease. The right to a court hearing also gives you valuable time to develop your case and perhaps resolve the dispute. Court hearings don't take place instantly. You usually have some breathing space in which to build your legal response.

Getting Out of a Lease

Suppose that your business doesn't work out or—more optimistically—that you outgrow the space that you've leased. How free are you to simply vacate the space and walk away from the lease? Unless your landlord has done something to make your space unusable, you're legally responsible for the entire rent for the remaining portion of the lease if the landlord can't find another suitable tenant.

But especially if you have desirable space and a favorable lease, getting out of it—or most of it, anyway—might be less difficult than you think.

If you find that you need to move out, you have two options:

- **Buy your way out.** Try working out a deal in which the landlord keeps all or a part of your security deposit (including, perhaps, the last month's rent) in return for releasing you from the lease. If the lease still has a fairly long time to run or it will be hard to find a new tenant, you might need to sweeten the deal by offering an additional month or two of rent.

- **Find a new tenant.** Find a new tenant to take over the space. Present the new tenant to the landlord along with information about the person's credit and business history. Especially if your lease says that your landlord can't unreasonably refuse to consent to a sublease, you're in a strong legal position if the new tenant has good financial credentials and runs a business of a type permitted by your lease. But again, even without this provision (or if your lease flat out prohibits subletting or assignment), the law in your state might recognize the landlord's duty to mitigate damages—that is, try to find a replacement tenant and minimize his or her loss. If so, you're in a pretty good legal position. If the landlord accepts a new tenant who agrees to pay as much or more than you do, you're free of the lease at no further cost. If the landlord turns down the new tenant and then sues you for lost rent, you can argue that the landlord acted unreasonably and that the landlord—not you—should absorb any losses.

In addition, in states that recognize the landlord's duty to mitigate damages, the landlord must make a good-faith effort to fill the space. Some landlords claim to meet this duty by placing a few ads on Craigslist and listing the property with a real estate agent (why should they do more if you're still obligated?). You're better off using your own efforts to find a new tenant if possible.

When You Need Professional Help

A basic lease that sticks to routine clauses like those listed earlier in this chapter and is written in clear English should be no problem to negotiate yourself. However, it still might be prudent to have a lawyer with small business experience look over the final draft of the lease before you sign it. A visit of an hour or so should be sufficient.

A real estate or small business expert might also be able to assist you. But make sure the person you check with doesn't stand to profit from putting the deal together—a circumstance that all but guarantees you won't get objective advice.

For nonroutine leases, seek assistance earlier in the game. You might need considerable help in negotiating and drafting some critical clauses.

This might cost a few dollars, but compared to a confusing lease that heavily favors the landlord, a fair, well drafted lease that contains the provisions you need is almost always a bargain.

RESOURCE

Looking for a lawyer? Asking for a referral to an attorney from someone you trust can be a good way to find legal help. Also, two sites that are part of the Nolo family, Lawyers.com and Avvo.com, provide excellent and free lawyer directories. These directories allow you to search by location and area of law, and list detailed information about and reviews of lawyers.

Whether you're just starting your lawyer search or researching particular attorneys, visit www.lawyers.com/find-a-lawyer and www.avvo.com/find-a-lawyer.

Home-Based Business

One of the major business trends, especially in light of the ongoing coronavirus pandemic, is the dramatic increase in the number of consultants, artists, craftspeople, therapists, mail-order specialists, professionals, and others who use their homes as a business base.

One reason that working from where you live is more feasible than ever is the array of technologies that makes it possible to be productive and in touch with the rest of the world without leaving your home. You can now duplicate conditions that until recently were practical only in leased commercial space.

But the upsurge in home-based businesses also reflects a new emphasis on the quality of life. Working at home gives you the chance to spend more time with your family, be more flexible in the hours that you work, and avoid the gridlock of the highway.

From a legal standpoint, a home-based business isn't much different from any other business. You still need to pick a business name, decide whether to be a sole proprietor or to form a partnership, LLC, or corporation, purchase insurance, pay taxes, sign contracts, and collect from customers. But a few special legal issues are peculiar to the at-home business, including land use restrictions, insurance, and special tax provisions.

Ways to Document Your Home Business Deduction

Here are some steps you can take to help establish your legal right to deduct home-related business expenses:

- Photograph your home office and draw a diagram showing the location of the office in your home.
- Have your business mail sent to your home.
- Use your home address on your business cards and stationery and in all business ads.
- Get a separate phone line for the business.
- Have clients or customers visit your home office—and keep a log of those visits.
- Keep track of the time you spend working at home.

Running a Home-Based Business in the Timeof Coronavirus

If you're thinking about running a home-based business and plan on dealing with customers or clients in person, take reasonable precautions, like wearing a mask and practicing social distancing, while the coronavirus crisis continues. You might also want to consider using alternatives to in-person appointments when possible, like phone calls, texts, emails, and video meetings.

Zoning Laws

Is it legal to run a business in your home? The answer depends on where you live and what you do. To understand how this works, let's start with the case of Bob Mullin (*Metropolitan Development Commission v. Mullin,* 339 N.E.2d 751 (Ind. App. 1979)), whose plight made its way into the lawbooks.

Bob ran his insurance business from his two-bedroom home in Indianapolis. He thought he was on safe legal ground. After all, unlike in some cities, the local zoning ordinance allowed people to use their homes for "home occupations." As long as a home was used primarily as a residence, it could also be used for "professions and domestic occupations, crafts or services." The ordinance specifically allowed homes to be used for such occupations as law, medicine, dentistry, architecture, engineering, writing, painting, music lessons, and photography. Also, people could use their homes for such businesses as dressmaking, tailoring, hair grooming, washing, ironing, and cabinetmaking. So why not an insurance business?

Bob Mullin used his living room as a reception room and office, complete with a secretary's desk and filing cabinet. He put his own desk in the dining room in place of a dining room table. The photocopier stood in the kitchen next to the stove and refrigerator, and he converted one of the bedrooms into an office.

The zoning board took Bob to court, claiming he'd gone too far. The Indiana Court of Appeals agreed. The court ruled that it was okay for Bob to conduct an insurance business at home, but that Bob's usage was excessive. The business had taken over the house to the point that the primary use was no longer residential. The court told Bob to cut back or close down.

This case demonstrates but one of the many ways that local zoning ordinances can have a devastating effect on a home-based business. The good news is that by learning the law and using discretion, you might find that zoning isn't a real problem for your business.

How Zoning Ordinances Are Organized and Applied

Most cities have zoning ordinances. Areas outside of cities are usually covered by zoning ordinances adopted by county, village, or township governments.

Zoning ordinances come in many shapes and sizes, but they all do basically the same thing: They divide the area into districts in which various types of activities are allowed or prohibited. For example, there are usually residential districts for single-family and two-family homes and other districts for apartments. Other areas or zones are earmarked for commercial usage. Ordinances often break down the types of commercial usage; in some zoning districts, only offices or retail and service businesses are allowed. Usually some part of town is reserved for manufacturing operations, which are typically broken down into light and heavy industrial.

In some areas, more than one use is allowed in a district; for example, commercial and light industrial, or residential and commercial. Outside of cities, zones allow various types of agricultural activities.

Some zoning ordinances, especially in affluent areas, exclude home-based businesses. More commonly, zoning ordinances restrict—but don't prohibit—using a home for a business. An ordinance might say, for example, that in general you can't run a business from your home, but then go on to list several types of businesses that are permitted. The Indianapolis ordinance mentioned earlier specifically allowed professions such as law, medicine, and architecture, as well as painting, music lessons, and photography. Some ordinances are vague, simply allowing "customary home occupations"—a term that must be interpreted by a judge if a given use is challenged.

Zoning ordinances that regulate home businesses frequently also limit:

- the amount of car and truck traffic
- outside signs
- on-street parking
- the number of employees, and
- the percentage of floor space devoted to the business.

It's not always easy to tell whether or not a particular business is allowed in a home under the zoning ordinance you're looking at. Some zoning ordinances were written years ago and don't adequately deal with many contemporary businesses that people wish to operate from home—especially sophisticated businesses that depend on high-tech communications equipment.

The level of enforcement varies widely. In more enlightened communities, zoning officials recognize that residential zoning is intended primarily to preserve the residential character of a neighborhood—not to prohibit low-profile businesses. Officials don't go out looking for violations but take their cues from the neighbors: If people living near a home-based business don't complain, why search for a possible technical violation? Even where it's clear that there's a violation, these officials work with the business owner to see whether changes can be made to make the business conform to the ordinance before ordering the owner to end the business or taking administrative or court action.

On the other hand, you might have the misfortune of living in a community that strictly enforces all ordinances. If so, your home-based business might be at the mercy of fairly rigid bureaucrats—although you can fight arbitrary or unreasonable action.

If municipal officials are determined to close down your home-based business, their first step is to write you a cease and desist letter. If you ignore this, you'll probably get another letter or two followed eventually by a misdemeanor prosecution (seeking a fine or, in an extreme case, a jail term) or a civil lawsuit requesting an injunction—a court order prohibiting future violations of the ordinance. If you violate such an injunction, the judge can fine you for contempt of court or even put you in jail.

Investigating Zoning Laws

Before setting up a home-based business, it's a good idea to learn not only what your local zoning ordinance provides but also to find out about enforcement attitudes. If you're in a strict enforcement community and you file for a local business license or tax permit, this might trigger an inquiry about whether you comply with the zoning ordinance. Talk to people who run other home-based businesses, local contractors, your city's business development office, small business advisers, and lawyers about how to make the fewest legal waves.

You might find yourself in a gray area. Your planned home-based business might or might not violate a vaguely worded local ordinance—for example, an SEO consulting business in an area that allows traditional home-based businesses.

It's hard to predict whether the local zoning officials will take action against you or not. One approach is to just go ahead and chance it. If you're simply planning to set up your desk and computer in an unused room in a home you already own, you have little to lose.

This approach is far less sensible if you plan to buy or renovate a house to accommodate your business. Before you spend a significant sum to house your business, you want assurance that you won't be closed down. It's best to approach the city, explain your plans, and ask for an official green light. If a purchase is involved, put a clause in your offer making the deal contingent on getting approval from the zoning authorities. Then, if your use isn't approved, you're free to cancel your purchase.

Law From the Real World

Get the Neighbors on Your Side

Ted operates a business in his home helping non-lawyers prepare their own divorce and bankruptcy forms. Several customers come and go each day, often in the early evening and on Saturdays. One of Ted's neighbors, who has no idea of what Ted is doing, jumps to the conclusion that he's dealing drugs.

She calls a meeting of other neighbors and convinces the others that there can be no other explanation for all the coming and going. They complain to the police and zoning board. When the truth comes out, the police laugh and leave.

The zoning officials are another matter. They cite a local ordinance prohibiting businesses that generate traffic and tell Ted to close down. Eventually, when Ted gets all his chagrined neighbors to sign a statement saying a few cars a day aren't a problem, the zoning officials reverse their position.

Ted could have avoided this time-consuming, anxiety-producing process if he'd simply told folks what was going on when he began his business.

If you plan to operate out of your existing residence and decide that your business is doubtful legally, or that you could be closed down if the ordinance were strictly enforced, you can minimize the risks. Start by being a good neighbor. Make sure that your business has little if any impact on the people who live around you.

For example, if all you do is convert one room to an office equipped for a consulting business, it's unlikely that anyone will complain—as long as you have no employees and see only an occasional client or customer at your home. This is true even if you generate $1 million a year in gross income. You'll also be in a better position if you cleared your plans with your neighbors or if several of them also have home-based businesses.

What kinds of things are most likely to get you in trouble? Anything that a neighbor can see, hear, or smell outside of your home that causes inconvenience or smacks of a commercial venture. Increased traffic, parking problems, signs, outside storage of supplies, noises, or unpleasant odors emanating from your home—any of these can lead to neighborhood complaints. Pollution is another red flag.

EXAMPLE: A craftsman who worked at home with stained glass and even taught classes there was doing quite well until he started dumping lead-laced fluids down a storm drain. The neighbors properly insisted that the city attorney put him out of business.

Dealing With Zoning Officials

Suppose you receive a complaint from the city. What steps can you take? Start by going to City Hall and talking to the person who administers the zoning law—someone in the zoning or planning department. There are both practical and legal reasons for attempting to resolve zoning matters without filing a lawsuit. On the practical level, administrative (agency) relief is quicker, less expensive, and often more flexible than a judicial solution. And the law usually requires you to pursue your available administrative solutions before you go to court; this is known in legal lingo as "exhausting your administrative remedies."

The kind of response you can hope for at City Hall depends greatly on community attitudes. If some home-based businesses are allowed, you clearly want to show that yours meets the spirit of the criteria for allowing businesses. Emphasize how small and unobtrusive your business is. When faced with the facts, the city might become more reasonable. Or you might be able to negotiate a settlement under which you scale down your operations. For example, you might agree to limit your business to weekdays from 8 a.m. to 5 p.m. and to provide off-street parking for your one employee.

If you can't negotiate with the city staff, there are more formal approaches. Most places have a planning or zoning board with power to grant exceptions (variances or conditional use permits) if compliance with an ordinance would cause unreasonable hardship. For example, a zoning board might allow a physically handicapped person to operate a therapy practice at home even though some traffic is generated.

The board might also have the power to overturn a zoning official's interpretation of an ordinance. If you appeal to a local zoning or planning board, try to get neighbors to attend the hearing to speak on your behalf. If that is too inconvenient, ask as many neighbors as possible to write letters or sign a petition stating that they support your business use. Neighborhood support or opposition is likely to be crucial to the success or failure of your appeal. Also, come to the hearing with any photographs or documents that accurately show the nature and extent of your business.

In many cities, if you're turned down by a zoning or planning board or commission, you can appeal to a second board—often the city council itself. While it's less likely that you'll prevail at this level, it does happen.

Going beyond administrative channels, you might be able to get the zoning ordinance amended by the city council or county legislative body. For example, in some communities, moves are afoot to change ordinances that allow "traditional home-based businesses" to include those based on the use of computers and other high-tech equipment— businesses that are unobtrusive, but hardly traditional.

To push through an ordinance change, you'll probably have to lobby some city council members or planning commissioners. You might also need to enlist the local chamber of commerce and other groups representing businesspeople. With increased use of homes for businesses, the time might be ripe in your community for ordinance revisions of this sort. It's politically attractive to revamp an archaic ordinance to allow more home-based businesses, especially if the city is struggling with traffic and parking problems.

Also consider trying to get your property rezoned. This works best if your home is on the edge of a commercial district. Ask the city to move the boundary line separating the two zoning districts so that your home falls within the commercial district—which, of course, would give you much greater latitude to run your business out of your home.

Going to Court

If you decide municipal officials are being unreasonable in attempting to close down your home-based business and you can't get administrative relief or an ordinance amendment, you might want to take the matter to court yourself—before the city starts a prosecution or requests an injunction. By acting first, you have a chance to frame the factual and legal issues more favorably, putting the municipality on the defensive.

At this stage, you'll probably need a lawyer's help; zoning cases are relatively complicated and specialized. Consulting and perhaps hiring a lawyer who works in this area regularly will be well worth the fee. Make sure you find a lawyer who's familiar with zoning practices.

RESOURCE

Looking for a lawyer? Asking for a referral to an attorney from someone you trust can be a good way to find legal help. Also, two sites that are part of the Nolo family, Lawyers.com and Avvo.com, provide excellent and free lawyer directories. These directories allow you to search by location and area of law, and list detailed information about and reviews of lawyers.

Whether you're just starting your lawyer search or researching particular attorneys, visit www.lawyers.com/find-a-lawyer and www.avvo.com/find-a-lawyer.

You needn't turn the whole case over to a lawyer —there's plenty you can do to organize support from neighbors and other home-based businesses as well as researching how courts have decided other similar cases.

You can assert several legal theories in a zoning lawsuit, including the following:

- The city's legal interpretation of its zoning ordinance was incorrect. For example, you might claim that your graphic design business is a "home occupation" even though the zoning officials decided that it isn't. You'd ask the judge to issue a judgment declaring that your business does qualify as a home occupation.

  EXAMPLE: Dr. William Brady lived in Beverly Hills, California. He wrote a syndicated column and, with the help of secretaries, mailed out 150,000 pamphlets a year from his home office. The city tried to close his business because the local zoning ordinance prohibited home businesses that involved the purchase or sale of materials for profit. But the court ruled that the doctor wasn't violating the zoning ordinance; sending out the pamphlets was basically the same as a person answering his or her mail. (*City of Beverly Hills v. Brady*, 215 P.2d 460 (Cal. 1950).)

- The ordinance is invalid because it violates the state statute (called an "enabling law") that gives cities authority to enact zoning ordinances. For example, you might claim that the zoning ordinance is invalid because it doesn't permit homeowners to have "reasonable accessory uses" or "home occupations" as required by the state enabling law.

- The ordinance is invalid because the city didn't use proper procedures in adopting or enforcing it. For example, the city might not have held the necessary public hearings before it amended the zoning ordinance to prohibit certain types of home-based businesses.

- The authorities have acted in a discriminatory manner by enforcing the ordinance against you. For example, they've allowed similar home-based businesses for years but now have singled you out for special treatment.

You aren't limited to just one legal theory. Your lawsuit can allege as many theories as apply.

Lawsuits are expensive, but yours might be settled before there's a full-scale hearing or trial. The city might agree on an acceptable compromise to avoid the expense or inconvenience of fighting your lawsuit or it might not want to put its zoning ordinance in jeopardy just for the sake of closing down one in-home business.

Private Land Use Restrictions

Zoning ordinances are not the only source of potential problems for a home-based business. You must also check out private restrictions on your use of your home, condo, or co-op unit. Depending on the part of the country and the type of ownership arrangement, use restrictions commonly are found in the following documents:

- property deed (the restrictions are called "restrictive covenants")
- a subdivision's declaration of building and use restrictions or covenants, conditions, and restrictions (CC&Rs)
- planned unit development (PUD) rules
- condominium regulations
- co-op regulations, and
- leases.

Language in these and similar documents is likely to restrict or even prohibit business uses. If your residence is covered by a title insurance policy (virtually every piece of real estate is), use restrictions might be identified there. If you've lost your deed or your subdivision, condo, or co-op restrictions, get a copy from your association or go to the county office where title papers are recorded (usually the county recorder or register of deeds) and purchase a copy.

If your neighbors believe you're violating these restrictions, they might take action to stop you. Often—especially for condo, co-op, or PUD units—they can take you before an owners' association board empowered to enforce regulations. If you don't come into compliance, you might lose privileges and face other penalties. Beyond these private sanctions, your neighbors can take you to court and try to stop your business. Judges can be very strict in enforcing these private restrictions. Here are three real-life instances where a judge sided with the neighbors.

EXAMPLE 1: Salvador, a field manager for a brush manufacturer, supervised a staff of door-to-door salespeople and supplied them from his residence in Metairie, Louisiana. He interviewed prospective salespeople at his home and received stored merchandise in his garage. The court ruled that merely receiving samples wouldn't violate the restrictive covenants in the deed to Salvador's property. But Salvador had a problem because he used his home to hire and outfit new employees with samples stored at home. He wasn't using his home "for residential purposes only" as required by the restrictive covenants. (*Woolley v. Cinquigranna*, 188 So.2d 701 (La. App. 1966).)

EXAMPLE 2: Sheldon and Raye practiced psychotherapy in their home in Illinois. The subdivision restrictions covering their home said that "No lot shall be used except for single residential purposes." Their neighbors took them to court, claiming a violation of that restrictive rule. The judge ordered Sheldon and Raye to discontinue their professional use of their home even though the exterior appearance of the home as a single-family home hadn't been altered. (*Wier v. Isenberg*, 420 N.E.2d 790 (Ill. App. 1981).)

EXAMPLE 3: Myrtle operated a part-time beauty parlor in her Sunnyvale, California, home, receiving six customers per day. Myrtle didn't advertise her services, there was no external evidence of her business, and neighbors weren't inconvenienced. Still, the judge ruled that Myrtle violated the subdivision restriction that said "No lot shall be used except for residential purposes." (*Biagini v. Hyde*, 3 Cal.App.3d 877, 83 Cal.Rptr. 875 (Cal. App. 1970).)

If you're taken to court, you have two main lines of defense. The first is that your neighbors or the condo association are misinterpreting the restrictions and that your business use is allowable. Second, if the neighbors did not object to prior business uses, they have, in legal effect, waived the right to do so now. In other words, their inaction in the past has nullified the restrictions.

Judges are often sympathetic to homeowners seeking to enjoy the use of their property. If neighbors have been lax or the restriction is vague, you have a good chance of getting a favorable ruling if your business use doesn't really hurt your neighbors or change the residential character of your neighborhood. On the other hand, if the legal restrictions are tightly drafted and your neighbors acted swiftly to enforce them whenever a violation came to their attention, even a sympathetic judge won't be able to help you.

But slugging it out in court should be a last resort. If you're both dogged and diplomatic, you might be able to find a way to operate your home-based business. Look first at the rules to see how restrictive they are. Some specifically allow certain types of home-based businesses while others simply adopt the standard in your municipality's zoning ordinance, which in turn might be fairly permissive. If you don't qualify under the rules, consider trying to change them. Other people in your subdivision might also feel they are too restrictive. Often the document creating restrictive covenants says that restrictions can be changed if a certain number —say 70%—of the homeowners in the subdivision agree. Similarly, condo regulations can often be changed by agreement of a specified number of owners.

> **CAUTION**
> **If you live in a rented house or apartment, read your lease carefully.** Your landlord might have the right to evict you if you use the premises for business. It's best to get clearance in advance and have it written into the lease. Most landlords won't care if you use the property partly for business as long as you don't cause any damage or create any problems with your neighbors.

Insurance

Chapter 12 discusses insurance coverage for small businesses. The same general principles apply to home-based businesses, but there are also some special considerations you should be aware of.

Never rely exclusively on your normal homeowner's policy. If you do, bad things can happen:

- After your computer is stolen, you might find out that it's not covered by your homeowner's policy because business property is excluded.
- After your house burns down, you might find that the fire coverage is void because you didn't disclose your business use to the insurance company.
- After the UPS delivery person slips on your front porch and breaks his back, you might find you're not covered for injuries associated with business deliveries.

It's easy to avoid these nasty surprises. Sit down with your insurance agent and fully disclose your planned business operations. It's relatively inexpensive to add riders to your homeowner's policy to cover normal business risks. You might need separate policies for other business-related coverage.

When it comes to business equipment and furnishings, figure out how much it would cost for replacements after a fire, theft, or other disaster. Don't overlook things such as the specialized business software you run on your computer. Depending on the nature of your business, replacing equipment and furniture could run into many thousands of dollars. Ask your insurance agent what it takes to insure this valuable property, allowing for a good-sized deductible to keep costs down. Make sure that the coverage on equipment and furnishings is for the full replacement cost—not just the depreciated value, as can be the case in some homeowner's policies.

Your homeowner's policy also might not adequately protect you from liability to business visitors. Accidents—such as people getting hurt when they trip and fall—are more likely to happen at home than in a well-planned office building. Your homeowner's policy probably protects you if you're sued by a social guest or someone at your home for a nonbusiness purpose—a florist's truck driver delivering flowers or the meter reader who's checking on gas usage. But it might not cover a business associate, employee, customer, or delivery person who is injured on your property.

Some home-based businesses need special kinds of insurance. If you render professional services, look into professional liability insurance. If you manufacture, distribute, or sell products that could hurt someone, think about product liability insurance. Also, if you have employees, you'll need to provide workers' compensation coverage. (All this is covered in Chapter 12.)

If you do some business away from your home, be sure that your car insurance covers injuries that occur while you're on business errands. And see about the extent of your general liability coverage if you should accidentally injure someone or damage their property while away from home on business. You might need a rider or special policy to cover this risk.

TIP

Policies to cover both your home and home business. Several insurance companies have developed special policies that cover both your home and a business run from your home. Typically, these policies cover your computer equipment and other business property— whether used in your house or elsewhere—and protect you from business liability lawsuits and loss of income. These policies can be less expensive than either adding riders to your home insurance or buying separate policies for home and business. But check the coverage carefully, as these policies tend to primarily address home offices and might not adequately insure you if, for example, you're a small manufacturer or a wholesaler who stores inventory in the basement.

CAUTION

Operating as a separate entity can affect your insurance coverage. Although the typical home-based business is organized as a sole proprietorship or partnership, you might have organized yours as a corporation or an LLC to get the benefit of limited personal liability. That's fine, but remember that your homeowner's

policy—even if it has riders—insures you personally and might not insure a separate business entity. This can present a coverage problem if your corporation owns the $3,000 computer that gets stolen or the delivery person falls down your front stairs while delivering an overnight letter to your LLC. Check with your insurance agent or broker to make sure your business entity is covered in the insurance policy—as well as yourself. It's usually a simple matter to have your business added as an insured party.

Deducting Expenses for the Business Use of Your Home

You might be able to take a tax deduction for business use of your home. The deduction is available not only for a home office but for other business uses as well, such as a workshop or studio at home.

Basically, if you meet the technical requirements of the tax law, you can deduct a portion of the cost of utilities, rent, depreciation, home insurance, and repairs when you use part of your home for business. For a detailed explanation, see IRS Publication 587, *Business Use of Your Home,* which also spells out the limitations on the amount you can deduct. It's available online at www.irs.gov.

Ways to Document Your Home Business Deduction

Here are some steps you can take to help establish your legal right to deduct home-related business expenses:

- Photograph your home office and draw a diagram showing the location of the office in your home.
- Have your business mail sent to your home.
- Use your home address on your business cards and stationery and in all business ads.
- Get a separate phone line for the business.
- Have clients or customers visit your home office—and keep a log of those visits.
- Keep track of the time you spend working at home.

Keep in mind that whether or not you can deduct expenses that relate specifically to your home, such as rent, utilities, home insurance, and repairs, you can still take a deduction for regular business expenses, such as photocopies, stationery, paper clips, wages, travel, equipment, professional memberships, and publications. (See Chapter 8.) You can also deduct the cost of long distance calls you make from home and a separate phone line used for business calls.

According to the IRS, your "home" can be a house, a condo, or an apartment unit—or even a mobile home or boat. But wherever you live, before you can deduct expenses for using part of your home as a business, you must meet two tax law requirements.

Requirement #1: You must regularly use part of your home exclusively for a trade or business.

Requirement #2: You must be able to show that you:

- use your home as your principal place of business
- meet patients, clients, or customers at home, or
- use a separate structure on your property exclusively for business purposes.

 RESOURCE

For more coverage of tax issues for home-based businesses, see *Home Business Tax Deductions: Keep What You Earn,* by Stephen Fishman (Nolo).

Regular and Exclusive Use

The first requirement for taking deductions related to your home is that you regularly use part of your home exclusively for a trade or business. The notion of regular use is a bit vague. The IRS says it means you're using a part of your home for business on a continuing basis—not just for occasional or incidental business. A few hours a day on most days is probably enough to meet this test.

Exclusive use means that you use a portion of your home only for business. If you use part of your home for your business and also use it for personal purposes, you don't meet the exclusive use test.

> **EXAMPLE:** Brook, a lawyer, uses a den in his home to write legal briefs and prepare contracts. He also uses the den for poker games, watching TV, and hosting a book club. Result: Brook can't claim business deductions for using the den.

Principal Place of Business

In addition to using part of your home regularly and exclusively for business, to take deductions relating to your home, your home must be your principal place of business—or, alternatively, if your home isn't your principal place of business, you can qualify for the deduction if you meet clients or customers at home or if you use a separate structure on your property exclusively for business purposes.

Establishing that your home is your principal place of business is simple if you have only one type of business and conduct it only at home. It gets more complicated if you have several businesses or conduct a business from more than one location.

The IRS says that you can have a principal place of business for each trade or business in which you engage. This means that if you use your home for a part-time enterprise, it might qualify as a principal place of business for that business.

> **EXAMPLE:** Alma teaches school. As a teacher, her principal place of business is the school where she teaches. She also runs a public relations consulting company and uses a part of her home as the headquarters for that business; her expenses for this business use of the home should be deductible.

If you have more than one business location, including your home, for a single trade or business, you must figure out whether your home is your principal place of business for that enterprise. Again, if it isn't, you can't take a deduction for the business use of your home.

Your home qualifies as your principal place of business if you:

1. conduct the administrative or management activities of your business there, and
2. have no other fixed location where you conduct those activities.

Your home doesn't have to be the place where you generate most of your business income. It's enough that you regularly use it to do such things as keeping your books, scheduling appointments, doing research, and ordering supplies. As long as you have no other fixed location where you do such things—for example, an outside office—you can take the deduction.

> **EXAMPLE:** Ellen, a wallpaper installer, performs services for clients in their homes and offices. She also has a home office that she uses regularly and exclusively to keep her books, arrange appointments, and order supplies. Ellen is entitled to deduct expenses for that part of her home.

CAUTION

Home-connected expenses. As noted earlier, the IRS rules discussed in this chapter apply only to home-connected expenses such as utilities, rent, depreciation, home insurance, and repairs. You needn't conform to these rules in order to deduct other business expenses. If you have a bona fide business and don't qualify for deducting home-connected expenses, you can still deduct many other business expenses—for example, the cost of supplies, postage, advertising, and long-distance phone calls.

Meeting Clients or Customers at Home

If your home isn't your principal place of business, you might still be entitled to deduct expenses for business use of your home if you regularly use part of your home exclusively to meet with clients, customers, or patients. Doing so even one or two days a week is probably sufficient. You can use the business space for other business purposes as well—doing bookkeeping, for example, or other business paperwork—but you'll lose the deduction if you use the space for personal purposes, such as watching movie DVDs.

> **EXAMPLE:** Julie, an accountant, works three days a week in her downtown office and two days a week in her suburban home office, which she uses only for business. She meets clients at her home office at least once a week. Because Julie regularly meets clients at her home office, she can take a home office deduction. This is so even though her downtown office is her principal place of business.

Adjusting Your Business Practices During the COVID-19 Crisis

Throughout this chapter and book, we discuss situations that might involve dealing with customers and other individuals in person. Again, while the coronavirus pandemic continues, use appropriate precautions and consider using an alternate communication method, like phone, email, text, or videoconferencing, which doesn't involve a face-to-face meeting.

TIP

Keep a log of the clients or customers you meet at home. Good records can be key if the IRS challenges your right to deduct home-related business expenses. Keep a record (hard-copy or online) of all appointments, carefully noting the name of the client or customer and the date and time of each meeting at your home. Save these records for at least three years; they can be crucial to documenting business usage if your tax return is audited by the IRS.

Using a Separate Building for Your Business

If your home isn't your principal place of business, and you don't meet clients or customers at home, you can deduct expenses for a separate, freestanding structure that you use regularly and exclusively for your business.

This might be a studio or a converted garage or barn, for example. The structure doesn't have to be your principal place of business or a place where you meet patients, clients, or customers. But be sure you use the structure only for your business: you can't store garden supplies there or, at least in theory, even use it for the monthly meeting of your investment club.

> EXAMPLE: Norm is a self-employed landscape architect. He has his main office in a professional center near a shopping mall, but most weekends he works in his home office, which is located in a converted carriage house in his backyard. Because Norm uses the carriage house regularly and exclusively for his landscape architect work, it qualifies for the home office deduction.

Amount of Deduction

If you meet the tests for deducting expenses for the business use of your home, the next step is to figure out how much you can deduct. You can use what the IRS calls the "regular method," but you might prefer the "simplified option."

The Regular Method of Deducting Expenses for the Business Use of Your Home

The tax law lets you deduct only a portion of your home expenses—not 100%. Begin by determining how much of your home you use for business. There are two common methods for doing this:

Square Footage Method. Divide the number of square feet of space used for your business by the total number of square feet in your home. For example, if your home contains 1,200 square feet and you use 240 square feet for your business, then your business percentage is 20%.

Number of Rooms Method. If the rooms in your home are about the same size, figure the business percentage by dividing the number of rooms used for business by the number of rooms in the home. If you use one room in a four-room home for business, then 25% of the total area is used for business.

Storing Inventory or Product Samples at Home

If you sell retail or wholesale products and you store inventory or samples at home, you can deduct expenses for the business use of your home. There are two limitations, however: First, you won't qualify for the deduction if you have an office or other business location away from your home. Second, you have to store the products in a particular place—your garage, for example, or a closet or bedroom. It's okay to use the storage space for other purposes as well, as long as you regularly use it for inventory or samples.

> EXAMPLE: Jim sells heating and air-conditioning filters to small businesses. His home is the only fixed location of his business. Jim regularly stores his inventory of filters in half of his basement. He sometimes uses the storage area for working on his racing bikes. Jim can deduct the expenses for the storage space even though he doesn't use that part of his basement exclusively for business.

The deduction for business use of your home has several components. Using the percentage arrived at by either of the above methods, you can deduct from your gross income the business portion of:

- your rent, if you rent your home, or
- depreciation, mortgage interest, and property taxes on your house, if you own your home—although you might prefer to deduct all of your mortgage interest and property taxes as part of your itemized personal deductions.

In addition, as either an owner or renter, you may deduct this same percentage of other expenses for keeping up and running an entire home. The IRS calls these indirect expenses.

They include:

- utility expenses for electricity, gas, and heating oil
- service expenses for snow removal and trash pickup
- homeowner's or renter's insurance
- home maintenance expenses that benefit your entire home, such as roof and furnace repair and exterior painting
- casualty losses if your home is damaged— for example, in a storm, and
- security system maintenance.

You may also deduct the entire cost of expenses you incur for the part of the house you use for business. The IRS calls these direct expenses. They include, for example, painting your home's business area or paying someone to clean it. If you pay a housekeeper to clean your entire house, you may deduct your business percentage of the expense.

> **EXAMPLE:** Rudy rents a 1,600-square-foot apartment and uses a 400-square-foot bedroom as a home office for his newsletter publishing business. His percentage of business use is 25% (400 ÷ 1,600). He pays $12,000 in annual rent and has a $1,200 utility bill for the year. He also spends $200 to paint his home office. Rudy can deduct 25% of his rent and utilities and 100% of the painting expenses, allowing him to write off a total of $3,500.

The Simplified Method of Deducting Expenses for the Business Use of Your Home

If your business occupies 300 square feet or less of your home, and you want to avoid the burden of detailed record keeping (under the "regular method," described above), you have another alternative. Under the simplified option, you may deduct a standard $5 per square foot of home business usage. If, for example, your business occupies 250 square feet of your home, you could deduct $1,250 (250 x $5 = $1,250). You make this deduction on IRS Schedule C (Form 1040), *Profit or Loss From Business*. As with the regular method described above, you can only take the deduction for space you use regularly and exclusively for business purposes.

Unlike the regular method, you can't deduct depreciation with the simplified method, but that's not all bad: When you sell your home, you won't have to worry about the recapture of depreciation, described in the tip (below), "Know the consequences of selling your home."

You can still use Schedule A (Form 1040), *Itemized Deductions*, to deduct your mortgage interest and real estate taxes. You won't need to allocate these deductions between personal and business use, as is required under the regular method. And you can still deduct business expenses unrelated to your home, such as advertising, supplies, and employee wages.

What if your home business workspace exceeds 300 square feet? You can still use the simplified option, but you'll be limited to a $1,500 deduction (300 x $5 = $1,500). However, that might suit you just fine.

> **EXAMPLE:** Julia, a psychologist, sees patients in her home office that measures 350 square feet. She has reviewed the rules for using the regular method to compute her tax deduction—and she's put off by the record-keeping requirements. Julia decides to use the simplified option. Even though she might save a few more bucks in taxes by using the regular method, Julia is satisfied with getting the $1,500 deduction, and knows she won't need to sweat the paperwork details.

RESOURCE

Complete information on the home business tax deduction. IRS Publication 587, *Business Use of Your Home,* includes the rules for switching from one method to the other.

TIP

You're always able to deduct the normal business expenses not associated with your home use. Remember that this section addresses only the expenses you can deduct for business use of your home. As discussed earlier, whether or not you qualify for or take a home business deduction, you're able to claim as business expenses—and deduct from gross income—the cost of such items as supplies, postage, long distance charges, and so on. You don't need to qualify to take deductions for your business use of your home in order to write off these items. And you can also depreciate or expense (under Section 179) the cost of office furniture, computers, copiers, and other tangible property you use for your business and keep at home.

TIP

Know the consequences of selling your home. If you live in your home for at least two of the five years before you sell it, the profit you make on the sale— up to $250,000 for single taxpayers and $500,000 for married taxpayers—isn't taxable. (See IRS Publication 523, *Selling Your Home.*)

You will, however, have to pay a capital gains tax on any depreciation deductions you took after May 6, 1997 for your home office. These are the deductions you may have taken each year for the decline in value due to wear and tear on the business part of your home. The IRS taxes these recaptured deductions at a 25% rate (unless your income tax bracket is lower than 25%). As Stephen Fishman points out in *Home Business Tax Deductions: Keep What You Earn* (Nolo), this might not be a bad deal. The tax is probably no more—and is often less—than the tax you'd have paid if you didn't take the depreciation deductions and, instead, paid tax on your additional taxable income at ordinary income tax rates.

Employees and Independent Contractors

Many small businesses start as solo acts, with the business owner playing every role from executive decision maker to receptionist. At some point, however, you might need some help. You might be looking for temporary seasonal help (for example, someone to package and send your specialty food products during the holidays), expert assistance (a Web designer to set up your website, for example), or even a team of employees (a sales force to make your product known to the world).

Other small businesses—such as new stores or restaurants—have employees right from the start. In fact, these businesses might have to hire a large group of employees before they can open their doors to the public.

No matter which group you fall into, you need to know the rules that govern how you treat employees and contractors. Employment is a very heavily regulated field, with numerous federal, state, and even local laws coming into play. This chapter provides basic information on your obligations when you become an employer. It also explains the rules relating to independent contractors, including how to avoid costly misclassification mistakes.

 RESOURCE

For an in-depth treatment of your legal obligations, see *The Employer's Legal Handbook,* by Fred S. Steingold (Nolo). For a variety of articles on hiring employees and independent contractors and numerous other employment law topics, check out Nolo's Employment Law Center at www.nolo.com/legal-encyclopedia/hr-employment-law. For links to state and regional Department of Labor programs and information on state labor laws, including minimum wage, see the U.S. Department of Labor website at www.dol.gov/dol/whd/state/state.htm.

Hiring Employees

You can steer clear of legal peril when hiring employees by following the guidelines outlined below.

Avoid Illegal Discrimination

Federal and state laws prohibit all but the smallest employers from discriminating against an applicant or employee because of race, color, gender, religion, national origin, disability, citizenship status, or age (if the person is 40 years old or older). Also, many states and cities have laws prohibiting employment discrimination based on marital status, sexual orientation, gender identity, and a variety of other characteristics.

But antidiscrimination laws don't dictate whom you must hire. You remain free to hire, promote, discipline, and fire employees and to set their salaries based on their skills, experience, performance, and reliability.

Some illegal practices should be obvious, such as advertising a job for people ages 20 to 30 only —which on its face violates age discrimination laws—or paying lower wages to women than men for the same work in violation of equal pay laws. But antidiscrimination laws also can bar employment practices that seem innocent but end up having a disproportionate and discriminatory impact on certain groups. For example, if you automatically disqualify any applicant who doesn't have a college degree, that might have a disproportionate impact on certain racial groups (depending on the demographics of the region where you do business). Unless it's a business necessity for employees to hold a degree, this type of requirement could be discriminatory.

To avoid violating antidiscrimination laws at the hiring stage:

- Advertise job openings in a variety of places so they come to the attention of diverse people.
- Determine the skills, education, and other attributes that are truly necessary to perform the job so that you don't impose requirements that unnecessarily exclude capable applicants. Avoid screening techniques that have an unfair impact on any group of applicants.

Respect the Applicant's Privacy Rights

Though it's wise to screen potential employees, there's a potential problem in mounting intensive background checks. Your attempt to assess applicants by gathering information about their past can conflict with their right to privacy. Before you send for high school or college transcripts and credit reports, you must obtain the applicant's written consent. If the applicant won't consent, you're free to drop that person from further consideration, as long as you follow that policy with all applicants.

Don't Promise Job Security

Most employees in the United States work "at will." This means that they are free to quit at any time, for any reason, and that you are free to fire them at any time, for any reason that isn't illegal. It's illegal to fire even an at-will employee for discriminatory reasons, in retaliation for complaining of a workplace safety violation, or in violation of public policy, for example.

At-will employment gives you a lot of leeway to make personnel decisions that you feel are right for your business. However, you can unwittingly lose the right to fire at will if you promise an employee or applicant job security, whether in an employee handbook, other written documents (such as an offer letter or application for employment), or even a conversation or job interview. Promises like these could create an employment contract that limits your right to fire.

Employment at will is the "default" relationship between employer and employee, but it can be changed by contract. For example, let's say you need to hire someone to sell your company's software. You're looking for a top-notch salesperson who already has an extensive network of potential clients, is willing to travel extensively, and can understand and demonstrate the software's technical features. To land the right applicant, you might well have to offer a written contract promising that the person won't be fired for a set period of time—a year or two, for example—absent serious misconduct. You might

even propose this type of contract yourself, to make sure that the employee doesn't quit right away, after you spend significant time and money on training.

Not all employment contracts are in writing, however. If you tell an employee, "I won't fire you as long as you're doing a good job," or "I like to give new employees at least a year to get up to speed," a court could interpret that as a contract that limits your right to fire at will. Statements like these are especially common in the hiring process when employers are trying to sell strong applicants on the benefits of working for their company. To avoid problems, don't make any assurances or promises about job security. Make sure your application forms and offer letters clearly state that employment is at will, and have the applicant sign an acknowledgment to that effect.

Prevent Negligent Hiring Claims

You have a legal duty to protect your customers, clients, visitors, and the general public from injuries caused by employees who might harm others. When you hire someone for a position that might expose customers or others to danger, you must use special care in checking references and making other background checks. If someone gets hurt or has property stolen or damaged by an employee whose background you didn't check carefully, you might face a lawsuit for negligent hiring.

Be especially vigilant when hiring maintenance workers, delivery drivers, and others whose jobs give them easy access to homes and apartments.

If you hire people for sensitive jobs, investigate their backgrounds as thoroughly as possible and look for any criminal convictions. Make sure any employee who will be driving is currently licensed and has a decent driving record. And where state laws require an occupational license—for asbestos removal, for example, or tending bar—check to see that the applicant is properly licensed.

Contact previous employers. Insist that the applicant explain any gaps in employment history. Consider turning over the prehire investigation to professionals with experience in screening job applicants.

Protect Against Unfair Competition

Employees sometimes leave to start a competing business or go to work for a competitor. Obviously, you needn't be too concerned about the employee you hire to scoop ice cream or the clerk you hire to work behind the counter at your dry cleaning shop. But employees who have access to inside information about product pricing or business expansion plans, for example, might pose competitive risks. The same goes for employees who handle valuable and hard-won customers—a salesperson, perhaps, who handles a $200,000 account.

Consider asking new hires to sign agreements not to take or disclose trade secrets or other confidential information. Also, you might ask selected employees to sign covenants not to compete with your business.

Trade Secrets

Some business owners need to protect their unique assets from misuse—assets such as:

- a restaurant's recipe for a special salad dressing
- a heating and cooling company's list of 500 customers for whom it regularly provides maintenance, or
- a computer company's unique process for speedily assembling computer boards.

If they are treated as such, the recipe, customer list, and assembly process are all "trade secrets." Other examples are an unpatented invention, engineering techniques, cost data, a formula, or a machine. To qualify for trade secret protection, the business information you seek to protect must meet two requirements.

The information must truly be secret. The information must not be freely available from other sources. If the recipe for a restaurant's award-winning custard tart can be found in a standard American cookbook or recreated by a competent chef, it isn't a trade secret. On the other hand, if the restaurant's chef found the recipe in a medieval French cookbook in a provincial museum, translated it, and figured out how to adapt it to currently available ingredients, it probably would be considered obscure enough to receive trade secret protection.

You must have protected the secrecy. You must show that you've taken steps to keep the information secret—for example, by:

- keeping it in a secure place such as a locked cabinet
- giving employees access to it on a need-to-know basis, and
- having employees acknowledge in writing that the information is a trade secret.

EXAMPLE: Sue works at Speedy Copy Shop. She has daily access to the list of larger accounts that are regularly billed more than $2,000 per month. She quits to open her own shop. Before she does, she copies the list of major accounts. One of her first steps in getting her new business going is to try to get their business away from her former employer. Speedy sues Sue for infringing on its trade secret. At trial, Speedy shows that it keeps the list in a secure place, permits access only to selected employees who need the information, and has all employees—including Sue—sign nondisclosure agreements. In light of these precautions, the judge orders Sue not to contact the customers on the list and requires her to compensate Speedy for any profits she's already earned on those accounts.

Covenants Not to Compete

It's always disappointing and often quite costly when a high-level employee leaves your business and begins competing with you—especially if you've trained the employee and shared valuable inside information. Consider having high-level employees sign a covenant not to compete. In a typical covenant, the employee agrees not to start or work for a business that competes with yours for a specific time and within a specific distance from your established business.

The best time to secure a covenant not to compete is when you hire an employee. An employee who is already on the payroll might be more reluctant to sign anything—and you'll have less leverage to negotiate the agreement.

Battles over the legality of these agreements must usually be resolved in court. Judges are reluctant to deprive people of their rights to earn a living, so the key to a legally enforceable covenant not to compete is to make its terms reasonable. Focus on three questions:

- **Is there a legitimate business reason for restricting the particular employee?** There probably is if you expect to spend significant time and money training a high-level employee and plan to trust that person with sensitive contacts or lucrative accounts.

- **Is the covenant reasonably limited in time?** Courts tend to favor short covenants—the shorter the better. A one-year covenant might be reasonable for a particular employee. A three-year limit might not be.

- **Is the covenant reasonably limited as to geographical scope?** For a local business, a 50-mile limit or one that excludes competition in a few counties might be reasonable. For a regional business, a limit spanning several states might be deemed reasonable.

EXAMPLE: When Mariah hires Sydney to be the office manager for her profitable travel agency, she realizes that Sydney will have access to major corporate accounts and daily contact with the corporate managers who make travel arrangements. Mariah also knows that she'll spend considerable time in training Sydney and invest more than $4,000 in specialized seminars that she'll require Sydney to attend. She has Sydney sign a covenant not to compete, in which Sydney promises that while working for Mariah and for two years afterward, she won't work for or own a travel agency within 50 miles of Mariah's agency. After six months, Sydney quits and starts a competing agency one mile from Mariah's. The judge enforces the covenant not to compete by issuing an injunction forbidding Sydney from operating her new business and by awarding damages to Mariah as well.

CAUTION

Not all states honor noncompete agreements. Noncompete agreements can be difficult—or impossible—to enforce. In California, for example, courts virtually never enforce noncompete agreements, and other states enforce them only in very limited circumstances. Even in the states where they are enforced, it can be hard to overcome a judge's reluctance to interfere with an employee's ability to earn a living. One way to avoid this problem is to ask employees to sign a nonsolicitation agreement and nondisclosure agreement instead. Courts are more willing to enforce these agreements, which prevent former employees from taking your employees or using your company's confidential information. With these protections in place, you don't lose much by not having a noncompete agreement.

Job Descriptions

Write a job description for each position you're seeking to fill. Listing the skills and qualifications you're looking for in applicants will make the hiring process more objective. It will also give you ready standards to measure whether applicants are qualified—and which ones are most qualified—for the position.

A well-drafted job description should include:

- a summary, which briefly describes the most important aspects of the job
- a list of job functions, which provides a detailed description of duties
- a requirements section, which lists any education, certifications, licenses, and experience necessary to do the job, and
- a section for other information, where you can provide any other facts job applicants should know (for example, that the job has odd working hours or requires travel).

When you come up with your list of job functions, think carefully about whether each is essential to the job. The Americans with Disabilities Act (ADA) prohibits discrimination against applicants with disabilities, as long as they can perform the job's essential functions with or without a reasonable accommodation. This provision is intended to make sure people aren't excluded from a job simply because they can't perform some of the marginal duties associated with that position. For example, a receptionist who spends the day answering phones and greeting visitors at a front desk might also replace the large water bottles in the waiting room's machine when they're empty. But this probably isn't an essential function of the position: It takes only a couple of minutes a week, could easily be handled by someone else, and could well screen out applicants with disabilities.

RESOURCE

Need more information on job descriptions? You'll find tips for coming up with essential job functions, troubleshooting your job descriptions for legal problems, and using job descriptions in every aspect of employment in *The Job Description Handbook*, by Margie Mader-Clark (Nolo).

Job Advertisements

After you write a job description, summarize it in a job advertisement. Be careful because nuances in an ad can be used as evidence of discrimination against applicants of a particular gender, age, or marital status.

There are a number of semantic pitfalls to avoid in job ads.

Don't Use	Use
Salesman	Salesperson
College Student	Part-time Worker
Handyman	General Repair Person
Gal Friday	Office Manager
Married Couple	Two-Person Job
Counter Girl	Retail Clerk
Waiter	Waitstaff
Young	Energetic

In any ad, stick to the job skills needed and the basic responsibilities. Some examples:

"Fifty-unit apartment complex seeks experienced manager with general maintenance skills."

"Midsized manufacturing company has opening for accountant with tax experience to oversee interstate accounts."

"Cook trainee position available in new vegetarian restaurant. Flexible hours."

Job Applications

Develop a standard application form to make it easy to compare applicants. Use the form to let the job seeker know the basic terms and conditions of the job. Because an applicant signs the application, it can be a valuable piece of evidence if a question comes up later about what you actually promised or what experience and qualifications the applicant claimed to have.

You can also use the job application to obtain the employee's consent to a background investigation and reference check. If the applicant consents to your investigation, it will be tough to later claim an invasion of privacy.

Limit the form to job-related information that will help you decide who's the best person for the job. Consider requesting the following information:

- Name, address, and phone number
- Are you legally entitled to work in the United States?
- What position are you applying for?
- What other positions would you like to be considered for?
- If you are hired, when can you start work?
- Education—high school, college, graduate, and other (including school names, addresses, number of years attended, degree, and major)
- Employment history—including name, address, and phone number of each employer, supervisor's name, date of employment, job title and responsibilities, and reason for leaving, and
- Special training or achievements.

If the job involves handling money or calling on customers at home, ask whether the applicant has ever been convicted of a crime and the details of the conviction. Similarly, in an application for a job that requires driving, ask about the applicant's driving record.

Preemployment Inquiries

The chart below outlines the type of information you can ask for in applications and during job interviews as specified in federal laws. The chart might also be sufficient for complying with the laws of your state, but double-check with your state's civil rights department.

In addition to the areas covered in the chart, the Americans with Disabilities Act (ADA) prohibits you from asking any preemployment questions about a disability—including medical history or treatment—or requiring a medical exam. However, before you make a job offer, you may ask questions about an applicant's ability to perform specific job functions.

Postoffer Inquiries

After you make a conditional job offer, you're free to gather more details on health matters. You can at that point require a medical exam or ask health-related questions—but only if you require this for all candidates who receive conditional offers in the same job category.

Interviews

Before interviewing applicants for a job opening, write a set of questions focusing on the job duties (as listed in the job description) and the applicant's skills and experience. Some examples:

"Tell me about your experience running a mailroom."

"How much experience did you have making cold calls on your last job?"

"Explain how you typically go about organizing your workday."

"Have any of your jobs required strong leadership skills?"

By writing down the questions and sticking to the same format for all interviews for the position, you reduce the risk that a rejected applicant will later complain about unequal treatment.

During an interview, focus on job requirements and company policies. Suppose you're concerned that an applicant with young kids might spend too much time talking with them on the phone. You can't ask: "Do you have children?" or "Who watches the kids when you're at work?"

But you can say to the applicant: "We don't allow personal phone calls during work hours. Do you have a problem with that?" The applicant then knows the ground rules and will let you know if a problem exists. Just make sure you apply your phone policy to all employees.

RESOURCE
Want more information? Get the lowdown on interviews, wages, hours, employee benefits, workplace safety, and much more in Nolo's *The Employer's Legal Handbook*, by Fred S. Steingold (Nolo).

Testing

Testing job applicants is most common in larger businesses. Testing can include skills testing, aptitude testing, honesty testing, medical testing, and drug testing. But even if your business is small or midsized, you might have needs you feel could best be met by testing. If so, you should know the legal limitations.

Preemployment Inquiries		
Subject	**Lawful Preemployment Inquiries**	**Unlawful Preemployment Inquiries**
Name	Applicant's full name Have you ever worked for this company under a different name? Is any additional information relative to a different name necessary to check work record? If yes, explain.	Original name of an applicant whose name has been changed by court order or otherwise Applicant's maiden name
Birthplace	None	Birthplace of applicant Birthplace of applicant's parents, spouse, or other close relatives Requirements that applicant submit birth certificate, naturalization, or baptismal record
Age	Are you 18 years old or older? (This question may be asked only for the purpose of determining whether applicants are of legal age for employment.)	How old are you? What is your date of birth?
Religion or Creed	None	Inquiry into an applicant's religious denomination, religious affiliations, church, parish, pastor, or religious holidays observed
Race or Color	None	Complexion or color of skin Inquiry regarding applicant's race
Photograph	None	Any requirement for a photograph prior to hire
Height	None	Inquiry regarding applicant's height (unless you have a legitimate business reason)
Weight	None	Inquiry regarding applicant's weight (unless you have a legitimate business reason)
Marital Status	Is your spouse employed by this employer?	Requirement that an applicant provide any information regarding marital status or children. Are you single or married? Do you have any children? Is your spouse employed? What is your spouse's name?
Gender	None	Mr., Miss, Ms., or Mrs. or an inquiry regarding gender; inquiry as to the ability to reproduce or advocacy of any form of birth control
Disability	These [*provide applicant with list*] are the essential functions of the job. How would you perform them?	Inquiries regarding an individual's physical or mental condition that are not directly related to the requirements of a specific job

Preemployment Inquiries (continued)		
Subject	**Lawful Preemployment Inquiries**	**Unlawful Preemployment Inquiries**
Citizenship	Are you legally authorized to work in the United States on a full-time basis?	Questions below are unlawful but applicant might have to provide information as part of the federal I-9 process: • Country of citizenship • Whether an applicant is naturalized or a native-born citizen; the date when the applicant acquired citizenship • Requirement that an applicant produce naturalization papers or first papers • Whether applicant's parents or spouse are naturalized or native-born citizens of the United States; the date when such parent or spouse acquired citizenship.
National Origin	Inquiry into language applicant speaks and writes fluently	Inquiry into applicant's lineage, ancestry, national origin, descent, parentage, or nationality (unless part of I-9 process) Nationality of applicant's parents or spouse Inquiry into how applicant acquired ability to read, write, or speak a foreign language
Education	Inquiry into the academic, vocational, or professional education of an applicant and public and private schools attended	
Experience	Inquiry into work experience Inquiry into countries applicant has visited	
Arrests	Have you ever been convicted of a crime? Are there any felony charges pending against you? Such inquires are banned in some states and cities.	Inquiry regarding arrests that did not result in conviction (except for law enforcement agencies)
Relatives	Names of applicant's relatives already employed by this company	Address of any relative of applicant, other than address (within the United States) of applicant's father and mother, husband or wife, and minor dependent children
Notice in Case of Emergency	Name and address of person to be notified in case of accident or emergency	Name and address of nearest relative to be notified in case of accident or emergency
Organizations	Inquiry into the organizations of which an applicant is a member, excluding organizations the name or character of which indicates the race, color, religion, national origin, or ancestry of its members	List all clubs, societies, and lodges to which you belong

Source: *The Employer's Legal Handbook,* by Fred S. Steingold (Nolo).

Skills Tests

Most small businesses—especially new ones—operate on a slim profit margin and need to know that employees will be up to speed from day one. If you're hiring a person to be a clerk in your bookstore, you might want to test the applicant's knowledge of literature. If you're hiring a driver for a delivery van, a road test would be appropriate—and a cooking test for a chef is quite reasonable. As long as the skills you're testing for are genuinely related to job duties, a skills test is generally legal.

Aptitude and Psychological Tests

Few small employers are tempted to use written tests to get additional insight into an applicant's abilities or psyche. That's fortunate, because these tests are usually a poor idea. A written aptitude test might discriminate illegally against certain applicants because it really reflects test-taking ability rather than actual job skills.

A personality test can be even riskier. In addition to its potential for illegal discrimination, such a test might invade an applicant's protected privacy rights—by inquiring, for example, into religious beliefs or sexual practices.

If you do decide to use aptitude or personality tests, make sure they've been screened scientifically for validity and are related to job performance.

SEE AN EXPERT

Get professional advice. Because testing is such a sensitive legal issue and it's easy to make mistakes, it makes sense to check with an experienced employment lawyer before testing applicants.

RESOURCE

Looking for a lawyer? Asking for a referral to an attorney from someone you trust can be a good way to find legal help. Also, two sites that are part of the Nolo family, Lawyers.com and Avvo.com, provide excellent and free lawyer directories. These directories allow you to search by location and area of law, and list detailed information about and reviews of lawyers.

Whether you're just starting your lawyer search or researching particular attorneys, visit www.lawyers.com/find-a-lawyer and www.avvo.com/find-a-lawyer.

Honesty Tests

Lie detector or polygraph tests—rarely used by small businesses anyhow—are virtually outlawed by the federal Employee Polygraph Protection Act. With just a few exceptions, you can't require job applicants to take lie detector tests and you can't inquire about previous tests. The only private employers who can use lie detector tests to screen applicants are businesses that offer armored car, alarm, and guard services or that manufacture, distribute, or dispense pharmaceuticals—and even in those situations there are restrictions on which applicants can be tested and how the tests must be administered.

About the only time the typical employer can use a lie detector test is when an employee is reasonably suspected of being involved in a workplace theft or embezzlement.

Some employers are intrigued by written "honesty tests" as a way to screen job applicants. Because these tests are often inaccurate and sometimes invade an applicant's privacy or have a discriminatory impact, their legality is doubtful in most states.

Drug Tests

You have a legal right to insist on a drug-free workplace. The only problem is that testing to weed out drug users might conflict with workers' rights to privacy. The laws on drug testing vary widely from state to state and are changing quickly. In states having such statutes, your right to test for drugs might turn on whether or not the employee's job poses an unusual risk of danger to the employee, coworkers, or the public.

 TIP

Check your state law on drug testing. Before you initiate any program of testing job applicants or employees, be sure you know exactly what your state law provides. A trade association might have information about the current status of the drug-testing laws in your state or you can do your own legal research. To learn how to do your own legal research, get Nolo's *Legal Research: How to Find & Understand the Law*, by Stephen Elias (Nolo). Another good resource is the "State Drug and Alcohol Testing Laws" chart in Appendix B of *The Essential Guide to Workplace Investigations*, by Lisa Guerin (Nolo). A brief consultation with an experienced employment lawyer should also give you the information you need.

You generally have much more leeway in screening job applicants than in testing employees who are already on board. If your state permits testing applicants or employees and you plan to do such testing, use the job application form to inform applicants of this policy. State law might also require you to give applicants a written policy statement that's separate from the application. When applicants are told up front about drug testing, it's harder for them to later claim an invasion of privacy.

Background Checks

Because some people give false or incomplete information in their job applications, it's a good idea to verify application information. To reduce the risk of an invasion of privacy claim, inform the applicant in the job application that you will be requesting information from former employers, schools, credit reporting sources, and law enforcement agencies.

Ask the applicant to sign a consent form as part of the application process.

Former Employers

Contact as many former employers as possible to get the inside story about an applicant. But understand that former employers are often reluctant to say anything negative for fear that if they speak frankly, they might be hit by a lawsuit for defamation.

In speaking with former employers, you'll often have to read between the lines. If a former employer is neutral, offers only faint praise, or repeatedly overpraises a person for one aspect of a job only— "really great with numbers" or "invariably on time"— there's a good chance some negative information is hiding in the wings. Ask former employers: "Would you hire this person back if you could?" The response might be telling.

If references aren't glowing and don't take in all aspects of the job, consider calling the applicant back for a more directed interview.

 TIP

Tell former employers if your state protects reference providers. In response to the legal perils of providing an informative reference, many states have passed laws that allow former employers to speak more frankly without risking a lawsuit. These laws, sometimes called "qualified privileges," typically protect former employers who provide reference information as long as they act in good faith. If your state has such a law (you can find out from your state's labor department), let the former employers you call know about it. They might be willing to provide more information if they aren't worried about getting sued.

School Transcripts

On-the-job experience generally is more relevant to employment than an applicant's educational credentials. Still, you might have good reasons for requiring a high school diploma or college degree for some jobs—especially for younger employees who don't have a lot of job experience. If so, you might want to see proof that the applicant really received the diploma or degree or took the courses claimed in the job application.

If you wish to see these records, ask the applicant to sign a written release giving you the right to obtain them. Federal law prohibits schools that receive federal funds from turning over transcripts without such as release; many schools take it a step further and refuse to deliver the records to anyone but the former student.

Credit History

Credit information might be relevant in the rare cases when you hire someone who will handle money. An applicant who can't keep his or her personal finances in order is probably not a good choice for a job requiring management of your company's finances.

In most situations, however, a credit check is an unnecessary intrusion into an applicant's personal life. What's more, unless you have a good reason for doing a credit check for a particular job, you might run afoul of antidiscrimination laws. According to the EEOC, requiring an applicant to have good credit might subtly discriminate against some minority groups. State laws, too, might limit your use of credit information in deciding whether to hire someone.

Assuming that you have a good business reason to order a credit report on a job applicant, be sure to get the applicant's written consent first. In addition, the federal Fair Credit Reporting Act requires you to let an applicant know if you decide not to hire the applicant because of something in a credit report.

TIP

When ordering a credit report, make it clear that your request is part of a hiring investigation. Your request will then be treated as a "soft inquiry," meaning it won't affect the applicant's credit score. (By contrast, an inquiry for purposes of lending credit is treated as a "hard inquiry," which can lower the applicant's credit rating.)

RESOURCE

Authoritative information about the Fair Credit Reporting Act is available at the Federal Trade Commission's website, at www.ftc.gov.

Criminal History

Asking an applicant about his or her arrest record or making a hiring decision based on that record can violate state and federal antidiscrimination laws. Criminal charges are often dropped or found to be without merit.

Convictions are another matter. Antidiscrimination laws generally allow you to inquire about an applicant's conviction record and to reject an applicant because of a conviction record that suggests the applicant wouldn't be a good fit for the job. If you're hiring a delivery truck driver, for example, it wouldn't violate antidiscrimination laws to reject an applicant based on a drunk driving conviction.

In some states you can't ask about convictions for minor offenses, juvenile records, or misdemeanors that go back more than five years if the applicant has had a clean slate since that time.

Driving Records

When a job requires an employee to drive, it's wise to check applicants' driving records. You usually can obtain driving records for a modest cost from the state authority that issues driver's licenses. Check, too, with your insurance company to be sure you meet the requirements for bringing new employees under your vehicle insurance coverage.

Immigration Law Requirements

Immigration laws, enforced by the Department of Homeland Security (DHS), prohibit hiring aliens who don't have government authorization to work in the United States. There are specific procedures you must follow when hiring employees to make sure that they meet these requirements.

You and the new employee must complete Form I-9, *Employment Eligibility Verification.* This one-page form is intended to ensure that the employee can work legally in the United States and has proof of his or her identity.

RESOURCE

Form I-9 and further information are available on the website of the DHS U.S. Citizenship & Immigration Services (USCIS) at www.uscis.gov.

Personnel Practices

The vast majority of job disputes can be resolved within the workplace if you listen patiently to what employees have to say and are prepared to make adjustments when legitimate complaints surface. However, there's always the chance that a dispute will get out of hand and an employee will sue your small business for some perceived abuse of his or her rights. Or an unhappy employee might file a complaint with a government agency alleging that you violated a statute or an administrative regulation.

If that happens, you'll have to prove to a judge or jury or an arbitrator or investigator that you met your legal obligations to the employee. That can be harder than you think. Key paperwork might have been lost—or never prepared in the first place. And witnesses might have forgotten what happened or moved on to new jobs.

To maintain a solid legal footing, establish good written policies and then maintain a paper trail indicating how they are implemented. Written policies and an employee handbook explaining employee benefits and responsibilities provide cogent points of reference when you discuss problems with an employee—and increase the likelihood of reaching an amicable resolution.

Employee Handbooks

An employee handbook can be of practical help in running your business. Once you give it to an employee, there can be no dispute over whether you gave the employee a list of paid days off or explained your vacation policies. It's all there in writing and everyone has the same information.

If your handbook is good, you get a bonus: a measure of legal protection if you're challenged by an employee in a court or administrative proceeding. A handbook can be an objective piece of evidence showing that you've adopted fair and uniform policies and have informed your employees of exactly where they stand in their employment.

A good handbook should tell your employees how to let you know if they have a workplace problem. This gives you a chance to react before a small misunderstanding erupts into a full-blown legal dispute.

If yours is a very small business, keep your handbook short and sweet at the start. Then, as your business grows, the framework necessary for a more detailed version will be in place.

Check with your state department of labor to make sure your handbook complies with the laws in your state. Keep the handbook up to date as laws change. If you have specific legal questions, a brief consultation with a lawyer should be sufficient to clear them up.

TIP

Make sure your handbook doesn't promise more than you can deliver. Your handbook might be treated as a contract that can actually limit your right to fire employees. To avoid that result, state in the handbook that:

- employees don't have employment contracts—and can't have them in the future—unless they're in writing and signed by the company president, and
- your company reserves the right to terminate employees for reasons not stated in the handbook or for no reason at all.

RESOURCE

Want an easy way to prepare a professional, legally safe handbook? See *Create Your Own Employee Handbook: A Legal & Practical Guide for Employers*, by Lisa Guerin and Amy DelPo (Nolo).

Performance Reviews

Most large companies review and evaluate their employees periodically. This is a sound management practice and one that you should consider—especially for new employees.

Evaluating new employees periodically gives them a chance to improve if they're not performing well. If you later find it necessary to discipline or fire an employee, it won't come as a surprise to the employee. By putting your evaluations in writing and saving them in the employee's file, you have a credible history of documented problems you can use if an employee claims termination for an illegal reason.

RESOURCE

Want help with performance evaluations? See *The Performance Appraisal Handbook*, by Lisa Guerin and Margie Mader-Clark (Nolo), which provides all of the forms and information you need to review and document employee performance.

Illegal Discrimination

To give workers a fair opportunity to get and keep jobs, Congress and state legislatures have passed laws prohibiting discrimination in the workplace.

Title VII of the Civil Rights Act

Title VII (42 USC §§ 2000 and following) applies to your business if you employ 15 or more people—either full time or part time. State laws, with similar prohibitions against discrimination, generally cover smaller employers, too.

Under Title VII, you can't use race, color, religion, gender, or national origin as the basis for decisions on hirings, promotions, dismissals, pay raises, benefits, work assignments, leaves of absence, or just about any other aspect of employment. Title VII applies to everything from help wanted ads, to working conditions, to performance reviews, to giving references to other prospective employers.

Sexual Harassment

Sexual harassment in the workplace is a form of prohibited sex discrimination. Illegal sexual harassment occurs when unwelcome sexual advances, requests for sexual favors, and other verbal or physical conduct of a sexual nature create a hostile or abusive work environment.

Under federal law, it's clearly sexual harassment for an employer or a manager to make unwelcome sexual advances or to demand sexual favors in return for job benefits, promotions, or continued employment.

But sexual harassment in the workplace can consist, as well, of many other activities including:

- posting sexually explicit photos that offend employees
- telling sex-related jokes or jokes that demean people because of their gender

- commenting inappropriately on an employee's appearance
- requiring employees to dress in scanty attire
- repeatedly requesting dates from a person who clearly isn't interested
- having strippers perform at a company gathering, and
- stating that people of one gender are inferior to people of the other gender or can't perform their jobs as well.

In short, any hostile or offensive behavior in the workplace that has a sexual component can constitute sexual harassment—and is illegal.

Your business can also be held responsible for sexual harassment if you or a supervisor know, or should know, it's being committed by one coworker against another—or even by customers or vendors on your premises.

You're also under a legal duty to take all necessary steps to prevent sexual harassment. No matter the size of your business, start by adopting a formal policy stating clearly that sexual harassment won't be tolerated. Post it on a bulletin board and place it in your employee handbook. Let employees know who within your company they can complain to if they've been sexually harassed.

Once you learn of potential harassment, investigate right away. If you decide that harassment occurred, take appropriate disciplinary action against the wrongdoer. You might also consider sexual harassment training for your workforce.

Age Discrimination

The Age Discrimination in Employment Act (ADEA) prohibits discrimination against those 40 years old or older. It applies to businesses with 20 or more employees—but similar state laws generally apply to businesses with fewer employees. Age discrimination is prohibited in all aspects of

employment: hiring, firing, compensation, and all other terms of employment.

Another law, the Older Worker's Benefits Protection Act, makes it illegal to use an employee's age as the basis for discrimination in benefits. Like the ADEA, this act covers employees who are 40 years old or older. Under this law, you cannot, for example, reduce health or life insurance benefits for older employees, nor can you stop their pensions from accruing if they work past their normal retirement ages. The law also discourages your business from targeting older workers when you cut staff.

The law also regulates the legal waivers that some employers ask employees to sign in connection with early retirement programs. For details, see *The Employer's Legal Handbook,* by Fred S. Steingold (Nolo).

Pregnancy

The Pregnancy Discrimination Act (PDA) applies to businesses with 15 or more employees. Under the PDA, it's a form of gender discrimination to treat an employee differently because of pregnancy, childbirth, or related medical conditions. If a woman is affected by such a condition, you must treat her just as you treat other people in the workforce who are either able or unable to work.

You violate the PDA, for example, if you fire a woman whose pregnancy keeps her from working, but you don't fire other workers who are temporarily unable to do the job because of other physical problems. Similarly, if a pregnant worker is able to do the job, you can't lay her off because you think it's in her best interests to stay home. On the other hand, you don't violate the PDA if you apply medically based job restrictions to a pregnant woman—as long as you apply those same policies to employees who are not pregnant but who are under medical restrictions.

Citizenship Status

The Immigration Reform and Control Act of 1986, which applies to businesses with at least four employees, makes it illegal to discriminate against a person for not being a U.S. citizen or national. The law forbids you from discriminating against aliens who have been lawfully admitted to the United States for permanent or temporary residence—and aliens who have applied for temporary residence status.

Disability

The Americans with Disabilities Act (ADA) applies to businesses with 15 or more employees. Basically, the ADA states that, in making hiring and employment decisions, it's illegal to discriminate against anyone because of a disability. If a person is qualified to do the work, or to do it once a reasonable accommodation is made, you must treat that person the same as all other applicants and employees. During the hiring process, make sure your job descriptions focus on core tasks. You don't want to eliminate a person with a disability from consideration based on an inability to perform a marginal job duty.

You might have to provide a reasonable accommodation to enable a disabled person to perform the job, unless this would cause undue hardship for your business. For example, a reasonable accommodation might consist of rearranging a workstation to make it possible for a person in a wheelchair to do the work. Or you might need to install a phone accessory for an employee who is hard of hearing. Sometimes, it might be reasonable to allow an employee to work from his or her home. This could be the case with a telemarketing or proofreading job if the employee doesn't need direct supervision.

Sexual Orientation and Gender Identity

In a momentous victory for LGBTQ workers, the U.S. Supreme Court held in *Bostock v. Clayton County*, Georgia (590 U.S. ___ (2020)) that employers who discriminate against employees due to their sexual orientation or gender identity violate Title VII of the Civil Rights Act. So employers nationwide are barred from discriminating against workers on the basis of sexual orientation or gender identity in any aspect of employment, including hiring, training, promotion, compensation, discipline, and termination. Because harassment is a form of discrimination under federal law, the ruling also prohibits workplace harassment based on sexual orientation or gender identity.

Before the Bostock ruling, over half the states and hundreds of cities and counties had laws barring workplace discrimination and harassment against gay and transgender people.

Wages and Hours

Federal and state statutes regulate workplace wages and hours, including the minimum wage, overtime rules, and more. Because fines and back wage awards can be expensive, it pays to know the law.

Here's an overview of laws covering wages and hours. For details on federal laws, check out the Wage and Hour Division (WHD) of the U.S. Department of Labor website at www.dol.gov/whd. To find your state rules, check with your state department of labor; you'll find yours on the WHD website (see "WHD Local Offices").

The Fair Labor Standards Act

The main law affecting worker's pay is the federal Fair Labor Standards Act (FLSA), which Congress passed in 1938. In addition to setting a minimum wage, the FLSA requires premium pay for overtime work and equal pay for men and women doing the same work. The law also contains special rules for hiring young workers.

Virtually all businesses and employees are covered. There are just a handful of specific exemptions, including most small farms. For details, check with the nearest office of the U.S. Labor Department's Wage and Hour Division. Even though your business is covered by the FLSA, some employees might be exempt from that law's minimum wage and overtime pay requirements.

Most employees who are exempt from the minimum wage and overtime pay requirements fall into one of five categories:

- executive employees
- administrative employees
- professional employees
- outside salespeople, and
- people in certain computer-related occupations.

There are a few miscellaneous categories of workers who are exempt as well.

Who's Exempt and Who Isn't?

Job titles alone don't determine whether someone is an exempt executive, administrative, or professional employee. The actual work relationship is what counts. Still, it's possible to make some generalizations about who's exempt and who isn't. Typical exempt jobs include such positions as department head, financial expert, personnel director, credit manager, account executive, and tax specialist. Typical nonexempt jobs include such positions as clerk, bank teller, administrative assistant, warehouse worker, data entry person, bookkeeper, and trainee.

RESOURCE

Need to learn more about exempt employees? For links to the fine points of these exemptions, go to www.dol.gov/elaws and click on "Employment Law Guide."

Pay Requirements

If your business is covered by the FLSA (which it probably is), you must pay all covered employees at least the minimum wage, which is $7.25 an hour.

The amount will be higher if your state has established a higher minimum wage. In California, for example, the minimum wage for 2021 is $13 an hour for employers with up to 25 employees and $14 an hour for employers with more than 25 employees, with additional increases set for subsequent years. In states that have a lower minimum, the federal rate controls. Each state has its own—often complex— rules for who's covered by its minimum wage law.

A person who's exempt from the federal minimum wage requirements might be entitled to a minimum wage under the state law. To learn the details, contact your state's department of labor.

The Equal Pay Act, an amendment to the FLSA, requires you to provide equal pay and benefits to men and women who do the same jobs, or jobs that require equal skill, effort, and responsibility. Job titles aren't decisive in assessing whether two jobs are equal; it's the work duties that count. The Act makes it unlawful, for example, for the owner of a hotel to pay its janitors (primarily men) at a different pay rate than its housekeepers (primarily women) if both are doing essentially the same work.

The Equal Pay Act doesn't prohibit pay differences based on:

- a seniority system
- a merit system
- a system that bases pay on the quantity or quality of what a worker produces, or
- any factor other than the worker's gender— starting salaries, for example, that are based on the worker's experience level.

Overtime Pay

The FLSA requires you to pay nonexempt workers at least one and one-half times their regular rates of pay for all hours worked in excess of 40 hours in one week. The FLSA doesn't require you to pay an employee at an overtime rate simply for working more than eight hours in one day (although some state laws do). Generally, you calculate and pay overtime by the week. Each workweek stands alone; you can't average two or more workweeks. And you can't manipulate the start of the workweek merely to avoid paying overtime.

As of January 1, 2020, the overtime rules say that you don't need to pay overtime to the following exempt employees:

- **White-collar employees:** Salaried employees who earn $455 a week or more and primarily perform executive, administrative, or professional work, as defined by the U.S. Department of Labor

- **High earners:** Salaried employees who earn $107,432 or more, whose primary duties include office or nonmanual work, and who also regularly perform at least one executive, administrative, or professional function.

- **Outside salespeople:** Employees who work away from your place of business to make sales or obtain orders.

- **Computer professionals:** Computer analysts, programmers, software engineers, and similarly skilled workers who earn at least $27.63 an hour, or are paid a salary of $455 a week or more.

Note that no exemptions are allowed for manual laborers or others who perform repetitive operations with their hands, physical skill, and energy, regardless of how much they're paid. Such workers are always entitled to overtime pay.

These are the federal rules for overtime pay. Be aware that the law in your state might require overtime pay for additional classes of workers and might require such pay when someone works more than eight hours in a single day. Your state's department of labor can give you details.

Overtime Rule Changes Are Coming, but When?

To qualify under some of the overtime exemptions covered above, an employee must make a minimum salary. For many years, the salary threshold was $455 per week. But under a new rule passed in 2019 and effective as of January 1. 2020, the threshold increased to $684 per week. While this change is important, under the Obama administration, the Department of Labor passed a final rule revising the FLSA overtime pay provisions, which was set to take effect on December 1, 2016. This rule would have increased the salary threshold to $913 per week and would have made millions of additional workers eligible for overtime pay. But several states and business groups challenged the final rule, and a federal court struck it down. The court also issued a permanent injunction. The Department of Labor appealed the permanent injunction and later filed a motion to stay the appeal pending new rulemaking.

This area of law could change in the coming years. For updates, go to Nolo's Legal Updates for Employment Law section at www.nolo.com/legal-updates/legal-updates-for-employment-law. You should also check the Wage and Hour Division website (www.dol.gov/whd) for the latest overtime rules.

Compensatory Time Off

The practice of granting hour-for-hour compensatory time—for example, giving a worker six hours off one week as compensation for six hours of overtime work the previous week—isn't usually allowed for private sector employees covered by the FLSA. (The rule is different for public employees.)

Employers and employees are often puzzled when they learn that comp time isn't permitted in the private sector, because it seems like a sensible and mutually beneficial way to handle overtime in many situations. You do, however, have a few options for avoiding premium overtime pay by giving a worker time off instead of money. One way is to rearrange an employee's work schedule during a workweek.

> **EXAMPLE:** Margaret, a paralegal at the law firm of Smith and Jones, normally works an eight-hour day, Monday through Friday. One week, Margaret and the lawyers need to meet a deadline on a brief due in the court of appeals. So that week, Margaret works ten hours per day, Monday through Thursday. The law firm gives Margaret Friday off and pays her for a 40-hour week at her regular rate of pay. This is legal because Margaret hasn't worked any overtime as defined by the FLSA; she has worked only 40 hours for the week.

If an employee works more than 40 hours one week, it's sometimes possible to reduce the worker's hours in another week so that the amount of the employee's paycheck remains constant. This is legal if:

- the time off is given within the same pay period as the overtime work, and
- the employee is given an hour and a half of time off for each hour of overtime work.

> **EXAMPLE:** Frames and Things, a shop that specializes in framing pictures, employs Jared and pays him $640 at the close of each two-week pay period. Because a week-long street art fair is expected to generate a great demand for framing services, the shop's owner wants Jared to work longer hours that week. However, the owner doesn't want to increase Jared's paycheck. She asks Jared to work 50 hours during art fair week and gives him 15 hours off the next week. Because Jared is paid every two weeks, Frames and Things may properly reduce Jared's hours the second week to keep his paycheck at the $640 level.

Because state regulations might further restrict the use of comp time, check with your state's labor department before implementing this type of arrangement.

Calculating Work Hours

You must pay covered employees for all of their time that you control and that benefits you. In general, time on the job doesn't include the time employees spend washing themselves or changing clothes before or after work, or meal periods when employees are free from all work duties.

You needn't pay employees for the time spent commuting between their homes and the normal job site, but you do have to pay for commuting time which is actually a part of the job. If you run a plumbing repair service, for example, and require workers to stop by your shop to pick up orders, tools, and supplies before going out on calls, their work day begins when they check in at your shop.

You must count as payable time any periods when employees are not actually working but are required to stay on your premises while waiting for work assignments. If you require employees to be on call but you don't make them stay on your premises, then two rules generally apply:

- You don't count as payable time the on-call time that employees can control and use for their own enjoyment and benefit.
- You do count as payable time the on-call time over which employees have little or no control and which they can't use for their own enjoyment or benefit.

> **EXAMPLE 1:** Spotless Auto Detailing provides vehicle cleaning services to individuals and companies. Spotless hires Ryan to clean from 8 a.m. to 5 p.m., Monday through Friday and also requires him to be available one night a week so he can handle occasional cleaning assignments after normal working hours. Because Ryan is free to pursue personal and social activities during nonworking hours, Spotless doesn't have to pay him for his on-call time.

> **EXAMPLE 2:** AirTec provides mechanical services for small planes at a local airfield. Joe is an AirTec mechanic. The company requires him to be on call every fourth Saturday. When he's on

call, he must stay within a five-minute drive to the airfield, keep his cell phone free for calls from the company, and refrain from drinking alcohol. Because Joe isn't free to use his on-call time as he pleases, the company must pay him for the time.

Unless there's an employment contract that states otherwise, you can generally pay a different hourly rate for on-call time than you do for regular work time. But keep in mind that employees must be paid at least the minimum wage.

About half the states have laws requiring employers to provide meal and rest breaks and specifying minimum times that must be allowed. You don't have to pay a covered employee for time spent on an actual meal. But the employee must be completely relieved from work during that period to enable enjoyment of a regularly scheduled meal. If, for example, you require employees to remain at their desks during the meal period or keep an eye on machinery, you must pay for the meal time.

Child Labor

The FLSA has special rules for younger workers. These rules are designed to discourage young people from dropping out of school too soon and to protect them from dangerous work, such as mining, demolition, wrecking, logging, and roofing. Check with the local office of the U.S. Department of Labor's Wage and Hour Division for the current rules and a list of jobs that are considered to be hazardous to young people. State laws—available from your state department of labor—might impose additional restrictions in hiring young workers.

Occupational Safety and Health

The Occupational Safety and Health Act (OSH Act) is designed to reduce workplace hazards. It broadly requires employers to provide a workplace free of physical dangers and to meet specific health and safety standards. Employers must also provide safety training to employees, inform them about hazardous chemicals, notify government administrators about serious workplace accidents, and keep detailed safety records.

Although there can be heavy penalties for not complying with the OSH Act, such penalties are usually reserved for extreme cases in which workplace conditions are highly dangerous and the employer has ignored warnings about them. If your workplace is inspected, the Occupational Safety and Health Administration (OSHA), which enforces the OSH Act, will work with you to eliminate hazards. Inspections of small businesses are rare unless the business is especially hazardous—an auto paint shop, for example, or a welding business.

The OSH Act won't apply to your workplace if you're self-employed and have no employees or if your business is a farm that employs only your immediate family members. Similarly, you won't be covered if you're in a business that is already regulated by other federal safety laws, such as mining.

When Employees Telecommute

Generally, when you allow an employee to work at home, the OSH Act doesn't require you to make sure that the home is safe. This is true if the employee is just doing office work—filing, typing, computer research, reading, and writing. Your employee's activities might include using typical office equipment: a phone, computer, scanner, and copier. In that case, you won't be responsible for conditions in the employee's home. OSHA officials won't inspect the home.

The situation is different, however, if your employee is expected to engage in manufacturing or other potentially hazardous work. Here, you are responsible for hazards caused by materials, equipment, or work processes that you provide or require the employee to use. And OSHA officials will inspect the working conditions if it gets a complaint or referral indicating a safety or health problem.

The OSH Act requires that you provide a place of employment that's free from recognized hazards that are causing or likely to cause death or serious physical harm to employees. OSHA has set additional, more specific, workplace standards covering concerns such as:

- exposure to hazardous chemicals
- first aid and medical treatment
- noise levels
- protective gear—such as goggles, respirators, gloves, work shoes, and ear protectors
- fire protection
- worker training, and
- workplace temperatures and ventilation.

Most small businesses are inspected by OSHA only if:

- an employee has complained to OSHA
- a worker has died from a job-related injury, or
- three or more employees have been hospitalized because of a workplace condition.

Every state has an agency, funded mostly by OSHA, that offers free, on-site consultations about how you can comply with the law. In addition to consultants, a trade association in your industry might often be able to provide advice on complying with the OSH Act.

RESOURCE

More information on OSHA. For details on federal laws and links to your state OSHA agency, check out www.osha.gov.

Workers' Compensation

The workers' compensation system provides replacement income and medical expenses to employees who suffer work-related injuries or illnesses. Benefits might also extend to the survivors of workers who are killed on the job.

Workers' compensation is a no-fault system. The employee is usually entitled to receive stated benefits whether or not the employer provided a safe workplace and whether or not the worker's own carelessness contributed to the injury or illness. But the employer, too, receives some protection, because employees are limited to fixed types of compensation—basically, partial wage replacement and payment of medical bills. The employee can't get paid for pain and suffering or mental anguish and usually can't file a private lawsuit.

Each state has its own workers' compensation statute. While the details differ among those laws, one thing is clear: If you have employees, you generally need to obtain workers' compensation coverage. Your state workers' compensation office can tell you about any legal requirements you'll need to follow to inform your employees of their rights. The U.S. Department of Labor website has a list of state workers' compensation offices at www.dol.gov (search "State Workers' Compensation Offices").

To cover the cost of workers' compensation benefits for employees, you usually are required to pay for insurance—either through a state fund or a private insurance company. Although self-insurance is a possibility in some states, the technical requirements usually make this an impractical alternative for a small business.

Premiums are based on two factors: industry classification and payroll. If your premium exceeds a certain amount—$5,000 in many states—your actual experience with workers' compensation claims will affect your premiums. Your rate can go up or down, depending on how your claims compare with those of other businesses in your industry. The number of claims your employees file, more than their dollar value, affects your premium. That's because if you have a lot of accidents, it's assumed that you have an unsafe workplace and the insurance company eventually will have to pay out some large claims.

To keep your workers' compensation costs down, emphasize safety in the workplace. Provide proper equipment, safety devices, and protective clothing. Make sure desks, chairs, and keyboards are up to ergonomic standards and that employees know how to use them properly. Train and retrain your employees in safe procedures and in how to deal with emergencies. Consider setting up a safety committee made up of both managers and workers. And promote employee health by offering wellness and fitness programs.

Termination of Employment

Firing someone—even a person who is demonstrably incompetent—can be a risky endeavor. Do it for the wrong reason or in the wrong way and you could be facing a costly legal battle.

Cases in which former employees claim they were terminated for an improper reason or that an employer bungled the process are known as "wrongful discharge" cases—and they're based on such legal theories as violation of an anti-discrimination law, breach of contract, failure to deal in good faith with an employee, and violation of public policy.

Guidelines for Firing Employees

As noted above, the at-will doctrine theoretically gives you the right to fire an employee at any time as long as it's not for an illegal reason. Even so, most employers don't fire employees without a good reason. From a practical perspective, firing employees who are doing a good job is an obvious waste of time and money. Why would you take the time to find, hire, and train an employee, only to terminate the relationship on a whim? And why would you want to bring down workplace morale by causing other employees to fear that they could lose their jobs at any moment?

From a legal perspective, it's always a good idea to fire only for good cause, even if you're an at-will employer. The at-will theory will protect you from having to prove your reasons for firing in most cases: As long as you can show that you're an at-will employer and the employee can't show any illegal reasons for the termination, you probably won't find yourself in a courtroom. However, if an employee

claims that you acted illegally—for example, that you fired the employee for discriminatory or retaliatory reasons—then you will be very well served by having a legitimate, business-based reason for your decision.

Some Employees Have Contract Rights

Before you fire an employee, check into whether you've made an oral or written contractual commitment that might limit your right to fire. Consider the following:

- Is there a written or oral contract that promises the employee a job for a fixed period of time?
- When you hired the employee, did you make any statements about job security?
- Have you assured the employee that good cause would be the only reason for termination?
- Have you listed causes for termination—in a contract, employee handbook, or elsewhere —in a way that limits you to those specified causes?
- Do your employee handbook, written policies, and memos make any promises about job security?

Your answers to these questions will help you identify whether you've limited your ability to fire. If your employee handbook or your handouts to new employees restate your right to fire a worker at any time and say that all contracts must be in writing, you should be in good shape.

 TIP

Written employment contracts can be a two-way street. Although employment contracts may limit your right to fire an employee, the flip side is that they usually spell out the employee's obligations to your business. An employee who isn't performing satisfactorily could well be in breach of the contract, giving you the legal right to terminate the relationship. Because interpreting contract terms can involve legal subtleties, consider having a brief conference with a lawyer before firing an employee who has a written contract.

To head off the possibility that an employee might try to base a wrongful termination action on alleged illegal conduct or motives in your workplace, be prepared to show the real reason for the firing.

Reasons that might support a firing include:

- performing poorly on the job
- refusing to follow instructions
- abusing sick leave
- being absent excessively
- being tardy habitually
- possessing a weapon at work
- violating company rules
- being dishonest
- endangering health and safety
- engaging in criminal activity
- using alcohol or drugs at work
- behaving violently at work
- gambling at work, and
- disclosing company trade secrets to outsiders.

Depending on the nature of your business, you might have other legitimate reasons to fire employees as well. Whatever reasons you use as a basis for firing people, it's absolutely essential that you treat your employees evenhandedly. If you regularly let some employees engage in prohibited conduct, you'll be on shaky legal ground if you claim good cause for firing others for the same reason.

> EXAMPLE: Andrew, an African American patient attendant, is a half-hour late for work three days in a row. His employer, a medical clinic, fires him. In suing for wrongful discharge based on illegal discrimination, Andrew shows that two white attendants had been similarly tardy in recent weeks but received only a verbal warning to shape up. Even though excessive tardiness is a valid business reason for firing someone, the jury awards damages to Andrew because the employer applied the rules unevenly and unfairly.

Final Review

Because firing is such a drastic and traumatic step—and one having potentially serious legal consequences for a small business—it makes sense for the owner or president to have the final say. If you're unsure about any aspect of the firing, seek advice from an experienced employment lawyer—especially if the employee might claim illegal discrimination or other legal violation.

Your final review should verify that:

- the firing wouldn't violate antidiscrimination or other statutes
- the firing wouldn't be a breach of contract, including oral assurances of job security or statements made in an employee handbook
- your company has given the employee adequate and documented warnings of possible termination—except where the conduct would clearly warrant immediate firing
- you have followed your stated personnel practices, and
- you have followed the same procedures in similar situations involving other employees.

 **RESOURCE**

For more on firing practices, see *Dealing With Problem Employees: A Legal Guide,* by Amy DelPo and Lisa Guerin (Nolo).

Unemployment Compensation

State laws generally require employers to contribute to an unemployment insurance fund. Your rate is normally based on the size of your payroll and the amount of unemployment benefits paid from your account. Employers with smaller payrolls and low levels of unemployment claims will, over time, pay lower taxes.

Employees who are terminated because of cutbacks or because they are not a good fit for a job are generally entitled to payments from the unemployment fund. Employees who are fired for serious misconduct—stealing or repeated absenteeism, for example—or who voluntarily leave a job without good cause are not entitled to unemployment payments.

Think Twice Before Fighting Claims

Contesting all questionable claims might not be the wisest policy. Some claims you might think are questionable probably are allowed under unemployment compensation laws, which are made deliberately lenient to give unemployed workers a transitional source of income and keep them off welfare. Unless there's strong evidence that the employee pilfered from the company or engaged in other fairly extreme conduct, such as quitting for no reason, the employee will usually win in a claims contest.

What's more, fighting a claim can be time-consuming, emotionally draining, and costly for you —especially when balanced against the fact that a few unemployment claims spread over several years are unlikely to greatly increase your insurance rate.

Perhaps most important, fighting an unemployment claim will guarantee an angry former employee—a person far more likely to file a lawsuit or try to harm you or your business in some other way. This might happen anyway, of course. But your challenge to the employee's right to receive unemployment benefits might be the irritant that prompts the former employee to strike back.

Balance the benefits of saving on unemployment taxes against the trouble it takes to fight the claim and the risk of inviting a lawsuit against your business.

Applying these categories to a particular termination isn't always easy. For example, suppose you get into an argument with an employee who leaves shortly afterward. If the employee quits, benefits are not legally due. An employee who is fired, however, is entitled to unemployment benefits absent truly bad conduct. It's sometimes difficult to discern whether a termination is a quitting or a firing.

The claims process varies in each state. Typically, the process starts when a former employee files a claim with the state unemployment agency. You receive written notice of the claim and can file a written objection—usually within seven to ten days.

The state agency makes an initial determination of whether the former employee is eligible to get unemployment benefits. You or the former employee can appeal the initial eligibility decision and have a hearing before a referee—a hearing officer who is on the staff of the state agency. Additional appeals might also be available.

> **CAUTION**
>
> **Serious charges might be raised.** The referee's decision sometimes influences what happens in a related civil lawsuit. For example, if the referee rules that the employee quit because of sexual harassment, that ruling might be decisive in a later case that the employee brings against your business. Consult a lawyer if you anticipate that complicated legal issues—such as sexual harassment, illegal discrimination, or retaliation for complaining about a workplace hazard—could surface at the hearing.

Independent Contractors

Many businesses hire independent contractors rather than employees to perform at least some work. There are often advantages to such an arrangement, but there can be a downside, too. If you mistakenly classify a worker as an independent contractor rather than an employee, you could face potentially serious legal problems, particularly when it comes to taxes. The IRS prefers to have workers classified as employees rather than independent contractors: Unlike independent contractors, who are responsible for paying their own taxes, employees pay their income taxes automatically, through payroll withholding. This means the IRS gets its money faster, with fewer possibilities for evasion.

True independent contractors are in business for themselves, offering their services (which are often quite specialized) to a number of companies. Independent contractors differ from employees in two main ways:

- Independent contractors control not only the outcome of a project but also how the job gets done.
- Independent contractors control their own economic destiny to a large extent, making decisions and business investments that affect how much profit they'll earn and whether they'll suffer a loss.

Typically, a small business hires many independent contractors. Common examples are a lawyer, an accountant, a painter who spruces up your office, or a computer consultant who installs specialized software at your store and teaches employees how to use it.

Independent contractors generally have special skills that you need to call on only sporadically. But sometimes your company might have ongoing needs that can be filled equally well by an employee or an independent contractor. If you weigh both possibilities and conclude that you can save money and reduce paperwork by using an independent contractor rather than an employee, fine. But be sure the worker really qualifies for independent contractor status.

If the IRS or a state unemployment or labor department office decides that you misclassified a worker as an independent contractor when the worker should have been treated as an employee, you can wind up having to pay the taxes that should have been withheld, together with interest and penalties.

 RESOURCE
Working With Independent Contractors, **by Stephen Fishman (Nolo),** provides clear and comprehensive guidance on all aspects of using independent contractors in your business.

Advantages and Disadvantages of Hiring Independent Contractors

When you hire an employee, you assume financial burdens that you don't have if you hire an independent contractor. For example, you must make an employer's contribution for the employee's Social Security. You're also responsible for withholding federal and state income taxes and for keeping records and reporting these items to the federal and state governments. Each year, you must send the employee a Form W-2 showing how much was earned and how much was withheld. (See Chapter 8 for details on an employer's tax responsibilities.)

That's not all. As an employer, you must carry workers' compensation insurance for the employee and might have to make payments into an unemployment protection fund. Health insurance, retirement plans, and other fringe benefits might add to the cost. Finally, although not legally required, most employers provide paid vacations and sick leave for employees, further driving up costs.

Now, contrast this situation with hiring an independent contractor. When you hire an independent contractor, you're not required to withhold taxes from the amount you pay the worker, and you don't have to pay any portion of the worker's Social Security taxes. Your only responsibility is to complete a Form 1099-MISC at the end of the year if you paid the independent contractor $600 or more during the year. The form is sent to the IRS and the independent contractor.

When you hire an independent contractor rather than an employee, you normally also save the expense of providing an office or other work space for the worker and the ongoing expenses of fringe benefits and insurance. Furthermore, if you become unhappy with the person's work, you can turn to another independent contractor without going through the trauma often associated with firing an employee who works each day on your premises.

Another benefit of hiring someone as an independent contractor is that your company generally won't be liable for his or her negligence.

If you hire employees, however, you would be liable if, for example, the employee carelessly injured someone while at work.

Of course, there are trade-offs. A business doesn't enjoy as much day-to-day control over the work of an independent contractor. And not having the worker always available might also be inconvenient. Furthermore, to charge enough to cover the costs of doing business and still make a profit, an independent contractor might charge a higher price for services than an employee could demand. And if an independent contractor is injured because of some dangerous situation at your business premises or in a place that you have control over, the independent contractor can sue your business, claiming negligence. By contrast, an employee in the same situation would be limited to often lower workers' compensation benefits. But if you carry adequate liability insurance to protect you from injury claims, this isn't a significant drawback.

Given a choice, many workers prefer to be treated as independent contractors rather than employees. Some like the fact that there's no withholding of taxes; they feel that they have a better cash flow, even though they're ultimately responsible for paying their taxes, and the employer isn't picking up any part of the Social Security tax. Workers might also see benefits in being treated as independent contractors because of the opportunity it affords them to charge a higher rate and to deduct business expenses, including money spent on cars, home offices, and travel and entertainment.

On the other hand, some workers prefer employee status, which gives them paid vacations, medical care, and other fringe benefits at the employer's expense—and freedom from worry about the paperwork required of people who are in business for themselves.

How to Avoid Classification Problems

Because the IRS is the government agency most likely to challenge your classifying a worker as an independent contractor, we'll focus here on how

to stay within the IRS guidelines. Fortunately, a worker who qualifies as an independent contractor under the IRS tests will almost certainly qualify as well under the rules of most state agencies, even though the state rules might be slightly different.

 RESOURCE
For details on the various legal tests for independent contractor status, see IRS Form SS-8 (and related instructions), *Determination of Worker Status for Purposes of Federal Employment Taxes and Income Tax Withholding*, and IRS Publication 15 (Circular E), *Employer's Tax Guide*, both available at www.irs.gov. For a full discussion on the subject, as well as contracts you can use to hire independent contractors, see *Working With Independent Contractors*, by Stephen Fishman (Nolo).

For a variety of online independent contractor agreements, see the Business Suite section of the Nolo store at www.nolo.com.

It might surprise you to learn that there's no law or court case to precisely guide you in deciding whether it's legally safe to treat a worker as an independent contractor for federal tax purposes. In fact, the most authoritative guidance is found in an unlikely place—the manual the IRS uses to train its audit examiners. Fortunately, by following a few basic rules derived from the principles discussed in this manual, you're likely to steer clear of most problems.

The Easy Cases

As a practical matter, you can hire a wide range of independent contractors with virtually no worries about whether they should be treated as employees. These "no sweat" situations involve workers who clearly are in business for themselves, demonstrated by the fact that they share most of the following characteristics:

- The worker is available to perform services for many businesses.
- The worker has a fixed base of operations— a commercial location perhaps, or a home office—and ongoing business expenses.

- The worker lists the business in the phone book and may also drum up business through newspaper ads, radio commercials, or a website.
- The worker hires and pays for assistants as needed.
- The worker has invested significant money in the business for equipment, vehicles, and supplies.
- Depending on how the business goes, the worker might earn a large profit, a small profit, or none at all—perhaps even suffering a loss.
- The worker incurs expenses in doing a job that won't be reimbursed by the client.

A few examples will help you identify what a classic, easy-case independent contractor looks like.

EXAMPLE 1: Lydia runs a billing service for a number of law firms. She purchases a computer for her home office, along with sophisticated billing software, which she upgrades from time to time. Lydia advertises her business in an online forum that serves lawyers, does work for several law firms, and is continually looking for more clients. She goes to lawyers' offices weekly to collect their time and expense records so she can enter them into her computer system and produce bills and reports. During these visits, she sometimes consults with the managing partners about their special problems and needs, but she's free to devise solutions to meet the lawyers' needs. She pays for billing paper and other supplies and for her transportation to and from the lawyers' offices, and she isn't directly reimbursed for these expenses.

EXAMPLE 2: Joe does lawn maintenance work in the summer and snow removal in the winter for local businesses, advertising for clients by sending out a circular twice a year to members of the chamber of commerce. He owns a truck, two lawn mowers, a leaf blower, fertilizer spreader, two shovels, and a snow blower, as well as a scraper that attaches to the front of his truck. Joe has a schedule of charges based on the size of the grounds to be serviced and the number of times he provides his services. Sometimes, to meet his commitments to clients, Joe hires his brother to help mow grass or remove snow, paying him as his part-time employee. During a mild winter, when Joe gets fewer calls, he might have trouble covering his expenses.

EXAMPLE 3: Elsie, a catalog designer, works out of a studio in her apartment. She does freelance work for three local ad agencies, who have major retail clients. The ad agencies pay her a flat fee for each catalog she lays out. The agencies send her basic materials to be featured and suggest a theme for each catalog but rely on Elsie's judgment on how best to present the material. She uses her own cameras, computers, and art supplies to produce the camera-ready pages for the catalogs. In busy times, she farms out some of the artwork to colleagues in a nearby town and pays them herself.

In each of these examples, the small business owners (Lydia, Joe, and Elsie)—not the companies that hire them—determine how to do the work. In addition, Lydia, Joe, and Elsie control how they run their business. It's highly unlikely that a business hiring any of these three as an independent contractor would have any difficulty justifying its position if challenged.

The Tougher Cases

Other workers might be harder to classify as independent contractors. Not infrequently, a worker might be in an ambiguous area where the distinction between an employee and an independent contractor gets fuzzy. Though you might see some advantages in treating the worker as an independent contractor, you might at the same time feel nervous about the legal risks involved, because any penalties for misclassification will fall squarely on your shoulders and not those of the worker.

The possible ambiguity in a worker's status can be seen in the following examples.

EXAMPLE 1: During the week, Rocco is employed as a custodian at a research firm. Hoping to earn additional money, he checks the help-wanted ads, where he sees that a small company is looking for someone to come in every Sunday to perform janitorial services. Rocco applies for the work and learns that the company would provide mops, brooms, and pails, but that Rocco would be expected to bring his own vacuum cleaner. The company would pay Rocco $100 per cleaning session and would reimburse him up to $10 per session for cleaning supplies. The company would provide Rocco with a checklist of cleaning duties and the sequence in which they were to be performed. If the company president were to decide that the work on a given Sunday wasn't satisfactorily performed, Rocco would have to come back on Monday night to touch up.

EXAMPLE 2: Alice is offered work delivering flowers and plants for a local florist shop from 2 p.m. to 5 p.m., Monday through Friday. Alice will drive her own van and be responsible for gas and maintenance, which is offset by the fact that she'll earn $20 an hour for her work. The business owner will give Alice a delivery list each day, indicating the priority deliveries that need to be accomplished first. Otherwise, Alice will be free to decide the timing of the deliveries and to choose what route to follow. The business will also provide Alice with a cell phone to take with her on her deliveries so she can call in periodically to see if she needs to return to the shop to pick up last-minute orders. While making deliveries, Alice will have to wear a jacket bearing the name of the florist shop.

EXAMPLE 3: Edgar teaches art and design at a community college. He is approached by a clothing store owner who is known for eye-catching window displays that change weekly. The store owner wants Edgar to come in each Tuesday—a day when Edgar doesn't teach— and change the window display under the owner's supervision. This is similar to work that Edgar is already doing for a bookstore on Saturday mornings. Edgar would be expected occasionally to construct some of the displays in his basement shop, because there's limited space at the clothing store to do so. He'd be reimbursed for the supplies used in the displays, but not for the tools he'd need to do the work.

In these three examples—and thousands of similar cases—the work arrangements share some characteristics of an employment relationship and some characteristics of an independent contractor relationship. It's difficult to predict whether the IRS would agree with the business owner's decision to treat the worker as an independent contractor.

In these ambiguous situations, you have two safe ways to proceed—and a third way that involves a measure of risk.

Treat the worker as an employee. If you want to be super safe and avoid any risk that the IRS—or other governmental agencies—will determine that you've mistakenly classified the worker as an independent contractor, always treat the worker as an employee. This will protect you from possible penalties. The problem is that both you and the worker will lose the advantages that can flow from an independent contractor relationship. And some independent contractors won't be willing to go along with this, because it could imperil their independent contractor status on other jobs.

Require the worker to form an entity. If you and the worker are both motivated to go the independent contractor route in an ambiguous situation, there's a way to do it that's practically risk-free: Simply have the worker form a corporation or an LLC, which will employ the worker. The IRS will almost always treat this as a valid arrangement and accept the fact that the worker isn't your employee but an employee of his or her own entity. As described in Chapter 1, it's legal in every state to form a one-person corporation or LLC—and the process can be simple and relatively inexpensive.

Sample Contract With Independent Contractor .

Independent Contractor Agreement

This AGREEMENT is made on _____ , 20xx, between _____

[Name of Client]

of _____ (Client) and

[Business Address]

_____ of

[Name of Contractor]

_____ (Contractor).

[Business Address]

1. **Services to Be Performed.** Contractor agrees to perform the following services for Client:
   [Describe services]

2. **Time for Performance.** Contractor agrees to complete the performance of these services on or before _____ , 20[xx.]

3. **Payment.** In consideration of Contractor's performance of these services, Client agrees to pay Contractor as follows:
   [Describe how payment will be computed]

4. **Invoices.** Contractor will submit invoices for all services performed.

5. **Independent Contractor.** The parties intend Contractor to be an independent contractor in the performance of these services. Contractor will have the right to control and determine the method and means of performing the above services; Client will not have the right to control or determine such method or means.

6. **Other Clients.** Contractor retains the right to perform services for other clients.

7. **Assistants.** Contractor, at Contractor's expense, may employ such assistants as Contractor deems appropriate to carry out this agreement. Contractor will be responsible for paying such assistants, as well as any expense attributable to such assistants, including income taxes, unemployment insurance, and Social Security taxes, and will maintain workers' compensation insurance for such employees.

8. **Equipment and Supplies.** Contractor, at Contractor's own expense, will provide all equipment, tools, and supplies necessary to perform the above services and will be responsible for all other expenses required for the performance of those services.

Contractor   Client

_____   _____

Date _____   Date _____

Here is how this strategy works:

- The worker forms a corporation or an LLC under state law and obtains an Employer Identification Number from the IRS.
- You sign a contract with the entity, under which the entity agrees to provide specified services for your business.
- The entity hires the worker (who owns the corporate shares or LLC membership interests) as an employee to perform the services required by your contract with the entity.
- The entity bills you as services are performed for your business under the contract.
- You pay the entity—not the employee—for the services billed to your business.
- Each time the entity issues a paycheck to its employee, the entity withholds federal income taxes, along with the employee's share of Social Security and Medicare taxes, as outlined in Chapter 8.
- Periodically, the entity (using its own Employer Identification Number) pays the IRS the withheld taxes along with the employer's share of Social Security and Medicare taxes.

RESOURCE
You'll find numerous easy-to-use contracts in *Working With Independent Contractors*, by Stephen Fishman (Nolo). In filling out these contracts, be sure to indicate that you're hiring the entity (corporation or LLC) as an independent contractor. The entity's owner should sign the contract as an officer of the entity (as president, for example) rather than as an individual.

Accept a measure of risk. Suppose the worker's status as an independent contractor is ambiguous and, for one reason or another, the safer courses of action—treating the worker as an employee or requiring the worker to form a corporation or an LLC—are not practical. Then you must recognize that if you move ahead and hire the worker as an independent contractor, you're opening yourself up to some legal risk.

One way to reduce the risk is to get professional advice. See a tax expert—a lawyer or an accountant who's familiar with the worker classification issues.

Another way to reduce the risk is to follow as many of the following suggestions as you can:

- Sign a contract with the independent contractor spelling out the responsibilities of each party and how payment is to be determined for each job. The contract should allow the independent contractor to hire assistants and to have as much say as possible as to how the work is to be performed. A sample contract appears above.
- Require the independent contractor to furnish all or most of the tools, equipment, and material needed to complete the job.
- Avoid a commitment to reimburse the independent contractor for business expenses; if necessary, pay the independent contractor a little more to cover these costs.
- If feasible, arrange to pay a flat fee for the work rather than an hourly or weekly rate.
- Don't provide employee-type benefits such as paid vacation days, health insurance, or retirement plans.
- Make it clear that the independent contractor is free to offer services to other businesses.
- Specifically state in your contract that the contractor will carry insurance, including workers' compensation coverage.
- Keep a file containing the independent contractor's business card, stationery samples, ads, and Employer Identification Number. These items can help show that the contractor has an established business.

CAUTION
Protect your trade secrets. In some situations, you might need to disclose trade secrets of your business to an independent contractor. If so, include a clause in the agreement prohibiting the independent contractor from disclosing or making any unauthorized use of the trade secrets.

Special Categories of Workers

In most situations, a worker's status is determined by the guidelines described above. Certain workers, however, fall into special categories, and the usual IRS criteria don't apply to them. For example, the federal tax law says that the following workers are automatically treated as employees as far as Social Security taxes, Medicare taxes, and federal unemployment taxes (FUTA) are concerned:

- officers of corporations who provide service to the corporation
- food and laundry delivery drivers
- full-time salespeople who sell goods for resale
- full-time life insurance agents working mainly for one company, and
- at-home workers who are supplied with material and given specifications for work to be performed.

For these workers, you must withhold the worker's share of Social Security and Medicare taxes and you must also pay the employer's portion of those taxes. But you might or might not have to withhold income taxes; it depends on whether the worker qualifies as an employee or independent contractor under the usual IRS guidelines.

Federal law also provides that for tax purposes, licensed real estate agents and door-to-door salespeople are generally treated as "nonemployees"—which is another way of saying they're independent contractors. People in these occupations may, however, be treated as employees for the purpose of state payroll taxes and workers' compensation coverage.

As a sole proprietor or partner in your own business, you're neither an employee nor an independent contractor. You're responsible for paying your own income tax and Social Security self-employment tax. If you're a shareholder in a corporation but provide services to the corporation, you're generally an employee.

A Worker's Status Might Change

Don't assume that once you've determined that a worker is an independent contractor, you can forget about the matter. If there's a shift in the working arrangements, you might have to reclassify the worker.

EXAMPLE: John operates a small desktop publishing shop specializing in writing and designing brochures, flyers, and other promotional materials for small businesses. At first, John does most of the work himself, turning any overload over to others with similar skills. John collects from the customer and pays these people as independent contractors. So far, so good.

As John's business grows, he arranges for part-time help on a fairly regular basis. Sue, Ted, and Ellen regularly handle the overflow, working in John's offices under his broad supervision an average of about two days per week each. The rest of the time they work for themselves. John continues to treat them as independent contractors. By law, he shouldn't.

Because John is exercising significant control over these workers and using their services in-house on a regular basis, he's tempting fate—and the IRS. To be safe, John should treat them as part-time employees, which requires that he withhold income taxes, pay the employer's share of Social Security taxes, carry workers' compensation insurance, and pay into the state's unemployment fund.

Additional State Rules

The IRS analysis of who qualifies as an independent contractor is similar to the standards followed in most states for state taxes and unemployment rules, but there can be some differences. For example, in California, a person working for a licensed contractor who performs services requiring a license (for example, erecting a building) is considered to be an employee unless the worker also has a valid contractor's license. If you plan to hire independent contractors, check with the employment office in your state to see if special rules apply.

The Risks of Misclassification

There are at least four ways for the IRS to learn about your hiring and classification practices:

- The IRS may look into the affairs of an independent contractor who hasn't been paying income taxes.
- Disgruntled employees might complain to the IRS if they think independent contractors are getting favored treatment.
- During tax audits, the IRS routinely checks to see if workers have been misclassified as independent contractors.
- A worker asserting misclassification as an independent contractor may file IRS Form 8919, *Uncollected Social Security and Medicare Tax on Wages*, which will alert the IRS to take a closer look at the situation.

The presumption is that the worker is an employee unless proven otherwise. If the status of a worker is questioned, it's up to you to prove that the worker is an independent contractor rather than an employee.

If it turns out that an employee was in fact misclassified, the cost to your business will be heavy. You'll be responsible for paying the employee's Social Security tax, federal income tax, and federal unemployment insurance for up to three years. In addition, the IRS can add penalties and interest.

State government officials are also interested in businesses that misclassify employees as independent contractors. A state employment office might audit your business to see if there's been any misclassification. The audit can be the result of a spot check by the state employment office or a request by an independent contractor for unemployment or workers' compensation benefits. You might wind up owing money to a state unemployment insurance fund. And if the IRS learns of the state's action, you'll probably face a federal audit as well.

> **CAUTION**
>
> **Be careful if you change a worker's status from employee to independent contractor.** The IRS will take a close look if you give a worker a Form W-2 and a Form 1099 for the same year. This might happen, for example, if an employee retired and then started working for you as an independent contractor. To avoid problems with the IRS, be able to show that following the worker's retirement, you had less control over the worker's performance or that the worker had different duties.

Employers' Health Care Insurance Requirements Under Obamacare

The Affordable Care Act (ACA), also known as "Obamacare," creates certain requirements for businesses to offer health insurance (often referred to as the "employer mandate"). As of 2016, businesses with 50 or more full-time employees are required to offer "affordable" health insurance that is of "minimum value" to employees and their dependents. (Generally, an employee who works an average of at least 30 hours per week or 130 hours per month is considered full time. For more on the specific definition of full-time employee, search www.irs.gov for "Affordable Care Act.")

According to the federal health insurance marketplace, a health insurance plan provides minimum value if:

- it covers at least 60% of the total cost of medical services for a standard population, and
- its benefits include substantial coverage of physician and inpatient hospital services.

Along with providing minimum value, an acceptable health insurance plan must not cost more than 9.66% of an employee's annual income.

Employers who fail to provide employee health insurance as required under the ACA are subject to penalties. While the amount of these penalties can vary, and deductions might apply, in many cases they can be $2,000 or $3,000 for each full-time employee the employer does not cover.

Businesses with fewer than 25 full-time employees that pay average salaries of $50,000 or less and offer employee health insurance usually qualify for a federal tax credit through the Small Business Health Options Program (SHOP). To get the credit, you must file IRS Form 8941, *Credit for Small Employer Health Insurance Premiums*. Businesses with 50 or fewer full-time employees also can use SHOP to search for group health plans.

One other important element of the ACA for small businesses is that it raises the amount of employee withholding. More specifically, withholding for Medicare Part A hospital insurance is increased from 1.45% to 2.35% for single employees with income over $200,000 and married employees filing jointly with income over $250,000 (as of 2016). The amount of employer withholding, however, remains at 1.45%.

RESOURCE

More information on Obamacare. For details about the Affordable Care Act's requirements for small businesses, check healthcare.gov.

16

The Importance of Excellent Customer Relations

Customers (you might call them clients or patients) are the lifeblood of any small business or professional practice. To thrive, you not only need a steady stream of people who keep coming back for more goods or services; you also need them to enthusiastically recommend your business to their friends. To build a loyal following, you must do more than just give people what the law requires. Yes, knowledge of your legal rights and those of your customers is important, but it's even more important not to let legal technicalities take priority over a key objective of your business: to keep happy customers coming back and sending other people your way.

EXAMPLE: When Sandra brought her white wool blazer home from the dry cleaner's, she was dismayed to see that it had a very slight pink tint. Sandra reported the problem to Mark, the owner of the cleaning shop. Mark could have legally responded in a number of ways, including the following:

- "The problem is scarcely noticeable. You're being fussy."
- "How do I know the blazer wasn't like this when you brought it in?"
- "Didn't you see our sign? We're not responsible for any problems once you take the cleaned garment from the shop."
- "That's a two-year-old blazer. Used clothing isn't worth much. I'll pay you $20 for the damage—not a penny more."
- "I've never had this type of complaint before. I want to send the blazer to an independent testing lab to see if the fabric is substandard. If it is, it's your problem—not mine."

But Mark was a wise businessperson. He didn't stand on his legal rights. Instead he told Sandra: "I'm sorry this happened. We use state-of-the-art cleaning processes, but apparently something went wrong. In any case, we guarantee your complete satisfaction. Because we can't fix this type of damage, let me know

the purchase price of an equivalent new blazer." Sandra did, and Mark reimbursed her the full amount.

As a result of his enlightened attitude, Mark had a happy customer. In the two years since the blazer problem, Sandra and her husband have taken more than $500 worth of cleaning business to Mark's shop. They not only continue to be loyal customers, but—even more important—every time Sandra wears her new blazer, she tells the story of how Mark bought it for her and she recommends his business. Because Mark treated Sandra well, the blazer now ranks as one of Mark's all-time best investments.

Now consider what would have happened if Mark had responded with a strictly legalistic approach, offering Sandra the value of a two-year-old blazer. Sandra might have grumbled and accepted the $20 payment or she might have taken Mark to small claims court and perhaps have won a few dollars more. But this much is certain: Sandra and her husband would never have taken any more cleaning to Mark's place. Even worse, they'd likely have told others about Mark's inadequate service for years to come and might have complained to local better business and state regulatory agencies. So while Mark was thinking of himself as a tough businessperson who knows his legal rights and never lets customers rip him off, he actually would have foolishly lost many thousands of dollars of business.

Dealing With Customers During the COVID-19 Crisis

Since the start of the coronavirus pandemic in early 2020, many companies have had to rethink their usual in-person methods of conducting business. Remember, while the pandemic continues, use appropriate precautions when you're dealing with others in person, like wearing a mask and practicing social distancing. Also, consider using an alternate communication method, like phone, email, text, or videoconferencing.

State Rules on Refunds

Several states have laws governing refund policies. Here are three examples:

California. You must post your refund policy unless you offer a full cash refund or credit refund within seven days of purchase. If you don't post your policy as required, the customer is entitled to return the goods for a full refund within 30 days of purchase.

Florida. If a business does not offer refunds, that fact must be posted. If the statement isn't posted, the customer can return unopened, unused goods within seven days of purchase.

New York. Stores must post their refund policy. If a store doesn't do so, state law requires the store to accept a customer's return within 30 days of purchase.

To learn if there's a similar law in your state and to check exceptions to refund policies (for example, final sales), contact the consumer protection division of your state's attorney general's office. To find yours, check out www.usa.gov/state-consumer.

Whether you run a restaurant, a hardware store, or a sand and gravel business, if a customer complains about your product or service, don't quibble. It's much smarter to point to your customer satisfaction policy as you eliminate or reduce the charges—and maybe even give the customer something extra as a reward for putting up with the problem. Maybe you won't make any money on that transaction; you'll probably even take a small loss. And yes, once in a blue moon someone will take unfair advantage of your policy. So what? When you consider the good feelings that customers will have about your business—and the fact that you'll receive positive rather than negative word of mouth from everyone you treat generously—it's a bargain. Consider, too, that a customer whose problem you resolve is unlikely to complain to any agency or board with power to license or otherwise oversee your business. Nor is that customer likely to post a complaint on a website such as Yelp. Anyone who has had to cope with an investigation knows that even if the complaint that triggered the inquiry has no merit, the process can be worrisome and, if lawyers are involved, expensive.

Legal relationships with customers are covered in the next three chapters. Chapter 17 covers the legal rules for handling advertising, retail pricing, returns, warranties, and other customer transactions. In Chapter 18, you'll find information about checks and credit cards. Chapter 19 explains how to extend credit and get prompt payment.

Developing Your Customer-Satisfaction Policy

Whether you're selling products or services, go further than is legally required in anticipating and responding to the problems of your customers. How you do this depends in part on the nature of the products or services you offer. But for starters, consider the policy of Eddie Bauer—a highly successful national company that sells outdoor goods through its catalog and retail outlets:

Our Guarantee

Every item we sell will give you complete satisfaction or you may return it for a full refund.

Our Creed

To give you such outstanding quality, value, service, and guarantee that we may be worthy of your high esteem.

Over the years, my family and I have bought many items from Eddie Bauer. We've never had to return anything for a refund. But just knowing that the company stands behind what it sells has given us confidence in Eddie Bauer products. And that, of course, is the point: By reassuring customers in advance that they control the resolution of any problems, Eddie Bauer's good customer service is a marketing advantage.

Some department store chains such as Nordstrom have also built solid businesses based in large part on their guarantee of customer satisfaction. But it's not just the big-time operators who successfully use a customer recourse policy as a business building technique. Nolo—the California company that published this book—has more than held its own in the highly competitive book business in part because of its consumer-oriented policies.

Law From the Real World

Listening to Your Employees

Rose, the owner of a retail store, overhears clerk Ned tell an unhappy customer that there is nothing he can do—the time to return a particular item ran out yesterday. Rose intervenes to solve the customer's problem by graciously taking the merchandise back. Now, Ned is unhappy. "I was just following your policy," he tells Rose. "You undercut me and made me feel really stupid." Rose realizes it is unwise to adopt a strict policy and then throw it out on a whim. After all, if she hadn't overheard the conversation, she would have lost a customer and made an employee feel bad about being a tough guy. Rose meets with her employees, and together they come up with a much more customer-friendly policy. They post it conspicuously in the store so that everyone knows what the new, fairer rules are.

Businesses that treat customers generously can reap an unexpected dividend: higher morale among workers. Employees are not robots. They hate defending miserly policies that result in stressful confrontations with customers. They make great ambassadors for businesses they truly feel good about.

Businesses that offer services have different problems than restaurants and retail outlets. But they still have many opportunities to enhance customer satisfaction and favorable word of mouth. On longer-term jobs, you can set time-performance standards in advance so that both you and the customer can judge whether everyone's expectations are being met. Often this consists of little more than committing yourself to meeting interim deadlines.

For example, a toxic materials contractor removing asbestos from heating ducts in a three-story building might agree to get the entire job done in 30 days with the first floor clean and ready to reoccupy in ten days and the second floor in 20 additional days. A home remodeling or painting company might go further and commit to meticulously cleaning up its work area each day.

Another good approach is to regularly ask for feedback from customers or clients. For example, if you run a bookkeeping service, a copy shop, or a janitorial service that does regular business with larger accounts, ask your customers from time to time whether your high standards—and the customer's needs—are being met. I was favorably impressed when the landlord who owned the building where my law firm practiced asked me to evaluate the interior and maintenance services we were receiving. We periodically renewed our lease—even when there was a glut of office space in my town. We knew that the landlord seemed sincerely concerned about keeping the building spic and span. It was only after more than two decades in the building that I moved elsewhere to join a new law firm.

You might think that a business offering a service as intangible as a seminar would have a hard time developing an effective customer satisfaction policy—but you'd be wrong. Here's a guarantee from the American Management Association that serves as an excellent model:

> 100% Satisfaction Guaranteed—At AMA, we guarantee the quality of our seminars. In fact, 98% of our participants say they would recommend the course they have taken to their colleagues. If, for any reason, you are not satisfied with a seminar for which you have paid, AMA will give you credit toward another seminar of comparable price or will refund your fee.

Get Help to Solve Customer Disputes

Sometimes, despite your best efforts to treat customers fairly, a dispute starts to get out of hand. At that point, consider bringing the Better Business Bureau or another respected third party into the picture. I recommend the BBB because according to various national polls, it's usually the first agency that consumers turn to for help when they're trying to solve a problem with a business.

Your local government might also offer mediation as a means of resolving consumer-business disputes without going to court. This is true, for example, in many counties in California. Also, many communities have neighborhood dispute programs that might be helpful for some types of small business disputes.

For more on dispute resolution techniques, including negotiation, mediation, arbitration, and litigation, see Nolo's Mediation, Arbitration & Collaborative Law section at www.nolo.com/legal-encyclopedia/mediation and Nolo's Business Litigation section at www.nolo.com/legal-encyclopedia/business-litigation.

Telling Customers About Your Policies

Every communication between you and your customers is an opportunity to let them know that you're sincerely interested in their complaints and comments. Show your concern through signs in your business place, questionnaires and surveys mailed to them, and by simply inquiring from time to time whether their needs are being met.

Use your imagination. Labels, receipts, catalogs, and packaging afford you the chance to let people know what their rights are and exactly how you'll deal with any problems. And don't use small print. Although it's sometimes hard to accept, you want your customers to know that you welcome the chance to fix problems. Also, see Chapter 17 for advice on how your website can best convey your policies to customers.

And now, a few words on how not to communicate with customers. We've all seen stores that have negative signs next to the cash register, with unfriendly messages such as:

> No returns without receipt
>
> No cash refunds
>
> No out-of-town checks

Often, the owner has then added a few Scotch-taped signs with more negative messages such as "$10 is charged for every returned check—no exceptions" or "If you break it, you own it." Not only is this offensive—it's stupid. Your statement of a customer's responsibilities doesn't have to be put in confrontational language. To take one example, even if you decide not to give cash refunds (a policy you might want to rethink), there are friendlier ways to state your policy, such as:

> We are pleased to accept all returns within 30 days for full store credit.

This statement has a positive tone but makes the customer responsible for returning the goods within 30 days to receive credit.

The law in many cities and a few states requires that you post your policies on returns and other customer recourse. In many of those locations, if you don't post your policy, your customers have the right to a full cash refund. But even if the law doesn't require you to post your policy, it makes excellent business and legal sense to do so.

Legal Requirements for Dealing With Customers

Many legal problems can be avoided by adopting enlightened policies for dealing with your customers. Customer-friendly policies, however, can't anticipate every problem. Consequently, you must understand the legal rules that apply. This chapter covers advertising, retail pricing and return practices, warranties, and consumer protection laws.

RESOURCE

Details on consumer protection laws. For federal law, check out the Federal Trade Commission (FTC) Bureau of Consumer Protection Business Center website at www.ftc.gov/tips-advice/business-center. For state law, contact your state consumer protection agency; find yours at www.usa.gov/state-consumer. You'll also find lots of useful information in the Consumer Protection area of www.nolo.com (in the Personal Finance section).

Advertising

Before we get into the legal rules for advertising, consider a more fundamental question: Do you really need to advertise?

Is Advertising Necessary?

People starting a small business often assume they must advertise to attract customers. This always made good sense to me—until I read and thought about some eye-opening ideas in *Marketing Without Advertising: Easy Ways to Build a Business Your Customers Will Love & Recommend,* by Michael Phillips and Salli Rasberry (originally published by Nolo, but now out of print). Phillips and Rasberry argue convincingly that for small businesses, most money spent on conventional advertising, like radio and TV spots, is wasted. You're competing with thousands of other advertisers, and your message is unlikely to produce a profitable level of sales.

Here's more from *Marketing Without Advertising:*

> The best and most economical way to attract and hold customers is through personal recommendation. A customer who is prescreened and prepared for what you have to offer is far more likely to appreciate you and use your business than is someone responding to an ad offering a low price. The essence of marketing without advertising is to encourage personal recommendation. How do you do this? Lots of ways, all of which start with creating an atmosphere of trust. Central to doing this is to run an honest business.

Phillips and Rasberry recommend marketing strategies that don't rely on traditional advertising. For example, they discuss the importance of the physical appearance of your business (insist on scrupulous cleanliness and avoid clutter and unpleasant smells). They point out that listing your products or services where customers expect to find them—such as local business directories and trade publications—is often extremely cost effective.

Interestingly, Phillips and Rasberry believe you should judge advertising and listing options not on the basis of cost (although advertising does usually cost considerably more), but on whether customers are prescreened to see your message. For example, someone who checks a local free classified newspaper for a drain cleaning service needs that type of business. By contrast, someone who hears a radio advertisement for the same business is unlikely to need that service immediately or to remember the ad months or years later when the need does arise.

Legal Standards for Advertising

Advertising is regulated by both federal and state law. Under the law, your ad is unlawful if it tends to mislead or deceive. This means the government doesn't have to prove (at an administrative hearing or in court) that the ad actually fooled anyone—only that it had a deceptive quality. Your intentions don't matter, either. If your ad is deceptive, you'll face legal problems even if you have the best intentions in the world. What counts is the overall impression created by the ad—not the technical truthfulness of the individual parts. Taken as a whole, your ad must fairly inform the ordinary consumer.

In addition, if your ad contains a false statement, you have violated the law. The fact that you didn't know the information was false is irrelevant.

The Federal Trade Commission (FTC) is the main federal agency that takes action against unlawful advertising. State and local governments also go after businesses that violate advertising laws; usually this is the responsibility of the state attorney general, consumer protection agency, and local district attorney. Consumers and competitors might also be able to sue the advertiser.

Over the years, the FTC has taken action against many businesses accused of false and deceptive advertising. A significant number of those administrative actions have been tested in court. By and large, courts have upheld even the most stringent FTC policies. For the most part, the FTC relies on consumers and competitors to report unlawful advertising.

If FTC investigators are convinced that an ad violates the law, they usually try to bring the violator into voluntary compliance through informal means. If that doesn't work, the FTC can issue a cease-and-desist order and bring a civil lawsuit on behalf of people who have been harmed. The FTC can also seek a court order ("injunction") to stop a questionable ad while an investigation is in progress. In addition, the FTC can require an advertiser to run "corrective ads"—ads that state the correct facts and admit that an earlier ad was deceptive.

Most states have laws—usually in the form of consumer fraud or deceptive practices statutes—that regulate advertising. Under these laws, state or local

officials can seek injunctions against unlawful ads and take legal action to get restitution to consumers. Some laws provide for criminal penalties—fines and jail—but criminal proceedings for false advertising are rare unless fraud is involved.

Consumers often have the right to sue advertisers under state consumer protection laws. For example, someone who purchases a product or services in reliance on a false or deceptive ad might sue in small claims court for a refund or join with others (sometimes tens of thousands of others) to sue for a huge sum in another court.

A competitor harmed by unlawful advertising or faced with the likelihood of such harm, generally has the right to seek an injunction and, possibly, an award of money ("damages") as well, although damages are often difficult to prove.

How to Stay Out of Trouble

The following rules will help keep your ads within safe, legal limits.

Rule 1—Be Accurate

Make sure your ads are factually correct and that they don't tend to deceive or mislead the buying public. Don't show a picture of this year's model of a product if what you're selling is last year's model, even if they look almost the same.

Be truthful about what consumers can expect from your product. Don't say ABC pills will cure headaches if the pills offer only temporary pain relief. Don't claim a rug shampooer is a wizard at removing all kinds of stains when in fact there are some it won't budge.

"Waterproof" or "fireproof" means just that—not water resistant or fire resistant under some circumstances. The term "polar," when attached to winter gear, suggests that it will keep people warm in extreme cold, not that it's just adequate when the temperature drops near freezing.

> **TIP**
>
> **Make sure you have scientific evidence to back up health or safety claims.** You'll need this evidence if the FTC challenges your ads. For example, the FTC went after Tropicana Products for claiming its "Heart Healthy" orange juice would produce dramatic effects on blood pressure and cholesterol levels, reducing the risk of heart disease and stroke. The FTC alleged that Tropicana's claims went well beyond any scientific support. To settle the FTC complaint, Tropicana agreed it would not make similar health claims in the future, unless the claims could be substantiated by reliable scientific evidence.

Rule 2—Get Permission

Does your ad feature someone's picture or endorsement? Does it quote material written by someone not on your staff or employed by your advertising agency? Does it use the name of a national organization such as the Boy Scouts or Red Cross? If so, get written permission.

Under U.S. copyright law, the "fair use" doctrine allows limited quotations from copyrighted works without specific authorization from the copyright owner. In some circumstances, this doctrine provides legal justification for the widespread practice of quoting from favorable reviews in ads for books, movies, and plays—and even vacuum cleaners. However, with the exception of brief quotes from product or service reviews, you should always seek permission to quote protected material. For more on the fair use doctrine and many other aspects of copyright law and practice, see *The Copyright Handbook: What Every Writer Needs to Know,* by Stephen Fishman (Nolo).

Rule 3—Treat Competitors Fairly

Don't knock the goods, services, or reputation of others by giving false or misleading information. If you compare your goods and services with those of other companies, double-check your information to make sure that every statement in your ad is accurate. Then check again.

Rule 4—Have Sufficient Quantities on Hand

When you advertise goods for sale, make every effort to have enough on hand to supply the demand that it's reasonable to expect. If you don't think you can meet the demand, state in your ad that quantities are limited. You might even want to state the number of units on hand.

State law might require merchants to stock an advertised product in quantities large enough to meet reasonably expected demand, unless the ad states that stock is limited. California, for example, has such a law. Some states require merchants to give a rain check in certain circumstances if they run out of advertised goods. Make sure you know what your state requires.

Rule 5—Watch Out for the Word "Free"

If you say that goods or services are "free" or "without charge," be sure there are no unstated terms or conditions that qualify the offer. If there are any limits, state them clearly and conspicuously.

Let's assume that you offer a free paintbrush to anyone who buys a can of paint for $10.95 and that you describe the kind of brush. Because you're disclosing the terms and conditions of your offer, you're in good shape so far. But there are pitfalls to avoid:

- If you usually charge less than $10.95 for this kind of paint, the brush clearly isn't free.
- Don't reduce the quality of the paint that the customer must purchase or the quantity of any services (such as free delivery) you normally provide. If you provide a lesser product or service, you're exacting a hidden cost for the brush.
- Disclose any other terms, conditions, or limitations.

For more information on the use of the word "free," see "Deceptive Pricing," below.

Rule 6—Be Careful When You Describe Sales and Savings

You should be absolutely truthful in all claims about pricing. Because this point is so important, I discuss it in more detail in "Deceptive Pricing," below.

Rule 7—Observe Limitations on Offers of Credit

The law closely regulates advertisements that offer credit. You may advertise only credit terms that you actually offer. In other words, you may not "bait and switch" consumers by advertising favorable terms that you aren't prepared to make good on. You can also get in trouble by characterizing your credit terms or policy in ways that might be misleading (for example, "free money" or "easy credit").

If you advertise certain credit terms, you have to include specific information in the ad. The purpose of this rule is to make sure consumers understand all of the relevant credit terms up front, so they can compare various credit offers. For example, if your advertisement includes information about the required down payment ("only $10 down!"), you must also provide details on the terms of repayment and the annual interest rate.

Retail Pricing and Return Practices

In addition to regulating advertising, the federal government and most state governments have laws and rules that address several types of retail practices.

Deceptive Pricing

The Federal Trade Commission (FTC) has jurisdiction over deceptive pricing practices. At the state level, usually the attorney general's office or, in bigger cities, the district attorney's consumer fraud unit enforces laws dealing with deceptive trade practices. Two of the major problems they encounter concern retailers who (1) make incorrect price comparisons with other merchants or with their own "regular" prices, and (2) those who offer something that is supposedly "free" but in fact has a cost.

Offering a reduction from your usual selling price is a common and powerful sales technique. But to satisfy legal requirements, it's essential that the former price be the actual price for which you sold the item. Otherwise, the pricing is misleading.

> EXAMPLE: WizWare, Inc., produces computer software and announces a new product for $129. But the company sells the product to wholesalers for $79 and similarly discounts it to direct customers. The $129 price has never really existed, except to mislead customers into thinking they were receiving a discount.

Price comparisons often use words such as "regularly," "usually," or "reduced." For example, it's common to see a price tag that says, "Regularly $200, Now $150." Or sometimes a sign says "⅓ off our regular price." These comparisons are fine legally—if you in fact offered the sale merchandise at the old price for a reasonable length of time. They're not okay if you've brought in a special batch of merchandise especially for the sale and created a fictional "regular" price or one you adhered to for only a day or two.

If your ad compares your price with what other merchants are charging for the same product, be sure of two things:

- the other merchants are selling the identical product, and
- there was a sufficient number of sales at the higher price by merchants in your area so that you're offering a legitimate bargain.

In other words, make sure that the higher comparison price isn't an isolated or unrepresentative price.

Finally, remember that when you offer "free" products or services, they must actually be free. You can't recoup the cost by, for example, charging more than usual for the product that must be purchased in a "buy one, get one free" promotion. And, if there are any conditions the purchaser has to meet to get the free item (such as purchasing another product or participating in a survey), you must disclose them.

Sales Away From Your Place of Business

A customer has three days—a "cooling-off period" —to cancel any sale not made at your usual place of business. For details (including exceptions), see the FTC's trade regulation rule called "Cooling-Off Period for Sales Made at Homes or at Certain Other Locations" (16 CFR § 429). Here's how the FTC defines these sales:

> A sale, lease, or rental of consumer goods or services in which the seller or his representative personally solicits the sale, including those in response to or following an invitation by the buyer, and the buyer's agreement or offer to purchase is made at a place other than the place of business of the seller … and which has a purchase price of $25 or more if the sale is made at the buyer's residence or a purchase price of $130 or more if the sale is made at locations other than the buyer's residence, whether under single or multiple contract.

If you do any selling covered by the FTC definition, you must do two things. First, give the buyer a fully completed receipt or a copy of the sales contract. These documents must contain the date of the transaction and your name and address. They also must be written in the same language used during the sales presentation (for example, Spanish). They must also include the following words in large boldface type near the signature on the contract or the front of the receipt:

> You, the buyer, may cancel this transaction at any time prior to midnight of the third business day after the date of this transaction. See the attached notice of cancellation form for an explanation of this right.

Second, you must also give the buyer a completed form, in duplicate, labeled "notice of cancellation." This notice must be in the language of the sales pitch and in boldface type that's at least ten-point size. See the Notice of Cancellation below for the required language.

Sample Notice of Cancellation

Notice of Cancellation

[*Enter date of transaction*]

You may cancel this transaction, without any penalty or obligation, within three business days from the above date.

If you cancel, any property traded in, any payments made by you under the contract or sale, and any negotiable instrument executed by you will be returned within ten business days following receipt by the seller of your cancellation notice, and any security interest arising out of the transaction will be canceled.

If you cancel, you must make available to the seller at your residence, in substantially as good condition as when received, any goods delivered to you under this contract or sale; or you may, if you wish, comply with the instructions of the seller regarding the return shipment of the goods at the seller's expense and risk.

If you do make the goods available to the seller and the seller does not pick them up within 20 days of the date of your notice of cancellation, you may retain or dispose of the goods without any further obligation. If you fail to make the goods available to the seller or if you agree to return the goods to the seller and fail to do so, then you remain liable for performance of all obligations under the contract.

To cancel this transaction, mail or deliver a signed and dated copy of this cancellation notice or any other written notice or send a telegram, to [*name of seller*] , at [*address of seller's place of business*] NO LATER THAN MIDNIGHT OF _____ .

I hereby cancel this transaction.

Date: _____

Buyer's signature: _____

CAUTION

State laws and regulations. Most states also have laws and regulations dealing with door-to-door sales. Some of them go beyond the federal requirements. For example, in some states, the cooling-off period is five days. Check your state consumer protection agency for your state rules. Find yours at www.usa.gov/state-consumer.

Law From the Real World

Selling at Trade Shows

Do you sell consumer goods at trade shows or fairs? If so, you should give customers notice about their right to cancel their purchases. Otherwise, you might be violating the FTC's three-day cooling-off rule.

The FTC devised the rule to protect homebound, unsophisticated consumers from fast-talking door-to-door salespeople. At the time, most transactions at trade shows and fairs were business to business; the cooling-off period didn't apply. Over the years, however, trade shows and fairs have expanded considerably. In fact, many shows—featuring everything from computer software to outdoor equipment and housewares—are geared primarily toward consumer sales.

The FTC has "prosecutorial discretion" in pursuing merchants who sell at trade shows and fairs without giving customers a notice of cancellation rights. In most instances, the FTC doesn't stroll the halls of convention centers to shut down noncomplying businesses. But it has that power. And an unhappy (and savvy) customer could report you to the agency, which would investigate and could take action against you.

Refunds

Strictly speaking, once a sale (other than an offsite sale, as described above) is complete, you don't have to give a refund to a customer who has a change of mind. This is based on traditional contract law,

which says that a sale is a completed contract. Unless there's been a significant breach of the contract (for example, the goods or services you sold were seriously flawed), or some provision allows one of the parties to cancel, you're both stuck. So a customer who buys a product from you doesn't have the legal right to cancel the contract later and automatically get a refund. By the same token, if you discover that you could have charged a higher price, you can't cancel the sale either.

So much for the legalities. In real life, most retailers give customers the option of returning merchandise for either a cash refund or at least a store credit. Sometimes retailers impose conditions. For example, the customer must return the merchandise within a certain number of days; the merchandise must be unused; or the customer must show a receipt or another proof of purchase.

A liberal refund policy can give your customers confidence in your business and can be an effective marketing technique. (See Chapter 16.) Whatever you decide to do about a customer return policy, state your rules as positively as possible and post them conspicuously in your store. (This statement pertains to brick-and-mortar stores. For a discussion of online sales, see "Dealing With Customers Online" later in this chapter.)

Some states have laws that require merchants to post their refund policies if they don't accept certain types of returns. For example, California merchants must post their return policies if they don't give a cash refund, credit refund, or exchange for items returned within seven days of purchase. To find out whether there's a similar law in your state, contact your state's consumer protection agency.

Mail Orders

If you take orders by mail, telephone, fax, or the Internet, you need to become familiar with the Federal Trade Commission's rule dealing with this subject. The best source is the booklet *Business Guide to the FTC's Mail, Internet, or Telephone Order Merchandise Rule*. It's available at the

FTC's Business Center website at www.ftc.gov/tips-advice/business-center. Do a search using the guide's title as your search term. Here are some important features of the FTC rule:

- You must ship the merchandise within 30 days after you receive a properly completed order and payment, unless your ad clearly states that it will take longer.
- If there's going to be a delay, you must notify the customer in writing. You must give the customer the option of a new shipment date (if known) or the opportunity to cancel the order and receive a full refund. You must give the customer a way to reply at your expense. You may assume that a customer who doesn't reply has agreed to the delay.
- If the customer cancels, you must refund the customer's money within seven working days. If the customer used a credit card, you must issue the credit within one billing cycle.
- If there is a further delay—that is, if you can't ship by the later date to which the customer agreed—you must send a second notice, again seeking the customer's consent. This time, however, you have to cancel the order and send the customer a refund unless the customer responds and accepts the second revised shipping date.

The mail order rule doesn't cover:

- services (such as mail order photofinishing)
- magazine subscriptions (except for the first shipment)
- sales of seeds and plants
- COD orders, or
- book and music clubs and other subscription plans in which the seller ships items and bills the subscriber unless the subscriber returns them within a specified time limit.

Unordered Merchandise

With only two exceptions, federal law (and the law in most states) makes it illegal to mail unordered merchandise. The exceptions are:

- free samples that you clearly and conspicuously mark as such, and
- merchandise mailed by a charitable organization to solicit contributions.

It's illegal to send the recipient a bill or dunning letter for any unordered merchandise. A person receiving unordered merchandise is legally entitled to treat it as a gift.

Warranties

Basically, a warranty is a guarantee that the manufacturer and retailer will stand behind a product. Sometimes a warranty is made through an oral or written statement of the seller. This is called an "express warranty."

Even if you don't make an express warranty, however, a warranty might be imposed by law; this is called an "implied warranty." The law holds the manufacturer or retailer responsible for these warranties even if they've said nothing on the subject. Sometimes you can get rid of an implied warranty by making a disclaimer.

Although I focus on the sale of goods, it's also possible for services to be warranted. For example, a TV repair service might warrant that a repair job will be good for at least six months; an auto mechanic might warrant the repairs on a car's electrical system for one year; and a lawn maintenance company might warrant that certain weeds won't reappear during the current season. Warranties for services are almost always express and not implied, and they're not as widely regulated as product warranties.

Express Warranties

Express warranties are statements and promises that a manufacturer or retailer makes about a product or about its willingness to remedy defects and malfunctions in the product. If the statements are untrue or if the stated commitments are not honored, the manufacturer or retailer might be legally liable to the buyer for breach of warranty.

Express warranties take a variety of forms, from advertising claims to a printed certificate that accompanies the product and specifically guarantees it. Express warranties can be made either orally or in writing.

Oral Warranties

If a seller makes an oral promise to a buyer, that is an express warranty.

> EXAMPLE: A seller says, "This TV set is new" or "This oven heats to over 600 degrees." If the TV set is used or if the oven heats only to 500 degrees, the seller will be liable for breach of warranty, whether or not the seller knew that the claims were false.

If the seller shows a customer a sample or a model of goods being sold, there's an express warranty that the goods the customer purchases will be basically indistinguishable from the sample. For example, if a salesperson shows a customer some samples of printer paper and the customer orders a dozen packages based on the sample, the entire order must conform to that sample. And if a dealer shows a customer a small-scale model of a garage door, the door the customer receives must look like and be constructed like the model.

But not everything that a seller says as part of a sales transaction is a warranty. Merely giving an opinion about the goods or praising them doesn't create a warranty. For example:

- Martha is at a drugstore looking at hair coloring products. The clerk says, "I recommend this brand. It works very well, and I believe you'll be satisfied with it." Martha uses the product and develops a severe allergic reaction on her scalp.
- Phillip tries on a new suit. The store owner says, "It looks good on you. You'll be wearing it for a long time." In fact, the suit is a size too big and wears out after a year.

These statements would be considered opinions, not promises or statements of fact. They wouldn't constitute express warranties.

Written Warranties

A statement doesn't have to be called a warranty or guarantee to be legally treated as such. And warranties needn't be part of a formal written contract. Statements made in advertisements or in product literature distributed by the manufacturer or retail store can constitute binding warranties.

If a sales contract or order form contains a description of the goods, that constitutes an express warranty by the seller that the goods will be as described. So if the product is described as an Ear Play Model 400 stereo receiver and it turns out to be a different brand or model, the seller has breached an express warranty.

Written warranties on consumer products are covered by state laws and a federal law, the Magnuson-Moss Warranty Act. You can read the text of the federal law on the FTC's Business Center website at www.ftc.gov/tips-advice/business-center. Do a search for "Magnuson-Moss." That law is designed to make it easier for consumers to understand and deal with warranties. It doesn't replace state warranty laws but does add certain requirements.

The Magnuson-Moss Warranty Act covers consumer products normally used for personal, family, or household purposes. It doesn't require a manufacturer or seller to give any written warranty at all. But if a written warranty is given, it must comply with the statute and with rules of the Federal Trade Commission.

For a product costing the consumer $15 or more, the written warranty must be in simple, understandable language. Also, the seller must make the terms of the warranty available to the buyer before the sale occurs. You can comply with this requirement in one of two ways:

- clearly and conspicuously display the warranty on or near the warranted product, or
- post prominent signs letting customers know that warranties are available on request, then providing them to customers who ask to see them. (This section addresses brick-and-mortar stores. For a discussion of online sales, see "Dealing With Customers Online" later in this chapter.)

If a product costs $10 or more, the written warranty must state that it's either a full warranty or a "limited warranty." Naturally, a consumer who sees the words "full warranty" believes that a large measure of protection is being provided. To qualify as a full warranty, a written warranty must meet these requirements:

- Implied warranties (see below) can't be limited in time.
- The warranty must be good for anyone who owns the product during the warranty period.

- Warranty service must be provided free, including the cost of returning, removing, or reinstalling the product, if applicable.
- The customer must be entitled to a choice of either a replacement or a refund if you are unable to repair the product after a reasonable number of tries.
- Customers cannot be required to do anything unreasonable to get warranty service, beyond letting you know that service is necessary.

Any written warranty that doesn't qualify as a full warranty must be labeled as a limited warranty. You can restrict the duration of implied warranties, as long as the restrictions are not "unconscionable" (that is, shockingly unfair). Restrictions must be stated clearly, and the implied warranties must last for a reasonable time.

The Magnuson-Moss Warranty Act doesn't supersede state laws that give consumers greater rights or laws that permit people to recover damages for injuries caused by defective products, despite a disclaimer of liability. For example, in California the Song-Beverly Consumer Warranty Act contains more stringent warranty provisions than the Magnuson-Moss Warranty Act. Among other things, the California statute provides that a manufacturer who provides a written warranty (full or limited) must maintain service and repair facilities in California reasonably close to all areas where its products are sold. The manufacturer can delegate repair and service facilities to retailers or independent repair shops. Repairs to motor vehicles must be completed within 30 days, except in unusual circumstances.

Implied Warranties

Implied warranties don't come from anything a seller says or does. They arise automatically when a product is sold. Under the Uniform Commercial Code, there are two kinds of implied warranties:

- that the product is fit for its ordinary use, and
- that the product is fit for any special use the seller knows about.

Merchantability

A seller automatically makes an implied warranty that new (not used) goods sold are fit for their ordinary purpose—in other words, that the product will work the way similar products ordinarily work. This implied warranty is also called a "warranty of merchantability."

Here are some examples:

- A lawnmower will cut grass that is four inches tall.
- A stepladder will support a 275-pound person.
- A toaster will make both dark and light toast.
- A bicycle's brakes will work in a light rain.
- A bottle of ginger ale won't have loose glass in it.

The manufacturer and retailer of a product that's not fit for ordinary purposes are liable to the purchaser for breach of the implied warranty.

Fitness for a Particular Purpose

There's a special implied warranty if the seller has reason to know that (1) the goods are required for a particular purpose, and (2) the buyer is relying on the seller's skill or judgment to select suitable goods. In that situation, the seller is bound by an implied warranty that the goods will be fit for that purpose.

Here are some examples:

- Joanne goes to a paint store and asks for two gallons of white paint that will work well on plaster walls. The store owner selects paint for her. Unfortunately, it's intended solely for metallic surfaces and ruins her walls.
- Morton asks an air-conditioning contractor to pick out and install an air-conditioning unit for a part of his plant. He explains that the room contains extensive electronic equipment and must be kept at 55 degrees or cooler at all times. The air conditioner is installed but leads to costly problems, because in hot weather it can't keep the temperature below 62 degrees.
- Wilma goes to a sports retailer and asks for a sleeping bag that will be adequate to

10 degrees Fahrenheit. The retailer selects a model for Wilma, and she buys it, but it won't keep a normal person warm below freezing.

In these examples, each seller is liable to the buyer for breach of the "implied warranty of fitness for a particular purpose." Each seller knew the buyer needed the goods for a particular purpose and that the buyer was relying on the seller's skill or judgment to furnish suitable goods.

This is different from the implied warranty of merchantability discussed in the preceding section. An air conditioner that cooled a room to 62 degrees in hot weather would be fit for the ordinary purposes for which an air conditioner is used. It wouldn't violate the implied warranty of merchantability. But because the seller in the second example knew the buyer had special requirements and was relying on the seller to meet them, this special implied warranty took effect.

Disclaimers of Implied Warranties

The Uniform Commercial Code allows sellers, in many cases, to disclaim implied warranties through a conspicuous written notice. Typically, to disclaim implied warranties, you must inform consumers in a conspicuous manner, in writing, that you won't be responsible if the product malfunctions or is defective and that the entire product risk falls on them. To do this, you must specifically state that you don't warrant "merchantability" or use a phrase such as "with all faults" or "as is."

There are, however, major exceptions to the general rule that make it impossible to disclaim implied warranties in some circumstances.

Exception 1: State law restrictions. In some states, you might not be able to avoid implied warranties. Despite its name, the Uniform Commercial Code isn't completely uniform; state legislatures have tinkered with parts of it, including the part about disclaiming implied warranties. Some states don't let you sell consumer products "as is" or require you to follow strict rules to do so.

Exception 2: Injuries. A disclaimer of implied warranties won't shield you from legal liability if your product is so defective it injures someone.

Exception 3: Federal law restrictions. If you offer a written warranty for a consumer product or offer a service contract on it, you can't disclaim any implied warranty. (This restriction is imposed by the Magnuson-Moss Warranty Act.)

> **CAUTION**
>
> **Implied warranties are difficult to disclaim.** If you're going to enter this legal thicket, you'll likely need a lawyer's advice on whether you can disclaim implied warranties in your situation and, if so, how best to do it. Even if the law permits a disclaimer of warranties, if you and a customer slug it out in court, you'll find that judges often tend to favor the consumer. Unless a seller is absolutely clear, this warranty disclaimer will be disallowed.

Some sellers are interested not in getting rid of implied warranties entirely but only in limiting the remedies in case of a breach. For example, the seller might want to say that in case of a product defect, the buyer can either (1) return the goods and get a refund, or (2) have any defective parts replaced or repaired, but cannot collect monetary damages. Although this sort of limitation on damages is normally effective, it won't always work, particularly where the limitation is found to be highly unreasonable. Suppose the seller of a $2,000 stereo set puts this language in the warranty: "Seller is obligated only to replace defective parts." After Melissa buys a stereo, a protective circuit fails, causing it to overheat. This destroys several key parts and ruins the stereo. Will a court allow the seller merely to replace the $5 part that didn't work? Perhaps not. The buyer might be able to convince the court that the limitation shouldn't be enforced because it is unfair to do so in these circumstances. And remember that a disclaimer can't shield you from liability for personal injury to a consumer hurt by a defective product.

What Happens If a Warranty Is Breached

Federal and state laws give consumers certain rights when an express or implied warranty is breached.

The Buyer's Options

Under the Uniform Commercial Code, if there's a breach of warranty, the customer usually can return the merchandise and get a full refund. The manufacturer or retailer bound by the warranty, however, has the right to correct the problem ("cure the breach") by fixing the merchandise or replacing it with nondefective merchandise. A customer who prefers to keep the merchandise can do so and sue for the direct economic loss—generally, the reduced value of the product because it's defective.

In addition to damages for the reduced value of a defective product, a buyer might also be entitled to damages for:

- consequential economic losses (such as lost profits) resulting from the product's failure to meet requirements and needs that were foreseeable at the time of sale

  EXAMPLE: Meadowbrook Golf Course buys 12 golf carts, all of which are defective. As a result, Meadowbrook loses $20,000 in profits over the eight-week period it takes to get the carts fixed. (It proves impractical to get substitute carts on short notice.) It can successfully recover these losses.

- injury to people and damage to property caused by the defective product

  EXAMPLE: Marissa buys a CutAbove power lawnmower. One day when her teenage son Reggie is mowing the lawn, the mower propels a small stone into one of his eyes. Reggie loses his sight in that eye. Because the mower doesn't contain normal safety features, Reggie is entitled to collect damages for his injury.

Who Is Liable?

Who is liable if a customer buys a product from a retailer and the product fails to live up to the warranty? Sometimes the manufacturer, sometimes the retailer, and sometimes both. Although liability depends on the circumstances, here are some general rules:

- **Manufacturer's express warranty.** If an express warranty made by the manufacturer was breached, the manufacturer is responsible for making good on the promise. The retailer usually isn't liable, unless it "adopts" the manufacturer's warranty by its conduct at the time of sale.

  EXAMPLE: Maria goes to Pete's Fitness Mart and looks at HomeBody, a $3,000 set of exercise machines manufactured by Health Horizons, Inc. She's interested but wants to be sure it's backed by a broad warranty. To clinch the sale, Pete calls the president of Health Horizons and has the company send an extensive written warranty.

  Nine months after Maria buys the Home-Body, it fails; meanwhile, Health Horizons has gone out of business. Pete's Fitness Mart is bound by the warranty, because it was part of the inducement that Pete used to convince Maria to buy HomeBody.

- **Retailer's express warranty.** If the warranty was made independently by a retailer, the retailer is liable. The manufacturer isn't bound unless the retailer was acting under the authority (in legal lingo, as an "agent") of the manufacturer in making the warranty.

- **Breach of implied warranty of merchantability.** If there is a breach of the implied warranty that the goods are fit for ordinary purposes, both the manufacturer and the retailer are liable— but if the customer sues the retailer, the retailer

in turn will usually have the right to recover against the manufacturer for supplying a defective product.

- **Breach of implied warranty of fitness for a particular purpose.** If the customer relied on the retailer to select the goods for a particular purpose and the goods aren't satisfactory for that purpose, the retailer is liable.

- **Personal injury.** A buyer who's injured by an unfit product can usually sue the manufacturer, even though the injured person didn't deal directly with the manufacturer. What's more, it's not only the buyer who can sue for personal injuries from a defective product. In most states, members of the buyer's family or household or house guests who are injured can also sue the manufacturer if it's reasonable to expect that these persons would use or be affected by the product.

Whether or not an injured person can sue the retailer as well as the manufacturer depends on court decisions in your state and the extent of the retailer's involvement in the sale. In many states, a retailer who simply sells an unopened box and makes no statements about the product won't be liable if the product later injures someone. But some states hold the retailer liable even under these circumstances.

> **CAUTION**
>
> **Get legal advice.** Liability for breach of warranties is one of the most complex areas of commercial law. Because liability depends on many factors and because the law is somewhat unsettled, use this book for general background only. Also, it's important to understand that in a lawsuit, a person who has suffered a serious injury or significant economic loss because of a defective product will probably rely on additional theories of legal liability (such as negligence and strict liability) besides breach of warranty. See a lawyer for specific legal advice.

Consumer Protection Statutes

Remember "caveat emptor"—let the buyer beware? That used to be the law of the marketplace. Not anymore. Today, consumers have clout.

For example, in Florida, a Chevrolet dealer promised a "free four-day, three-night vacation to Acapulco" to anyone who bought a car or van. Relying on this special promotion, Peter bought a van from the dealer. When the vacation voucher arrived, Peter found that the so-called free vacation was really a time-share sales promotion. The vacation trip was loaded down with conditions, restrictions, and obligations. Believing he'd been cheated, Peter sued the dealer. The jury awarded Peter $1,768 in compensatory damages (the value of the trip) plus $667,000 in punitive damages. (*Bill Branch Chevrolet, Inc. v. Burkert*, 521 So.2d 153 (Fla. App. 2d Dist. 1988).)

This case was brought under a state consumer protection statute. Such statutes are meant to protect consumers from unfair or deceptive practices and often go beyond the traditional legal remedies available for breach of warranty. Laws like these are on the books in nearly every state, although the details vary.

Consumer protection laws place a potent weapon in the hands of buyers. In an ordinary contract lawsuit, a plaintiff can recover only for actual losses. For example, the man who sued the car dealer about the free vacation won punitive damages amounting to many times the value of his trip. The potential for large verdicts gives buyers and their lawyers an incentive to sue if it looks like a law has been violated.

"Big deal," you might say. "I'm an honest and ethical businessperson. None of this affects me." Well, that might not be so. For one thing, you need to know the details of your state's consumer protection laws so that you can tell your employees about practices that could get you in trouble. Furthermore, these state laws often allow a customer to sue even if the violation was not intentional. If you sell a product manufactured by a U.S.-based company (say, a Schwinn bike) and mistakenly advertise that the product was made in the United States when in fact it was made in Taiwan, you might be legally liable.

Hundreds of cases have been brought under consumer protection laws, including these:

- A man sued a department store that ran out of an advertised waffle iron and didn't give him a rain check—a violation of the consumer protection law in his state.
- A homeowner sued a roofing contractor who falsely advertised that it could arrange financing for roof repair jobs.
- A woman sued a health spa that backed out on its promise to return her deposit and cancel her contract if she changed her mind within three days.

Most consumer protection laws contain a broad prohibition on "unfair or deceptive practices." In addition, many statutes list specific practices that are forbidden, such as bait-and-switch and deceptive pricing.

Dealing With Customers Online

For the most part, the same legal rules apply when you do business online as when you sell to customers in a brick-and-mortar store or by mail. As long as you don't overstep federal and state statutes and regulations, you have quite a bit of latitude in establishing your business policies and making them legally binding on your customers. You can set rules covering issues such as what forms of payment you accept, when and how customers can return items, and what warranties you offer.

In a store, you might do this by posting your policies in a prominent place or by having customers agree to them on an order form. When selling by mail, you can include your policies in your catalog or, again, on an order form. But obviously, the mechanics of informing customers of your policies are different when you're selling over the Internet.

In this section, I'll provide information to help you establish legally enforceable policies for your website. For more information, see the eCommerce area of www.nolo.com (in the Small Business section).

Why Bother to Post Policies?

With just one major exception, there are no laws requiring e-commerce websites to post their terms and conditions or mandating how and where such conditions should appear. The exception is the Children's Online Privacy Protection Act (COPPA), which requires you to post a privacy policy if your Web content is directed at children. The Federal Trade Commission enforces COPPA, so check its website for more information (www.ftc.gov/tips-advice/business-center).

Even with no general requirement that a business post its policies, posting can offer business and legal benefits. On the business side, being straight with visitors and customers builds trust, credibility, and loyalty. On the legal side, a well-thought-out set of terms and conditions can help limit your legal liability and avoid disputes over the details of transactions.

True, if a disgruntled customer sues you, your terms and conditions might not give you 100% protection, but at least you and your lawyer should have some solid arguing points to present to the judge.

Policies Worth Posting

If you'll be selling goods or services online, below are some topics you might want to cover in the policies you post.

Credit card use. If your website will offer direct sales via credit cards, it's wise to reassure customers that their credit card information will be kept confidential. Advise them of any steps you've taken to ensure the security of their credit card purchase. Customers will probably expect your web address to have an "s" in "https" and will look for the padlock symbol, which means the site is encrypted and

payment information will be secure. Also, under federal law, a credit card user is liable only for the first $50 of unauthorized purchases, assuming that the user promptly notifies the credit card issuer about the unauthorized use. Some businesses offer to pay up to the $50 limit if the credit card issuer fails to do so.

Warranties. You might already offer a warranty that explains what you will and will not do for the customer if there's a problem with the products you sell. Your warranty can both reassure the customer and limit your liability, so I recommend that you post your warranty on your website. When you sell goods that carry a manufacturer's limited warranty and the goods sell for more than $15, federal law requires you to post the warranty or tell customers how they can view it.

Returns and repairs. It's important to develop a return and repair policy and post it online. For example, perhaps you're prepared to give a full refund, but only if the product is returned within 30 days and is in salable condition. If customers know this in advance, they won't be surprised if you refuse to give a refund 45 days after the purchase. While you have a great deal of discretion in how you deal with returns and repairs, a generous policy can build tremendous goodwill among present and prospective customers.

Legal jurisdiction. Because people from all over the country—or the world—might buy from you online, you might want to say that the law of your state will apply to any dispute and that the courts of your state will have exclusive jurisdiction. Be aware, however, that some judges balk at enforcing this type of restriction, especially in a consumer transaction involving a claim of $50 or more. Still, posting this type of provision can do no harm.

Sales limited to the United States. You might want to limit your exposure to laws (and lawsuits) in distant places by selling only to people in the United States. If so, you can post a notice to that effect—but also take polite and reasonable steps to reject orders from people outside the country.

Limited liability. You can use your postings to limit the financial damages for which your business will be legally responsible if there's a problem with the products, services, or information you offer online. Understand that language limiting your liability won't always have the desired effect; judges might balk at limitations that are unfair or that try to cut off the amount a person can receive for bodily injuries. But in many situations, judges do enforce limitations that customers have agreed to. Your posting might include language such as this: "Protobiz LLC will not be liable to a customer for any damages beyond what the customer has actually paid to Protobiz."

> **TIP**
>
> **Do some no-cost research: Read the terms and conditions posted on websites that you respect.** The sites that you've personally used and come to trust will probably have well-written, customer-friendly policies that you can adapt for your own site. If you've never studied their fine print before, now's the time to do so. Then, after you've drafted your own set of policies, consider having a lawyer look over your handiwork and possibly tweak it for maximum legal impact.

How and Where to Post Your Terms and Conditions

Easy navigation will be important throughout your website, and access to your terms and conditions is no exception. You'll want to provide prominent links that take customers right to the relevant information. This, by itself, will provide a reasonable level of legal protection.

How to Link Prominently

Linking to your terms and conditions on your site's home page is a good place to start. You might also add links on other important pages, including the order page. You can call your link "Terms and Conditions" or anything else that's reasonably descriptive—for example, "Our Policies," "Customer Policies," or "Terms of Service."

Here are some other ways to make your links and other information grab the customers' attention:

- Put the link where users can see it without having to scroll down.
- Put the link in large type and a distinctive color.
- Include a link on all other pages, if possible. But at a minimum, put the link on the pages where customers place orders so they can read your terms and conditions first.
- Write your terms and conditions in plain English so customers can easily understand their meaning.
- Put your terms and conditions in large type that's easy to read.

Requiring Actual Assent

If a dissatisfied customer sues you, you'd like the judge to treat your terms and conditions as a binding contract. Some judges will find a contract if you've followed the above guidelines—the assumption being that the customer read and accepted your terms. But other judges might rule that a conspicuous posting is not enough. They'll find a contract only if the customer specifically accepted your terms.

One way to protect yourself is to present your terms to your customers, then require them to click a button at the end that says "I Accept" or "I Agree" before they can complete the transaction. That way, if a dispute ever ends up in court, you'll have evidence that the customer not only had the opportunity to read your terms and conditions, but presumably did read them, right before actually agreeing to them.

Cash, Credit Cards, and Checks

This chapter considers the three most common ways that businesses get paid for the goods and services they sell: cash, credit cards, and checks. If you extend credit directly to customers, clients, or patients, you should also read Chapter 19, which explains how to avoid collection problems.

Cash

Cash includes not only currency but also equivalents that are as good as cash—certified checks, cashier's checks, and (less common these days) traveler's checks and money orders. It also includes payments through mobile payment services, like Venmo and Zelle.

If you have very large cash transactions, you might have to report them to the IRS. The reporting requirements are intended primarily to deter money-laundering schemes by customers (often drug dealers) who want to conceal income.

If you receive more than $10,000 in cash—or in traveler's checks or money orders—in one transaction or two or more related transactions, you must provide information about the transaction to the IRS. (Certified, cashier's, business, or personal checks aren't covered by this requirement.) The necessary information includes the buyer's name, address, and Social Security number. In addition, if you're a retail merchant, you must report:

- cash transactions in which you receive more than $10,000 in installment payments in one year
- transactions of more than $10,000 in which part of the payment is in cash, traveler's checks, or money orders, and
- any suspicious transaction, no matter what the amount.

In calculating whether a transaction or related transactions involve more than $10,000 in cash, you must include not only cash, but also each cashier's check, traveler's check, bank draft, or money order that is part of the transaction and is made out for $10,000 or less.

EXAMPLE 1: Gloria buys a boat from Todd, a boat dealer, for $16,500. She pays Todd with a $16,500 cashier's check payable to him. The cashier's check isn't treated as cash because the face amount is more than $10,000. Todd doesn't have to report this sale to the IRS as a cash transaction.

EXAMPLE 2: Donald buys gold coins from Maryanne, a coin dealer, for $13,200. Donald pays Maryanne $6,200 in $100 bills and the remaining $7,000 by cashier's check. Because the cashier's check is less than $10,000, it's treated as cash, so Maryanne must report this to the IRS as a cash transaction.

Use IRS Form 8300, *Report of Cash Payments Over $10,000 Received in a Trade or Business*. The form must be filed within 15 days after the transaction occurs, or within 15 days after a customer's transactions over a 12-month period add up to $10,000.

In addition, before February 1 of the year following the year when you received the cash, you must give the customer a written statement that includes:

- the name, telephone number, and address of a contact person at your business
- the total amount of reportable cash the customer gave you, and
- notice that you're reporting this information to the IRS.

You can send the statement electronically if the customer agrees to receive it that way. Keep a copy.

Credit and Debit Cards

Depending on the business you're in, your customers or clients might want to pay with plastic—the familiar Visa, MasterCard, Discover, American Express, and other cards. Technically, there's a distinction between "credit cards" (such as Visa or MasterCard) and "travel and entertainment cards" (such as American Express and Diners Club), also called "charge cards." For most practical purposes, the same legal concepts apply, so I'll simply use "credit card" to cover both types.

In deciding which credit cards to recognize, take into account the preferences of your customers and clients, as well as the size of the discount exacted by the credit card issuer and how quickly you get paid.

When a customer charges goods or services using a bank-administered credit card, the bank credits your account with the amount of the sale less a discount—2% is considered a good rate for merchants—which is the bank's fee for handling the transaction and accepting the risk that the customer doesn't pay. In addition, the bank might charge you a start-up fee and a fee for the card-swiping or point-of-sales machine.

If you're in a retail or other business where customers or clients expect to pay on credit, credit cards are often more cost-effective than directly extending credit. In general, if you follow the bank's rules—such as checking the credit card to make sure it hasn't expired and getting approval for all or at least larger transactions—the credit card issuer (not you) absorbs the loss if the customer doesn't pay up. Electronic systems used by credit card issuers do most or all of the checking for you and get the money into your bank account almost immediately.

However, there are still a few exceptions to the general rule that if you follow the bank's procedures, you're sure to get your money. For example, if the goods are defective and the customer refuses to pay the bank, you might have to bear the loss. This will be spelled out in your contract with the bank. Read it carefully.

Some states restrict your ability to record personal identification information about a credit card holder. The laws on this subject differ from state to state, but the California statute provides a good illustration of the kinds of restrictions that might apply to you. In California, in most circumstances you can't require the cardholder to give you personal identification information such as an address or phone number. There are, however, a few exceptions. For example, you can require the cardholder to provide this information if you need it for a special purpose related to the transaction, for example, shipping, delivery, servicing, or installation of the merchandise, or for special orders.

There can be hefty penalties for violating these statutes, so learn the rules in your state and make sure that your employees know them.

Even if your state does permit you to record this information, ask yourself if you really need it. After all, if the customer doesn't pay the bill, it's a problem for the bank that issued the credit card, not for you. And because some customers regard making a request for personal information as an invasion of their privacy, doing so might be poor customer relations. If your main reason to gather this information is to build a mailing list, it's better simply to ask your customers if they'd like to be added to your list.

Many customers prefer to use a debit card that withdraws money from their bank account and transfers it to yours at the time of purchase. As with a credit card, you'll pay a small fee on each transaction. Often, the same piece of plastic serves as both a debit card and a credit card, so before ringing up the sale, you'll need to ask: "Debit or credit?"

TIP

If you do business online, look into the PayPal program. Services like PayPal make it easier to process transactions and inspire consumer confidence. Go to www.paypal.com for details.

CAUTION

Don't unwittingly aid the identity thieves. As you know, if a credit or debit card receipt with the full account number and card expiration date falls into the wrong hands, it can lead to misery for the customer. An important provision of the Fair and Accurate Credit Transactions Act deals with this problem. It requires you to shorten the information on the credit and debit card receipts you print. You can't include more than the last five digits of the card number, and you must omit the expiration date. (Up-to-date receipt printers are programmed to meet this federal law.) You needn't comply with this provision if you give only handwritten receipts or receipts that imprint or copy the card—methods that are becoming less common.

Checks

In any business—and especially in a service or wholesale business—you're likely to find that some customers or clients want to pay using personal or business checks. Obviously, accepting payment by check is riskier than accepting payment by cash or credit card. Millions of bad checks are written each year.

Avoiding Bad-Check Problems

Checks can be bad for a number of reasons. Here are the main ones:

- The account has insufficient funds to cover the amount of the purchase.
- The account has been closed—or perhaps it's a fictitious account that never existed.
- The signature of the person who signed the check is a forgery.
- In the case of a third-party check (such as a paycheck) names or dollar amounts on the check have been altered, or the endorsement is a forgery.
- A person signing or endorsing a check on behalf of a partnership or corporation doesn't have legal authority to sign for the business.

Faced with these many possibilities for losses, some retail businesses adopt a simple policy: No checks. But such a policy often carries its own risks—mainly that you might lose perfectly solvent customers or clients who like the convenience of writing checks. After all, it's customary for most retail, wholesale, service, and manufacturing industries to accept checks. And because the bank doesn't keep a percentage of each transaction (as is the case with credit cards), you might actually want to encourage regular customers to pay by check rather than credit card.

No matter what type of business you're in, the best way to approach the potential bad-check problem is to adopt sensible rules and stick to them. How stringent you want to be depends on the nature of your business and how well rules will be accepted by your customers and clients. It boils down to a business decision about how much risk you're willing to accept.

If yours is a retail business, here are some policies to consider:

- Require that checks be written and signed in your presence.
- Accept checks drawn on local banks only.
- Be sure the checks have the customer's name, local address, and phone number preprinted on them.
- Don't accept checks written for more than the purchase price; in other words, don't give change for a check. (Some small businesses, such as grocers, build customer loyalty with minimal losses by issuing check-cashing cards allowing regular customers to write a check for up to $20 more than the price of goods purchased.)
- Wait until the check has cleared before giving a cash refund for returned goods.
- Don't accept third-party checks—paychecks, Social Security checks, and other checks that someone else has made out to the customer, who then endorses them.

> **EXAMPLE:** Laurie offers you a check made out to her from her employer, Amalgamated Products. She endorses it on the back. The check might be a forgery, or maybe the company doesn't have funds in the account to cover the check.

- Don't accept postdated checks.
- Set a limit on the check amount you will accept, or at least call the bank and verify that larger checks are good.
- Require a manager's approval for checks over a certain amount.
- Write the customer's phone number on the check, if the law in your state allows it.
- Ask to see ID—including something that contains a photo and signature. A driver's license is a good choice. Record key information (such as the driver's license number) on the check; it will help you locate the customer if the check is no good.

Restrictions on ID requirements. Find out if your state has a law restricting the kind of ID you can require. In some states, for example, you can't require a customer to show you a credit card as condition of accepting a check. If you violate laws of this type, you might face a fine, a civil lawsuit, or both. No matter what your state law is, avoid using credit cards as a form of ID. For one thing, you can't charge the client's credit card account if the check bounces. For another, bank personnel or others seeing a credit card number might use this information improperly. Why subject your customers to this risk?

If you're presented with a check drawn on a business account, be sure that the person signing it has authority to do so. If a check is signed by someone other than the owner, a partner, or a corporate officer, call the bank to see if the person presenting the check is an authorized signer.

Some businesses post a sign saying that they charge a specified fee for any check that bounces. In many states, you can't collect such fees without advance warning to customers. And some business owners think that such notices deter bad-check writers. Still, I generally recommend against posting signs. It's insulting to the customer, and there's no evidence that it will cut down the bad checks you receive. And remember, your main goal is to avoid getting bad checks in the first place—not to try to collect them later plus a $10 fee. But if you do post such a sign or charge such a fee, check the law in your state to see how much you can legally charge.

RESOURCE

Solve Your Money Troubles: Strategies to Get Out of Debt and Stay That Way, **by Amy Loftsgordon and Cara O'Neill (Nolo),** is addressed primarily to people who owe money, but the information on bad-check laws is also helpful to businesses receiving money.

Once you accept a check, stamp it with an endorsement stamp (available from your bank) and deposit it in your business account the same day. Every day you wait increases the chances that

the check writer will have emptied or closed the account. Under the Uniform Commercial Code, a statute adopted in every state that governs most banking transactions, there's a presumption that a check becomes "stale" six months after the date it's signed. The bank may refuse to honor it after that period—although in actual practice, they'll usually honor older checks as long as the account is solvent.

When the Customer Stops Payment

Sometimes a customer stops payment on a check, claiming that the goods you sold were defective. If there's a legitimate dispute, the customer's good faith will be a valid defense to a prosecution or a civil lawsuit for multiple damages. And if it turns out that the goods were in fact defective, the customer will be entitled to a reduction of the amount owed—or even, in extreme cases, a cancellation of the debt. But if the customer's allegations are a trumped-up excuse to get something for nothing, you'll be entitled to your full legal remedies in court. Often, however, in dealing with a customer who is unhappy with the merchandise purchased, the best policy is simply to have the customer return the goods and to call it a day.

Dealing With Bad Checks

Even if you take reasonable precautions, a bad check will occasionally slip through your system. A bank might return a check to you with the notation "insufficient funds" or "NSF," which means the same thing: The customer has an active account but there's not enough in it to cover the check. Or a bank might inform you that the account has been closed.

Here are some steps you can take to get your money, many of which apply primarily to bad checks from individuals. Other techniques might be more appropriate when the bad check comes from another business. (See Chapter 19.)

Step 1. Call the Customer

Call the customer and ask that the check be made good or you be paid in cash. (This is one reason why you should write down the customer's phone number when you take a check, if permitted by state law.) But be careful about when you call the customer—and how often. Laws in several states limit what you can do to collect debts. (See Chapter 19.) To avoid problems, call only between 8 a.m. and 9 p.m., don't discuss the debt with the customer's employer, and make sure your request for payment is polite.

Step 2. Write a Letter

Send a certified letter—return receipt requested—making the same demand. This sets the stage for a possible criminal prosecution if the check writer intentionally attempted to defraud you. Also, many states have bad-check laws that are particularly favorable to businesses. In such states, if you send a written demand for payment, you might be able to collect extra damages in court (often two or three times the value of the check) if the check writer doesn't come through.

> **EXAMPLE:** Monica, the owner of a Florida gift shop, receives a bad check from Norbert. She sends Norbert a notice demanding payment in full plus a service charge of $25 or 5% of the check, whichever is greater. If Norbert doesn't pay within 15 days, Monica can sue him under Florida law for the amount of the check plus additional damages of three times the amount of the check (at least $50). This is in addition to court costs, reasonable attorneys' fees, and any bank fees that she incurs.

The sample notice and demand for payment shown below here is derived from the Florida bad-check statute (Crimes, § 832.07). Because the law in each state is different, find out the specific requirements where you do business.

Sample Bad-Check Notice (Florida)

You are hereby notified that a check, numbered _____ , in the face amount of $_____ , issued by you on _____ , ____ , drawn upon (*name of bank*), and payable to _____ , has been dishonored. Pursuant to Florida law, you have 15 days from receipt of this notice to tender payment of the full amount of such check, plus a service charge of $25 if the face value does not exceed $50; $30 if the face value exceeds $50 but does not exceed $300; $40 if the face value exceeds $300; or an amount of up to 5 percent of the face amount of the check, whichever is greater, the total amount due being $_____ . Unless this amount is paid in full within the time specified above, the holder of such check may turn over the dishonored check and all other available information relating to this incident to the state attorney for criminal prosecution. You may be additionally liable in a civil action for triple the amount of the check, but in no case less than $50, together with the amount of the check, a service charge, court costs, reasonable attorney fees, and incurred bank fees, as provided in Florida Statutes § 68.065.

Step 3. Contact the Bank

If the customer's bank account is still active, wait a few days and then inquire to see if the check is now good (the customer might have deposited a paycheck after the check was dishonored). You can normally check the status of an account by calling the bank and saying you hold a check for a certain dollar amount and asking whether there is enough in the account to cover it. If so, take the returned check to the bank and draw out the cash. Another alternative is to ask the customer's bank for "enforced collection." If the bank offers this service, the bad check will be held in a special category. The next money deposited in the customer's account will go to you. Procedures and costs vary; get details from the bank.

Payment in Full

Be careful about accepting and depositing checks that say "payment in full" or something similar. If the check writer owes more, you might be barred from collecting the additional amount.

Where there's a good-faith dispute about how much the check writer owes you, depositing a full-payment check usually means that you accept the check in complete satisfaction of the debt. Crossing out the words "payment in full" generally won't help; you could be cut off from suing for the balance. If you don't want to accept the check as full payment, you must send it back rather than depositing it.

However, a number of states have changed this rule to help creditors. In those states, if you cash a full-payment check and explicitly reserve your right to sue for the balance, you can go after the check writer in court. If your state has modified the rule, you normally can preserve your right to sue for the balance by writing the words "under protest" or "without prejudice" with your endorsement.

Step 4. Request Prosecution

Intentionally writing a bad check is a crime. As noted above, before you contact the local district attorney's or prosecuting attorney's office to request prosecution, you might have to give the check writer a written notice. After all, the bad check might have been an innocent mistake. The police department or district attorney can tell you whether you must send a notice and what the notice must contain. But again, in any oral or written communication with the customer who passed the bad check, avoid the temptation to threaten prosecution. Such a threat might constitute harassment or extortion under some state statutes.

What are the chances of law enforcement officials taking action? Some police departments and prosecuting officials drag their feet on these kinds of cases, saying that they don't want to be used as a collection agency. Others are far more cooperative. Some of the best have bad-check programs under which the person who has written the check is contacted and given a chance to avoid being prosecuted by making the check good and, in some counties, by attending special classes.

Step 5. Use Small Claims Court

If you still haven't been paid, consider suing in small claims court, as long as the check is for less than the maximum amount you can sue for in small claims—or close enough that you don't mind giving up your right to collect the rest. Most states have limits between $5,000 and $15,000. As noted in Step 2, if you've followed the bad-check procedures in your state, you might be entitled to two or even three times the amount of the check as damages, as well as your court-filing and service-of-process costs. And if the check writer has a job, you'll generally be able to use postjudgment proceedings to get paid out of the worker's wages—although it's difficult to collect from the wages of low-income people. You might also be able to collect from bank or other deposit accounts. In most states, you can also cheaply and easily put a lien against the debtor's real estate. Chances are you'll ultimately be paid when the property is sold or a loan on the property is refinanced.

 RESOURCE
Learn how to represent yourself in small claims court. For information, tips, and strategies on how to sue someone in small claims court, see *Everybody's Guide to Small Claims Court* by Cara O'Neill (Nolo).

Step 6. Use a Collection Agency

Turning a bad check over to a collection agency is often worth considering. For smaller checks, going to small claims court might not be worthwhile. Or perhaps, despite the huge cut a collection agency takes, you might want to put your time and energy elsewhere. And while some states make small claims court fairly friendly to businesses (for example, you might be able to send an employee to court with business records), other states require that the business owner appear to testify in person. That might make suing the check writer more trouble than it's worth. So if you want to keep your personal involvement in the collection process to a minimum, stay open to the possibility of letting a collection agency do most of the work.

Extending Credit and Getting Paid

n this chapter, you'll find out how to establish credit practices that help ensure that you get paid when you should. You'll also learn how to comply with federal and state credit laws and what to do if customers, clients, or patients don't pay when they're supposed to.

The Practical Side of Extending Credit

Some businesses give customers 30 or 60 days to pay for goods and services. They might even let customers make installment payments over a longer period. For example, a small wholesaler of children's music products might require retail customers to pay at the time of sale but extend 30 days' credit to wholesale customers. Similarly, many professionals and other service providers extend short-term credit to clients and customers, who are expected to pay after receiving a monthly invoice.

If you extend credit, you need to set up a well-organized, accurate, easy-to-use system of accounts, send out bills periodically, and keep after those who pay slowly or not at all—all of which takes time, money, and effort.

Many small business people fantasize about avoiding the whole mess by requiring customers to pay cash. Unfortunately, this sort of daydreaming is normally just that; in many businesses and professional practices, it's almost impossible to operate if you don't extend credit.

Professional and Personal Service Businesses

In many professional or consulting practices, it used to be considered unusual to require a client or patient to complete a formal credit application. No longer. Today, credit applications are becoming routine, because businesses simply can't afford to provide services unless they get paid. But if you shy away from a formal application, you can still gather much pertinent information from your new client or patient intake sheet. Ask where the person works and banks. Ask for the name of the "nearest relative not living with you"—useful information if the client or patient skips out.

Health care professionals will, of course, want to inquire about insurance or Medicaid/Medicare coverage. Consider offering a modest discount (say, 5%) for payment at the time services are rendered—it usually leads to prompt payment. Also, if you accept credit cards, there's really no reason for the patient not to pay on the spot.

Lawyers, accountants, appraisers, engineers, dentists, and other professionals may appropriately ask for advance payment to be applied against the first batch of services, especially if a new client or patient needs extensive services. One way to do this is to present a fee letter to each new client. The letter might state that new clients are asked to pay a retainer and that future payments are due ten days from billing. (See "Putting Professional Relationships on a Sound Financial Footing," below.)

Another positive thing a professional or consultant can do is to routinely record bank account data about the client or patient as payment is received. Then, if you have to sue the client or patient, you have one more place to turn to try to satisfy your judgment.

If you're worried that someone isn't creditworthy —particularly if the bill is likely to mount rapidly —you can run a quick credit check with a credit reporting agency. Credit checks are so routine these days that this won't drive away business. However, you should notify the client or patient beforehand. Also, before using credit reports, familiarize yourself with the federal Fair Credit Reporting Act and similar state laws. (See "Laws That Regulate Consumer Credit," below.) For example, if you reject credit for a client or patient based on a credit report, you need to disclose this to the person, as well as the name, address, and phone number of the credit reporting agency that gave you the negative information.

Putting Professional Relationships on a Sound Financial Footing

If you have a professional practice or run a consulting or personal service business, consider giving each client or patient a written statement of your billing procedures, so that they know what to expect.

It is also businesslike and inoffensive to prepare a letter of retention spelling out the services you'll be performing, how much you'll be charging, when you'll be billing, and when payment is due. Such letters might even be legally required. In California, for example, lawyers and clients must sign a fee agreement if the expected fee is more than $1,000 or the fee is contingent on the outcome of a lawsuit.

You could even take the retention letter one step further by providing payment envelopes for the patients to use in sending their monthly checks. This approach works for professionals where fairly predictable services are delivered over a defined time period.

Your letter should state when you expect to be paid—usually within ten days of the statement date. Also, list the amount of any interest or finance charges you'll assess (as permitted by state law) if payment is late, and reserve your right to stop rendering services. (In a few professions, rules of professional ethics might affect how and when you can terminate the relationship.) Have the client or patient acknowledge in writing receipt of your letter and agreement to its terms.

Wholesale and Manufacturing Businesses

If you're a wholesale or service business—a shoe wholesaler, software company, or clothing manufacturer, for example—you should have a credit policy and you should insist that customers complete a formal application for credit. The details of your credit policy will depend on the kind of business you're in and the type of customers you serve. Here are some issues to think about:

- How many days after billing is payment due?
- Is there a discount for early payment?
- Do you require prepayment or "COD" ("cash on delivery") terms for certain classes of customers?
- Do you add interest or finance charges? If so, how much?
- When are credit checks required? (For example, you obviously wouldn't require a credit check if the customer is the government and probably wouldn't for a major, well-established company. On the other hand, you likely would want to check on the credit of a new small business or an individual making a large purchase.)
- How are credit limits determined?
- When and how often do you send past-due notices and follow up with phone calls?
- Do you keep selling to a customer whose account is overdue?
- At what point will you begin aggressive credit efforts?

When you approve credit for new trade accounts, let them know the maximum credit you're allowing and when they're expected to pay—as well as other relevant features of your credit policy.

A sample credit application form designed for trade accounts is shown below.

Sample Credit Application

Credit Application

The undersigned company is applying for credit with ABC ELECTRICAL, INC., and agrees to abide by the standard terms and conditions of ABC ELECTRICAL, INC., as printed on the reverse side.

Company name _____

DBA (if different) _____

Contact person _____

Address _____

Phone (____) _____ Fax (____) _____ Email (____) _____

Federal Tax ID or Social Security no. _____

Type of business_____

No. of employees _____ Date business established _____

Types of products you will purchase _____

_____ Amount of credit requested $_____

Are You a:

☐ Corporation

State of incorporation _____

Names, titles, and addresses of your three chief corporate officers _____

_____

_____

Name and address of your resident agent _____

_____

☐ Limited Liability Company (LLC)

State where formed _____

Names, titles, and addresses of your three chief managers or members _____

_____

_____

Name and address of your resident agent _____

☐ Partnership

Names and addresses of the partners_____

_____

_____

☐ Sole Proprietorship

Are you sales tax exempt?   ☐ Yes   ☐ No

Have you ever had credit with us before?   ☐ Yes   ☐ No

If yes, under what name? _____

Authorized purchasers _____

Purchase order required?   ☐ Yes   ☐ No

Sample Credit Application (continued)

Trade References

Reference #1   Name _____

Address _____

Email _____   Phone (____) _____

Reference #2   Name _____

Address _____

Email _____   Phone (____) _____

Reference #3   Name _____

Address _____

Email _____   Phone (____) _____

Bank References

Bank #1   Account #_____   Phone (____) _____

Contact person _____

Name of bank _____

Address _____

Bank #2   Account #_____   Phone (____) _____

Contact person _____

Name of bank _____

Address _____

I represent that the above information is true and is given to induce ABC ELECTRICAL, INC., to extend credit to the applicant. My company and I authorize ABC ELECTRICAL, INC., to make such credit investigation as ABC ELECTRICAL, INC., sees fit, including contacting the above trade references and banks and obtaining credit reports. My company and I authorize all trade references, banks, and credit reporting agencies to disclose to ABC ELECTRICAL, INC., any and all information concerning the financial and credit history of my company.

I have read the terms and conditions stated below and agree to all of those terms and conditions.

Authorized signature: _____

Printed name: _____

Title: _____

Date: _____

Sample Credit Application (continued)

Personal Guarantee of Corporate or LLC Officer

In consideration of ABC ELECTRICAL, INC., extending credit to _____

_____ , I personally guarantee payment for all items and

services purchased on credit by that corporation or LLC.

Signature: _____

Printed name: _____

Date: _____

General Terms and Conditions

1. Bills are sent on the first day of each month. You may take the 5% discount as indicated on the bill if you pay the invoice by the 10th of the month.

2. All bills become payable in full on the 11th day of the month and, if not paid by the end of the month, are considered past due.

3. A service charge of 2% per month will be added to all amounts billed if not paid by the end of the month.

4. No additional credit will be extended to past-due accounts unless satisfactory arrangements are made with our credit department.

Should You Charge Interest?

Most businesses don't charge interest or impose finance charges in exchange for granting credit. More typically, interest is charged when bills aren't paid within the agreed time, often between ten and 30 days. If you decide to impose these charges, you must inform the customer how the charges will be computed. The Truth in Lending Act, which applies primarily to sales to consumers, prescribes the disclosures you must make—but not the rates you can charge. That's done by state law.

One reason to consider adding interest or finance charges after a certain date is that customers who are short of cash tend to pay first the bills that carry such charges. Other incentives for early payment include:

- discounts for prompt payment—for example, 5% off if the customer pays the bill on the spot or within ten days
- free shipping and handling (a big item these days) for customers who prepay
- making the customer responsible for paying for court costs and reasonable attorneys' fees required to enforce collection if the customer doesn't pay as agreed. The customer must agree to this, either in a credit application or a separate contract.

Extending Credit to Businesses

When the customer is another business, it's wise to get information about whom you're really dealing with—especially if the business wants a substantial amount of credit. Is the customer a sole proprietor? A partnership? A corporation? The answer determines who's liable for the debt. If the business is owned by an individual who hasn't incorporated or formed a limited liability company (for example, Bill Jones doing business as Jones Products), the owner's own assets—as well as those of the business— are available to satisfy the debt. With a general partnership, you can go after the assets of the individual partners, if necessary, so it's a good idea to have the names of all the partners listed on the credit application. A limited partnership, on the other hand, consists of general partners and limited partners; only the assets of the general partners are available to satisfy the debts of a limited partnership. (See Chapter 1 for more information.)

With a corporation or an LLC, you usually are limited to collecting from the business assets. Because you can't collect from the personal bank accounts of the officers and shareholders, there's good reason to seek personal guarantees when dealing with a new or small corporation that wants substantial credit. In some businesses, however, it's completely against trade practices to ask for a personal guarantee. It's your job to learn the practices in your industry before using a personal guarantee like the one shown in the sample credit application above. If you do decide to seek personal guarantees, check out whether or not a signature on a credit application is sufficient in your state. The law might require that you obtain a new guarantee each time you extend credit to a company.

You might also want to ask for the personal guarantees of others if someone who applies for personal credit has weak financial status. Maybe a friend or family member will agree to be responsible if the customer doesn't pay on time. This is often called "cosigning." You can obtain the personal guarantee or cosignature on the credit application form or on a separate document called "Guarantee of Payment."

As noted above, in some states, a personal guarantee on an application form or a one-time separate document might not suffice. You might need to get a signature from the guarantor each time you extend credit.

References and Credit Checks

Your credit application should provide space for the applicant to list several other businesses that will vouch for the fact that the applicant pays on time. Check these references carefully, even though the credit applicant will probably list people who will say positive things. Your job is to try to penetrate the facade many credit applicants are sure to present that everything is just fine.

If the amount of credit you're extending is large, don't stop with checking a few references. Purchase a credit report on an individual from a national credit reporting agency such as TransUnion, Experian, or Equifax or, on a business, from Dun & Bradstreet. Check their websites for more information.

To get a report on an individual, most agencies want the name, address, phone number, Social Security number, and date of birth, if possible, of the person you're asking them to search—information you should get on your credit application form.

Be wary of negative information in credit reports, which might be inaccurate or out of date. If an individual seems to be otherwise well qualified for credit, consider extending a chance to explain the negative stuff before you deny credit.

CAUTION

Guard against misuse of credit report information. To comply with an FTC rule, you should store credit reports—and information you derive from them—in a safe place, such as a locked cabinet. Use a secure password for computerized versions of the information. You want to prevent identity theft and other illegal use of the information. At some point, you won't have a legitimate business need for the information. When that time comes, shred the physical documents and delete the computer file.

Signatures for Receipt of Goods

Have customers sign receipts when they receive merchandise on credit. If you provide services, have customers sign an acknowledgment of services performed. This avoids arguments about whether or not the customer actually received the goods or services.

Laws That Regulate Consumer Credit

Many small businesses don't extend credit directly to consumers. With the widespread availability of credit cards, this is often the safest and most cost-effective way to go. However, if yours is a business where credit must be granted, you must comply with federal laws affecting credit sales to consumers for personal, family, or household purposes. States have also adopted consumer credit laws that mirror many provisions of federal law.

Here's an introduction to the major federal laws that affect consumer credit.

The Truth in Lending Act

This statute requires you to disclose your exact credit terms to people who apply for credit, so they'll know what they're expected to pay. It also regulates how you advertise consumer credit. Among the items you must disclose to a consumer who buys on credit are:
- the monthly finance charge
- the annual interest rate
- when payments are due
- the total sale price, which includes the cash price of the item or service, plus all other charges, and
- the amount of any late payment charges and when they'll be imposed.

The Equal Credit Opportunity Act

You may not discriminate against an applicant on the basis of race, color, religion, national origin, age, sex, or marital status. The act does leave you free to consider legitimate factors in granting credit, such as the applicant's financial status (earnings and savings) and credit record. Despite the prohibition on age discrimination, you can reject a consumer who hasn't reached the legal age in your state for entering into contracts.

The Fair Credit Reporting Act

This law deals primarily with credit reports issued by credit reporting agencies. It's intended to protect consumers from having their eligibility for credit thwarted by inaccurate or obsolete credit report information. The law gives consumers the right to a copy of their credit reports. If they feel something is inaccurate, they can ask that it be corrected or removed. If the business reporting the credit problem doesn't agree to a change or deletion or if the credit bureau refuses to make it, the consumer can add a 100-word statement to the file explaining the other side of the story. This becomes a part of any future credit report.

The law also deals with a denial of credit. If your business denies credit to a consumer based wholly or partly on something in that person's credit report, you must give the consumer a written notice that you've done so. Your notice must include the name, address, and phone number of the agency that provided the report. The consumer can then seek a correction of inaccurate information or can add an explanation to the credit report, as noted above.

The Fair Debt Collection Practices Act

This statute addresses abusive methods used by third-party collectors—bill collectors you hire to collect overdue bills. Small businesses are more directly affected by state laws that apply directly to collection methods used by a creditor. (See "Collection Problems," below.)

RESOURCE
Want to learn more about consumer credit?
Check out the Credit & Finance section of the FTC's Business Center website at www.ftc.gov/tips-advice/business-center/credit-and-finance; be sure to see the helpful guide called *Complying with the Credit Practices Rule.* You'll also find useful information in the Personal Finance section of www.nolo.com.

A fine Nolo book discusses these issues from the perspective of the consumer: *Solve Your Money Troubles: Strategies to Get Out of Debt and Stay That Way,* by Amy Loftsgordon and Cara O'Neill.

Becoming a Secured Creditor

If you sell major amounts of merchandise or equipment to a customer on credit, look into becoming a secured creditor. If a debt is secured by property ("collateral"), you can seize that property if the customer doesn't pay the debt as promised. Businesses commonly take a "security interest" in the goods they sell on credit.

For example, a store that sells furniture on credit keeps a security interest in the furniture. If the buyer gets behind on payments, the store can take the furniture back, without having to file and win a lawsuit to collect the debt. Under federal and state laws dealing with billing problems, the store might still be subject to penalties for failing to comply with the required procedures.

Sales of Merchandise or Equipment

The Uniform Commercial Code (UCC), which has been adopted by all states, allows you to acquire a legal (security) interest in the property that you sell to the customer—or in other property of the customer—so you can sell or take back the property if the customer doesn't pay. Typically, you have the customer sign a financing agreement and you file a UCC *Financing Statement* with the appropriate public office, such as the county clerk or the secretary of state (it varies from state to state).

Also, if the customer files for bankruptcy, you'll have a big advantage over general (unsecured) creditors—those who didn't take a security interest in the customer's property. The property in which you have a security interest will be earmarked for your benefit. Unsecured creditors get only a share of the bankrupt's unsecured assets—which might repay only a tiny portion of what's owed or (often) nothing at all.

Obviously, it takes time and requires some paper-work and expense to create a security interest. It might not be worth it if you sell someone a $500 washing machine (it's a lot easier to take credit cards and require full payment)—but definitely worth doing when the product is a $10,000 computer system. Banks routinely obtain a security interest when they lend money to a customer to purchase equipment.

Incidentally, as an alternative to extending credit on larger purchases, one option is to refer the customer to a bank or leasing company—particularly one with whom you've established a working relationship. These organizations are in business to take credit risks and can absorb losses better than you can.

Special Rights for Those in the Construction Business

A "lien" is a legal claim on someone's property. Under state law, you may have a mechanic's, materialman's, or construction lien on real estate if you provided materials or labor on a construction or renovation project—for example, if you supplied the lighting fixtures or installed the roofing for a new house. If your bill isn't paid, you can "foreclose" on your lien. This means the real estate can be sold to pay your bill.

To take advantage of this powerful weapon to protect your rights, many states require you to file certain legal documents claiming ("perfecting") a lien within a short time after you complete your work or supply the materials. Speak to a construction industry trade association or, if necessary, a lawyer about how to do this.

Collection Problems

Despite your best efforts to screen your customers, if you extend credit, sooner or later you're going to run into people or businesses who are slow in paying. It can be one of the most frustrating aspects of running a business. Part of the reason is that you might be pursuing several objectives that are not compatible. Here's what I mean:

- You want to be paid in full, of course, but—
- you'd also like to continue doing business with the customer, if possible; what's more—
- you don't want to run afoul of laws that restrict or prohibit aggressive collection tactics, and
- you don't want to waste your resources on a wild goose chase.

It's not an easy problem, but a number of techniques can help keep your losses to a minimum.

Strategies for Avoiding or Reducing Losses

Following these suggestions should help you hold down your losses on credit transactions:

- Send bills promptly and rebill at least monthly. There's no need to wait for the end of the month.
- Make sure your bills clearly state the goods sold or the services provided. It's a great idea to include on the bill a request to the customer to contact you if there are problems with the goods or services. If the customer fails to do so and later tries to excuse the failure to pay by claiming the goods or services were unsatisfactory, you have a good argument that the customer is fabricating a phony excuse. Another benefit is that if your goods or services are in fact prone to problems, you open up lines of communication and usually can keep the customer happy.
- Enclose a self-addressed envelope (preferably stamped) to facilitate payment.
- Keep a record of the checking account that the customer uses to pay you.
- Send past-due notices promptly when an account is overdue. Ask clearly for payment. Many people worry that the word "pay" sounds too blunt. Here are a few alternate phrases, courtesy of collection expert Leonard Sklar, author of *The Check Is NOT in the Mail* (Baroque Publishing):

"We'd appreciate it if you would *clear your account.*"

"You can *take care of this* by cash or check, whichever you prefer."

"Please *bring your account current.*"

- If this doesn't work, promptly telephone to ask what's wrong. The customer needs to know that you follow these matters closely. Do not extend more credit, no matter what the hard luck story. This is particularly important. Lots of businesses facing tight finances pay only when they need more merchandise. If you let them have it without payment, you're showing them that you're a pushover.

- Have a series of letters to use in routine cases. These letters should escalate in intensity as time goes by. (See the discussion of collection letters later in this section.)

- If the customer has genuine financial problems, find out what the customer realistically can afford. Consider extending the time for payment if the customer agrees in writing to a new payment schedule. Call the day before the next scheduled payment is due to be sure the customer plans to respect the agreement.

- Save copies of all correspondence with the customer and keep notes of all telephone conversations.

- Watch out for checks for less than the full amount that say "payment in full." In some states, if you deposit the check—especially if the amount owed is in dispute—you might have wiped out the balance owed. (See Chapter 18 for more information.) Learn the law in your state before you deposit such a check.

- Continue to keep in contact with—but don't harass—the customer.

- If an account is unpaid for an extended period and you're doubtful about ever collecting, consider offering in writing a time-limited, deep discount to resolve the matter. This way, the customer has the incentive to borrow money to take advantage of your one-time, never-again offer to settle.

- When collection starts to put heavy demands on your time and your chances of recovery are slim because you know the customer is on the skids, consider turning the debt over to a collection agency so you can get on with more productive activities. (But first consider the collection alternatives described at the end of this chapter.)

Collection Letters

You might find it useful to develop a set of past-due notices to use when customers fall behind. Although these are form letters, it's easy to customize them using your computer and word processing software. In writing to an individual customer, use the customer's name. In writing to a company, address your letter to the owner or chief operating office. It's less effective to start out with "Dear Customer" or "Dear Accounts Payable Supervisor."

Your first letter might suggest that perhaps the bill was overlooked and that payment should be sent now so that the customer can maintain a good credit rating. Your second and third letters should be polite but increasingly firm. Vary the format of your letters. Each one should look a little different. Samples are shown below.

Sample Collection Letter 1

Account no. _____

Dear _____ :

Our records show that you have an outstanding balance with our company of $450. This is for (*describe the goods or services*).

Is there a problem with this bill? If so, please call me so that we can resolve the matter. Otherwise, please send your payment at this time to bring your account current. I'm enclosing a business reply envelope for you to use.

Until you bring your account current, it's our policy to put further purchases on a cash basis.

Sincerely,

P.S. Paying your bill at this time will help you to maintain your good credit rating.

Sample Collection Letter 2

Re: Overdue bill ($_____)

Account no. _____

Dear _____ :

Your bill for $450 is seriously overdue. This is for the (*describe the goods or services furnished*) we supplied to you last (*state the month*). More than 60 days have gone by since we sent you our invoice. You did not respond to the letter I sent you last month.

We value your patronage but must insist that you bring your account up to date. Doing so will help you protect your reputation for prompt payment.

Please send your check today for the full balance. If this is not feasible, please call me to discuss a possible payment plan. I need to hear from you as soon as possible.

Sincerely,

Sample Collection Letter 3

Re: Collection action on _____

Overdue bill ($_____)

Account no. _____

Dear _____ :

We show an unpaid balance of $450 on your account that is over 90 days old. This is for the (*describe the goods or services furnished*) that we supplied you over (*insert number*) days ago.

I have repeatedly tried to contact you, but my calls and letters have gone unheeded.

You must send full payment by (*date*) or contact me by that date to discuss your intentions. If I do not hear from you, I plan to turn over the account for collection.

As you know, collection action can only have an adverse effect on your credit rating, and, according to our credit agreement, you will be responsible for collection costs. I hope to hear from you immediately so that the matter can be resolved without taking that step.

Sincerely,

Prohibited Collection Practices

Because of abuses, Congress passed the Fair Debt Collection Practices Act to regulate the activities of collection agencies. The federal law applies only to third-party collection agencies, not to small businesses that collect their own bills. Many state laws, however, do crack down on the aggressive collection techniques of such businesses. And in states where the legislature hasn't yet acted, court decisions often penalize businesses that harass debtors or use unfair collection tactics.

Most business owners know intuitively the kind of behavior that's out of bounds. Here are some debt collection practices specifically outlawed by California's Fair Debt Collection Practices statute:

- using or threatening to use physical force to collect a debt
- falsely threatening that the failure to pay a consumer debt will result in an accusation that the debtor has committed a crime
- using obscene or profane language
- causing expense to the debtor for long distance calls
- causing a phone to ring repeatedly or continuously to annoy the debtor
- communicating with the debtor so often as to be unreasonable and to constitute harassment, or
- communicating with the debtor's employer regarding a consumer debt, unless the communication is necessary or the debtor has consented in writing. (A communication is "necessary," according to the statute, only to verify the debtor's employment, to locate the debtor, or to carry out a garnishment of wages after you have sued and won a judgment.)

The list goes on and on. If there's a similar statute in your state, get a copy and read it carefully. Like California's, most state laws in this field are modeled on the federal law. Some statutes, however, are more specific than others; for example, some list specific hours during which you can call the debtor.

Collection Options

Suppose you can't get the customer to pay up voluntarily. What next? If you're not willing to write off the debt (which is sometimes the wisest thing to do), you have three collection options:

- sue in small claims court
- hire a lawyer, or
- turn the account over to a collection agency.

Each choice has pros and cons.

Small claims court is inexpensive and speedy. The downside is that it can take a good chunk of your time. Furthermore, any judgment that you receive might be worthless if the debtor lacks a job or bank account.

Lawyers can be effective, but they're expensive. Consider using a lawyer to write collection letters. Many lawyers are willing to do this for a nominal charge.

Collection agencies are good at tracing elusive debtors, but they take a big percentage of what they collect for you.

Put It in Writing: Small Business Contracts

As the owner of a small business, it's likely that you'll often encounter both written and oral contracts. The most important piece of advice about contracts is obvious: Put all important agreements in writing. This chapter shows you how and tells you what to do if something goes wrong.

What Makes a Valid Contract

A valid contract requires two and sometimes three elements:

- an agreement ("meeting of the minds") between the parties
- "consideration"—a legal term meaning the exchange of things of value, and
- something in writing, if the contract covers certain matters, such as the sale of real estate and tasks that can't be completed in one year. (See "Must a Contract Be in Writing?" below.)

For example, suppose you're opening a new store. You meet with Joe, a sign maker, to discuss the construction and installation of a five-foot-by-three-foot sign. Joe offers to do the work for $450 and to have the sign ready for your grand opening on June 15. "It's a deal," you say. You now have a legally binding contract, enforceable in court or by arbitration. All the necessary elements are present:

- **An Agreement.** Joe offered to build and install the sign at a certain price by a certain date. You accepted the offer by telling Joe, "It's a deal."
- **Consideration.** The two of you are exchanging something of value. You're giving your promise to pay $450. Joe is giving his promise to build and install the sign.
- **Written Agreement Not Required Here.** Normal business contracts that can be performed in less than a year don't have to be in writing to be enforceable.

To understand why "consideration" is important, let's explore the difference between a contract and a gift. Assume that Joe installs the sign on time and you pay him $450 as agreed. Impressed by the high quality of his work, you say: "Joe, to thank you for the great job you did, I'm going to send you a $100 bonus next week." Can Joe enforce your promise to pay the bonus? No. He got what he bargained for—the $450 payment. He didn't promise you anything (consideration) for the extra $100 payment. If you pay it, fine. If not, Joe can't force you to.

Negotiations

Negotiations, which might or might not lead to an agreement, do not constitute a contract. Let's say you call Joe and describe the job. He says he can probably do it for about $450. You say, "Thanks, let me think about it." There was no agreement, so you don't have a contract.

Offer and Acceptance

If after negotiations, two people reach an agreement, a contract is formed. Say that after discussing the job with you by phone, Joe promptly sends you a letter in which he says: "I can build and install the sign shown on the enclosed sketch for $450. I'll have it in place by June 15 when you open. You can pay me then." You send back a fax saying: "Sounds good. Go ahead." This is a valid contract. Joe has made a clear offer. You've just as clearly accepted that offer. The fact that you and Joe didn't meet face to face and didn't even use the same type of communication medium doesn't alter this conclusion.

In this example, you accepted Joe's offer promptly. But what if you'd waited two weeks or two months to accept? The legal rule is that an offer without a stated expiration date remains open for a reasonable time. What's reasonable depends on the type of business and the facts of the situation. If you're offered a truckload of fish or flowers, it might be unreasonable to delay your acceptance more than a few hours or even minutes, while an offer to sell surplus wood chips at a time when the market is glutted might reasonably be assumed to be good for a month or more. But there's really no need to tolerate any uncertainty in this regard. Include a clear deadline for acceptance when you present an offer. If you want to accept an offer, do it as promptly as possible.

Counteroffers

In the real world, negotiations aren't usually as simple as making an offer and having it accepted. And until an agreement is reached, there's no contract.

For example, say Joe sends you the letter offering to provide your sign for $450. You call his office and leave a message on his voice mail saying: "Go ahead, but I can only pay $400." So far, there's no contract. By changing the terms of Joe's offer, you've rejected it and made a "counteroffer." The two of you are still negotiating. If Joe calls back and says, "Okay, I'll do it for $400," you now have a binding contract. Joe has accepted your counteroffer. Again, the fact that you and Joe weren't in the same room or never spoke to each other isn't significant. What is key is that one of you made an offer (in this case, in the form of a counteroffer), and the other accepted it.

Revoking an Offer

Until an offer is accepted, it can be revoked by the person who made it. So if you're about to write Joe a letter accepting his offer, and Joe calls to revoke his offer because he's decided $450 isn't enough, you're out of luck. Joe revoked his offer before you accepted it, so there's no contract.

Option to Keep Offer Open

If you want someone to keep an offer open while you think about it, you might have to pay for the privilege. If you do and the person who made the offer agrees to keep it open, your agreement (which is itself a contract) is called an "option." Options are commonly used when real estate or businesses are sold.

To stay with our sign example, say that when Joe sends you the letter offering to provide your sign, you tell him you're not ready to respond yet, but you want to be sure the offer will stay open while you think about it. Joe responds that if you pay $100 now, he'll keep his offer open for two more weeks. You pay the $100 and accept the offer within the two-week period. The resulting contract would be valid even if Joe tried to withdraw his offer before the end of the two-week period. You and Joe already have a contract (an option), which consists of your right to purchase his services at the $450 price if you act within the two-week period. He received something of value (your $100) in return for granting you this option.

How an Offer to Contract Ends

1. The person who made the offer revokes it before it's accepted.
2. The offer expires.

   EXAMPLE: "This offer will expire automatically if I don't receive your acceptance by noon on May 10." But unless you've been paid something to keep the offer open (as is common for an option to buy real property or a business), you (the offeror) can still revoke the unaccepted offer before the period for acceptance expires.

3. A reasonable time elapses. There are no hard and fast rules as to what's reasonable. It all depends on circumstances and the practices in your industry.
4. The offer is rejected. If you reject an offer and then change your mind, it's too late. To get the deal going again, you'll need to make a new offer to the other party.
5. Either party dies before the offer is accepted.

How Offers Are Accepted

Usually, offers are accepted either in writing or orally. But that's not always necessary. It is an area of considerable legal complexity, but generally an offer can be accepted by a prompt action that conforms with the terms of the offer. For example, you might leave the sign builder Joe a note at his workshop, saying "Please add a red border to this sign today; I'll pay you an extra $100." Joe comes back that afternoon and adds the red border. You're obligated to pay him.

An Advertisement as an Offer

Under traditional contract law, ads are considered only invitations to negotiate or to make an offer; you have no obligation to go through with the deal just because someone offers to meet your advertised price. So if a customer appears and says she wants to buy the house, land, or business that you advertised in the classifieds for $200,000, there's no binding contract. One major exception to this rule involves rewards. Generally, an ad offering to pay a reward is binding if someone performs the requested act.

Consumer protection laws have also changed this traditional rule. For example, the law in many states requires merchants to stock advertised items in quantities large enough to meet reasonably expected demand, unless the ad states that stock is limited. And some states require the merchant to give a rain check allowing the consumer to purchase the same merchandise at the same price at a later date. (See Chapter 17 for more on consumer transactions.)

Unfair or Illegal Contracts

What if a person makes a bad bargain? Suppose you agree to pay $800 for a used laser printer that's worth only $200. Can you call off the deal on the ground that the contract was grossly unfair? Probably not. As long as there's a valid contract, it doesn't usually matter whether or not the item is objectively worth the price paid for it.

Sometimes, however, a court sets aside a contract if the terms are unconscionable. For example, a judge or an arbitrator might release an unsophisticated consumer (say a recent immigrant who isn't fluent in English) from a grossly unfair contract extracted by a sophisticated, high-pressure salesperson. Applying this principle of law, a contract to sell a $500 television for $5,000 might be set aside. But even though a judge might cite contract law, the decision would probably be based more on the doctrine of fraud or misrepresentation. Or the decision might be based on a state consumer protection statute that prohibits taking advantage of people who can't protect their interests because of disability, illiteracy, or a language problem. (See Chapter 17 for more on this type of statute.)

When it comes to reasonably experienced businesspeople working out contracts with each other, however, unfairness is rarely if ever a legal ground for setting aside a contract. Usually, a party who negotiates a bad deal is stuck with it.

If a contract clause is illegal or against public policy, the judge or arbitrator won't enforce it. For example, a remodeling contract stating that neither party will obtain a legally required building permit would be void as a violation of public policy, as would a similar contract obligating a party to bribe a building inspector.

Misrepresentation, Duress, or Mistake

If, before you sign a contract, the other person tells you a false statement about something important, and you rely on that statement in signing the contract, you can go to court and have the contract "rescinded" (canceled). This is so even if the other person doesn't realize that the fact is untrue. For example, say you buy a pickup truck for your business, relying on the seller's assertion that the truck can carry loads up to two tons. It turns out that the seller got the numbers wrong, and the truck can only carry one-ton loads. You can have the contract rescinded. If you have a contract rescinded, you must return any benefits you already received. In this example, you'd have to return the pickup truck to the seller to get your money back.

If you accept "an offer you can't refuse"—because, for example, the offer is made at gunpoint—the contract isn't legally enforceable. The same is true of any other contract made as a result of unlawful threats. For example, if one party threatens to report the other party to the IRS or a state agency if a one-sided contract isn't signed, the contract isn't enforceable.

Breach of Warranty
Sometimes a buyer can return goods to the seller and get a refund based on a breach of warranty. While the practical result in such cases might be the same as setting aside a contract for the reasons mentioned in this section, a different legal concept is at work.
An action for breach of warranty assumes that there's a valid contract. A buyer who seeks a refund based on breach of warranty is saying: "I acknowledge that we have a binding contract. I want to enforce my rights under that contract for breach of warranty." (See Chapter 17.)

A mistake is the other ground for rescission of a contract. You thought you were buying a two-year-old computer. The seller thought you were buying her five-year-old computer. If you were both acting in good faith and simply miscommunicated, a judge or an arbitrator would probably set aside the contract. But you can't avoid liability if you simply used bad judgment and paid too much for a five-year-old computer that doesn't provide the quality or speed you need.

Must a Contract Be in Writing?

Unless a contract falls into one of several specific categories, it is binding even if it's not in writing. You should put all important contracts in writing anyway. Otherwise, you run the risk of a dispute as to exactly what was promised, how much was to be paid, when the contract was to be performed, and on and on. And if you argue so long that you end up in court, it can be somewhere between difficult and impossible (not to mention expensive) to prove the existence and terms of an oral contract.

Contracts That Must Be in Writing

Each state has a statute (usually called the "statute of frauds") listing the types of contracts that must be written to be valid. A typical list includes the following:

Contracts Involving the Sale of Real Estate or an Interest in Real Estate

Examples are a contract to purchase a building or parking lot or a contract to sell someone the right to use part of your land for a certain purpose (an "easement").

Leases of Real Estate Lasting Longer Than One Year

An example is a three-year lease for retail space in a neighborhood shopping plaza.

A Promise to Pay Someone Else's Debt

This generally involves guarantees of payment. For example, the president of a corporation personally guarantees to pay for any goods you sell to the corporation; or an uncle guarantees to pay the rent for his nephew's new store.

Contracts That Will Take More Than One Year to Perform

This provision of a statute of frauds applies only to contracts that cannot be performed within one year; for example, a contract to provide landscaping services to a hotel for a two-year period.

If performance of a contract is possible within one year, the contract doesn't have to be in writing. How about a contract to plant three maple trees within the next two years? Because the trees could be planted right away, the contract doesn't have to be in writing to be enforceable. Here are several more examples of oral contracts performable within one year (and therefore enforceable):

- a contract to teach four new employees within the next 18 months how to use a software program
- a contract to cater a total of ten sales banquets for a corporation at dates to be selected by the corporation during the next three years, or
- a contract to remove debris from the sites of five new homes to be completed within the next two years.

Contracts for the Sale of Goods (Tangible Personal Property) Worth $500 or More

A contract to sell you a laptop computer for $2,000, for example, must be in writing to be enforceable. If you call a computer store and they agree over the phone to sell you the computer for $2,000 but raise the price to $2,500 when you get there, you don't have an enforceable contract.

Under the Uniform Commercial Code (UCC), however, the written contract doesn't have to state the price or time of delivery—only that the parties agree on the sale of goods and the quantity of goods being sold. And in some cases, if the seller simply sends a written confirmation of an oral order and the buyer doesn't promptly object, a contract has been formed. These UCC exceptions are very important; be sure to read "The Sale of Goods: Special Uniform Commercial Code Rules," below, which explains them in more detail.

There's an important exception to the rule that contracts for the sale of goods worth $500 must be in writing: If an oral contract is partially performed, the whole contract becomes binding. For example, say a salesperson offers to sell you a computer for $2,000 and to throw in a modem when the store gets its next shipment in a week. You pay the $2,000 and take the computer home. When you return to the store the next week to pick up your modem, the store denies that it owes you one. You could sue successfully for breach of contract even though you don't have a written contract for a sale of goods over $500. The reason is that partial performance of the oral contract (your payment and the store's partial delivery of the merchandise) removes the transaction from the written contract requirements in the statute of frauds. Of course, as a practical matter, it would have been better to get the whole deal in writing.

What Constitutes a Written Contract

When state law does require a contract to be in writing, it doesn't mean you need a long-winded document labeled "contract" or "agreement" and signed by both parties. Especially in a business context, judges recognize and enforce writings that contain few details. All that's typically required is a letter, memo, or any other writing signed by the party against whom the contract is being enforced. The writing must identify the parties and generally describe the subject and the main terms and conditions of the agreement. That's all. The rules for what the writing must contain are even more relaxed for transactions covered by the Uniform Commercial Code, which automatically fills in many missing details. (See "The Sale of Goods: Special Uniform Commercial Code Rules," below.)

I don't recommend that you settle for the bare-bones legal requirements. Because businesspeople's memories—like everyone else's—are imperfect and because putting a contract in writing tends to highlight erroneous assumptions and because not everyone you deal with is completely trustworthy, you want important contracts to contain a reasonable amount of detail.

> **EXAMPLE:** Arnie, a fish shop operator, meets Phyllis, a phone equipment salesperson, at a trade show. Arnie becomes enthusiastic about purchasing a new telephone system for $3,000, which he believes covers the installation, including all wiring and control panels. Phyllis, the sales rep for FoneTek, thinks her company is providing just the phones themselves. If they go ahead on the basis of an oral contract, disaster clearly looms. If, however, Arnie and Phyllis sit down to write up a contract, the issues that haven't really been agreed on are sure to come out, and Arnie and Phyllis will have ample opportunity to make necessary adjustments or call the deal off.

The Sale of Goods: Special Uniform Commercial Code Rules

The Uniform Commercial Code (UCC) contains special rules affecting contracts for the sale of goods. It loosens up the requirements for creating a binding contract when goods are being sold.

The UCC requires you to produce something in writing if you want to enforce a contract for a sale of goods and the price is $500 or more. However, the UCC says that this writing can be very brief—briefer than a normal written contract. Under the UCC, the writing need only:

- indicate that the parties have agreed on the sale of the goods, and
- state the quantity of goods being sold.

If items such as price, time and place of delivery, or quality of the goods are missing, the UCC fills them in based on customs and practices in the particular industry.

CAUTION

Don't rely on sketchy contracts. Just because the UCC makes legal some very sketchy contracts for the sale of goods doesn't mean it's a good idea to routinely use such contracts. It's far better to put together a good written contract. (See "Writing Business-to-Business Contracts," below.)

Remember, if a customer comes to a store, pays for merchandise, and takes it away, there's no need for a formal written contract—the deal is done. (For larger purchases, it makes sense for the retailer to have the customer sign a receipt acknowledging delivery of the goods.) Under the UCC, having some writing is important when the seller merely promises to deliver the goods.

In most situations, the UCC requires that when a contract must be in writing to be enforceable, it must be signed by the person against whom the other party is seeking to enforce the contract. Stated another way, if A wants to sue B for breach of contract and a writing is required, A must show that B signed something showing an intent to be contractually bound.

But when merchants—people who sell goods—are involved, there doesn't always have to be a signed document. If a seller sends a confirmation of an order and the buyer doesn't object in writing within ten days after receiving it, nothing more is required to satisfy the written contract requirement.

Where the UCC Came From

In 1940, someone came up with a brilliant idea: Why not put together a comprehensive code (statute) covering all the branches of commercial law and get it adopted in all states? That way, businesses in Michigan, Illinois, Georgia, or Oregon would all follow the same rules.

It took 11 years to carry out this proposal, which resulted in a set of model statutes called the Uniform Commercial Code, or UCC. Every state except Louisiana has adopted it; Louisiana has adopted key portions of it. The UCC covers these areas of law:

- sales (including warranties; see Chapter 17)
- commercial paper (drafts, checks, certificates of deposit, and promissory notes)
- bank deposits and collections
- letters of credit
- warehouse receipts, bills of lading, and other documents of title
- investment securities, and
- secured transactions.

EXAMPLE: Nandita owns a retail store that sells shoes. Runner's Choice, Inc., a manufacturer, sends Nandita a notice saying: "This is to confirm that you agreed to buy 1,000 pairs of men's jogging shoes from this company." Under normal written contract rules, this wouldn't be enough to permit Runner's Choice to enforce a contract against Nandita, because she's signed nothing. But under the UCC, if Nandita doesn't object in writing within ten days after receiving the notice, she can't complain about the lack of a written document bearing her signature.

In this example, the notice from Runner's Choice satisfies the requirement that the contract be in writing. But if Runner's Choice sues Nandita for rejecting the shipment of shoes, it will still have to convince the judge or arbitrator that before Runner's Choice sent Nandita the notice, the parties actually reached an oral agreement regarding the shoes. In short, the notice, by itself, is not conclusive evidence that the parties reached a meeting of the minds. A contract signed by both sides is always preferable.

Valid contracts with no writing at all. Where specially manufactured goods are ordered, the UCC says you don't need something in writing to enforce a sales contract if the seller has already made a significant effort toward completing the terms of the contract.

> **EXAMPLE:** A restaurant calls and orders 500 sets of dishes from a restaurant supply company. The dishes are to feature the restaurant's logo. If the supply company makes a substantial beginning on manufacturing the dishes and applying the logo, the restaurant can't avoid liability on the contract simply because it was an oral agreement.

Checking Out the UCC

Your state laws (statutes) should be available in any law library in your state, in the reference section of many public libraries, and at Cornell University's Legal Information Institute website at www.law.cornell.edu/uniform/ucc.html. The Uniform Commercial Code is probably indexed under "uniform," "commercial," or "commerce." For most small businesses, the section on sales (Article 2) is the most helpful part of the UCC. The UCC changes fairly often; be sure you have the latest version that's been adopted in your state.

Writing Business-to-Business Contracts

Whatever your business, you'll need to write contracts from time to time. You'll probably need a written contract if you want to:

- buy or sell goods
- perform services as an independent contractor or consultant
- lease real estate or equipment
- manufacture, distribute, or license products
- enter into joint ventures
- grant credit, or
- advertise.

Checklist of Contract Clauses

The content of a contract depends, of course, on the type of transaction you're getting into. The checklist below includes items to consider when you draft a contract.

Additional Requirements for Specialized Contracts

Many states require specific provisions in contracts that cover certain types of transactions. Areas where special requirements are likely include:

- sales of new and used vehicles and mobile homes
- home improvement services
- motor vehicle repairs
- apartment and home rentals
- door-to-door sales, and
- funerals, burials, and cremations.

If you're in one of these regulated businesses, you not only need to use a written contract—you also need to make sure it conforms to your state's legal rules. Among other things, you might have to put certain information or warnings in type of a certain size, including a statement about the customer's right to cancel the deal under certain conditions. In some states, you might have to print the contract in Spanish as well as English.

> **EXAMPLE:** In Michigan, a statute requires a funeral director to insert the following language in boldface type in every prepaid funeral contract:

> This contract may be canceled either before death or after death by the buyer or, if the buyer is deceased, by the person or persons legally authorized to make funeral arrangements. If the contract is canceled, the buyer or the buyer's estate is entitled to receive a refund of ___ % of the contract price and any income earned from investment of the principal less administrative or escrow fees.

Checklist of Contract Clauses

☐ **Names and addresses of the parties.**

☐ **Date that the contract is signed.** (See "Signing Your Contracts," below, for suggestions about signing a contract.)

☐ **A short preamble ("recitals").** This provides some of the background of the agreement. For example, a contract might recite that Discs Unlimited is a retailer of compact discs and has three stores in the metropolitan area; that Stewart has an inventory management business; and that Discs Unlimited wishes to retain Stewart as an independent contractor to establish and maintain the company's inventory control system.

☐ **What each party is promising to do.** Pay money, provide a service, sell something, build something, or so on. Often this section of the contract—particularly if it involves a product or a construction project—is labeled "specifications." In many situations, such as designing software, constructing a building, or providing consulting services, the specifications require lengthy attachments that may include drawings, formulas, or charts. (See "Attachments to Contracts," below, for more information.)

☐ **When the work will be done or the product delivered.** If strict compliance with contract deadlines is important, be sure to include the phrase: "Time is of the essence." Otherwise, a judge might allow reasonable leeway in enforcing the deadlines.

☐ **How long the contract will remain in effect.**

☐ **The price—or how it will be determined.**

☐ **When payment is due.** Will there be installments, and will interest be charged? In contracts for consulting and other services, it's common to have a payment schedule tied to interim completion deadlines. For example, a contract for architectural services might provide for payment of one-third of the architect's fees when drawings and specifications are finished and approved;

one-third after bids have been received on the construction project and a contract signed with the general contractor; and one-third when the project is completed and a certificate of occupancy is issued by the building department.

☐ **Warranties.** If one party guarantees labor and materials for a certain period of time, what steps will be taken to correct warranty problems?

☐ **Conditions under which either party can terminate the agreement.**

☐ **"Liquidated damages" if performance is delayed or defective.** In cases where actual damages for breach of contract would be difficult to compute, the parties can establish in advance a fixed dollar amount (called liquidated damages) to be paid by a party who fails to perform its contractual obligations properly. (See "Enforcing Contracts in Court," below.)

☐ **Whether or not either party can transfer ("assign") the contract to another person or company.** A contract that allows assignment of contract rights might be okay if it involves just the right to receive money, but not if it means that some other, unknown party will wind up performing skilled services called for by the contract.

☐ **Arbitration or mediation of disputes.**

☐ **Whether or not a party who breaches the contract is responsible for the other party's attorneys' fees and legal costs.**

☐ **Where notices of default or other communications concerning the contract can be sent.** Typically, the notices are sent to the parties' business headquarters.

☐ **What state law applies if questions about the contract arise.** If the parties have operations in different states or the contract will be performed in more than one state, you can avoid potentially knotty legal issues by specifying which state law applies.

How to Design Your Contracts

You need contract forms that reflect the specialized nature of what you do, be it creating software, selling produce, publishing books, or cleaning buildings. This is especially true if your business is subject to consumer laws that require specific contract language. Typically, you'll need several basic types of contracts for your business, each with spaces to fill in the details of the specific transaction.

EXAMPLE: Brian is setting up a direct mail consulting business. He plans to work with local businesses to show them how to stay in better contact with customers by announcing sales, new merchandise, and seasonally extended hours. Brian needs a contract that covers what he'll do, when he'll do it, what he expects his small business clients to provide, warranties, responsibilities for proofreading and signing off on mailings, and payment.

Brian will also need to hire independent contractors—graphic designers, artists, and computer wizards—to help him carry out his contracts, so he'll also need a basic "work-for-hire" contract. Finally, Brian plans to use his experience to develop customized software for sale to similar businesses and so will need a basic software licensing agreement.

If you're new to your business, start by gathering copies of contracts used by other people in your field. Some kinds of contracts, such as commercial leases, are widely available. For other kinds, you might have to dig a bit. Trade associations, which commonly publish material containing sample contracts, are one good source. Other people in your line of work might be willing to share their contracts with you. Form books published for lawyers are an excellent starting point for developing your own specialized contract. Talk to the librarian at any major law library to find some suitable books.

Once you find a simple contract that's more or less suitable, make sure that you understand every word. Obviously, contracts written in plain English are better than those filled with legalese—but if the latter type is all you can find, it might not be too difficult to rewrite it. Next, write a rough draft of any additions you might need.

CAUTION

Professional help. If you plan to use a form contract for major transactions, consider reviewing it with a lawyer who has small business experience—ideally, one who knows something about your field. It can help you see whether or not the contract does what you want it to do and includes everything you need. Because you have done most of the work, your adviser's advice should be reasonably priced.

RESOURCE

Looking for a lawyer? Asking for a referral to an attorney from someone you trust can be a good way to find legal help. Also, two sites that are part of the Nolo family, Lawyers.com and Avvo.com, provide excellent and free lawyer directories. These directories allow you to search by location and area of law, and list detailed information about and reviews of lawyers.

Whether you're just starting your lawyer search or researching particular attorneys, visit www.lawyers.com/find-a-lawyer and www.avvo.com/find-a-lawyer.

Attachments to Contracts

It's common to use attachments (often called "exhibits") to your contract to list lengthy details that don't fit neatly into the main body of the contract. For example, in drawing up a contract with a sign maker, you could attach a sketch of the sign and a list of detailed specifications, including materials to be used. Simply refer in the main contract to Attachment A or Exhibit A and note that you "hereby incorporate it into this contract." By referring to the attachment in the contract itself, you make it a part of the contract.

If you're a consultant or routinely contract for your services, consider using a short basic contract and then adding your performance specs in an attachment. That way you can use the same basic contract form over and over with only slight modifications.

 RESOURCE

Here are some books that can help you make your own contracts:

- *Legal Forms for Starting & Running a Small Business*, by Fred S. Steingold (Nolo). This book includes forms and agreements for use in preparing a variety of business documents, including commercial leases; contracts for the purchase of a business or real estate; contracts for hiring employees and independent contractors; and contracts for buying, selling, manufacturing, renting, and storing goods.
- *Contracts: The Essential Business Desk Reference*, by Richard Stim (Nolo), provides plain-English advice on common contract terms, and how to understand (and change) contracts.

In addition to the books listed above, Nolo offers many downloadable contracts for sale on www.nolo.com, including sales contracts and independent contractor agreements.

Signing Your Contracts

Many contracts take the form of a single document containing a series of numbered clauses. Each party signs two copies and each keeps a copy. But as discussed throughout this chapter, some written contracts are much less formal. Commonly, they're in two—or more—parts. For example, A sends B an offer; B accepts by a separate letter, fax, or email. Or A sends B an offer; B sends back a counteroffer; A accepts the counteroffer by letter or fax. As long as there's a genuine meeting of the minds, a contract contained in several documents is valid.

Sample Contract in Letter Form

September 10, 20xx

Dear Maddie:

I'd like to summarize our agreement for you to redecorate our store at 123 Main Street. We agreed that for $2,000, you'll apply wall covering to the south wall of our sales areas and apply two coats of paint to the remaining walls. The paint will be XYZ brand latex semigloss, and the wall covering will be ABC brand vinyl, pattern #66.

In addition to the $2,000 payment, I'll promptly reimburse you for the paint and wall covering at your cost (when you present invoices from RacaFrax Wall Coverings), but you'll be responsible for the cost of all other tools, equipment, and supplies.

I'll pay you $1,000 before you start work and the balance within seven business days after the work is completed. You'll do the work on the next two Sundays so that our business isn't interrupted. The quality of your work will meet or exceed the job you recently completed for the Ski Shoppe next door.

We also agreed that if any problems come up about this job and we can't resolve them ourselves, we'll submit our dispute to Metro Mediators, Inc., for mediation and, if that doesn't resolve the problem, to binding arbitration—and we'll split the cost 50-50.

If I've accurately stated our agreement, please sign the enclosed copy of this letter and return it to me by noon Wednesday.

Sincerely,

Jim Dalton

Jim Dalton

d/b/a Jim's Fitness Shop

The above terms are acceptable to me.

Date _____   _____

Maddie Walz

Another form of contract is a letter that pulls together the details of your deal and is accepted by the other person by a signature at the bottom. This is typical when you and the other party (perhaps someone you've worked with often) have worked out the deal over lunch or through a series of phone calls and don't feel the need for a formal contract. An example is shown above.

Revising a Contract Before You Sign

In negotiating a contract, it's common for the parties to go back and forth through several drafts, refining the language. You can easily revise your agreement using your word processing program. If you take this approach, just print out a fresh copy before signing the agreement. For minor changes, you can cross out the old wording and write in the new. Each party should initial each change to establish that the changes were agreed upon.

Another way to handle changes is to put them in an addendum. If you use an addendum, state that in case of a conflict between the addendum and the main contract, the wording in the addendum prevails. Both parties should sign the addendum and the main contract.

If a contract has gone through several revisions, it's a good idea to have both parties initial each page so that you're sure everyone has a correct copy of the final draft.

Signatures

How a contract should be signed depends on the legal form of your business:

- **A Sole Proprietor's** own name is sufficient because a sole proprietorship isn't a separate legal entity. But there are two other ways to do it, either of which is just as legal.

Method 1:

> _____
> Jim Dalton
> D/B/A Jim's Fitness Shop
> [_D/B/A means "doing business as."_]

Method 2:

> Jim's Fitness Shop
> By: _____
>   Jim Dalton

- **For a Partnership,** the following format is commonly used:

> ARGUS ELECTRONICS,
> A Michigan Partnership
> By: _____
>   Randy Argus, a General Partner

Only one partner needs to sign on behalf of a partnership.

- **For a Limited Liability Company,** use this format:

> REALTY APPRAISAL SERVICES, LLC
> By: _____
>   Sheila Martin, Member [_or Manager_]

- **For a Corporation,** use this format:

> KIDDIE KRAFTS, INC.,
> A California Corporation
> By: _____
>   Madeline Arshak, President

A person signing as a corporate officer doesn't assume personal liability for meeting contractual obligations. (See Chapter 1 for a discussion of how using the corporate form of doing business can limit the personal liability of people operating the corporation.) If the other party to a contract is a corporation, you might (particularly in a major transaction) want to see a board of directors' resolution or corporate bylaws authorizing the particular officer to sign contracts on the corporation's behalf. You can omit this step if the contract is signed by the corporate president; a president is presumed to have authority to sign contracts for a corporation.

If you're entering into a contract with a corporation and want someone (such as a corporate officer or major shareholder) to sign a personal guarantee, you can use a clause like this one at the end of the contract:

> In consideration of Seller entering into the above contract with Starlight Corporation, I personally guarantee the performance of all of the above contractual obligations undertaken by Starlight Corporation.
>
> Liz Star

Witnesses and Notaries

"Notarization" means that a notary public certifies in writing that you:

- are the person you claim to be, and
- have acknowledged under oath that you have signed the document.

Very few contracts need to be notarized or signed by witnesses. The major exceptions to this rule are documents that are going to be recorded at a public office charged with keeping such records (usually called the "county recorder" or "registrar of deeds"). These documents are described in the next section. Occasionally—but very rarely—state laws require witnesses or notaries to sign other types of documents.

Recording

The great majority of business contracts don't have to be publicly recorded—and, in fact, are usually ineligible for recording. Here are the exceptions:

- documents that affect title to or rights in real estate. This includes deeds, mortgages, "trust deeds" (a form of mortgage used in many states), and easement agreements.
- long-term real estate leases or memoranda summarizing them, and
- some documents dealing with tangible personal property, such as UCC financing statements or chattel mortgages, when the seller or a third party is financing part of the purchase price and receiving a security interest ("contingent ownership") in the property. Banks, for example, routinely record security interests when making equipment loans.

Dates

When you sign a contract, an offer, a counteroffer, or an acceptance, include the date—and make sure the other person does too. This helps to establish that there was agreement (remember, a meeting of the minds is an essential element of any valid contract). A simple way to do this is to always put a date line (Date: _____ , 20xx) next to the place where each person will sign. Don't worry if the dates of signing differ by a few days or even a week, as is common when the parties exchange documents by mail.

> **EXAMPLE:** If you sign on Monday and the other party signs a week later, you have a valid contract unless (1) you revoked your signature before the other person signed, or (2) you stated in the contract or offer that the other person must accept the offer before that date.

Originals and Photocopies

A contract is an "original" as long as the signatures are originals. So a photocopied document that both parties then sign is an original. So is a carbon copy or computer-printed copy that both parties sign.

If you enter into a traditional written contract—one document that contains the full agreement of the parties and is signed by both of them—it's best if each party has a copy of the contract with the original signatures of both parties. This is easy if you sign at the same session; simply sign two originals, so each party can keep a fully signed one.

A photocopy or faxed copy of a signed contract can still be enforced as long as the judge or arbitrator is convinced that what you have is an accurate reproduction of the original.

Storing Contracts

Store your contracts and other important documents in a fireproof safe or file cabinet. Another precaution is to keep photocopies of all important documents at another location. This might seem like overkill—but not if you have to prove what's in a contract and all copies have been destroyed, stolen, or lost.

Revising a Contract After Both Parties Sign

Once a contract has been signed, any changes must be agreed to by both parties. In essence, this means they're forming a new contract. The simplest way to make fairly minor revisions to a signed contract is through an addendum—or a second or third addendum if necessary. When you write an addendum, follow these steps:

- Refer to the earlier contract by date, names of the parties, and subject matter.
- State all of the changes.
- State that in case of a conflict between the terms of the original contract and the addendum, the terms of the addendum prevail.
- Make it clear that all terms of the original contract, except those that you're changing, remain in effect.
- Sign and date the addendum and keep it with the original.

Electronic Contracting

For centuries, business contracts have been written on paper. Today, you have an alternative: forming contracts electronically. Electronic contracts are enforceable if they meet the usual requirements of contract law—for example, there must be a meeting of the minds and an exchange of things of value (called consideration). See "What Makes a Valid Contract" at the beginning of this chapter for details. Electronic contracts can be especially helpful if you're selling goods or services online.

Your first task is to come up with a set of contract terms to post on your website. Your terms become an offer. If the buyer accepts your terms, you have formed a legally binding contract. The content of your contract terms will vary, depending on what kinds of goods or services you're selling. You'll probably want to state the nature of any warranty you're offering. And you might also want to include disclaimers that limit your liability. Consider hiring a lawyer to draft the contract terms—or perhaps to review the ones you've written. To get a head start, check the terms offered online by businesses similar to yours.

Make your contract terms easy to find on your website and have the buyer acknowledge that those terms are binding. Typically, you'll do this by having the buyer click on a button that says "I Agree" to the contract terms, or "I Accept" them.

Arrange for your contract terms to appear automatically on the buyer's screen before the buyer can agree to them. Or require the buyer to click on a link to your terms before the buyer can accept them. You don't want the buyer to later claim that your terms were hidden away somewhere on your site.

The contract terms should appear clearly on the buyer's computer screen—and should print out in legible form if the buyer chooses to print them. And make sure the marketing materials you display on your site don't contradict the terms you've posted. For example, don't offer a six-month warranty in your contract terms online but promise a one-year warranty elsewhere.

Just before the place where the buyer agrees to your terms, emphasize that this will be a legal contract. You might say, for example, "When you click the 'I Agree' button, you'll be entering into a binding contract." It's wise to require the buyer to read—or at least scroll through—the terms before being able to agree.

Offer the buyer a choice of accepting your terms or rejecting them. For example, alongside the "I Agree" button, you might have an "I Reject" button. Of course, if the buyer rejects your terms, that should be the end of the transaction. You don't want to provide goods or services to someone who refuses to accept your terms. Make the rejection wording as clear as the acceptance wording. Instead of the words "I Reject," you might prefer "I Do Not Agree" or "I Decline."

There might be business deals that don't lend themselves to the buyer's acceptance by clicking. In those situations, a signer might paste a scanned signature at the end the contract. Or a person might sign electronically using cryptographic "scrambling" technology.

To comply with federal law, let consumers know whether paper contracts are available for transactions with your business and, if they are, what fees you impose if a consumer prefers paper.

For more on the subject, see the guide to the Electronic Signatures in Global and National Commerce Act at www.ftc.gov.

Enforcing Contracts in Court

Often, if there's a dispute about a claimed breach of contract, you can resolve it through negotiation. If that doesn't work, you'll need to use one of the other methods of resolving legal disputes: mediation, arbitration, or litigation. (For an overview on how each works, visit Nolo's Mediation, Arbitration & Collaborative Law section at www.nolo.com/legal-encyclopedia/mediation and Nolo's Business Litigation section at www.nolo.com/legal-encyclopedia/business-litigation.)

Most people prefer to resolve their contract disputes by mediation because it's an effective, cost-efficient, and less adversarial process than litigation. If mediation doesn't work and you resort to a more formal proceeding—arbitration or a lawsuit—you'll likely be focusing on two basic questions:

- Was there a breach of contract?
- If so, what relief should be awarded to the nonbreaching party?

We'll tackle the first question in this section, and the second one in "What Can You Sue For?" below.

Suppose your business sues or is sued for an alleged breach of contract or such a claim is taken to arbitration. What defenses can the defendant assert? Here are the main ones:

- **No valid contract was formed.** If there was no meeting of the minds (no legally binding offer and acceptance) in the first place or no consideration was given in exchange for one party's promise, no contract even exists. (See "What Makes a Valid Contract," above.) It's a lot easier to establish such a claim if neither side has begun to follow and rely on the so-called contract.
- **There's no written contract and, because of the subject of the contract, one is required by law.** (See "Must a Contract Be in Writing?" above.)
- **The contract is void because it's illegal or against public policy.** Contracts that call for criminal or immoral conduct might be unenforceable. (See "Unfair or Illegal Contracts," above.)
- **The contract should be rescinded (canceled) because the other side misrepresented the facts, the contract was induced by duress, or there was a mutual mistake.** (See "Misrepresentation, Duress, or Mistake," above.)
- **There was no breach of contract.** The defendant admits entering into a valid contract with the plaintiff but fully complied with its terms.
- **The other party suffered no damages.** The breach of the contract was minor or technical and didn't cause the plaintiff any actual loss or damage. For example, if your store delivered

a conference table and six chairs to a lawyer's new office a week later than promised, there's likely been minor inconvenience but no real damage—nothing serious enough to make you liable for breach of contract.

- **The plaintiff failed to limit the damages.** All parties to a contract have a legal duty to act reasonably and keep any damages to a minimum (called "mitigation of damages" in legalese). Or, put another way, it's not legally permissible to sit back and let damages add up when reasonable steps could be taken to stop or limit them. For example, suppose your company services refrigerators and you signed a two-year contract with a butcher. While you're on vacation, the butcher calls your company and requests that you immediately repair a breakdown in his refrigerator. Your chief assistant is sick, so the job doesn't get done until you return ten days later. The butcher sues for damages, claiming he lost $5,000 worth of meat due to lack of refrigeration. You can point out that the butcher could have mitigated his damages by calling another company to fix his refrigerator. Had he done this promptly, his loss might have been limited to $500 of particularly temperature-sensitive meat plus $300 for the extra service charged. You should be responsible for $800 in damages and not the full $5,000.

Enforcing Lost Contracts

What if a party wants to legally enforce a written contract, but neither party can find a signed copy? The contract is still legally enforceable if you can prove to the satisfaction of an arbitrator or judge that:

- a written agreement was actually signed, and
- it contained the specific terms you're seeking to enforce.

You might be able to reconstruct the terms from an unsigned photocopy or from a final draft stored on your computer.

RELATED TOPIC

Chapter 13 explains how the concept of mitigation of damages applies where a lease is involved. This information is generally applicable to all contracts.

What Can You Sue For?

In a breach-of-contract case, the court can award the plaintiff money damages and might also, in some cases, order the defendant to do—or stop doing—something.

Compensatory Damages

If a plaintiff proves that a defendant breached a contract, the usual approach is for the judge or arbitrator to award the plaintiff "compensatory damages." The goal is to put the parties in the same position as they would have been in if the contract had been performed—or to come as close to that as possible.

Let's return to the contract with Joe, the sign maker we discussed at the beginning of this chapter. If Joe failed to build the sign for your business, and it cost you $750 to have someone else do it, you'd be entitled to recover $300 from Joe for breach of contract. This is the difference between the contract price you and Joe agreed on ($450) and what you had to pay to get the job done ($750). This assumes that you made a reasonable effort to limit or mitigate your damages. In this situation, you'd have to show that you made a reasonable attempt to find a second sign maker to do the job at a fair price. You couldn't just go to the most expensive sign maker in the state and expect Joe to reimburse you for the top dollar.

Consequential Damages

A plaintiff might also be entitled to "consequential damages." These are damages that arise out of circumstances that the breaching party knew about or should have foreseen when the contract was made.

For example, what if Joe built your sign for you but didn't get around to installing it until a month after your business's grand opening? Can you sue for the profits you lost because potential customers didn't know your store was there? The usual rule is that you can recover for lost profits only if this issue is covered by your contract or if it was foreseeable to both parties when you signed the contract that you'd lose profits if the other person didn't carry out the contact. Whether or not a judge will award you damages for Joe's failure to install your sign on time is anybody's guess—unless you specifically dealt with the issue in the contract.

If the contract did provide for lost profits, there's another problem: The amount of lost profits you claim must be ascertainable with reasonable certainty. With a new store, you have no earnings history. This makes it difficult to prove and recover lost profits. But you might be able to show how much similar stores at similar locations earned when they first started and get a judge to accept this as a reasonable estimate of your losses.

Let's look at one more example. Say that the sign you ordered from Joe was to contain your store name plus the name of a major manufacturer of merchandise you planned to carry. You had a deal with the manufacturer that entitled you to a 10% discount if you put the manufacturer's name on your sign. Because Joe put up the sign a month after the store opened, you didn't receive the discount on the first batch of merchandise, which cost you an extra $1,000. Can you collect this money from Joe? Only if Joe knew about your deal with the manufacturer when you and he entered into your contract. Otherwise, Joe would have no reason to expect you to suffer this additional loss if he installed the sign late.

Liquidated Damages

In addition to or in place of compensatory and consequential damages, a plaintiff might be able to recover "liquidated damages." These are damages that the parties agree in the contract will be paid if there's a breach. That is, instead of trying to determine the money damages for a breach of contract after the fact, you do it in advance.

For example, because actual losses caused by late installation of your sign would be difficult to determine, you and Joe could agree in your contract that for each day of delay, Joe would owe you a $25 late fee. If the liquidated damages are a reasonable attempt to estimate the losses you'd suffer and are not intended as a penalty, a judge or an arbitrator will enforce this clause.

Contracts for the purchase of real estate commonly contain a liquidated damages clause. For example, if you put down $5,000 in "earnest money" when you sign a contract to purchase a building, the contract will likely allow the seller to retain the $5,000 as liquidated damages if you later back out for no good reason.

Injunctions and Other Equitable Relief

In addition to monetary damages, a judge might order "equitable" relief in some circumstances. This can come in a variety of forms, depending on the facts of the case and the judge's ingenuity. The idea is to reach a fair result and do justice in a way that can't be done simply by a monetary award. Here are some equitable remedies that a judge may order:

- **Injunctions.** An "injunction" is an order a judge issues that prohibits a person from performing specified activities. Occasionally, a judge issues an injunction to prevent a party from violating a contract. When time is of the essence, a judge may issue an emergency injunction (sometimes called a "temporary restraining order," or "TRO") without a hearing to freeze matters until a court hearing can be held.

EXAMPLE 1: Aggie accepts a job as the accounts manager for DDS Innovations, a dental supply house. As part of her employment contract, she signs a covenant not to compete in the same business in a four-county area for two years after leaving the company. After 18 months on the job, Aggie quits and starts a business in the same city, competing directly with DDS Innovations. The company sues Aggie for breach of her covenant not to compete. The judge, after conducting a trial, finds that the covenant not to compete is reasonable and legally valid and enjoins Aggie from continuing in that business for two years.

EXAMPLE 2: Maurice and Albert are business partners who have a falling out. Unable to resolve the dispute, Maurice sues Albert, claiming a breach of the partnership agreement. Albert countersues. The judge holds a preliminary hearing and issues a "preliminary injunction"—in force while the lawsuit is pending—prohibiting both partners from removing any property from the offices of the partnership and from taking any money from the partnership bank account.

EXAMPLE 3: Gilda and her landlord, Archie, have a dispute over who is to pay for electricity to Gilda's restaurant. On Friday afternoon, Archie threatens to shut off the power to Gilda's restaurant, which would ruin a private banquet for 200 guests that night. Based on Gilda's "affidavit" (sworn statement) showing the likelihood of immediate damage, the judge issues a temporary restraining order prohibiting Archie from shutting off Gilda's power. The judge schedules a hearing for 9 a.m. Monday, at which time the TRO might be dissolved or continued. Because a TRO is usually issued based on the statements of one party only ("ex parte" in legal lingo), such an order is signed only if there's an emergency. A court hearing is always scheduled promptly.

- **Specific Performance.** If a contract concerns a unique or special asset—such as a piece of real estate, a work of art, or a uniquely valuable item of jewelry—the judge may order the losing party to deliver the property to the other party to carry out the agreement. This remedy is rarely used in any other type of commercial transaction.

- **Rescission.** In an appropriate case a judge may "rescind" (cancel) a contract and order "restitution" (return) of any money already paid. This unusual remedy is generally reserved for situations where one party's breach has completely frustrated the objectives of the other party and the judge decides that it would be unfair to enforce the contract. To obtain rescission, the party getting a refund must give up any benefits already received. (Grounds for rescission of a contract are discussed earlier in this chapter.)

If a judge orders you to perform a contract or stop doing something that violates a contract, you can find yourself in deep trouble if you don't obey the order. You can be held in contempt of court, which is punishable by fines and even time in jail.

The Financially Troubled Business

A new business doesn't come with a guarantee. Even with the best planning, it's possible that your business will go through hard times and maybe even fail. Many an entrepreneur has weathered a number of shaky ventures before landing in a business that proved solidly successful. So if your business becomes troubled or even if it needs to be put out of its misery, it shouldn't be viewed as the end of the world.

And, although it's always unpleasant—and can be heartbreaking—to have your business go bad, it's important to understand that there are many steps you can take to limit your losses so that you can get back on your feet and move on to other, more productive ventures. Especially if faced promptly, business troubles don't have to be long-term financial disasters.

A key economic preservation strategy is to protect your personal assets from business debts to the greatest extent possible. How you organize and run your business can make a decisive difference in whether you're able to do this.

In addition, if your enterprise should find itself in financial trouble, your day-to-day management decisions should be guided at least in part by your knowledge of what legal and business actions can help or hurt your personal situation.

Finally, if your financial troubles become so severe that you consider ending your business and maybe even declaring bankruptcy, you'll need to know exactly what legal options and protections are available.

Thinking Ahead to Protect Your Personal Assets

Perhaps you personally own a home, a valuable car, stocks and bonds, or a savings account. Or maybe you own a second business or other valuable assets. Whatever you own, one thing is sure: You don't want to see everything you've acquired gobbled up by debts resulting from a failed business. Fortunately, with some advance planning, you can often protect many of your personal assets from your business creditors.

> **CAUTION**
>
> **Early planning is essential.** It's crucial that you develop your asset protection plan as early as possible—preferably before rather than after you begin doing business. Once your business is in operation—and especially after it runs into financial trouble—you'll be greatly restricted in the steps you can take to protect your personal assets.

Choice of Business Entity

As discussed in Chapter 1, when you start your business, insulating yourself from personal liability for business debts and liabilities is one important consideration. This is especially true if there's a strong possibility that the business's failure would leave you with a huge stack of bills or lawsuits for uninsured liabilities. If you organize your business as a sole proprietorship or partnership, you'll be personally liable for all obligations of the business. If, however, you organize your business as a corporation or a limited liability company (LLC), your personal liability will be substantially limited. Or to put this more bluntly, corporations and LLCs offer the greatest opportunity for protecting your personal assets from business obligations.

Beware of Penniless Partners

Another good reason to start your business as a corporation or an LLC rather than a general partnership—or to switch your existing partnership to a corporation or an LLC—is to protect yourself from the possible insolvency of any co-owners that could leave you stuck with all the business liabilities. The potential problem of working with co-owners in the context of a partnership is that if your business goes bad, you and your partners will be liable "jointly and severally" for business debts. This legal jargon means if any partners can't pay their shares of business debts, the others will have to make up the difference. So if you operate as a partnership, at least make sure your partners have enough assets to pay their shares of any partnership debts.

> **EXAMPLE:** Ginny has two partners when her partnership business fails, leaving $30,000 in unpaid bills. Creditors get a judgment for $30,000 against all three partners. Unfortunately, Ginny's partners don't have any assets. Under the doctrine of "joint and several liability," Ginny is legally on the hook to pay the entire judgment.

Assuming that Ginny pays the entire $30,000 judgment and the partnership agreement makes all the partners equally liable for business debts, she'll be able to collect $10,000 from each of the other partners if they come into some money in the future.

Personal Loan Guarantees

Even if you form a corporation or an LLC to insulate your personal assets from business debts, you might be asked to put your personal assets on the line if your business applies for a bank loan or line of credit. Commercial lenders particularly won't make a loan or extend a line of credit to new corporations or LLCs unless the business owners personally guarantee to repay it. Unfortunately, if you agree to do this and your business later is unable to make payments as they come due, the lender has a right to get a judgment and collect it from your personal assets exactly as if you hadn't formed a corporation or an LLC in the first place.

In some cases, the requirement that you personally guarantee a potential loan might be enough to dissuade you from borrowing the money in the first place. In unusual circumstances, a lender might agree to put a cap on the amount of your guarantee so your personal assets aren't fully at risk. Or, if you can't sell that idea, try for a written commitment that your personal guarantee will expire after a preestablished period of time—perhaps two years—if the corporation or LLC has made all payments on time and is profitable.

Having Your Spouse Sign Too

If a lender asks you to personally guarantee a line of credit or a loan for your corporation or LLC, the lender might also ask for your spouse to be a coguarantor. A lender might make a similar request whether you open a line of credit or take out a loan as a sole proprietor or partner. Be aware of the additional risk this entails.

In most states—except for the nine that follow the community property system—if you alone sign for a line of credit or a loan and don't pay on time, the creditor can get a judgment against you but not against your spouse. This means that, ordinarily, a creditor will be able to reach the property that you own in your own name, but not the property that you and your spouse own in both your names.

However, if you and your spouse both sign on the dotted line, the creditor's rights will be much greater. Now if you and your spouse own property in your joint names—a home or bank account, for example—the creditor will be able to sue and get a judgment against both of you if the debt isn't paid. Then the creditor can enforce the judgment by seizing your joint bank account or jointly owned securities or home in addition to property you own in your name alone. The creditor will also be able to go after property that's in your spouse's name alone—and even to garnish your spouse's paycheck.

 CAUTION

Both spouses are liable for most debts in community property states. Nine states follow the community property system: Arizona, California, Idaho, Louisiana, Nevada, New Mexico, Texas, Washington, and Wisconsin. In those states, a married couple's property accumulated after marriage is primarily community or jointly owed property regardless of the names in which it's held. Each spouse can also own separate property but, especially in longer marriages, this tends to be less important. In most instances, the rights of creditors vary, depending on the type of property involved, as discussed below:

- **Community Property.** Usually, property earned or acquired by either spouse after marriage—except by gift or inheritance—is at risk for a debt incurred by either spouse. This means a creditor can go after the community property of you and your spouse to pay off a debt, even if only you signed for the loan. In other words, you can't shield the community property from a creditor by not having your spouse sign for the loan.

- **Separate Property.** This usually is property a spouse owned before getting married, acquired later by gift or inheritance, or agreed in writing would be kept separate. It's also property—such as a business—acquired from separate assets. If, for example, someone gets married owning a piece of real estate, sells it, and uses the proceeds to open a business, the business is separate property. If your spouse has separate property and signs for a loan, that spouse's separate property will be at risk if you default—but if your spouse declines to sign, that separate property will normally be beyond the creditor's reach. Your own separate property, of course, will be at risk whether or not your spouse signs.

Pledging Collateral for Loans

In addition to asking you to personally guarantee a loan by signing a promissory note, a lender might ask you to pledge a personal asset—typically, your home—as collateral for a business loan. In the case of your home, this would be done through a second mortgage or deed of trust. Think long and hard before you agree to do this, because it means you'll lose your home if you can't repay the money and the lender exercises its right to foreclose.

It's important to understand that there can be a big difference between simply putting your personal signature on a promissory note (see "Personal Loan Guarantees," above) and giving the lender a security interest in property such as your home. The reason is that states have debtor protection laws (called "homestead laws") that protect your investment in your home. This means that being unable to pay a personal debt—one, for example, based on a promissory note that's not secured by your home—

won't automatically put you at risk of losing your home. By comparison, however, if you pledge your house as security for a loan, these homestead laws won't protect you.

CAUTION

Check the law in your state. In many states the homestead exemption is low—or even nonexistent. This means that if an unsecured creditor sues and gets a judgment, the creditor could possibly force the sale of your home to collect.

So much for the law. In the cold world of trying to raise money for your business, you might have no practical alternative to putting your home at risk. The truth is that the equity in your home might be your most accessible source of cash. The point is to ponder seriously what you and your family would do if you lost your home due to business reverses.

CAUTION

Be careful in using a home equity line of credit to finance your business. A home equity line of credit, of course, amounts to a second mortgage. Don't overlook the fact that if you write a $15,000 check against your line of credit to cover business expenses and can't later make your payments on time, the bank can enforce its lien rights and force the sale of your home.

Maintain Adequate Insurance

You never know when an injured person might sue your business, claiming that you or an employee acted negligently—for example, a customer who falls in your parking lot and fractures her hip might claim that you were negligent in not keeping the area properly lighted. A jury might agree that you were negligent and sock your business with a huge judgment. There are many other risks as well—such as an injured consumer suing your manufacturing business for producing a defective product or a suit by a pedestrian injured by one of your employees who was driving a company truck. In short, you absolutely need to carry adequate insurance because if you don't, your investment in the business could be wiped out by a huge verdict. Even if your personal funds or house aren't at risk, you'll have suffered a stunning financial loss.

If you're a sole proprietor or partner, be especially careful to carry adequate business risk insurance, because you're personally liable for paying the judgment. Another way to say this is if insurance proves too expensive or difficult to get, you'll almost certainly want to form a corporation or an LLC to at least limit your personal liability. (For more on insurance, see Chapter 12.)

Managing the Financially Troubled Business

So far, this chapter has reviewed things you can do in advance to limit potential liability. Now let's shift gears and assume your business is currently facing financial problems. My focus here is to present several practical strategies that will help legally protect both you and your personal assets.

Keep Taxes Current

Rule number one for the owner of any struggling business is to meticulously pay on time all taxes withheld from employees' paychecks. (See Chapter 8.) Even if you operate your business as a corporation or an LLC, the IRS and state tax authorities can hold you personally liable for these taxes—plus penalties—if they're not paid. And you're still legally on the hook to pay these taxes, even if the business goes bankrupt.

So if your business starts having financial problems, stave off the other creditors as best you can—and use whatever cash is available to take care of employment taxes. Paying these taxes is so crucial that if your business is financially disorganized, you should pay for any accounting help you need to be sure these taxes are computed accurately and paid on time.

And remember that you don't have to wait until the last day to deposit employment taxes. It's often

wise to deposit the employment taxes as soon as you know the figures, so the money will be out of your bank account and legitimately beyond the reach of any other creditor who is attempting to collect a court judgment against your business.

CAUTION

Don't pay employment taxes with a credit card. If possible, use a check or cash to pay employment taxes to ensure that the taxes are really paid. By contrast, if you use your personal credit card and can't pay the bill later, you'll continue to be responsible to the charge card company for the amount you charged for taxes—even if you go through personal bankruptcy. A discharge in bankruptcy won't cancel your personal liability for the portion of your credit card debt that's attributable to the tax payments.

Don't Lie About Debts

When a business starts to have financial troubles, its owner might frantically try to borrow more money. Before doing this, think carefully about whether your business is really likely to do better in the near future or if you're only likely to compound your debt problems. If you apply for a new loan or to consolidate old ones, be forthright in disclosing the financial condition of your business. If you misrepresent your debts to get a loan, you might not be able to get rid of your personal liability for the debt—even if you go through bankruptcy—because the law will regard your new debt as being obtained by fraud. Where big bucks are involved, the debt could haunt you for many years.

The key to avoiding trouble with lenders is to be very careful that all facts appear—and appear accurately—on any financial statement you give a potential creditor. Even if you borrow money or have credit extended to you without having to fill out a financial statement, it can be treated as fraud if you knew that the business was having financial trouble and didn't make all the facts clear to your creditor before obtaining the loan.

> ⚠ **CAUTION**
>
> **Don't rely on shortcuts suggested by the lender's agent.** Some finance company employees have been known to deliberately tell people—orally, of course —that they don't need to list all their debts. Often this is done because the person in the finance company office is under pressure to make loans and, therefore, has a motive to bend the rules to qualify you. Don't fall for this. If you later default on the loan and the company claims you obtained the money by fraudulently withholding information about your finances, chances are the employee will either be long gone or will say, "Of course I didn't say to deliberately omit debts." Either way, chances are you'll be unable to discharge the "fraudulent" debt in bankruptcy.

Also, be aware that the bankruptcy laws take a broad view of what constitutes fraud. Not disclosing negative financial information might be considered fraudulent even if you acted with the best of intentions.

> **EXAMPLE:** Jimmy, a sole proprietor, owns a secondhand furniture store. One day, the landlord raises the store rent by 50%. Based on past performance, Jimmy knows that with the rent increase, he'll have difficulty making a profit. Nevertheless, he decides to stay at that location because it would cost even more money to move elsewhere. At this time, he has a line of credit for $25,000 with a local bank of which only $10,000 has been used. A month later, already feeling the sting of the higher rent, he draws against the additional $15,000 and uses it to keep afloat. Because Jimmy neglected to tell the bank about the significant rent increase that put his business in a precarious financial condition, the additional draws can be considered a fraudulent use of credit and might well not be discharged in bankruptcy. If the bank sues Jimmy in bankruptcy court after he's gone through bankruptcy, Jimmy might still be liable for the $15,000.

This doesn't mean that drawing on a line of credit to meet the ordinary ebb and flow of business constitutes fraud. It doesn't. After all, the bank expects that you'll use your line of credit to cover leaner times. But you do need to disclose significant changes in your business, such as a lawsuit or the bankruptcy of your largest customer that threatens the financial well-being of your business.

Be Careful About Transferring Business Property

Occasionally, out of desperation, a business owner will consider trying to protect personal assets by hiding them. Because creditors are used to ferreting out such tactics, by and large they prove ineffective and are likely to give rise to civil and perhaps even criminal charges of fraud. Specifically, a business owner shouldn't:

- transfer assets to friends or relatives in any effort to hide them from creditors or from the bankruptcy court, or
- conceal property or income from a court.

Avoid Preferential Payments to Creditors

The bankruptcy code frowns on your preferring certain creditors over others by making what are called "preferential payments." If you file for bankruptcy, all payments you make during the year before the filing will be scrutinized by creditors to make sure that some creditors weren't given an unfair advantage by being paid while others received little or nothing. If you did improperly single out some creditors for more favorable treatment by paying money or transferring property to them, the bankruptcy judge can order those creditors to return the money or property so it can be added to the total (called your "bankruptcy estate") available to all of your creditors.

Fortunately, most payments you make as part of your business's ordinary operations won't be considered to be illegal preferences should you declare bankruptcy. Here's a brief overview of the types of payments that are safe and those likely to cause problems:

- **Payments in the ordinary course of business.** Neither you nor the payee has to worry about the payments you make in the ordinary course of business. These payments are considered to be safe and won't be undone—even if you made them the day before you filed for bankruptcy. Examples of payments you can safely make include:
  - utilities
  - rent
  - payroll deposits
  - retirement plan contributions
  - insurance premiums
  - payments to suppliers whom you pay on delivery or with 30- to 60-day terms, and
  - salaries—as long as they're kept at the same level you've been paying right along.
- **Payments to family members or insiders.** If you repay money or transfer property to a family member or an insider and then you file for bankruptcy within one year after the payment or transfer, the family member or insider will probably have to return the money or property to the bankruptcy court so it can be divided among your creditors. (An "insider "is some-one who's in or close to your business, such as a partner, a corporate director, or a corporate officer.)
- **Payments to other creditors.** When you repay money or transfer property to someone who's neither a relative nor an insider and the payment isn't in the ordinary course of business, the timing of the payment is crucial (Example: Paying off a bank loan that's not due for six months). If you make such payments or transfers of property during the 90 days before you file for bankruptcy, the recipient might have to return the money or property to the bankruptcy court to be added to the pool of funds available to your creditors.

Protect Your Bank Account

If you face serious financial problems and owe money to a bank, it's often wise to keep most of your checking and other accounts elsewhere. This is because typically your loan agreement gives the bank the right to take your deposited funds without prior notice if the bank thinks you're in financial trouble. (This is called a "setoff.") To put it mildly, it can be a rude surprise to learn that your favorite lender has suddenly drained your account.

Plan for Ongoing Insurance Coverage

If your business winds up in a Chapter 11 or Chapter 13 reorganization under the bankruptcy code, you might have a tough time finding a carrier that's willing to renew your business coverage or one that's willing to issue a new policy. So if you're planning to seek protection under either of those bankruptcy sections, make sure you have insurance in place that extends at least 12 months into the future. Make payments on the policy as they become due. As long as you pay on time, the insurance can't be canceled and you'll enjoy some peace of mind as you continue in business.

Don't Panic About Utilities or Your Lease

If you declare bankruptcy, the utility companies can't use your filing as an excuse for shutting off services—although they can require you to post a reasonable deposit if you want to keep the lights, phone service, and heat.

Similarly, as long as you continue to pay your rent, your landlord can't kick you out. Don't be spooked by the scary clause commonly placed in commercial leases that says you're automatically in default if you file for bankruptcy. You can't believe everything you read. These clauses are not enforceable.

Consider Returning Some Leased Property

If you're leasing equipment and know you won't want to retain it after you file for bankruptcy, consider giving it back to the leasing company before you file. If you do so and the equipment is currently worth less than what you owe under the lease, the deficiency will get discharged in bankruptcy.

On the other hand, if you prefer to keep the leased property, you'll need to continue making your lease payments on time. When you choose to hang onto leased property, the obligation to make lease payments isn't discharged by your going through bankruptcy.

Seeking an Objective Analysis

A business can get into financial trouble for a long list of reasons. One of the most common is simply that the business owner, over time, becomes less attentive to the needs of the business—perhaps as a result of getting tired of dealing with problems that have become tedious. It might help to think of a business much as you would a child: No matter how much work you put in early in life, both continue to need constant attention and are unlikely to thrive if that attention is absent for any extended time.

Early signs of financial trouble usually include the following:

- You've routinely begun to ask creditors for more time to pay bills.
- Creditors are beginning to require you to pay COD.
- Your bank line of credit is routinely maxed out.
- You need to delay cashing your own paycheck a few days because the money isn't there.

And red flags are obviously flying if:

- Impatient creditors are calling you repeatedly.
- You're getting cash advances on your credit card to keep your business afloat.
- You're starting to miss payments to your landlord.
- You're being sued or threatened with lawsuits.
- You're having trouble paying employment taxes.
- Other tax bills are piling up.

The fact that your business is having financial problems doesn't mean it will fail. Even a seriously ailing business might be savable if you recognize the true extent of its problems and seek help soon enough. One good approach is to get objective advice to help you determine how deep your financial problems are and what options are open to you. Maybe you're just facing a temporary downturn that you should be able to weather by cutting costs and fine-tuning your business operations. But it's also possible that your problems might be more serious, requiring you to take more drastic steps to avoid a complete financial disaster that eats up not only your investment in the business but your personal assets as well.

Turn first to an experienced accountant. A small business accountant can usually review your business numbers—your debt-to-equity ratio, for example, or the time it's taking you to collect receivables—and quickly take your business's financial temperature. Then, the accountant will try to identify some problem areas—such as overhead that's too high given your volume of sales. And an experienced business accountant often can provide practical advice for getting the business back on a solid financial track by suggesting, for example, ways to collect more of your receivables or quickly convert assets to needed cash.

If you conclude your financial problems are especially serious, you should also consult an experienced small business lawyer. For starters, the lawyer will probably have a good idea about what the creditors are thinking—insights that can be very valuable in managing these strained relationships. In addition, after information about your business's financial problems and legal structure is on the table, an experienced lawyer should be able to help you sensibly decide whether it's best to try to buy more time through negotiations with creditors, try to sell the business, use a bankruptcy proceeding to keep creditors off your back while you try to rebuild the business, or simply shut the business down and liquidate any remaining assets.

RESOURCE

Looking for a lawyer? Asking for a referral to an attorney from someone you trust can be a good way to find legal help. Also, two sites that are part of the Nolo family, Lawyers.com and Avvo.com, provide excellent and free lawyer directories. These directories allow you to search by location and area of law, and list detailed information about and reviews of lawyers.

Whether you're just starting your lawyer search or researching particular attorneys, visit www.lawyers.com/find-a-lawyer and www.avvo.com/find-a-lawyer.

It Might Pay to Have Your Business Appraised

It can often make sense to hire an appraiser to place a value on the business's real estate, equipment, and inventory. For one thing, a solid appraisal will provide realistic values for your business assets and, therefore, help you and your accountant analyze your financial predicament. Especially if you're considering trying to sell your business, this information can be extremely helpful.

An appraisal might also be helpful if you try to negotiate a nonbankruptcy "workout" with your creditors. Even though you're not legally required to disclose the results of an appraisal at this stage, doing so can definitely be in your interest if the appraisal shows you have valuable assets. This information is likely to reassure unsecured creditors and convince them to give you some breathing room. (See "Workouts," below, to learn more.)

What's more, knowing the value of business assets can be extremely helpful in making decisions about bankruptcy, if matters come to that. You'll have a good idea, for example, of how much debt will remain if the assets are liquidated in a Chapter 7 business bankruptcy and whether the remaining debt—which you might be responsible for paying—will force you into personal bankruptcy.

TIP

Seek out a good small business consultant. If you can find the right one, a small business consultant can often suggest more meaningful business operation strategies than an accountant or lawyer—new strategies, for example, for your product mix, marketing, location, and pricing. But check references carefully to be sure the person you're considering working with really helped others in similar circumstances. Almost anyone can set up shop as a business consultant and the last thing you want is bad advice.

How a Good Consultant Can Help

Ben opens a graphic design business, borrowing from his family to purchase necessary equipment and software and leasing the rest. Although his business is busy from the start and Ben is working long hours, after nine months, it's obvious he's losing money. Trying to figure out what to do, Ben considers increasing his sales or cutting his overhead. But because he and his employees are already overworked, this doesn't promise to solve the problem.

Finally, Ben turns to Sarah, a local small business consultant highly recommended by a neighboring business owner. After examining Ben's books for less than two hours, Sarah spots the problem. Ben isn't charging enough for his services.

After listening to Ben explain that graphic design is a very competitive business and that he will lose customers if he institutes a general price increase, Sarah helps Ben come up with a plan that involves keeping his current prices in effect for about one-half of his volume. But she also suggests that he raise prices significantly for rush orders and specialty work. With some adjustments over time, Sarah's plan works brilliantly. Customers remain loyal, because prices for routine work haven't changed. On rush orders and specialty work, it turns out that Sarah's insight that customers focus more on speed and quality and less on price is correct. Ben's customers pay his higher prices without much complaint, and within a month, his business is making money.

Workouts

In developing a plan of action for your financially troubled business, your objectives probably include one or more of the following:

- keeping the business alive
- salvaging as much as possible from your investment
- minimizing or eliminating your personal liability for business debts
- avoiding personal liability for IRS or other tax penalties
- retaining certain property—such as your house —that's been pledged as security to a creditor
- preserving your ability to get personal or business credit in the future, and
- protecting the assets of relatives and friends who have helped you financially.

Fortunately, several nonbankruptcy alternatives to cope with a failing business are worth considering. In this section, I explain one of these, which is commonly called a "workout." This normally involves developing a voluntary plan under which your creditors and others make concessions so you can keep your business in operation. The idea is that you will continue to zealously address its financial problems so that eventually your creditors can hope to receive all or most of their money.

But workouts aren't your only choice. The next section briefly covers two other nonbankruptcy possibilities: selling your business or simply shutting it down. And at the end of this chapter I summarize the bankruptcy alternatives of liquidating your business under Chapter 7 of the bankruptcy code or keeping it in operation under the protection of Chapter 11 or Chapter 13. You'll want to read all of these sections for an overview of the full range of choices available.

Sometimes it's hard to remember this when your business is going badly: There are bound to be a number of people who are pulling for your business to succeed—people such as creditors, suppliers, employees, customers, and even neighboring business owners who will benefit if you can stay in operation.

These people are "stakeholders," because they have a stake in whether your company lives or dies. Given their long-term self-interest, some of these folks might be willing to lend a helping hand. To take an example, creditors might be willing to make some financial concessions—usually as part of a well-defined business recovery plan (the workout)—to help you through your financial difficulties.

Creditors might give you more time to pay or otherwise help you because they understand that their chances of getting paid on past debts are better if they cut you some slack, such as extending the time for debt payment or even agreeing to forgive a portion of your debt. Valued customers who rely on the availability of your goods and services might also be willing to help out. For example, they might be willing to speed their payments to you so they won't have to turn to a less satisfactory business to fill their needs. Similarly, suppliers might realize that they need your future business as much as you need their supplies. As long as you can convince them that your business can be viable in the long run, they might extend the time for you to repay old debts and even extend more credit.

Your employees are obviously among your business's key stakeholders. Some might agree to work fewer hours or accept reduced wages and benefits until your business gets healthy again. After all, a job in the hand is worth two in the want ads.

Finally, local authorities might be willing to give you more time to pay property taxes—a better alternative than trying to squeeze cash from a defunct business, unless there are statutory tax-sale deadlines.

To get all your stakeholders to work together, you typically need to create a workout plan. This is an out-of-court agreement under which your major creditors agree to hold off on suing your business, collecting on court judgments they've already obtained, or forcing you into bankruptcy. Creditors might even agree to extend more credit while you try to jointly devise a realistic payment schedule. For creditors to go along with your proposal, they must, at a minimum, be convinced that they're likely to come out better financially under your workout plan than they would if they sued you or pushed you into bankruptcy.

To prepare a workout package, start by opening your books to your creditors. A good way to begin the full disclosure process is to prepare a list of all creditors and how much you owe each one. Then list the assets of your business along with estimates as to their value both if you liquidate and if you stay in business. It makes sense to include financial statements—and property appraisals if you have them—in your workout package, so that creditors can see what you're worth and what your problems are. Also, if you have created a business turnaround plan either on your own or working with a small business adviser, include it in your package.

Next, compare what the creditors will receive if you have to liquidate the business in a Chapter 7 bankruptcy with what they're likely to get if your workout plan succeeds. To do this, you might need some help from a bankruptcy lawyer or an experienced accountant in putting together the liquidation scenario.

Give time and thought to showing why your alternative proposal—your long-term workout plan—is likely to eventually put far more money in each of your creditor's pockets as compared to the meager returns they are likely to receive if you go through bankruptcy. While it makes sense to emphasize why your plan to turn around your business has a good chance of succeeding, you should be realistic. Creditors will be justly suspicious of any plan that's based on wishful thinking.

TIP

Put the facts on bankruptcy forms. For extra psychological leverage in trying to get creditors to negotiate a livable workout plan, you might want to prepare official bankruptcy forms (available at www. uscourts.gov; search for "bankruptcy forms") as if you actually planned to file. The filled-in forms will list your business debts and the value of your business assets. Show the forms to your creditors along with your workout plan. This sends the message that you're really prepared to file

for bankruptcy if you can't achieve a compromise. It also dramatically highlights how little the creditors will wind up with if they push you into bankruptcy.

In negotiating with creditors who have a mortgage or other security interest in real property, vehicles, or business equipment in your possession, be prepared to show them that you're continuing to keep the property in good condition. Otherwise, they'll likely conclude that they're better off repossessing the property quickly. Also realize that although suppliers might be willing to extend your time for paying past debts, most will expect you to pay in advance or COD for any new goods delivered to your business. To avoid this inconvenience, you'll need to convince them that your business is in the black on the basis of current operations and that you're routinely paying all new bills promptly.

Be sure your employees support you. If your long-time managers and other key employees are willing to take a temporary pay cut, it will go a long way toward convincing creditors that your business can slim down enough to become profitable. Also, be sure that disgruntled employees aren't badmouthing your recovery plan. Remember that most long-term creditors will almost surely know some of your employees and are very likely to contact them for the true lowdown on your business.

Try to get 100% of your major creditors to agree to your plan. Unfortunately, if there are a significant number of holdouts among your major creditors, your workout plan is probably doomed to failure. The holdouts will drain your time and energy—not to mention your checking account—as they push ahead with lawsuits and other collection efforts.

Once your creditors agree to your plan, quickly put the terms in writing. Each written agreement should state specifically that if you make agreed workout payments on time, the creditor will hold off on filing lawsuits and will terminate collection actions. In addition, if the creditor has agreed to accept less than 100% of what's owed, there should be a clear statement that if you pay the agreed amount, you and your business will be fully released from the debt.

Ideas for Business Workouts

Common elements of workout packages include:

- **Partial Liquidation of Assets.** You agree to sell specific business assets that are not essential to your current business and to use the money to partially pay creditors on a pro rata basis.

- **A Creditor Takes the Collateral.** You turn over to a secured creditor the property you pledged as security for the loan or line of credit. The creditor agrees that your total obligation is wiped out—even if the property is worth less than you still owe. Normally, the creditor will do this only if repossessing and selling the used property is likely to net more than letting you keep it and holding onto your debt. If a creditor really sees you as a long-term deadbeat, that creditor will be more likely to take the property and forget about the debt.

- **Lump Sum Payback.** The creditor accepts a lump sum payoff that's less than the full debt and in full satisfaction of the entire debt. This scenario can particularly make sense when you have a family member or friend who will lend you some new money only if a particular creditor will accept a partial payment. The important thing is to make creditors realize they might get little or nothing if they don't agree.

- **Monthly Payments.** You agree to make monthly payments on your debts, and the creditors agree to hold off on lawsuits and other collection actions. The total amount they agree to accept might be less than the amount owed—but if the debt is reduced, the creditors will probably want a larger monthly amount than they'd settle for on a lump sum payoff.

- **Creditors Become Owners.** In unusual situations, creditors might agree to take ownership rights—such as stock in your corporation—in exchange for forgiving some or all debts owed to them.

Source: *Holding Onto the American Dream: How Small Businesses Can Conquer Financial Problems,* by Marguerite M. Kirk (Odenwald Press).

 CAUTION

Make your peace with the IRS first. If you owe back taxes, pay them or come to terms with the IRS before you approach the other creditors. They're unlikely to agree to a workout if there's a chance the IRS might close down the business.

Selling the Business

Although selling your financially troubled business might seem like a long shot, it's always worth a try. Naturally, you won't get top dollar for your business when it's in distress—but if you arrange a sale, it might give you enough to pay creditors and come away with a few bucks. Selling an operating business, even one that's in trouble, almost always brings more money than closing it down and selling off the assets.

Before you give up and conclude that no one will buy your business, consider that people buy businesses—even those with financial problems— for all sorts of reasons, including:

- The buyer might have lower personal financial needs and expectations and might be willing to squeak by on a modest return that's wholly unacceptable to you.

- The buyer might have a similar business and by combining the two, operate more efficiently than you can.

- The buyer might be extremely eager to take over one or more of your business assets— its location, key employees, or name.

- The buyer might have better access to needed financing than you do and, therefore, be able to stay the course until your good business idea ultimately proves itself.

- The buyer might have greater expertise in your business than you do and see a way to turn a profit by changing how the business is run.

- The buyer might conclude that it's cheaper to buy your business and turn it around than to start a similar business from scratch.

TIP

Value is in the eye of the beholder. You might think that the buyer unrealistically claims greater expertise than yours or mistakenly believes the business has unrecognized potential, but these facts alone could be enough to produce a purchase offer. Don't let your ego get in the way of making the deal by defending your business decisions and strategy so forcefully that you talk the potential purchaser into withdrawing the offer.

If you have an opportunity to sell your business but the proceeds of the sale won't yield enough money to pay off all the business debts, look carefully at what remaining debts you'll be personally responsible for and what personal assets have been pledged as security for the business debts. Merely selling the business won't be enough to relieve you from your personal liability to creditors or the risk that creditors might take property that you've pledged as security.

To reduce or eliminate your personal liability or the danger of losing pledged property, there are some solutions worth looking into. On debts for which you're personally liable, see if the bank or another creditor is willing to substitute the purchaser of your business and release you. The creditor might be willing to do this if the person buying your business is financially stronger than you are or, in the case of a currently unsecured debt, is willing to pledge security. A buyer who's enthusiastic about the prospects of the business might be willing to be substituted for you.

If the creditor won't let you off the hook, another way of dealing with unsecured debts that you'll be personally liable for is to ask the buyer to agree in writing to pay the specified debts and to indemnify and save you harmless from those obligations. This means that if the bank or another creditor comes after you because the debt isn't paid, the buyer guarantees to pay the debt and protect you from any liability. Of course, this kind of guarantee is only as good as the buyer's financial condition, so you won't want to rely on such a guarantee if you have any reason to believe the buyer is financially shaky.

Where you've secured a business debt by pledging your personal property as collateral—for example, your home, car, or stocks—see if the creditor is willing to release your property as security if the buyer substitutes property of equal or greater value. The buyer, for example, might have as much or more equity in the family home than you do in yours, and the bank might be willing to substitute that home as security in place of yours, if the buyer consents.

RESOURCE

For in-depth guidance and a full set of forms on how to sell a business, see *The Complete Guide to Selling a Business*, by Fred S. Steingold (Nolo).

Closing the Business

So much for selling your financially troubled business. If you can't sell it, consider closing it down. Even if you can't pay all your debts immediately, this option at least allows you to avoid running up more. In addition, you'll normally want to negotiate with your creditors to pay them off for less than the full amount the business owes. Why should creditors accept this? It's often a better choice than either of their other options: suing you and chasing down your assets to collect every last dollar or taking what's available in a bankruptcy liquidation. This approach can be particularly sensible, too, if you have a corporation or an LLC and have personally guaranteed some business debts. If you can reach a negotiated settlement, you'll not only avoid a business bankruptcy, but also you won't have to go through personal bankruptcy to get out from under the debts you've guaranteed.

If you haven't personally guaranteed any debts of the corporation or LLC, one option is to simply close the business and pay the debts on a pro rata basis to the extent the business has funds. Then let the corporation or LLC die on its own. Because any remaining debts aren't your personal responsibility, this should, in theory at least, end matters. Sometimes, however, you might want to consider having the business file for bankruptcy in this situation. If the corporation or LLC hasn't gone through bankruptcy, some creditors might go ahead and sue the business and get judgments against it. If that happens, you might be subpoenaed and have to go to court to explain that the business used up all its assets. That can be a nuisance. So if you have a number of creditors who are likely to pursue you to the bitter end, putting the business through bankruptcy will save you from having to testify in multiple lawsuits. Creditors, of course, lose their right to sue once the corporation or LLC is bankrupt.

> **CAUTION**
>
> **Watch out for preferential treatment.** If at first you decide simply to close down your business but later decide to file for bankruptcy, you might have backed into trouble. If your business eventually has to file for bankruptcy, or if some creditors join together to put your business into involuntary bankruptcy, giving preferential treatment to some creditors in the months before you file by paying off all or part of their bills can create a problem. Creditors who didn't receive preferential treatment might complain, in which case the favored creditors will have to return the money or property they received so it can be part of an asset pool available for equitable distribution among all creditors. (See "Avoid Preferential Payments to Creditors," above.) So even if you hope not to file for bankruptcy, try to work out similar deals with all creditors.

Understanding Bankruptcy

If your business is in serious financial trouble, consider the possibility that you'll eventually need to file for bankruptcy if the other strategies mentioned in this chapter won't work for you. Fortunately, thoroughly understanding how bankruptcy works and how you can best cope with it if it becomes inevitable can result in major savings later on.

> **CAUTION**
>
> **Bankruptcy information straight from the source.** You'll find valuable information at the official bankruptcy site: www.uscourts.gov (click "About Bankruptcy").

Different Types of Bankruptcy

Bankruptcy is a legal proceeding handled in the federal court system. It's based on the federal bankruptcy code, which is divided into different chapters, each covering a different type of bankruptcy, as described below. Bankruptcy is usually voluntary, but be aware that one or more creditors may force you into bankruptcy by filing an "involuntary bankruptcy petition" against you. Because lawyers and others with bankruptcy knowledge refer to the various types of bankruptcy protection by their chapter numbers, you, too, will need to learn this jargon, which I explain below.

> **SEE AN EXPERT**
>
> **Legal advice could be essential.** If you're a sole proprietor and have a relatively small amount of business debt, you might be able to handle a bankruptcy yourself or with a limited amount of professional help. But be forewarned: A number of issues (whether certain property is exempt from being taken to pay debts, for example) can be complicated when business and personal affairs are intertwined. It generally makes sense to seek advice from a lawyer who specializes in small business bankruptcy. Professional help is essential for corporations and LLCs because you can't represent these entities in a bankruptcy proceeding unless you're a lawyer. Seek out an experienced bankruptcy lawyer who will take the time to explain all your options—both bankruptcy and nonbankruptcy—before filing papers for you. It might not be necessary for the business to file Chapter 7. It might be better to just shut it down.

Liquidating the Business Under Chapter 7

A Chapter 7 filing is sometimes called a "straight bankruptcy." It's available to businesses organized in all the usual ways—sole proprietorship, general partnership, corporation, and LLC. Under Chapter 7, your business property is sold, and the proceeds are used to pay off debts to the extent funds are available.

If your business is a sole proprietorship, you and the business are legally the same entity, and you are personally liable for all business debts. To put your sole proprietorship through Chapter 7 bankruptcy, you would have to personally file for bankruptcy.

Two Kinds of Creditors

Bankruptcy law distinguishes broadly between two types of creditors: secured and unsecured.

A "secured creditor" is either one to whom you or your business has pledged collateral in exchange for a loan or line of credit ("voluntary secured creditor") or one who has filed a lien (tax, judgment, construction, or mechanic's) against your property ("involuntary secured creditor"). Collateral pledged to a voluntary secured creditor may consist of business property, such as inventory and equipment, or your own property, such as your house, car, or boat. Whether voluntary or involuntary, the creditor ends up with a lien on the property. This means that if you or the business can't pay back the debt, the creditor can take the property to satisfy the debt.

An unsecured creditor is either one to whom no collateral has been pledged or one who hasn't filed a lien. Typically, these debts will include amounts your business owes for inventory, office supplies, minor equipment and furnishings, rent, and advertising, as well as what's owed for services such as maintenance contracts, equipment repair, and professional advice. Credit card charges, too, are unsecured.

In bankruptcy, the secured creditor is in a much more favorable legal position than one who is unsecured. If the bankrupt business has little or no money, the unsecured creditor is likely to wind up with little or nothing, whereas the secured creditor walks away with whatever the collateral is worth. A Chapter 7 bankruptcy gets rid of the debt but not the security interest.

If your business is a general partnership, each partner is personally liable for all partnership debts. Putting the general partnership through Chapter 7

won't do away with your personal liability for these debts. To accomplish that, you'd need to file for personal bankruptcy.

If your business is a corporation or an LLC, you're generally not personally liable for debts of the business, unless you've personally guaranteed a business debt or you've commingled business debt with personal assets. And if you've put up any property as collateral, the secured creditor can take the property unless you pay that creditor the value of the property or agree to have the debt survive the bankruptcy. To escape from personal liability for business debts, you'll have to file for personal bankruptcy after the corporate or LLC bankruptcy is wound up.

A personal filing under Chapter 7 will free you from personal liability for most business debts—but it bears some potential disadvantages. The fact that you've filed for personal bankruptcy remains on your credit record for ten years. This can cause trouble when you apply for a mortgage, a bank loan, a charge account, a credit card, or an apartment. What's more, employers sometimes use credit information to screen job applicants, as do some landlords in checking out potential tenants.

 CAUTION

Cosigners and guarantors are still on the hook. If a friend or family member has cosigned for a business loan or guaranteed payment of a business debt, putting the business or yourself through Chapter 7 bankruptcy won't relieve the cosigner or guarantor from personal liability for the debt. This can be an added reason to try to resolve your debt problems through a workout or other nonbankruptcy alternative. (See "Workouts," above.)

Before filing for personal bankruptcy under Chapter 7, you must undergo credit counseling—usually online or by phone. Failure to complete the counseling and file a certification of completion will result in a dismissal of the case. Also, before the bankruptcy is final, you'll have to take a two-hour course on budget management. If you fail to take this course and to file a certificate of completion within 45 days of the creditors' meeting, you won't be able to get a bankruptcy discharge. (A "creditors' meeting" is a meeting at which the bankruptcy trustee and your creditors get to ask you questions under oath about your bankruptcy petition and the documents you're required to provide to the trustee.) In other words, you'll still owe all the debts.

Generally, if you seek personal bankruptcy relief, you can file under either Chapter 7 or Chapter 13 (described below). But if your income exceeds certain limits, your only option will be to file under Chapter 13. In that case, you'll be seeking approval of a plan that lets you repay your debts over a number of years. The income limits for a Chapter 7 filing vary from state to state.

 RESOURCE

For in-depth guidance, including forms and instructions for filing, see *How to File for Chapter 7 Bankruptcy,* by Albin Renauer and Cara O'Neill (Nolo). Another excellent resource is *The New Bankruptcy: Will It Work For You?* by Cara O'Neill (Nolo).

Reorganizing Your Business Debts

As an alternative to liquidation under Chapter 7, you might prefer to reorganize your debts under Chapter 11, 12, or 13 so that you can continue to operate your business while the bankruptcy court protects you from the demands of creditors. In a reorganization, you can often reduce the amounts you must pay back to unsecured creditors. In addition, under a court-approved repayment plan, you can spread your payments over a number of years.

Among the situations in which Chapters 11, 12, and 13 are worth considering are these:

- You want to retain all your assets and keep the business going.
- You want to partially liquidate your assets and then keep the business alive on a scaled-down basis.
- You want to totally liquidate the business, either by selling it as a going concern or by selling any remaining assets.

- You want to buy time to put the business in decent shape so that it's more attractive to potential purchasers.
- You want to pay your taxes in installments to stave off the IRS or state or local tax collectors who are poised to seize your assets, which would put you out of business.

In each case, a Chapter 11, 12, or 13 proceeding might offer the possibility of helping you achieve your objectives.

Chapter 11

A Chapter 11 reorganization allows your sole proprietorship, partnership, corporation, or LLC to continue doing business while often reducing or even eliminating the amounts you must pay back to unsecured creditors. Under a court-approved repayment plan, you can spread your payments over a number of years. Five years is typical.

If you file for a Chapter 11 reorganization, you'll immediately receive the protection of the bankruptcy court. All lawsuits and other collection actions against your business will come to a screeching halt. You'll then submit a plan—called a "reorganization plan"—showing how you propose to pay past-due debts while keeping up to date on current ones. Your plan doesn't have to include payment to unsecured creditors unless those creditors would receive some payment if your business were to file for liquidation under Chapter 7.

After you file the plan, creditors vote on it. (Unsecured creditors participate in the Chapter 11 case through what's called a "creditors' committee.") Secured and unsecured vote separately. To be adopted, the plan must be approved by 51% of the creditors in each class. If your plan is carefully crafted, the creditors will likely accept it. But if the creditors reject the reorganization plan, all might not be lost. A solution could be found in the "cram down"—a phrase used to describe the last-resort powers of the bankruptcy court. If your plan is basically fair and equitable, the judge can cram it down the throats of all the creditors.

To help your business stay alive, the judge can terminate burdensome or unprofitable leases or contracts. If, for example, your business is occupying expensive space under a lease that runs for seven years, your business is contractually obligated to keep paying rent throughout those seven years. But in Chapter 11, the judge can allow your business to move to a less costly location, with no further obligation to your current landlord—or at least with a reduction in the amount you'd otherwise owe.

If you qualify as a "small business debtor" (you're engaged in business activities and your total non-contingent liquidated secured and unsecured debts are less than $2,566,050), you can use a fast-track version of Chapter 11 that simplifies procedures and gives the creditors less control than they have in a regular Chapter 11 reorganization. You'll be subject to a few additional requirements; for example, you must file periodic financial reports over the course of your case showing profitability and the use of cash receipts, and timely file tax returns and make the payments when due. (11 U.S.C. §§ 308, 1116.) And in your plan, secured creditors to whom your business has pledged collateral must receive the current value of either the collateral or the debt, whichever is less, or the collateral itself.

With these many benefits, Chapter 11 sounds like a good deal for a financially troubled business, but the grim truth is that it rarely succeeds. It's usually an overwhelming task for a typical business owner to keep up with current bills while simultaneously chipping away at large, past-due debts and paying chunky administrative and legal fees. The result is that more than 90% of businesses that file under Chapter 11 eventually switch to Chapter 7 and liquidate their assets—although the fast-track procedures might lead to a higher success rate.

> **TIP**
>
> **Compare the payoffs to creditors.** Basically, if you're convinced that you can get more money for the creditors by reorganizing under Chapter 11, 12, or 13 than by filing for a straight liquidation under Chapter 7, then

reorganize. Otherwise, don't waste your time, energy, and money. Proceed directly with a Chapter 7 filing. Why worry about how much the creditors get? Because the more they get, the less you might be personally liable for.

Chapter 12

A Chapter 12 bankruptcy is available to family-owned farming businesses. As in a Chapter 11 proceeding, the total amount of debt owed to unsecured creditors might be reduced in the Chapter 12 plan. In addition, the financially ailing farm operation is allowed to continue doing business under a court-approved plan for repaying its remaining debts over a number of years. A court-appointed trustee serves as the intermediary between the farm and its creditors. Because Chapter 12 bankruptcy is relatively rare and this book is primarily for nonfarm businesses, Chapter 12 won't be discussed further.

Chapter 13

Businesses, per se, are not permitted to file for Chapter 13 bankruptcy. A sole proprietor, however, may file as an individual and include the business debts that carry personal liability. You can file for Chapter 13 bankruptcy if you have no more than $1,257,850 in secured debts and no more than $419,275 in unsecured debts. (These limits are adjusted periodically to reflect changes in the Consumer Price Index.) "Contingent" or "unliquidated" claims—such as a sexual harassment claim against you that's not yet resolved—don't count against these limits. As in a Chapter 11 reorganization, the amount you must pay back to unsecured creditors is reduced (sometimes to as little as zero) and, under a court-approved plan, you continue to run the business while paying off debts over a period that can last up to five years. A court-appointed trustee—whose fees you pay—makes payments to creditors under the payback plan.

Before filing for bankruptcy under Chapter 13, you'll have to receive credit counseling, just as you would in a Chapter 7 proceeding. Then, after filing, you'll have to complete a two-hour course on personal financial management.

As noted in the next section, there can be advantages to filing under Chapter 13 rather than Chapter 11, if your business qualifies. Prospects for keeping your business afloat over the long term are better with a Chapter 13.

RESOURCE

See *Chapter 13 Bankruptcy: Keep Your Property & Repay Debts Over Time,* by Cara O'Neill (Nolo), for a clear and in-depth look at how to get a court-approved repayment plan—either with or without a lawyer.

Choosing Between Chapter 11 and Chapter 13

All types of business entities—sole proprietorships, partnerships, corporations, and limited liability companies—can choose to file under Chapter 7 for a straight liquidation bankruptcy or under Chapter 11 for a reorganization of their business debts. Because Chapter 11 and Chapter 13 both allow a business to remain in operation under a court-approved plan, a sole proprietor who qualifies for both might face the dilemma of choosing between the two. Generally, it's more advantageous to choose Chapter 13, for a number of reasons:

- A Chapter 13 reorganization plan is usually approved by the court in less time than a Chapter 11 plan.
- You don't have to deal with a creditors' committee. This means you'll expend a lot less time and energy on paperwork and meetings, and, possibly, attorneys' fees will be less. Creditors may object separately to your Chapter 13 plan, but they don't carry the same weight as a committee objection would in a Chapter 11.
- You might be able to pay less than 100 cents on the dollar for unsecured debts. The bankruptcy judge in a Chapter 13 can approve a plan which provides for partial debt repayment.
- A Chapter 13 filing will stop collection action against a cosigner or guarantor if the Chapter 13 plan treats creditors fairly. In short, this option can help you protect friends and relatives who have obligated themselves to pay your debts.

- Going the Chapter 13 route is usually less expensive than the Chapter 11 alternative. That's because the filing fees are lower, and, if you hire a lawyer to help you, the legal fees will be lower, too.

At times, however, Chapter 11 can be a better choice. For instance, there's no debt limit. Also, in a Chapter 13 reorganization, you can "strip" (get the court to remove) a second mortgage lien from your home if the value of the home is less than the amount owed on your first mortgage—but you can't modify the terms of any other type of property. By contrast, a different rule applies to Chapter 11 filings, creating the possibility of reducing the loan if the value of other types of real estate has dropped, such as a business property, rental, or vacation home.

Who's Who in Bankruptcy

In addition to understanding the various types of bankruptcy, you'll quickly need to understand who the major players are and at least some of the jargon involved in a bankruptcy proceeding. Here's a brief overview:

- **Debtor.** The "debtor" is the person or business entity that owes the money. This can be you, your business, or—in the case of a sole proprietorship—both. If your business isn't a sole proprietorship and you are personally liable for business debts, you and your business must each file separate sets of bankruptcy papers. Generally, it's the debtor that files for bankruptcy, although creditors can sometimes start the ball rolling in an "involuntary bankruptcy."
- **Creditor.** A creditor can be any person, business, or governmental agency that has or might have a claim against you or your business. A secured creditor has a lien (claim) against specific property—usually either in the form of a real estate mortgage or a security interest in a vehicle or other equipment. A secured creditor is usually in a better legal position than an unsecured creditor, because if money isn't available to pay the debt, the secured creditor is entitled to grab the assets pledged as security.

- **Trustee.** A "bankruptcy trustee" takes possession of the debtor's business assets in a Chapter 7 proceeding and liquidates them to pay creditors. In a Chapter 7 personal bankruptcy, the trustee gathers the debtor's nonexempt property, liquidates it, and distributes the proceeds to the unsecured creditors. In a Chapter 11 proceeding, the debtor usually retains control over the business assets while the business continues to operate. But, especially if the business owner has committed fraud or seriously mismanaged the business, the court may appoint a trustee to take over managing the business in a Chapter 11 proceeding so that the creditors' interests are better protected. In a Chapter 12 or 13 bankruptcy, the debtor remains in possession of the property; the trustee collects monthly payments and distributes them to creditors. Trustees are appointed by the Justice Department's Office of the U.S. Trustee.

- **Judge.** A "bankruptcy judge" is part of the federal district court and has broad control over bankruptcy proceedings, including authority to resolve all disputes between the business and its creditors, as well as any issues involving the business's property. Despite this broad authority, the judge may abstain from trying issues that can be litigated in a state court—for example, actions to foreclose on real estate or to gain possession of cars and equipment or cases involving environmental cleanups. Bankruptcies are supervised, for the most part, by the trustee where one's been appointed—but debtors and creditors who disagree with a trustee's decision can seek a ruling from the bankruptcy judge, who can overrule the trustee.

- **Creditors' committee.** In a Chapter 11 proceeding, an "unsecured creditors' committee" may be appointed to represent the interests of all the unsecured creditors. If the proceeding is complicated, there may be additional creditors' committees representing special interests—for example, pension and profit-sharing recipients, undersecured creditors, and secured creditors. A creditor's committee may object that a proposed plan writes off too much of the debt owed to its members or that it gives the debtor too much time to pay.

Key Bankruptcy Concepts

Unfortunately, your mini-education in how bankruptcy works isn't quite complete. Bankruptcy law is unique, with its own concepts, procedures, and jargon, so it's crucially important to understand the legal basics.

Bankruptcy Estate

Once you or your business file for bankruptcy, the property—called the "bankruptcy estate"—is controlled by the bankruptcy proceedings. Creditors can't get their hands on it without the court's permission. Property subject to court control includes not only the property your business owned when you filed the bankruptcy papers, but also money your business earned but hadn't collected before you filed for bankruptcy. Also, in a Chapter 11, 12, or 13 proceeding, if your business acquires property after your case is filed, that property becomes part of the bankruptcy estate. However, if your business holds money in trust for third parties—such as withheld taxes that are to be paid to the IRS—that money isn't part of the bankruptcy estate.

 CAUTION

You might need a separate bank account. If you don't pay the employment taxes immediately, keep them in a separate bank account designated as a "trust account" so that it's clear that these funds are separate from other funds of the business. Then you'll be able to use these funds to pay the taxes and avoid personal liability and penalties. In a Chapter 11 filing, you'll probably need to set up several separate new accounts—for example, accounts for payroll and general operations, in addition to the one for employment taxes.

The Automatic Stay

As soon as your business has filed a bankruptcy petition, creditors are "stayed" (stopped) from continuing their collection efforts against the business. In addition, creditors can no longer seize any property owned or leased by the business that secures its debts, such as a car, building, or equipment. Furthermore, it's illegal for creditors to contact you to push for payment, start a lawsuit against you, or pursue any other collection action without permission of the bankruptcy court. Utilities such as the power, phone, and water company must continue to serve your business as long as you can guarantee payment for future services—for example, by posting a deposit.

Be aware that the IRS can continue an audit, issue a tax deficiency notice, demand a tax return, issue a tax assessment, and demand payment, but it can't record a lien or seize your property.

The Bankruptcy Filing

To start a bankruptcy case, your business must file a form called a "petition for relief" with the clerk of the federal bankruptcy court. To learn the location of the bankruptcy court, call the clerk of the U.S. district court that's nearest your business.

If you are filing individually or with a spouse for personal bankruptcy, you'll first have to take a credit counseling course and file a completion certificate with the court. Then, early in the bankruptcy process, you'll need to take a debt management course and file a completion certificate. Otherwise, you'll still be liable for your debts.

A list of creditors (everyone your business owes money to) and their addresses should accompany your petition, using a special format so that copies of your creditor list can be used as a mailing list.

Within 15 days, you must also file lists of debts and assets and a history of your business. In bankruptcy jargon, these lists are called bankruptcy "schedules" and the "statement of financial affairs." Include all debts your business might owe and any claims that creditors might have against your business—even those you have some doubts about or dispute.

In addition, if you're filing for personal bankruptcy under Chapter 7 and your debts are not primarily business debts, you'll have to fill out a "means test" form in which your income is compared to the median state income for a family the size of yours. Things get complicated if your income exceeds the median.

Claims

Once notified of your bankruptcy, creditors may file "claims" for payment of their debts with the bankruptcy court. Your business—and, in a Chapter 7 or Chapter 13 filing, the bankruptcy trustee—can challenge a claim that seems to be improper. The judge will decide whether the claim is valid.

In a liquidation of a business, because there's almost never enough money to pay all allowed claims, the law establishes priorities. Your bankruptcy estate (any money or property salvaged from your business) is used to pay the highest priority claims first, then the next highest priority, and so on, as long as the money lasts. Because there isn't enough money to go around, creditors in the lowest category typically receive much less than the amount they're owed. In fact, it's not uncommon for unsecured creditors to receive nothing.

Some creditors can obtain a super-priority status. In a Chapter 11 bankruptcy where the trustee or debtor must borrow new money to keep the business running, the lender of these funds could obtain a super-priority claim and be first in line when assets are distributed. Next come the secured creditors who have liens on specific real estate, vehicles, equipment, or other property. After that come such claims as the expenses of administering the bankruptcy, wages and commissions earned during the 90 days before the bankruptcy started, money owed to an employee benefit plan, deposits made on consumer goods, and most taxes.

At the bottom of the heap are general, unsecured claimants who, if they're lucky, receive a pittance. Often, unsecured claimants get a few cents for each dollar they were owed or come away entirely empty-handed. In a Chapter 13, secured creditors with liens and holders of priority debts could be paid simultaneously through the Chapter 13 plan.

The Effect of Bankruptcy on Secured Debts

If you go through a Chapter 7 personal bankruptcy, your creditors will lose the right to get a personal judgment against you requiring you to pay the debt that's owed. But even though a creditor can no longer demand that you repay the debt, if you've pledged property as collateral, that creditor still has a lien on that specific property. Because the creditor can enforce the lien and take or sell the property, be aware of the three options available to you—which can be summarized as the Three Rs:

- **Relinquishment.** You can simply give up the house, car, or other property on which the creditor has a lien.
- **Redemption.** You may buy the property by paying the creditor its value, usually in a lump sum. If there's a dispute about how much the property is worth, the bankruptcy judge will determine the value.
- **Reaffirmation.** You may reaffirm your obligation to pay the debt secured by your property before the debt is discharged in bankruptcy. Then you continue to make payments as you had agreed before the bankruptcy. Of course, the lien will remain on the property and, if you later miss payments, the creditor will be able to enforce the lien by taking back property to pay for the balance of the reaffirmed debt.

CAUTION

Bankruptcy won't protect you if you've committed fraud. If a creditor proves in bankruptcy court that you've engaged in intentional fraud concerning a debt, you'll be stuck with that debt. It won't be wiped out ("discharged") by the bankruptcy.

Continuing a Commercial Lease

If you file for Chapter 11 or Chapter 13 bankruptcy, you can hang on to your commercial lease—if you act promptly. Let's assume that your lease is in force at the time you file for bankruptcy and that it has several more years to run. You can "assume" the lease for the remaining term so that it won't be canceled in the bankruptcy. But to do that, you must act within 120 days after you file your bankruptcy petition. The court can grant a 90-day extension if you have good cause.

Before you can protect your lease, however, you have to cure any defaults—for example, you'll have to pay any overdue rent. And you'll have to provide assurance that you'll be able to meet your lease obligations in the future. Once you've assumed the lease, you can continue to occupy the premises or you can assign the lease to a credit-worthy business—even if the lease says it can't be assigned.

In a Chapter 7 bankruptcy, the trustee has to assume the lease within 60 days, or it's deemed to be rejected.

Exempt Property

If you go through a Chapter 7 personal bankruptcy where your assets are liquidated to pay your debts, you don't have to give up all of your personal property to pay back creditors. The law allows you to keep some items (called "exempt property") to help you get a fresh start. Exempt property is listed in the federal bankruptcy code, but states also have laws listing exemptions. Generally, you'll rely on your state law exemptions—either because the state law exemptions are more advantageous or because, as is the case in most states, the state law gives you no choice. If you do have a choice, check the federal homestead allowance carefully; it's usually more generous than state law.

Most state exemptions allow you to keep property in these broad categories:

- motor vehicles, to a certain modest value
- clothing other than furs
- household furnishings and goods
- household appliances
- jewelry such as a wedding ring and a watch
- personal effects—personal possessions that don't fall into the categories of clothing and jewelry
- life insurance (cash or loan value or proceeds) to a certain value
- pensions for public employees or pensions that qualify under ERISA
- part of the equity in your home
- tools of your trade, to a certain value
- portion of unpaid but earned wages, and
- public benefits (welfare, Social Security, or unemployment compensation) accumulated in a bank account.

RESOURCE

For detailed information about exemptions, see *Solve Your Money Troubles: Strategies to Get Out of Debt and Stay That Way,* by Amy Loftsgordon and Cara O'Neill (Nolo).

Law From the Real World

Carl and Phyllis Save Their Home

Carl starts a neighborhood restaurant, organizing his business as a one-person corporation. To raise capital, Carl and his wife Phyllis borrow $50,000 from a bank on their signatures and additionally secure the loan by giving the bank a second mortgage on their home.

In its first year, the business runs up a pile of debts. With prospects of becoming profitable looking bleak, Carl decides to close down. Carl considers putting the corporation through bankruptcy to make a clean break with creditors. Unfortunately, this won't help with the bank loan since Carl and Phyllis are personally liable for that debt, and their home is at risk if they can't pay it. Because this is a secured debt, even if they go through personal bankruptcy, they'll lose their home.

So Carl and Phyllis reduce the bank loan with $10,000 of personal savings that Phyllis had set aside from her salary as a teacher. They then refinance their home by getting a new first mortgage that pays off both the old mortgages. (Fortunately, Carl is able to get his old job back, so he and Phyllis have income to qualify for the new mortgage.) Carl and Phyllis now have 30 years to pay off the new mortgage in monthly installment payments.

Carl closes the business, sells the corporation's few remaining assets, and before dissolving the corporation, distributes the proceeds to the business's unsecured creditors.

The business failed, but with this small-scale workout, Carl and Phyllis saved their home.

Checklist for Starting a Small Business

You can download a PDF of this checklist on this book's companion page at:

www.nolo.com/back-of-book/RUNS.html

When there are important changes to the information in this book, we'll post updates on this same dedicated page.

Checklist for Starting a Small Business

Evaluate and Develop Your Business Idea

☐ Determine if the business taps into your skills, experience, and interests.

☐ Use a break-even analysis to determine if your idea can make money.

☐ Write a business plan, including a profit/loss forecast and a cash-flow analysis.

☐ Investigate business financing. (See Chapter 9)

☐ Set up a basic marketing plan.

Decide on a Legal Structure for Your Business (See Chapter 1)

☐ Research the various types of ownership structures:

    ☐ Sole proprietorship

    ☐ Partnership

    ☐ LLC

    ☐ C corporation

    ☐ S corporation

☐ Identify the factors involved in choosing a business structure:

    ☐ the number of owners of your business

    ☐ how much protection from personal liability you'll need, which depends on your business's risks

    ☐ how you'd like the business to be taxed, and

    ☐ whether your business would benefit from being able to sell stock.

☐ Get more in-depth information from a self-help resource or a lawyer, if necessary, before you settle on a structure.

Choose a Name for Your Business (See Chapter 6)

☐ Think of several business names that might suit your company and its products or services.

☐ Check the availability of your proposed business names:

    ☐ If you will do business online, check if your proposed business names are available as domain names.

    ☐ Check with your county clerk's office to see whether your proposed names are on the list of fictitious or assumed business names in your county.

    ☐ For corporations and LLCs: Check the availability of your proposed names with the secretary of state or other corporate filing office.

    ☐ Do a federal or state trademark search of the proposed names still on your list. If a proposed name is being used as a trademark, eliminate it if your use of the name would confuse customers or if the name is already famous.

☐ Choose from the proposed names that are still on your list.

☐ Register your business name:

    ☐ as a fictitious or assumed business name, if necessary

    ☐ as a federal or state trademark (if you'll do business regionally or nationally and will use your business name to identify a product or service), and

    ☐ as a domain name (if you'll use the name as a Web address too).

Prepare Organizational Paperwork

☐ Sole proprietorship: N/A

☐ Partnership: (See Chapter 2)

    ☐ Partnership agreement

    ☐ Buyout agreement

☐ LLC: (See Chapter 4)

    ☐ Articles of organization

    ☐ Operating agreement

    ☐ Buyout agreement

☐ C corporations: (See Chapter 3)

    ☐ Preincorporation agreement
      (Create this document using Quicken Legal Business Pro.)

    ☐ Articles of incorporation

    ☐ Corporate bylaws

    ☐ Buyout agreement, a.k.a. stock agreement

☐ S corporations: (See Chapter 3)

    ☐ Articles of incorporation

    ☐ Corporate bylaws

    ☐ Buyout agreement, a.k.a. stock agreement

    ☐ File IRS Form 2553, *Election by a Small Business Corporation*

Find a Business Location (See Chapter 13)

☐ Identify the features and fixtures your business will need.

☐ Determine how much rent you can afford.

☐ Decide what neighborhoods would be best for your business and find out what the average rents are in those neighborhoods.

☐ Make sure any space you're considering is or can be properly zoned for your business. (If working from home, make sure your business activities won't violate any zoning restrictions on home offices.)

☐ Negotiate the best deal.

☐ Before signing a lease, make sure it adequately protects you and that you understand all its terms.

File for Licenses and Permits (See Chapter 7)

- ☐ Obtain a federal Employer Identification Number by filing IRS Form SS-4 (optional for a sole proprietorship or single-member limited liability company without employees).
- ☐ Obtain a sales tax license or permit from your state if you will sell retail goods.
- ☐ Obtain state licenses, such as specialized vocation-related licenses or environmental permits, if necessary.
- ☐ Obtain a local tax registration certificate, sometimes called a business license.
- ☐ Obtain local permits, if required, such as a conditional use permit or zoning variance.

Obtain Insurance (See Chapter 12)

- ☐ Determine what business property requires coverage in case it's damaged, stolen, or destroyed.
- ☐ Obtain liability insurance on vehicles used in your business, including personal cars of employees used for business.
- ☐ Obtain liability insurance for your premises if customers or clients will be visiting.
- ☐ Obtain product liability insurance if you will manufacture hazardous products.
- ☐ Contact an insurance agent or broker to answer questions and give you policy quotes.
- ☐ Choose realistic policy limits and deductibles.
- ☐ If you will be working from your home, make sure your homeowner's insurance covers damage to or theft of your business assets as well as liability for business-related injuries.

Set Up Tax Reporting and Accounting (See Chapter 8)

- ☐ Familiarize yourself with the general tax scheme for your business structure:
  - ☐ Sole proprietorship
  - ☐ Partnership
  - ☐ LLC
  - ☐ C corporation
  - ☐ S corporation
- ☐ Familiarize yourself with common business deductions and depreciation.
- ☐ Get the following information from the IRS:
  - ☐ IRS Publication 334, *Tax Guide for Small Business*
  - ☐ IRS Publication 583, *Starting a Business and Keeping Records*, and
  - ☐ IRS Publication 1518, *IRS Tax Calendar for Small Businesses and Self-Employed*.
- ☐ Set up your books:
  - ☐ Decide whether to use the cash or accrual system of accounting.
  - ☐ Choose a fiscal year if your natural business cycle does not follow the calendar year (if your business qualifies).
  - ☐ Set up a record-keeping system for all payments to and from your business.
  - ☐ Consider hiring a bookkeeper or an accountant to help you get set up; or purchase *Quicken Home & Business* (Intuit), *QuickBooks* (Intuit), or similar small-business accounting software.

Hire Workers (See Chapter 15)

☐ Consider whether you need to hire employees or whether independent contractors will suffice:

    ☐ Familiarize yourself with the difference between independent contractors and employees.

    ☐ If hiring an independent contractor, use a written independent contractor agreement.

☐ Register and prepare systems and procedures before hiring employees:

    ☐ If you haven't done so already, obtain a federal Employer Identification Number by filing IRS Form SS-4.

    ☐ Register with your state's employment department or similar agency for payment of unemployment compensation taxes and be prepared to file IRS Form 940 to report your federal unemployment tax each year.

    ☐ Set up a payroll system for withholding taxes and making payroll tax payments to the IRS. Obtain IRS Publication 15, Circular E, *Employer's Tax Guide.*

    ☐ Get workers' compensation insurance. (In addition, you must notify new hires of their rights to workers' compensation benefits.)

    ☐ Familiarize yourself with Occupational Safety and Health Administration (OSHA) requirements and prepare an injury and illness prevention plan, if OSHA requires it.

    ☐ Contact the federal Department of Labor and your state labor department for information on notices you must post in the workplace.

    ☐ Create a job description for each type of position you will fill.

    ☐ Create a job application that complies with the applicable antidiscrimination laws.

    ☐ Create an employee handbook.

    ☐ Look into employee benefit programs that can help you attract top applicants and boost workplace morale.

☐ Complete these tasks each time you hire a new employee:

    ☐ Report the employee to your state's new-hire reporting agency for child support purposes.

    ☐ Fill out Form I-9, *Employment Eligibility Verification*, from the Bureau of Citizenship and Immigration Services (BCIS, formerly known as the INS).

    ☐ Have the employee fill out IRS Form W-4, *Employee's Withholding Allowance Certificate.*

Index

 **NOLO**

More from Nolo

Nolo.com offers a large library of legal solutions and forms, created by Nolo's in-house legal editors. These reliable documents can be prepared in minutes.

Create a Document Online

Incorporation. Incorporate your business in any state.

LLC Formation. Gain asset protection and pass-through tax status in any state.

Will. Nolo has helped people make over 2 million wills. Is it time to make or revise yours?

Living Trust (avoid probate). Plan now to save your family the cost, delays, and hassle of probate.

Provisional Patent. Preserve your right to obtain a patent by claiming "patent pending" status.

Download Useful Legal Forms

Nolo.com has hundreds of top quality legal forms available for download:

- bill of sale
- promissory note
- nondisclosure agreement
- LLC operating agreement
- corporate minutes
- commercial lease and sublease
- motor vehicle bill of sale
- consignment agreement
- and many more.

www.nolo.com